Praise for

no one
cares
about
crazy
people

"Extraordinary and courageous...I'm not sure I've ever read anything that handles the decline of one's children with such openness and searing, stumbling honesty...[Powers] writes with fierce hope and fierce purpose to persuade the world to pay attention. No doubt if everyone were to read this book, the world *would* change."
—Ron Suskind, *New York Times Book Review*

"[A] heartbreaking tribute to [Powers's] sons...and an urgent plea for reform." —*People*

"One of the most engrossing accounts of raising a family I've ever read, one in which Mr. Powers makes universal his themes of parental love, bewilderment, and rage at the vagaries of biological fate."
—John Donvan, *Wall Street Journal*

"This hybrid narrative, enhanced by the author's considerable skills as a literary stylist, succeeds on every level."
—*Kirkus Reviews* (starred review)

"Powers gives us powerful stories of real suffering and societal apathy toward the plight of our fellow citizens. Their struggles must not be forgotten as we continue to debate reforming our health-care system."

—*Washington Post*

"Very emotional...[Powers] reminds us how apathetic and cruel society can be when it comes to mental illness."

—*Booklist* (starred review)

"*No One Cares About Crazy People* is a woefully necessary kick in the teeth to society's understanding and treatment of mental illness. Reading Ron Powers is always an event—you can expect expert research and rich reporting in an engrossing style—but what makes this book soar is the passion of Powers's conviction based off his own intimate experiences with schizophrenia...It's the rare book that breaks your life into a before and an after."

—Susannah Cahalan, *New York Times* bestselling author of *Brain on Fire*

"Ron Powers writes eloquently, passionately, and persuasively about the failure to properly treat mental illness in America. What makes this book really powerful is Powers's personal story—the harrowing, wrenching tale of his two sons wrestling with the unholy demon of schizophrenia."

—Evan Thomas, *New York Times* bestselling author of *Being Nixon*

"In telling this gripping and deeply personal story, Ron Powers puts chronic mental illness in the broad context of history, society, and public policy. His compelling account helps shake us out of the embarrassment and apathy that have tethered public discourse and lasting action to treat mental illness...The story he tells is not a comfortable one, but it's an important one." —U.S. senator Patrick Leahy (D-Vt.)

"Very readable and highly recommended."
—E. Fuller Torrey, MD, author of *Surviving Schizophrenia*

"*No One Cares About Crazy People* is an unforgettable, insistent call for a nationwide conversation and action, for embracing our most vulnerable benefits us all."
—Pamela Rotner Sakamoto, author of *Midnight in Broad Daylight: A Japanese American Family Caught Between Two Worlds*

"[Powers] shares his searingly personal, heart-wrenching account of the schizophrenia that overtook his two talented, promising sons. In loving detail, [he] describes the joys and unfathomable challenges inherent in parenting two such blessed and simultaneously cursed young men."
—*Library Journal*

"Whether Ron Powers is writing about Mark Twain, small-town life in the Midwest, the state of television, or crime, his books resonate. Now he has written the book he never wanted to tackle—about the schizophrenia of his sons and the cruel failures of the American mental health establishment."
—Steve Weinberg, author of *Taking on the Trust*

no one cares about crazy people

My Family and the Heartbreak of Mental Illness in America

RON POWERS

NEW YORK BOSTON

Hachette Books
Hachette Book Group
1290 Avenue of the Americas
New York, NY 10104
hachettebooks.com
twitter.com/hachettebooks

First Trade Edition: May 2018

Hachette Books is a division of Hachette Book Group, Inc.
The Hachette Books name and logo are trademarks of Hachette Book Group, Inc.

The publisher is not responsible for websites (or their content) that are not owned by the publisher.

The Hachette Speakers Bureau provides a wide range of authors for speaking events. To find out more, go to www.hachettespeakersbureau.com or call (866) 376-6591.

Library of Congress Cataloging-in-Publication Data

Names: Powers, Ron, author.
Title: No one cares about crazy people : the chaos and heartbreak of mental
   health in America / Ron Powers.
Description: New York : Hachette Books, [2017] | Includes bibliographical
   references and index.
Identifiers: LCCN 2016046019| ISBN 9780316341172 (hardback) | ISBN
   9781478940906 (audio download) | ISBN 9780316341103 (ebook)
Subjects: | MESH: Schizophrenia—history | Mental Health Services—history |
   Mental Health Services—legislation & jurisprudence | Mentally Ill Persons
   | United States | Personal Narratives
Classification: LCC RC514 | NLM WM 203 | DDC 362.2/6—dc23 LC record
   available at https://lccn.loc.gov/2016046019

ISBNs: 978-0-316-34113-4 (pbk.), 978-0-316-34110-3 (ebook)

Printed in the United States of America

LSC-C

10 9 8 7 6 5 4 3 2 1

In Kevin's Memory
For Dean
For Honoree

For all those struggling with chronic mental illness
For all those who are dedicated to healing its victims
For all those who are dedicated to finding a cure

Contents

I have come to present the strong claims of suffering humanity. I come to place before the Legislature of Massachusetts the condition of the miserable, the desolate, the outcast. I come as the advocate of the helpless, forgotten, insane men and women... confined in cages, closets, cellars, stalls, pens! Chained, naked, beaten with rods, and lashed into obedience...I beg, I implore you [to] put away the spirit of selfishness and self-seeking. Lay off the armor of local strife and political ambition. Forget, I beg you, the earthly and perishable, the thought without mercy... Gentlemen, I commit you to a sacred cause!

—Dorothea Dix to the Massachusetts state legislature,
December 1843[1]

No one cares about crazy people.

—Kelly M. Rindfleisch, deputy chief of staff
to then Milwaukee County executive
Scott Walker, September 1, 2010

Preface

This is the book I promised myself I would never write. And promised my wife as well. I have kept that promise for a decade—since our younger son, Kevin, hanged himself in our basement, a week before his twenty-first birthday in July 2005, after struggling for three years with schizophrenia. The promise was easy to keep in the first five years after Kevin's death, if only because I could not bring myself to think about such a project and the revisiting that it would make necessary. I wasn't able to think about much of anything at all, except that I dreaded each new season of "greening up," as it is called here in Vermont. ("It's a tragically beautiful summer," my wife, Honoree, managed to observe not long after that terrible July had passed.)

Over the second five years, the infernal process of "healing"—adaptation, really—had begun its unwelcome sterilizing work. And then the malady struck our family again. Symptoms of schizophrenia surfaced in our elder and surviving son, Dean. My wife and I witnessed the psychotic break on a Christmas morning that sent him knocking on doors through the neighborhood, announcing that he was the Messiah, until a police officer restrained him and took him to a nearby medical center.

Dean stubbornly surmounted the disease's worst effects and is functioning well as of this writing. Still, this second of two unthinkable blows to our family added to a list of reasons why I felt that I should really just leave the subject alone.

At the top of the list was privacy. My sons, even as robust and outgoing children, shared a powerful ethic of discretion, which they inherited from their mother. None of these three was what you would call a hearts-on-sleeves person. It wasn't a matter of secretiveness. Some things were just nobody else's business, that was all. When Kevin, our younger son, was away with his guitar at a music academy in Michigan, he emailed us a photograph of himself and his date for the spring dance. Kevin was wearing a white dinner jacket, his first. I was moved to use the photo as the basis of a commentary I wrote for the Vermont public radio station:

> The image of a white dinner jacket, especially one worn by a 15-year-old son nine hundred miles from home on a spring night at the prom with a very young woman on his arm—this image takes on a new and unexpected luster: a sweetness and fragility so unbearable that you lie there in your bed wishing the damned alarm would go off and restore you to the necessary cynicism of daylight.

One of Kevin's buddies back in Middlebury, where we lived, heard the commentary and ratted me out. Kevin let me know that he was wise to what I'd done, in terms that you would have thought were being used against somebody who'd stolen his black Martin electric.

So privacy was my top consideration, and I suppose it should have sufficed. But there were other reasons, strong ones.

The moral blemish of exploitation, for example. Even when "exploitation" is not the intended motive in a book such as this, it can seem the unintended consequence. My sons were and remain sacred to me. They are not for sale.

And, really, end of the day, who the hell wants to read about schizophrenia anyway?

Not me.

And that was the way things stood for the second five years. That is the way I thought things would stand for the duration. I was just not interested.

But to paraphrase Tolstoy: "You may not be interested in schizophrenia, but schizophrenia is interested in you." It turns out, schizophrenia was particularly interested in the Powers family, and no amount of disinterest on my part was going to change that. So I began, tentatively, to explore the malady.

Schizophrenia is a chronic and incurable disease of the brain. It is rooted (or so neuroscientists presently believe; nothing about it is yet a matter of settled truth) partly in genetic mutation and partly in external, or "environmental," experiences. It is the most dreaded of all the human mental illnesses, afflicting slightly more than one in one hundred people. Its name—a bit misleading, as we shall see—is a vernacular near synonym for its closely allied affliction, schizo-affective disorder. The latter disease is rarer, striking about 0.3 percent of the population; but worse: it incorporates severe mood swings as well as the loss of touch with reality wrought by schizophrenia. Some specialists believe there is no hard distinction between the two maladies.

Schizophrenia is a scourge, but it's only one of the many mental illnesses that sprawl across many categories, lengths of duration, and degrees of severity. The World Health Organization estimates that one-fourth of the globe's people will experience some kind of mental illness in their lifetimes. Two-thirds of these either do not recognize that they are ill or simply refuse treatment. Studies by the National Institute of Mental Health show that among Americans age eighteen or older, more than sixty-two million (26 percent of the population) require (but are not always given) counseling and medical treatment.

But even among the many devastating diagnoses of mental illness, schizophrenia stands unique in its capacity to wreck the rational processes of the mind. It is to mental health as cancer is to physical health: a predator without peer and impervious to cure.

My final resolve to refrain from writing this book came unraveled on the night of January 30, 2014.

In the late afternoon of that day, Honoree and I drove northward from our home in Castleton to the Vermont state capitol in Montpelier. We'd been invited to testify at a public hearing convened by the Senate Committee on Health and Welfare. The hearing was called to air out arguments on either side of a bitter, seemingly intractable clash of ideologies: whether or not mentally ill patients should be detained against their will (an "involuntary" intervention) in times of acute need and sickness, especially given the delays in treatment caused by the shortages of hospital beds and treatment facilities. It sounds benign in the abstract, but in practice an "intervention" generally means retaining such a person in the emergency room until a psychiatric bed becomes available, and medicating the patient with psychotropic drugs. Neurological research supports the view that early intervention is necessary to prevent the psychosis from deepening—but when that intervention is involuntary, a whole new array of issues (both legal and ethical) arises.

In Vermont as in some other states, "involuntary" patients can be placed in emergency rooms but cannot receive medication for their affliction without a court order authorizing a doctor to proceed. Some Vermont patients have waited in their psychoses as long as two or even three months for the case to work its way through the courts.

At first glance, speedy "involuntary treatment" might seem the least objectionable of measures, given that people in psychosis are virtually never capable of making rational decisions. And yet opponents of the process, whose ranks are reinforced by schizophrenia victims, bring passionate counterarguments to the debate. Among the most formidable is that "involuntary treatment" is by definition a violation of one's civil liberties.

Another motivation for opponents of involuntary care lies in their distrust of the medications themselves. It is undeniable that as they have evolved since the 1950s, antipsychotic drugs, experimental by their very nature, have at times further damaged patients rather than stabilized them; that even the effective ones can produce damaging side effects; and that widely despised "Big Pharma," the multibillion-dollar pharmaceutical industry, has made it lucrative for doctors and psychiatrists to prescribe medications as a preemptive cure-all for mental illness at the expense of scrupulous individual care and regardless of how well or ill the patient, or even whether the meds work.

The hearing at Montpelier that cold winter night in 2014 showcased both sides of this disagreement. Honoree and I testified in alliance with those advocating for shorter waits for "involuntary treatment." Like many families visited by schizophrenia, we did not base our position in ideology. We thought about, understood, and respected the motivating principles on both sides.

The state legislature debated the bill through the spring, and in June the governor signed a version of it, containing several compromises, into law.

My purpose in bringing up this hearing and legislation is not to reargue its merits or demerits. My purpose is to describe the awakening the event triggered in me.

I discussed my reactions with Honoree as we walked out of the chamber and the capitol building to our car, and I discovered that hers were similar.

I had found myself moved—riveted—by the people who spoke against involuntary treatment. They sat in an uncomfortable line at the long polished desk in the committee chamber, clearing their throats and stealing glances at the suited and scarved and coiffed legislative committee members. They had come dressed in the Vermont uniform of workaday jeans and flannel shirts and denim skirts, many of the women with their hair uncombed and men with their beards untrimmed. Their voices sometimes quavered and their handwritten notes trembled in their grip. Yet they were there: the faces and souls of the mentally ill, emerging from their prevailing invisibility to declare themselves.

The sheer presence of them, their *actualization* in the room, had affected me in the gut, not because I hadn't expected them, but because of the profound, elemental humanity of them. Full realization dawned on me only later: Like so many people, I had converted the mentally ill into abstractions. I had stopped seeing them. I'd looked away reflexively when I did see them. I had stopped thinking about them. I had stopped acknowledging their chimerical presence at the corners of my tight little sphere of "reality."

How thunderously ironic.

I, who had witnessed mental illness in as intimate and convincing a form as is possible to witness it; I, who had wept, sat unmoving, endured years of dreams—including the most exquisitely, diabolically "sweet" dreams that an agitated human mind could concoct; a recurring dream of Kevin alive but refusing ever again to play his guitar*—I, of all people, was shocked to behold mentally ill people in corporeal form.

Shame on me.

Just three weeks after that hearing in Montpelier, I was stunned by the disclosure of a ghastly remark in a series of emails made public by subpoena. The emails had been written in 2010, principally by an administrative aide to Scott Walker, then the Milwaukee County executive, who was running for the governorship. The aide's name was Kelly Rindfleisch. At the time, Milwaukee County Hospital was in the news for allegations of mismanagement of its mental health complex—allegations that included the death of a patient by starvation and sexual assaults on patients by other patients and by staff doctors, at least one of which resulted in a pregnancy. Earlier in the chain—on March 27—Walker, wary of the effect the scandal might have on his campaign, had written, "We need to continue to keep me out of the story as this is a process issue and not a policy matter."[1]

Walker's staff labored through the spring and summer to satisfy his wish. On September 2, Rindfleisch wrote, "Last week was a nightmare. A bad story every day on our looney bin. Doctors having sex with patients, patients getting knocked up. This has been coming for months and I've unofficially been dealing with it. So, it's been crazy (pun intended)."

Later, in an attempt to reassure a colleague on Walker's staff, Rindfleisch somehow found it in herself to write: "No one cares about crazy people."[2]

I began to rethink my determination not to write this book. I realized that my ten years of silence on the subject, silence that I had justified as insulation against an exercise in self-indulgence, was itself an exercise in self-indulgence. The schizophrenia sufferers in that hearing room had not been asking for pity, or for anyone to "feel the pain" of their victimhood. They were asking for understanding. They were insisting that

---

* I later learned that Honoree independently shared this torture-dream with me.

their humanity, so indelibly on display in the room, be acknowledged. They were demanding that their points of view be heard as legitimate and considered alongside the viewpoints of the general population.

They were determined, it seemed to me, to speak up, and back, to the voices of indifference and denial: the voices of "No one cares about crazy people."

That claim, of course, is an exaggeration. Not even the person who infamously typed it into an email could have believed it to be literally true. Many people care about the insane, even though their numbers in proportion to the total population are tiny. They include family members; neurosurgeons; consulting and research psychiatrists; psychiatric nurses; the clergy; members of organizations such as the National Alliance on Mental Illness and its ideological opposite, the Citizens Commission on Human Rights; and many thousands of social workers, unpaid hospital and care-center volunteers, and sympathetic law enforcement officers such as the young policeman who gently restrained Dean on that frantic Christmas morning in Castleton.

Good, conscientious, indispensable people, all of them. And woefully outnumbered.

In tackling the layered and complicated topic of mental illness, I am treading a path that has been traveled by hundreds of writers with far better credentials than I have: neuroscientists with expertise in schizophrenia's evolving nosology; scholars who have retraced its long history and the long history of mankind's attempts to understand and conquer it or, alternatively, to render it invisible by throwing those afflicted with it into dungeons where atrocities were the norm. (This particular remedy survives—thrives—in our time.)

My aim with this book is not to replace or argue with the existing vast inventory of important books on mental illness. Rather, I hope to reamplify a simple and self-evident and morally insupportable truth:

Too many of the mentally ill in our country live under conditions of atrocity.

Storytelling is my choice of action. As noted, writing this book has not been an easy choice, and it is one that I have deferred for nearly a decade.

Writing the book has tested the emotional resilience of my wonderful wife, Honoree, and of my brave surviving son as well. And of myself.

Yet I have concluded that in the end, it is among those books that cannot *not* be written. (Other writers and discerning readers will understand this.)

Nor can it be written in half measures, as I had briefly contemplated after deciding that I was duty-bound to tackle the subject.

I had planned for a while to write from a distance, confining my book to a survey of mental illness's historic contours and of the efforts and impediments in the last century and a half to understand, master, and eradicate it. Yet a hard and humbling truth arose in my path and would not budge. The truth was that such a book would have been hollow, redundant at best with the many good expositional books on the subject already in (and out of) print. Useless, at worst. It would have meant the squandering of a chance, my last and only chance, to make common cause with the untold numbers of people maimed by psychotic attack upon either themselves or a beloved friend or relative.

By opening up my family's intensely private loss and suffering, I hope to achieve two goals.

One goal is to persuade my fellow citizens in the Schizophrenic Nation that their ordeals, while awful, are neither unique to them nor the occasion for shame and withdrawal. The other is to demonstrate to those who fear and loathe "crazy people" that these victims are not typically dangerous, weak, or immoral, or in any other way undeserving of full personhood. On the contrary, like my adored sons, Dean Paul Powers and Kevin Powers, they tend to be people who have known love, laughter, inventiveness, hope, and the capacity to dream the same dreams of a future that other people dream. That they have been maimed by a scourge of inexplicable, malign destructiveness is not their fault.

Well, there is a third goal: to preserve that which is possible to preserve in words that describe the lives and soaring souls of Dean and Kevin. Another term for this goal is "consecration."

Finally: *No One Cares About Crazy People* is a call to arms on behalf of these people for any society that dares describe itself as decent.

America must turn its immense resources and energy and conciliatory goodwill to a final assault on mental illness. My sons, and your afflicted children and brothers and sisters and parents and friends, deserve nothing less. The passionate, afflicted people who testified in that hearing room in the Vermont capitol in January 2014 deserve nothing less.

I hope you do not "enjoy" this book. I hope you are wounded by it; wounded as I have been in writing it. Wounded to act, to intervene. Only if this happens, and keeps happening until it needs happen no more, can we dare to hope that Dean and Kevin and all their brothers and sisters in psychotic suffering are redeemed; that they have not suffered entirely in vain.

from ordinary human to savage beast: the fanged werewolf, emerging from human form under the full moon to prowl the landscape in Satan's service, murdering and bestowing the lycanthropic curse of its bite. Similarly the vampire, the witch, the warlock, the monstrous Mr. Hyde.

The madness metaphors are shot through with fear and loathing. And they have impelled human society to centuries of actual, nonmetaphorical persecution of the mentally ill.

Those among us who were believed to be mad have been imprisoned in basements and in fortresslike asylums. In the Dark Ages and before—and after—they were beaten and burned at the stake. They have been locked in chains in "bedlams," sometimes for decades, taunted by the guards, starved, left to go naked or in rags, forced to sleep on mattresses soaked with their urine, and put on display on Sundays for the paid amusement of visitors. The Enlightenment added more sophisticated remedies when the mad were belted into chairs and spun rapidly around, leeched until they were bled nearly dry, forced to swallow mercury and chloride, and drenched with scalding or frigid water. And then came the twentieth century, when things got bad.

The 1900s brought totalitarianism to bear upon the insane. It delivered lobotomization and attempts at wholesale eradication via eugenics, which promised to rid mankind of its "defectives" by neutering or eliminating those who showed signs of madness, weakness, or deformity, thus "purifying" the race. Nazi scientists can claim full credit for using the living bodies of mentally ill prisoners for human experimentation, but the United States is not morally exempt from those crimes against humanity; in fact, it was rock-solid Yankee business boosters who first popularized eugenic theories that turned human beings into mad-science experiments.

In the years after World War II came the problematic panacea of the so-called wonder drugs. These antipsychotic and psychotropic medications were and are intended to control the symptoms of schizophrenia and bipolarity (yet *not* the diseases themselves; no cure is yet available). They work by regulating flaws in certain chemicals in the brain, such as serotonin and dopamine, which affect behavior. Sometimes they work wonderfully and restore patients to functioning (if not completely normal) lives. Yet psychotropics remain far from perfect and have caused much inadvertent harm, via misdosage and debilitating side effects.

Wonder drugs and their salesmen also disastrously coaxed our leaders in government, health, and business to talk themselves into a historic and massive blunder of mental health care social policy: the shuttering of in-residence mental institutions and the exile of mental patients, presumably medicated, back into their community—into the streets. This historic blunder has a name that grotesquely fits the elegance of its design and effects. The name is deinstitutionalization. Deinstitutionalization uprooted what meager stability insane people clung to—the dismal care of state mental asylums—and drove tens of thousands into the streets, where they pioneered an entirely new urban subpopulation, the accursed demographic of the mad that we call the homeless.

The sudden mass visibility and eccentric behavior of the homeless have made them subject to demonization on a scale and intensity not seen since the Dark Ages. Now the police round them up—from the adolescents just emerging, bewildered, into insanity, to the veterans of madness, who are helpless not just before mental illness but before the injustices that compound it: minority racial status, class disability, crabbed opportunity, inadequate medical care, and family instability. The police round them up for their crimes of survival: for robberies of food; for possession of the illicit drugs used for self-destructive self-medication; for loitering, vagrancy, and street harassment; for bothering noninsane people with their monologues and declarations; for not having homes. Bereft of committed support from any quarter, they live marginal, miserable lives and die early deaths.

As for those few schizophrenics who commit acts of horrific violence in psychotic states, they, too, are rounded up. They are found guilty in a criminal court and ordered not to a mental hospital against their (irrational) will, for that would be a violation of their *civil liberties*. They are ordered instead, in most cases, to prison, or to one of our great sprawling metropolitan jails, where their civil liberties entitle them to beatings and rape by their fellow inmates, beatings and taunting by the guards, solitary confinement that drives them madder still, deprivation of prescription drugs for those few who had prescriptions, roasting or freezing in their cells by manipulated temperature, murder, or despair-induced suicide.

Or, if "rounding up" is too much of a challenge to law enforcement, they can then simply be shot dead on the street. Or in their homes. (*I saw him reach for something.*)

Whether locked in asylums or wandering the streets, for centuries those who have been struck by madness have always had their own cruel nomenclature to bear, names intended to separate them out, divide *us* from *them*: lunatics, imbeciles, loonies, dips, weirdos, wackos, schizos, psychos, freaks, morons, nutcases, nutjobs, wingnuts, cranks.

The mad one, then, is something between a clown and a demon.

Unless that mad one is a gift of God made flesh. Madness defined as demonic possession has its countermetaphor. The Bible is saturated with episodes, visions, and characters that might have emerged from the pages of the *Diagnostic and Statistical Manual of Mental Disorders*. Disembodied voices of prophecy, flashes of blinding light, a burning bush, a sea that parts, righteous murder, ladders to heaven, transubstantiation, reincarnation, a bodily ascent into the sky, the book of Revelation entire: all are paramount among the sacred textual evidence of the Christian God.

Moses is called into the mountains of Midian by a divine Voice, returns with the Ten Commandments, the sixth of which stipulates thou shalt not kill, and at once orders the execution of three thousand "idolators." Abraham journeys into the land of Moriah, with his son Isaac in tow, for the purpose of slaying the unsuspecting boy as a test of his faith in God, only to spare the child at the last minute thanks to a heavenly voice; the Angel of the Lord has been convinced of Abraham's faith. And the Bible's concluding book is a vision of judgment so intricate, elaborate, and grandiose that, if it were told by a patient in the psych ward of a modern hospital, it would likely prompt a prescription.

If "evil" madness and "godly" madness were the two forms most recognized through history, a third interpretive force arose in the mid-twentieth century to dismiss each of these opposing dogmas: simply denying that madness exists at all. While the belief that mental illness is a myth has lacked the backing of accepted science, it quickly aroused a large and passionate following that encouraged the deinstitutionalization movement, blunted the momentum of accelerating breakthroughs in the identification and humane treatment of the mentally ill, maimed the cultural prestige of psychiatry, and justified legal obstacles to the emergency care and treatment of people in psychosis.

My family and I have witnessed this denialism in action. It arises from a seductive appeal to individual rights and constitutional freedoms. But as psychiatrist John Edwards has told me, denialism also is rooted in what he believes is "primal fear." Edwards continued: "I think primal fear is the origin, regarding mental illness, of all the misinformation, the projections, the denial, the blaming of the victim or the patient, the lack of empathy toward the sufferers, treating adolescents as criminals, cutting budgets for treatment centers—all of it. Human beings are terrified of this disease, and they try to deny it out of existence."

Most of us accept the basic, grievous medical truth of schizophrenia and do not deny the disease exists. And it is likely we will not ascribe to a mentally ill person the voice of God or of angels—nor will most of us believe that he or she is possessed by evil spirits. Yet, while holiness and denial remain powerful and influential means of interpreting (or dismissing) madness, we still do demonize the mentally ill. Demonization remains the mode of history and of our time. It may never have enjoyed the cachet and the freedom from accountability that it does now. In our era, in our country, mentally ill people suffer and die because of our fear.

On the unseasonably warm Sunday of January 5, 2014, a businessman and parent named Mark Wilsey picked up the telephone in his family home and dialed 911. This was the first step in a chain of events that within half an hour would thrust the Wilsey family through the porous membrane separating the "ordinary" from the monstrous.

Mark Wilsey, a stocky man in his mid-forties with a trimmed white mustache and goatee, was the owner of a homebuilding company in Boiling Spring Lakes, North Carolina. Boiling Spring Lakes is an

isolated town of approximately fifty-three hundred people in Brunswick County, about twenty-two miles southwest of Wilmington. It is
surrounded by more than fifty small lakes. In summer, bass fishermen
in their sunglasses and ball caps glide along the lakes' placid surfaces
in their high-performance aluminum boats, tossing their hard-plastic
poppers and buzzbaits down into what lies beneath: limestone caverns
and shifting sinkholes and the currents of five underground springs
that inevitably burst, boiling to the surface.

For Mark and Mary Wilsey, dialing the emergency response number was not an unusual event. They had called for police and paramedic
help several times over the last couple of years, starting about the time
their teenage son Keith began showing signs of mental illness. Now, on
this Sunday, Keith seemed unable to recognize his mother; he called her
"John." He said that he'd "seen a sign" advising him to ask for money. He
asked Mary if she wanted to fight. In his hand, he gripped a small electron-
ics screwdriver.[1] Mary pleaded with her husband to make the call.

Keith had retained his natural father's last name, Vidal. He had
turned nineteen less than a month earlier. He measured five feet, five
inches tall and weighed less than a hundred pounds. A mop of dark
hair spilled onto his soft face. His left eye tended to squint a little when
he smiled, as if he were about to offer a conspiratorial wink. He liked
to play video games and to pound the drums, and his parents had given
him a new drum set for Christmas.

Normally a gentle and affectionate boy—photographs show him
and his mother hugging closely—Keith had occasionally exhibited
jumbled thoughts and spoken of bizarre visions. Twice he had been
involuntarily committed for psychiatric care. His mother and stepfather tried several times to secure prescription medications that would
help him. But the right meds required the right diagnosis, and a right
diagnosis was not yet forthcoming. Finally, Mary thought she had succeeded. A doctor diagnosed Keith as suffering from schizo-affective
disorder, the worst possible combination of hallucinations and manic
depression. This time, the prescription seemed to match the disease,
and Keith's behavior improved.

And then in late 2013 the symptoms worsened again. Within about four minutes of Mark's call, John Thomas, an officer with the Boiling Spring Lakes police department two miles away, pulled to a stop in front of the Wilsey house on President Drive and strode into the house. Officer Thomas was wearing a body microphone issued by his department. The only active recording device on the scene, the microphone captured thirty-five minutes of voices and incidental noise that afternoon in the Wilsey home.*

Family members later recalled that after appraising the situation, Officer Thomas stepped to the distressed boy and tried to "talk him down" into a calm state. The two locked arms and struggled. As Officer Thomas tried to reduce Keith's agitation, a second officer hurried into the Wilsey household: Brunswick County Sheriff's Office deputy Samantha Lewis-Chavis. Lewis-Chavis joined with Thomas in the effort to subdue the boy, and the two soon had him lying facedown on the Wilseys' hardwood floor. Keith still held the screwdriver in his right hand.

His parents believe that officers Thomas and Lewis-Chavis were on the verge of gaining Keith's cooperation. But then the door flew open again and a third officer burst into the living room, thrusting his way into the small cluster of people around the boy. This was Bryon Vassey, a broad-shouldered and barrel-chested detective sergeant with eleven years' experience in the Southport department, eight miles to the south. In the court trial that followed, Mary Wilsey testified that Vassey bellowed, "I haven't got time for this shit! Tase him! Take him down now!" (Vassey denied having said this, and local newspapers reported that an officer's body microphone did not pick up such words.)

Vassey's aggressive entrance into the house, it seemed to some on the scene, caused Keith to panic—about the worst possible result of an encounter with someone in psychosis. The boy struggled free of the first

---

* Audio from the digital device was played at the trial of Bryon Vassey and small portions were quoted in the region's newspapers, but at this writing, the Boiling Springs police department has not released the recording.

two officers, bolted into the bathroom, and then charged back into the hallway, where Thomas and Lewis-Chavis again forced him to the floor. But Keith was still grasping the small screwdriver. Deputy Lewis-Chavis obeyed Vassey's order to tase Keith—though, because he was from a separate department, he lacked the authority to issue such an order to her.

Seventy seconds later, Deputy Lewis-Chavis's ear was ringing from the concussion of a service revolver discharged at close range, and Keith Vidal, with two Taser prongs in his face, lay bleeding to death on his parents' hallway floor from a bullet wound in his right armpit.

On February 3, 2014, a Brunswick County grand jury indicted Bryon Vassey on one count of voluntary manslaughter. He was suspended from his department and released on bail.

It was at the bond hearing for Vassey that the "screwdriver" that young Vidal had been holding metamorphosed into something deadlier, at least in testimony. "Let's not pussyfoot around anymore," District Attorney Jon Payne demanded—perhaps a little ominously, in retrospect—to the hearing judge, whose name was Jack Hooks. "It wasn't a screwdriver, Judge, it was a pick."[2] Whatever the object, it was not produced in evidence.

A year after that, a local reporter raised the question of why no trial date for Vassey had been set.[3]

The trial date was finally scheduled for April 18, 2016, in Brunswick County Superior Court. In the meantime, the presiding judge, Richard T. Brown, granted Vassey's request for a bench trial, a proceeding with no jury in which the judge alone renders the verdict.

The lawyers agreed after a day of argument that the detective sergeant could not be found guilty if Judge Brown determined that he had reacted reasonably in his belief that Vidal was about to kill an officer with the screwdriver. Or pick, depending on who was testifying.

In the trial, Vassey testified that Vidal had the tool raised over his head and was going to stab Thomas in the temple. How the young man could have carried out this maneuver while facedown on the floor was not made clear.

On the ninth day of the trial, Judge Brown heard defense testimony from Moira Artigues, a forensic psychiatrist of seventeen years' experi-

ence with an office in Cary, North Carolina, about 150 miles north of
Brunswick County. She had been hired to testify by the North Carolina
Police Benevolent Association at a rate of $310 an hour. Dr. Artigues
had never interviewed or met Keith Vidal. She testified that she had
reviewed the boy's medical records from 2013 and found that he had
expressed "suicidal" thoughts then. She also stated her belief that Keith
harbored homicidal thoughts. Her evidence here seemed to be word of
mouth: from Vidal's mother and doctors' comments in the past two
years that Keith "had suicidal and homicidal ideations." (Mary Wilsey
herself testified that her son had been depressed but was not a danger to
others.) Under cross-examination, Dr. Artigues admitted that she had
not reviewed Vidal's most recent records, from two weeks before the
shooting, when his behavior had taken its sharp turn for the worse.[4]
Newspaper reports do not show the prosecution boring in on this statement of omission.

Vassey admitted in testimony that he had been taking blood pressure
medicine and sleeping medication at the time of the shooting, and also
hydrocodone, a painkilling drug prescribed for him after oral surgery.[5]
Artigues testified that she did not evaluate Vassey's mental condition,
"but could have."[6] Again, the remark's implications were left unexplored.

On Friday, May 6, 2016, Judge Brown delivered his verdict in the Bryon
Vassey case: not guilty. "This has been an extremely tragic and emotional
case," the judge remarked. Sheriff's deputy Samantha Lewis-Chavis, the
second officer on the scene, was in the Brunswick County courthouse
in civilian clothes on the day the verdict was announced. F. T. Norton
of the *Wilmington Star News* spotted the woman and reported that
Lewis-Chavis "emerged from the district attorney's office with wet eyes.
She declined to comment as she hurried alone into an empty elevator. Her
sobs could be heard coming from behind its closed doors."[7]

A young reporter named Lindsay Kriz had joined a small newspaper in the area called the *Brunswick Beacon* just before the trial, and
she took part in the massive local coverage. After it ended, Kriz found
herself musing over an all but forgotten peculiarity: that transformation of Keith Vidal's small screwdriver into a "pick," or, as some outlets

took to calling it, an "ice pick." This was the transformation that had begun with District Attorney Payne's admonition to Judge Jack Hooks.

Kriz laid out her disquiet over "unanswered questions" in an 850-word essay that the *Beacon* published on May 17. "One of my questions is: What's the deal with the screwdriver?" she wrote. "This has plagued me basically since I first heard about the case when I started this job in March."

Kriz described a telephone conversation with Mark Wilsey, in which Keith's stepfather acknowledged to her that the young man had been holding a screwdriver. A few minutes after that, Wilsey called Kriz back to ask her "why other news outlets were saying [Keith] was holding an ice pick instead of a screwdriver." Kriz replied that she didn't know. She hadn't previously been aware that an ice pick had been mentioned. As the trial started, "I learned the defense was claiming that Vidal had an ice pick." Kriz's doubts about the accuracy of the description of the tool increased as the trial went on. "I will never forget Boiling Springs Police Cpl. John Thomas, on the stand, being shown [an] ice pick by the defense and saying, 'Sir, I have never seen that before in my life.'"

Kriz became convinced of her doubts, she recalled, as the anomalies mounted. "Vassey testified he retrieved the pick from Thomas. Thomas [had taken] it from Vidal's hand and passed it to Vassey, who put it in his pocket and brought it to the Boiling Springs Police Department. You're not supposed to tamper with evidence, especially at a scene where somebody died. What Vassey said he did seemed valid as far as keeping the weapon away from anyone else who might want to use it, but this was never really addressed in court."

And finally, there was the matter of four words, spoken by Mark Wilsey, picked up on Officer Thomas's recorder, and included in the transcription heard at trial: "I've got the screwdriver!"

Then Kriz presented her own closing summation: "After Vassey was acquitted, Wilsey Sr. said he was not allowed in his house for hours after the shooting and that's when [Keith's] screwdriver would've been taken from the scene.

"He said that's when the cover-up for Vassey started."[8]

The ordeal of the Vidal family broke into the news at around the time I was commencing research for this book—that is to say, after the membranes of sanity had broken beneath both of my sons. I want to say that the case of Keith's death stood out in my mind because of the pathos it embodied. Yet pathos pervades every act of destruction against a person who is mentally ill. A likelier truth is that the story gripped me because I was looking for it.

To begin consciously searching into the world of mental illness is to see it snap into focus before your eyes. It is everywhere. It has been hiding in plain sight, awaiting notice. Its camouflage is little more than the human instinct to reject engagement with the pitiable, the fearsome, the unspeakable—and to close our eyes to the moral obligations that those states of being demand of us. To focus one's heart and consciousness on the mental illness is to see abstractions transmute to flesh and blood, as they did for me in the death of Keith Vidal, which occurred eight years after schizophrenia had tormented my own son Kevin into suicide.

Mention mental illness, and the friendly woman who has trimmed your hair for years opens up about her stricken son. The assistant principal nods and tells you of her aunt, once a promising pianist, who has been in and out of psychiatric hospitals. ("In and out"—that is a phrase you will encounter often.) Your cardiologist and his wife have sunk thousands into the care of his delusional sister. A man you'd thought you knew well mentions the son he'd never talked about before, who disappeared from home at age seventeen, wrote a semicoherent letter from San Diego a few weeks later, and has not been heard from since. The clerk at the hardware store is a stabilized schizophrenic, and you never had a clue. Or you had a clue and you didn't pick up on it. Or you had a clue and picked up on it and then put it aside. Out of mind, so to speak.

These are the kinds of stories you learn when you shift your focus a millimeter or so, until it aligns with what James Agee called "the cruel radiance of what is." Then the stories never stop. Newspaper and online reports that you might once have given a glance before skipping on now command your gaze in boldface. Television footage of a body lying facedown on a city street will hold your gaze and prod you to murmur, "Mentally ill?" and you will be surprised at how often the answer turns out to be yes.

Mental illness could not have been further from my thoughts on a May afternoon in 1976. That was the day I met the woman I would marry. I spotted her as she came down the aisle of a Boeing 707 that was taking on passengers at LaGuardia Airport. We were both walk-ons. Such a thing was still possible back then. I had already boarded and was watching the stream of new arrivals from my aisle seat, on the right, when there came Honoree Fleming. I loved her before she sat down next to me. She had Irish-green eyes and wore her Irish-auburn hair to her waist, and she was quite beautiful, but that was not all that captivated me. She moved with a palpable grace and serenity, and there was gravitas in those green eyes, and I sensed a tremendous intelligence, and also gentleness, and then she looked at her boarding pass, and then at the empty seat next to me, and I stood up and moved aside, and later, and ever afterward, I realized that everything that had happened in my life had to happen as exactly and minutely as it had happened to bring me to this moment when I stood up and stepped aside as this woman, whose own history had to have unfolded as precisely as mine, moved to sit next to me.

A pair of walk-ons.

Honoree had received her PhD in biophysics at the University of Chicago two years earlier, after earning Phi Beta Kappa honors at New York University, and she had remained on in a postdoctoral position to study steroid hormones. What I could not have imagined until she told me later—all that city-girl ease and assurance—was that Honoree had overcome a family legacy of poverty, hard immigration, and childhood bereavement. Her mother had grown up in a hamlet of three thatched-roof houses in County Mayo, Ireland. She was one of nine siblings in a house with a dirt floor, and she walked barefoot several miles to school and back each day. In 1928, at age seventeen, Honora Reilly left the desperate household to relieve its cash burdens. She sailed to America on her own and made her way by train to Omaha, Nebraska, where relatives lived. It had not taken long for this country lass to decide that Omaha's lights were not bright enough for her, and she boldly moved on to Chicago—where she was greeted by endless storefronts with signs taped to the insides of their windows: NO IRISH NEED APPLY.

The young immigrant found work on Chicago's South Side as a nanny. Sometimes on weekends she would pull together a small stack of books and wander the footways of the University of Chicago, clutching the books to her chest, just to get a sense of what it might be like. She told this story to Honoree not long before she died.

Honora later moved on to New York, where she met and married a maintenance man of English descent named Berkeley Fleming. She bore his four children—three sons and Honoree, the youngest—before alcoholism overtook him. One of Honoree's earliest memories is of standing by the kitchen sink in the family's Washington Heights apartment and watching her father pull all of his teeth out, one after another, with a pliers, to relieve the pain in his gums. He died the following year, when Honoree was five. Her first words to her mother upon learning the news were, "How are we going to survive?"

They survived. Despite her background of poverty, Honora maintained a fierce faith in the power of learning. Among them, Honoree and her three brothers earned four bachelor degrees, two master's degrees, and two PhDs. Honora herself, having put her husband through engineering school, returned to school at age fifty-nine to take courses in biology and other subjects that would allow her to become a practical nurse.

Honoree had boarded this flight from New York to Chicago following her successful interview for a position at a research laboratory at Mount Sinai Hospital. After the interview, she'd sat in on a few sessions of a science convention there. The last speaker of the afternoon had canceled, and so she had decided on impulse to head for LaGuardia early. At the ticket counter, another departee from the conference, a rather large fellow, had attempted to step in front of Honoree. Washington Heights fought back. Honoree pushed the line-jumper away and claimed the ticket that would have gone to him. I joked to her ever afterward that had she not stood her ground, I might have married a large, surly male scientist. As for Honoree, she remembers deciding against pulling her seven-hundred-page text on steroid hormones from her flight bag on the chance that it might intimidate the interesting-looking man in the aisle seat.

As for the interesting-looking man, I was returning to Chicago after completing several days of interviews with television executives for what was to be my first book, a critical examination of TV news. I had taken a leave of absence from my job as a newspaper columnist and rented a sublimely ugly old two-story fieldstone pile on the southern tip of Lake Michigan, ninety miles southeast of the city. It sat on a pinnacle that descended to a narrow beach, and faced a leafy gravel road chockablock with similar houses—summer residences for the Chicago Mob in the 1920s, as local legend had it. For two or three nights in August, the city's towers were silhouetted, tiny but visible, by the setting sun.

I had planned to use the house as my solitary writer's retreat. It did become my retreat, but not solitary. Honoree came to visit on weekends, taking the South Shore railroad to nearby New Buffalo, in Indiana. We invited friends and swam in the lake and grilled food and loafed and drank Chateau Margaux wine at a price that was, as we realized later, ridiculously cheap.

Within a few weeks we were discussing how to bring up our children. We agreed that we would be loving but firm. I jokingly conjured up a figure from then-recent presidential politics and assured Honoree that I would be as fiercely disciplinary as Nixon's crew-cut consigliere, the Watergate conspirator H. R. "Bob" Haldeman.

That summer ended with Honoree having to leave for New York and her new career. My book was finished, and I would soon give up the stone house and go back to Chicago. On a rainy night in late August, the two of us drank jug wine under dim yellow lamplight on the rear porch, the lake below us invisible under the wind, and wondered about our future. I was a little emotional. All right, I was a blubbering mess. The thought of our nine-hundred-mile separation worried me. Honoree was subdued, but serene. We were in love. We would find a way. She was right. We lived apart for a year, met up at least once a month, spoke by telephone every night. At the end of that year, I quit my media job in Chicago and packed up and went to New York to be with her. We shared her small apartment on East Eighty-Fifth Street. In front of the apartment was a manhole cover that clattered every time a car drove over it. I hate sharp noise. I have never cherished a noise as much as I cherished that one.

We were married in October 1978 at the Ethical Culture Society across from Central Park. After the ceremony we took a taxi to our new apartment on West Eighty-Sixth Street. At the apartment, still in her wedding dress, Honoree supervised the making of hors d'oeuvres for our guests. It was the best and only wedding I've ever had.

Dean Paul Justin Powers was born on November 18, 1981. He arrived three weeks late and on my fortieth birthday. I told Honoree that a necktie would have been just fine. But the fact is that I cherished this boy from the moment I saw his bright, questioning eyes. I'd never particularly expected to have children, or thought much about it, through my extended years of bachelorhood. Now, all my abstract notions of children as "options" that brought "responsibilities" and presented "challenges" and "impediments" evaporated against the reality of Dean's corporeal warmth, his sacred helplessness and gratitude for nourishment, the daily lengthening of his fingers and thumbs. I soon forgot what it had been like living for forty years without a child. A son.

Dean grew to be a dreamer in his toddler years, and he remains a dreamer. I'd found work, and I wrote my articles and manuscripts at home while keeping an eye on him, with Honora's help, in our seventeenth-floor apartment, just opposite the building where Babe Ruth had once lived. Across Central Park and a few blocks north, Honoree worked as a research associate at Mount Sinai Hospital, studying the effects of steroid hormones upon cultured uterine cells. Every day I loaded Dean into his canvas-and-aluminum carrier, strapped it to my back, and took him on trips up to Broadway for visits to the dry cleaner, the wineshop, the supermarket, the little Greek takeout where roasted ducks turned on a spit. When I came to live in New York I had brought with me a Midwesterner's wariness, but with Dean fastened to my back—I could feel his bouncing and rocking—an irrational feeling of indestructibility always enveloped me. Who, however depraved, could possibly bring harm to such a radiant, glad child? Who, or what?

By age two, Dean had taken on many of his lifelong physical characteristics: a head of thick tousled brown hair, hazel eyes that approximated Honoree's green ones, and a solemn expression that mirrored my own. Our daily excursions by now involved our meandering hand in hand the half-block from our building to West End Avenue and across it into Riverside Park. One of New York's thousands of iron sidewalk grates, probably once used for delivering coal, lay in our path to the street corner. Dean could not pass this grate without stepping on it, pausing, and bending over to peer down into its darkness. His peering could take awhile. This often caused a flash of anxiety in the Midwestern father: these grates were known to give way once every so often. Yet I never really worried. I still irrationally thought of my son as indestructible, and myself as indestructible in his vicinity. And only now do I find myself discovering—and resisting—a metaphor in his gaze into the depths.

Once inside the park, my son made straight for the playground equipment. He loved to climb the steps to the pinnacle of the slide. There he would pause and stand, casting his eyes across the Hudson into New Jersey, until the children following him were stacked up in a kind of kid gridlock. Usually I could snap him out of it, but sometimes his motionless gaze persisted. What was Dean looking for, or seeing, that the children behind him could not? By the time he was four, our excursions were growing into adventures—or as Dean would say, "vaventures." We walked up to Eighty-Sixth and Broadway and got on the IRT subway ("the sunway") for the long ride down to the tip of lower Manhattan, where we would catch the ferry to Ellis Island, craning our necks to admire the stately green woman holding the torch aloft, whom Dean called the Snatue Delivery. Or we cabbed it over to the Museum of Natural History to check out the giant fiberglass blue whale and the dinosaur skeletons, along with an obligatory stop at the African diorama that features the young baboon, having rounded a bush and skidded to a halt in front of the welcoming viper. Dean always became thoughtful looking at that one. I had to wonder what ideas a son assembled as he absorbed a scene of nature in all its drama and the imminence of ugly death.

Kevin Berkeley Powers rocketed into the world on July 21, 1984, emerging with such velocity that for an instant it looked as though he might shoot right through the obstetrician's gloved hands. He was ivory-skinned, whereas Dean was darker; and his hair, when it appeared, grew long and yellow and curly above his blue eyes. Velocity was his modus. Dean, more laconic, observed this rollicking new arrival with amusement and tolerance. Two years and eight months separated them in age; they became amiable playmates and, later, friends; and, later still, a dynamic guitar duo.

By the time of Kevin's birth we had moved from West Side Manhattan to a little two-story brick house in Yonkers, just north of the city.

Ever the one to find an excuse to worry, I fretted for a while that this incomprehensible little being could pry his way into a family that already seemed entirely complete in its bonds. I need not have worried. Kevin came supplied with his own built-in dynamo. Crowing lustily from the seat of his Jolly Jumper affixed to a doorway, the baby made himself right at home, bouncing and cackling, his arms in motion, riveting all our attention. Dean didn't seem to mind.

In fact, Dean took his role as big brother seriously. It seemed to give him gravitas. He liked to be in on important adult doings in the household. I recall coming home one afternoon to find him and Honoree in the kitchen, Dean with crumbs on his fingers and chin. He looked up and greeted me and announced in Important tones: "We're making chicken in *fancy* style!"

One mud-puddly autumn day before the Yonkers move, Dean and I were alone at the tiny playground in Riverside Park. Dean was on a swing, and I was standing a few yards away, watching him. Something made me shift my gaze and take in a shape on the playground's far border. A thin young stranger, rainwater dripping from his black, oily hair, stood watching my son. His hands were in the pockets of his mouse-colored raincoat. After a while he shifted his attention from

Dean to me. The two of us stood motionless, our eyes locked onto each other's. No other human being was visible except for Dean, who swung happily.

I tried to calculate whether, if I broke into a sprint, I could reach my son before the stranger did. I was maybe three long paces closer than he. I bent my knees a little and tensed for my lunge, but otherwise I did not move; not yet. I was waiting for motion from him. Our eyes remained interlocked. After perhaps half a minute, the stranger gave a brief half-smile, then he turned his back and walked away. I quickly closed the distance between my son and me.

After that, my delusions of invulnerability went away. The stranger would return, in a different shape. And I would never reach my son in time.

For several years I had been lecturing in nonfiction every August at the Bread Loaf Writers' Conference near the Green Mountain National Forest above Middlebury, Vermont. Dean's first visit to Bread Loaf occurred three months before he was born: Honoree, her hair still down to her waist and braided then, was radiant in a violet paisley ankle-length maternity dress. Through a stroke of good luck, our assigned lodging for the sixteen summers of visits there was the Homer Noble farmhouse, a nineteenth-century white wood-frame that sat atop a hillock less than a mile from the Bread Loaf campus. A dirt road bordered by blackberry bushes connected the farmhouse to the main road. Behind it, to the north, stretched a rising meadow, and beyond the meadow lay woods. Robert Frost purchased that farmhouse in 1939 as a summer residence, and he wrote there, and in the smaller log cabin near the woods, until his death in 1963. In 1968 the homestead was designated a national landmark.

The boys experienced Bread Loaf as a kind of Brigadoon, a nonesuch kingdom that swept into view every August around a mountain-road curve at the end of a five-hour car ride: a permanent summery little realm of right-angled wood-framed buildings (the residence dorms) painted in bright yellow with green roofs and shutters, and ringed in the distance by fog-crowned mountains. The dominating structure is the Inn (more dorm rooms, the long dining hall, the administrative office, a fragrant fireplace), whose original construction traces to the 1860s. In back of the Inn rises a grand old three-story structure with gigantic Alice-in-Wonderland doors. This was the Barn. Down the hill behind the Barn, which contains classrooms and a spacious main floor where participants go to read, and talk, and eat, and dance on Friday nights, is a final unexpected wonder: a small pond with a miniature island crowning its center, and a wooden raft for getting there.

Many grown-ups, alighting at the campus from their airport shuttles, are stunned to silence by the intensity of this abrupt transition to what seems a palpable, perfect past. For an urban child open to enchantment, it can seize the soul and never let go. Dean and Kevin were such children. They gave themselves to this kingdom populated by a couple hundred grown-ups of mysterious provenance to them: mellow, friendly, strolling people who tended to disappear en masse inside the Barn and the other outbuildings from time to time, only to emerge about an hour later, stroll some more, and then vanish back into the buildings. Some of these people had children of their own, and so a kind of kingdom-within-a-kingdom existed, with kids poking their heads out of the alfalfa fields, waiting their turn for a ride to the island on the raft piloted by a Bread Loaf staffer, or sharing a long table in the clattering laughing dining hall.

Our sons loved the Frost farmhouse as well—the "Hobo Nobo" as they called it—prowling its small upstairs rooms and letting its lace curtains billow through their fingers, and inhaling its ancient aromas of charred firewood and the petrified glue of old books. In the evenings, as the grown-ups sat in the Little Theater listening to, say, Paul Mariani rumble forth his poems of working-class grace in his Long Island workingman's baritone, or to Linda Pastan's piercing epigrammatic lines ("I made a list of things I have / to remember and a list / of things I want to forget, / but I see they are the same list"), the children frolicked in the safe Vermont night.

Within a few years we started to entertain thoughts of moving to Vermont. The conference director, a professor of English at Middlebury College, recommended Honoree to the department of chemistry, which immediately recognized her credentials and offered her an appointment as a visiting professor of biochemistry, with the strong possibility of a tenure-track position. Our idle dream was now at the threshold of reality.

Yet we hesitated. Honoree was a lifelong New Yorker. My livelihood was tied to the city. We had previously moved to Yonkers for greater residential space within proximity to the city. Then one night, running late for a chamber music performance at Alice Tully Hall and finding parking garages filled, we took a chance in leaving our car parked on Tenth Avenue. The resulting vandalism was not drastic—a broken window, some audiocassettes looted. But in the time-honored spirit of mugged urban liberals everywhere, Honoree and I looked at each other, and one of us said: "Let's go to Vermont."

We went to Vermont. Where it was safe, for us and for our sons.

Years later, after our time in Middlebury, after our sons each encountered his particular dark shadow, after Honoree and I had been thrust into darkness with them, the Homer Noble Farm itself was vandalized, young invaders stopping by its woods on a snowy evening. Where my sons had explored and slept and had their dreams and games, other people partied, leaving behind broken windows, broken chairs, broken dishes, beer and rum bottles, pools of vomit, spittle, and piss—ten thousand dollars in damages. No place is safe, but by then we had already learned that.

2

What Is Schizophrenia?

What if we are all potential schizophrenics? What if our ancestors were schizophrenic as a matter of course?

What if schizophrenia were the foundational state of human consciousness?

What if vestiges of this preconscious state remain embedded in the human brain, in all newborns' brains—dormant but viable, awaiting a collision with some random circumstance to be hurt into poetry—Yeats's phrase—if only the dark poetry of destruction and self-destruction? Or, perhaps equally disturbing, what if that spurred state *gave* us the luminous poetry of art? Or the poetry of God?

Such questions can seem outlandish, yet they have been posed by serious, scholarly men and women in modern times in attempts to answer an unanswerable question: What *is* schizophrenia?

So little is known about schizophrenia that neuropsychiatrists and researchers hesitate to offer a definitive theory of causation. Of its origins and causes, the writer and professor of psychology Richard Noll has suggested that "contemporary readers would do well to be humbled by our current state of scientific knowledge." He points out that more than thirty thousand articles on the disease were published between 1998 and 2007, and that the output since then has increased to about five thousand articles per year. This illness shares with cancer, its partner in catastrophic affliction, an almost otherworldly imperviousness to definitive understanding and cure.

Neuropsychiatrists and allied professionals have only recently moved toward agreement on several fundamental likelihoods. Among them:

What we call "schizophrenia" is not a single disease, or a "categorical illness," but a rare clustering of several distinct malfunctions in the brain.

These malfunctions are genetic in nature, yet in a far more complex way than direct genetic inheritances like hair or eye color.

These *genetic* malfunctions are unlikely to produce schizophrenia in an individual unless they are stimulated by *environmental* conditions. By far the most causative environmental factor is stress, especially during gestation in the womb, early childhood, and adolescence—stages in which the brain is continually reshaping itself, and thus vulnerable to disruption. Stress can take the form of a person's enduring sustained anger, fear, or anxiety, or a combination of these. Stress works its damage by prompting an oversupply of cortisol, the normally life-sustaining "stress hormone" that converts high-energy glycogen to glucose in liver and in muscle tissue. Yet when it is called upon to contain a rush of glycogen, cortisol can transform itself into "Public Enemy Number One," as one health advocate put it. The steroid hormone swells to flood levels and triggers weight gain, high blood pressure, heart disease, damage to the immune system, and an overflow of cholesterol. Stress is a likely trigger for schizophrenia.

Many scientists believe that stress is especially destructive during the natural adolescent process of "pruning"—a critical and necessary period of cell destruction that can leave the prefrontal cortex open to disruption. I will explain pruning in greater detail later.

Scientists generally agree that the disease produces three sets of symptoms: positive, negative, and cognitive. Positive symptoms of schizophrenia are the most dramatic. They beckon the sufferer into an imaginary world, a world of shapes and presences and, most commonly, voices. Some people with schizophrenia can construct those voices and hallucinations into an alternate identity that either speaks to them or that they inhabit, as when they come to believe themselves a great leader from history, or even a god. In extreme cases, the patient acts out these delusions, sometimes with violent, deadly, and self-destructive results.

Negative symptoms embrace a range of responses that manifest as generalized withdrawal. They can take the form of decreased motivation, cauterized emotions, a passive turning away from friends, and listlessness—symptoms that are distinct from symptoms of clinical depression. Cognitive symptoms can include a loss of memory, a lack of focus on what is happening or being said, and a diminished ability to process information and take useful action based on it.

Despite such increasingly authoritative theories, I cannot put aside my layman's fascination with a book that appeared at the dawn of neuro-psychiatric discovery, an era that would strongly interrogate the book's assumptions. Despite the perceptions of obsolescence, it remains a book that, as many of its critics concede, offers richly provocative speculation on the origin of madness within its larger theme: an exploration into what the author calls "the consciousness of consciousness."

The Origin of Consciousness in the Breakdown of the Bicameral Mind was written by the late psychologist Julian Jaynes and published in 1976. Despite the portentous tone of the title, it is an unusually audacious, original, and eloquently written speculation on why and how human beings think, especially about themselves. It probes the question of why people sometimes hallucinate images, hear disembodied voices, express fantastical thoughts, and behave in ways that make no sense to "ordinary" people.

Jaynes, the son of a Unitarian minister, drew upon the extraclinical viewpoints he gathered as a playwright and actor before he turned to psychology. He proposed that until as recently as three thousand years ago, human beings were not "conscious" in the way that consciousness is understood today. That is, they were not conscious of being conscious, with all the introspection that state implies. We were instead a largely instinctual species, according to Jaynes, subject to "the authority of sound." We believed and obeyed without skepticism the seemingly autonomous voices that came into our thoughts.

To oversimplify Jaynes's theory (and oversimplification is virtually the only way to discuss his arguments without quoting the 469-page book entire), three millennia ago the two halves of our brain, though connected by millions of fibers, functioned almost autonomously in a sharp division of labor. The left hemisphere contained (as it still does) three "speech areas" that enabled our understanding of language. This left half was what Jaynes called the "man (human) part." The ununified right hemisphere was the repository of something far more complex: the seedbed, perhaps, of mysticism and religion. Here lay Jaynes's "god" part: the received sounds, most importantly human speech, actual and imagined. The bicameral mind did not distinguish between the actual and the imagined. Remembered voices bore the same authenticity as voices of other people in the moment. They often were admonitory—the voices of the father, the village elder—and thus commanded obedience. Hence: voices as gods.

The halves of the bicameral brain functioned almost independently through the epochs of subsistence agriculture and nomadic exploring, epochs of scattered populations and relatively little social complexity. It was the increase in population density and intense social interactions—divisions of labor, inventions, warfare—that obliged the brain to evolve into self-awareness, and to recognize internal thoughts as internal thoughts, not messages from on high. Yet the voices of our thoughts still echoed in us as if they came from other entities. In fact, Jaynes argues, in our own times, even everyday voices command us to a kind of obedience. To understand someone speaking to us, "we have to become the other person; or rather, we let him become part of us for a brief second. We suspend our own identities." What also has survived even in our evolved time is "a vestigial godlike function in the right hemisphere," according to Jaynes. "If [my] model is correct," he writes, "there might be some residual indication, no matter how small, of the ancient divine function of the right hemisphere."[1] Later in the book he writes: "What we now call schizophrenia...begins in human history as a relationship to the divine, and only around 400 B.C."[2]

The nascent shift in awareness from the bicameral to the integrated brain, Jaynes believes, can be located in certain distinctions between the two great epics commonly attributed to Homer, the *Iliad* and the

Odyssey. The two poems—passed along orally at first—were composed probably a century apart between 750 and 650 BC. (Some scholars place the creations farther back.) As the science writer Veronique Greenwood explained in a profile of Jaynes, the characters in the *Iliad* have no ability to look inside themselves: "They do only what is suggested by the gods." But in the *Odyssey*, "the characters are capable of something like interior thought... The modern mind, with its internal narrative and longing for direction from a higher power, appears."[3]

Jaynes's assertions have struck neurologically trained readers as eccentric or, at best, fatally compromised by his unawareness of the discoveries just then commencing. For instance, he writes, "Whatever brain areas are utilized, it is absolutely certain that such voices do exist," adding that they are experienced exactly like actual sound. "They are heard by many completely normal people to varying degrees." He seems a bit suspiciously sure of himself at times. The bicameral voices of antiquity, he averred, "were in quality very much like auditory hallucinations in contemporary people."[4] Yet readers of Jaynes who have lived out some of these assertions remain a bit more open-minded. I have experienced such voices on perhaps half a dozen very brief occasions that I can only dimly recall. I do remember that they sounded real. Most of these, I think, occurred while I was slipping into sleep or emerging from it, but they were not dreams. I cannot, however, vouch for being what Jaynes called "completely normal."

A century after naming this multiheaded beast, science is beginning to understand the biological mechanisms underlying the symptoms of schizophrenia and the psychosocial factors that influence their expression. Yet a vast and tragic gulf still separates scientific understanding from the incomprehension of people in general, including relatives of the afflicted, taxpayers, and the chain-link network of law enforcement, the courts, and jails. This mass public confusion has resulted in uncounted millions of wasted resources, much of it vaporized due to lost economic production, but more of it expended on maintaining punitive institutions such as jails, which have become the country's largest de facto mental institutions and which specialize, however unwittingly, in making an inmate's mental illness worse. Enlightened systems of care would cost Americans far less than the thoughtless incarceration and the resultant recidivism among those who must struggle to manage their actions. America, it seems, is not yet ready for enlightenment.

The cost to America's human treasury—the miasma of disabling personal agony, bewilderment, and social ostracism felt by a victim and his or her loved ones—is beyond any system of counting. Yet the abstraction of "human treasury" tends to distract one from contemplating the ruined uniqueness and hopes of individual lives.

What if you raised a child who grew up sunny, loved, and loving, perhaps unaccountably talented, a source of family joy, only to watch that child slowly transform in adolescence into a mysterious stranger, shorn of affect, dull of gaze, unresponsive to communication—and perhaps worse?

What if you grew to understand that this stranger was indeed communicating—but with no one whom you could see or hear?

What if you were forced to commence the lifelong process of reckoning with the likelihood that this child you thought you knew might persist in living, yet would never really return?

What if this transformation deepened and grew malign? What if this offspring of yours believed that you meant him harm—or intended to harm you? Or wanted to harm others? Or herself?

What if all of this misfortune were compounded by primal fear and judgmental withdrawal on the part of friends and even relatives? What if you picked up on gossip, as you surely would, among these friends, and relatives, and casual acquaintances, that your child's madness was just an extension of his unhappiness, or weak character—or your own failures as a parent?

As if the symptoms of schizophrenia were not devastating enough in themselves, nature has added a cruel joke, a seemingly valueless yet powerful barrier between the sufferer and professionals reaching out to help. The cruel joke is called anosognosia. *Anosognosia*, a Greek term connoting a blockage of insight into one's self (literally, "without knowledge"), is the false conviction within a person that nothing is wrong with his mind. It stems from a physiological by-product of psychosis, and accompanies about 50 percent of schizophrenia occurrences and 40 percent of bipolar cases. Anosognosia disrupts the parietal lobe's capacity to interpret sensory information from around the body. It may also be present in victims of strokes or of physical trauma to the brain.

Kevin would never admit that he suffered from mental illness. The closest term that he would tolerate was "a condition." As his illness deepened, so did his anosognosia. At the outset of his treatment, he consented to a prescribed regimen of oral medications. But nearly three years later—when the end was near—he decided that he did not need them, and he calmly informed us that he was going to stop taking them. We could not budge him from this insistence. Predictably, his refusal to take his pills led to another break, which led to another of his several hospitalizations. After that, he agreed to resume his regimen of meds, or so we'd thought. But after his death we discovered some of these drugs concealed or scattered in our basement.

It was not until nearly a decade after Kevin's death that my family learned—far too late—that our son's suicidal impulses might have been suppressed by a well-established, but underused, alternative method of administering antipsychotic medications. This is the so-called "depot" method—"depot" from the French sense of "place of deposit." More recently the concept has been rebranded as LAIs, for "long-acting injectables."

"Depot" was introduced in the late 1960s precisely to neutralize anosognosia. It involves a periodic injection performed by a clinician, rather than a self-administered daily oral dosage, of the prescribed medication. (Not all antipsychotic meds, particularly among the "second generation" ones that will be examined in chapter 15, can be transferred from the oral to the depot method.) The deposit usually goes into the muscled tissue of the patient's buttocks. The density of the muscle tissue ensures that the injected substance will flow into the patient's system gradually, and in consistent quantities, over a period of time—usually about a month. The clinician serves as an outside monitor who keeps track of the patient's cooperation. Oral meds, on the other hand, must be taken daily, and the responsibility usually falls on the patient. And therein lies the biggest rub.

Among the most notoriously feckless and forgetful populations in the world is that of mid-adolescents. Stir in with those traits the twin poisons of schizophrenia and anosognosia, and you have what seems to be a near-guarantee of catastrophe.

The biggest question when comparing "depot" over oral dosage is whether that intuitive response is valid: whether "depots" actually reduce incidences of relapse into psychosis, as they were designed to do.

Advocates of the depot method tend to feel certain that the answer is yes. In 2007, two British investigators, Maxine Patel of the Institute of Psychiatry in London and Mark Taylor, lead clinician at Springpark Centre, Glasgow, made a flat assertion: "Depots overcome overt, covert, and unintentional nonadherence" to patients' medical regimens.[5] Statistical studies, however, have been less categorical. In 2011, a team of investigators reviewed ten recent studies of 1,700 participants and concluded: "Depot antipsychotic drugs significantly reduced relapse," pointing to "relative and absolute risk reductions" of 30 and 10 percent.[6] Another review of studies pointed out that *most* schizophrenia patients stopped taking their meds at some point—75 percent after only two years—and asserted that no strong evidence pointed to a decisive benefit of the depot method.[7]

As for the Powers family, we endured our own "study," one we would have given anything to avoid. Our younger son, Kevin, was prescribed oral antipsychotics by a series of psychiatrists over three years; he loathed taking them yet pretended not to; he went off them; eventually hiding the ones he assured us he'd taken; and destroyed himself in the midst of a psychotic break. Our older son, Dean, some years and some resistance later, accepted the shrewdly constructed arguments of his psychiatrist, agreed to "depot" injections of Haldol, and has lived, and has improved.

In the decade or so before the end of the nineteenth century, mind science was still struggling to free itself from the last tangles of superstition, supernatural explanation, and the use of metaphor as a means of explaining madness. The young Viennese thinker Sigmund Freud was building upon innovative work by his European contemporaries to give humankind a sophisticated if fanciful conceptual scaffold on which to build rational understanding of the irrational. Freud classified aspects and functions of the mind, introducing such new terms as "the unconscious," "libido," "repression," "denial," "catharsis," "parapraxis," "transference," "dream interpretation"; and "the id," "the ego," and "the superego." He hypnotized his patients and got them to recall things they didn't know they remembered. Exploring these recovered memories often relieved those patients of their symptoms of depression, hysteria, or compulsive behavior.

Freud's methods seemed to work, at least for a small and select circle of patients. He was thought a revolutionary; he had created something where nothing had existed before, a sweeping model of the mind, built upon internally consistent components. No one had ever previously attempted a unified theory of human thought and its intricacies. Yet the changing times were pleading for such a theory; the Western world was hurtling from rural to urban, religious to secular, uncritical assumption to sharp analytic skepticism. "Progress," founded on questioning the verities of received thought and wisdom, was becoming the new secular god. People were losing patience with the blandishments that until the late nineteenth century fed the hunger for comprehending the mind's mysteries: blandishments such as demons, "humours," planetary gravity, "energy," Scrooge's undigested bit of beef. All these faded before Freud's dense nosologies.

The problem remained that Freud's constructs were metaphors. They were intended to alleviate compulsive preoccupations of the mind—neuroses—via painstakingly coaxing memories from the patient: "psychoanalysis." Freud's categories did not describe anything physical, visible, tactile. Nothing he said was verifiable via the scientific method. His scaffolding, if powerfully persuasive, was a scaffolding of words, employed to extract words.

Much of what we believe about "the mind" we must express through metaphor. The mind is itself a metaphor. The brain, where the corporeal answers resided, lay inaccessible, surrounded by a hard layer of protective bone, the skull. Unlike blood or bodily tissue, it could not be extracted for inspection without killing the patient. Or without waiting until the patient was dead.

The only way into the brain, for millennia, was via autopsy. As the practice of dissecting dead bodies grew in sophistication, it proved invaluable in advancing medical knowledge, as when the German Rudolf Ludwig Carl Virchow used it to discover a large quantity of white cells in the body of a fifty-year-old woman; he called this condition *leukämie*.

Inevitably, autopsy led doctors to explore the most complex organ in the body, thanks to Emil Kraepelin, who was the first psychiatrist to apply empirical science to evaluate the brain. Almost no laypeople in America today would recognize his name, yet many in the profession still consider him to be the father of modern psychiatry instead of Freud, whose theories Kraepelin detested.

Born in 1856, the same year as Freud, Kraepelin made his mark early, in 1883, when at age twenty-seven he published his foundational *Compendium der Psychiatrie*, arguing his case for the organic causes of mental illness and setting out his groundbreaking systems of classification. He charged headlong at the established masters of "mind-cure." His great text dismissed the idea that a given illness could be inferred from a given symptom. Instead, it was constituted of particular, observable *combinations* of symptoms that became evident as the illness progressed and pointed to its specific nature. Kraepelin drew this conclusion from poring over thousands of medical case studies. As for psychiatry, he concluded it should be joined to medical science, given that severe mental illness was the result of flawed biological processes in the brain— measurable through the steady deterioration of the patient's thought processes and behavior in ways unprompted by external experiences.

From his studies in biology he assembled his pioneering classifications of mental affliction in essentially two overall categories. One he called the *exogenous*, which stemmed from the reversals of fortune that life can bring to people, of the kinds that many people brought to Freud. These patients, Kraepelin agreed, could be treated. He assigned this category the umbrella designation *manic-depressive*. The second classification was incalculably more foreboding, and what it described set Kraepelin apart from previous psychiatric thought—even, and especially, from his great contemporary—and bête noire—Sigmund Freud. This was the *endogenous*, the inner region of the physical brain. Here lay the zone of organic brain damage (unacknowledged by the Viennese master) that was caused by flawed organic patterns and deteriorating tissue.

The organic deterioration Kraepelin postulated was, and is, associated with extreme old age. It is called dementia. But Kraepelin noticed from the case studies that a significant number of patients had begun showing symptoms of dementia in their teens and early twenties. Something was going wrong with the brains of these young people, and it was going wrong decades ahead of normal expectations. What could it be?

In 1896, Kraepelin introduced a term to define his answer to that question: "dementia praecox." (That same year Freud coined "psychoanalysis.") This Latinate word has references to "precocious" and "premature." Kraepelin had no hesitation about defining this form of illness as biological in origin, the result, perhaps, of "toxic" secretions from the sex glands (take that, Sigmund!) or the intestines.

Other psychiatrists soon gravitated to the biological point of view. In 1903, a thirty-nine-year-old doctor left his practice in Frankfurt to join Kraepelin as an assistant at the Munich medical school. Alois Alzheimer had admired the Munich doctor's work from afar, and he saw that it converged with some of his own. Alzheimer was then treating a fifty-one-year-old woman who was beset by delusions, hallucinations, paranoia, and bursts of violent behavior—classic symptoms of senile dementia, for which she was, statistically, too young. Alzheimer had never seen a case like this. When the woman died in 1906 at age fifty-five, Alzheimer obtained consent from her family to examine her brain. What he found in his autopsy—peering at thinly sliced slivers of cortex matter—were deposits of plaque and decayed strands of nerve cells: common flaws in the brain of, say, a ninety-year-old, but virtually unheard of in someone so young.

Alzheimer's disease,* as it became known, is similar to senile dementia, though its onset before age sixty-five was and remains extremely rare. In a grossly unfair example of "unintended consequences," its frequency has greatly expanded exactly because of medical progress, which has eliminated or deferred the onset of many lethal diseases, thus allowing people to live longer, and thus bringing more and more of them into the age range for this excruciating, slowly progressing affliction. And it remains irreversible.

The scientific value of Kraepelin's and Alzheimer's discoveries is immense. They decisively ratified the existence of physical causes of mental illness, and thus legitimized decades of development of neurotechnology—culminating, thus far at least, in CAT and PET scans, EEGs, MRIs, and MEGs†—methods, all, of providing information about what is happening in the living brain, whether the presence of tumors, evidence of epilepsy, or—eventually—the glimmerings of the causes of schizophrenia.

A figure even more important than Alzheimer in building upon Kraepelin's ideas (often, paradoxically, by taking issue with them) was the Swiss psychiatrist Eugen Bleuler. Bleuler was born in 1857, a year after Kraepelin and Freud. Unlike the emotionally remote Kraepelin with his dependence upon case studies, Bleuler plunged directly into the lives of his psychiatric patients. Not only did he conduct analytical interviews with them, which partly rebridged the gap that Kraepelin

---

* Records suggest that Kraepelin himself diagnosed it; and scientists have speculated that he allowed his new colleague to take the credit because he did not want to be seen as the only psychiatrist successfully on the trail of mental illnesses that had organic sources in the brain.

† These are acronyms for computerized axial tomography, positron emission tomography, electroencephalography, magnetic resonance imaging, and magnetoencephalography.

had marked off from Freud, but he socialized with them, accompanied them on hikes, arranged theater productions in which he acted along with them, and sometimes supervised their financial interests.[8] These intimate encounters allowed Bleuler to gather analytic insights unavailable through the filter of abstract assessment. He came to believe that mental illnesses covered an even wider and more complex range than the types Kraepelin had laid out—that they could include not just organic but environmental components, such as the ravages of abuse, traumatic shock, stress, all events that roughly corresponded to Kraepelin's "exogenous" category.

Here was the essence of what would become the "spectrum" concept of differentiated mental disorders, and with ever-improving diagnostic technology, its principles were to light the way for tremendous gains in brain science.* But Bleuler left himself open for years of second-guessing, not least because of a single word choice. Perhaps a little dazzled by the promise of his own refinements, he persuaded his colleagues to drop "dementia praecox" from the lexicon and replace it with a word of his own. Getting rid of Kraepelin's term was not a bad idea in itself: Bleuler had grown convinced that it was not dementia that psychiatrists were seeing in young patients, but something else, something a great deal more complicated. In 1908 he summed up this something else with the term "schizophrenia." This was not a wise choice. The word's literal meaning, drawing upon the Greek, meant "a splitting of the mind." Its ambiguity

---

* Just in case the reader is beginning to hope that these progressions are leading toward final enlightenment, a small monkey wrench of further ambiguity should be tossed here. In their paper "Schizophrenia: A Conceptual History," published by the *International Journal of Psychology and Psychological Therapy* in 2003, the psychiatric researchers German E. Berrios, Rogelio Luque, and José M. Villagrán write: "It would seem that no crucial experiment has ever been carried out to demonstrate that 'latest means truest' or that 'high usage' constitutes adequate evidence for validity. Indeed, the only support for the 'recency' assumption is the view that in this paper will be called the 'continuity hypothesis.' By the same token, peer and medico-legal pressures are a better explanation of 'high usage' than 'truth-value.' In fact, there is no 'objective' or 'empirical' way to decide which of the various definitions (referents) of 'schizophrenia' should be considered as the definitive RRUS." Have a nice day.

practically pleaded for misinterpretation, especially among laypeople. By "split," Bleuler meant a "loosening of associations"—the associations being the physical conductors that unify thoughts and behavior. (In important ways, this term anticipates Julian Jaynes's formulations.) In other words, psychosis did not always arise from "dementia," or decaying cells and tissue. In people who were not decrepit, it usually was triggered by a cluster of genetic flaws, often the result of heredity.

Yet "a loosening of associations" was for many just a short step from "split personality," which itself was but a short step from the old, largely discarded ghost of demonic possession. The times were rife with images of it, especially from the Gothic precincts of the British Isles. The Scotsman Robert Louis Stevenson published *The Strange Case of Dr Jekyll and Mr Hyde* in 1886. In 1897, the Irish novelist Bram Stoker published *Dracula*. Even Freud, from far-off Vienna, joined the fun— albeit unintentionally—with his 1918 paper on the patient he called "the Wolf Man." The Wolf Man was not in fact a shape-shifter; he was a depressive Russian aristocrat who, while very young, had witnessed his parents having sex, started having dreams of trees filled with white wolves, and from then on never felt really great, though he lived until 1979. It may not be entirely insignificant that the parents were using a sex technique that involved canine resonances.

Bleuler accepted Freud's emphasis on the unconscious, his use of hypnotism, and his strong diagnostic interest in hysteria. But he held back from accepting psychoanalysis as the cure-all for mental illness. He posited that the affliction, or afflictions, presented both *basic* and *accessory* symptoms. Basic symptoms, probably passed along through heredity, involved the deterioration and ultimate breakdown of the ability to think. Accessory symptoms were manifestations of that breakdown: delusions and hallucinations. The fundamentals of his formulation retain their diagnostic dimensions today.

Both Kraepelin and Bleuler (despite their differences) seem to have possessed great gifts, including extraordinary intuition. As has been remarked, decades would have to pass before neurotechnology came along to ratify and fine-tune their pioneering proposals about physical contributors—*lesions*, in a word—to madness. The basics of brain formation, so inaccessible to their generation, are by now familiar to most educated people. Still, a brief summary here may help the reader comprehend the inception of schizophrenia as we presently understand it, following Kraepelin's and Bleuler's beacon.

The prefrontal cortex is a complex, fragile region of the brain. In its healthy state, it directs human impulses toward rational choices and away from destructive or self-destructive behavior. It allows us to deal with the present moment while storing plans for the future. Yet as the newest part of the brain to develop in human evolution, the prefrontal cortex is also the region that takes the longest time to reach maturity, or maximum operating efficiency. It will not be fully functional until the person is past the age of twenty.

This out-of-sync progress ranks among the most profound natural misfortunes of humanity. For while the prefrontal cortex is taking its time, other powerful components of the human-in-progress have raced across the finish line and function without the cortex's restraints. A young adult with a still-developing prefrontal cortex will have reached physical maturity, which of course means the capacity to reproduce and the strong hormonal drive to do so. The hormone testosterone emerges and unleashes aggressive urges. Given the formative turmoil of the prefrontal cortex, emotional behavior is under the inadequate jurisdiction of the amygdala, a small and primitive region near the center of the brain. The amygdala is about reactions—impulses—rather than rational thought, the great boon of the prefrontal cortex.

The activity holding back the prefrontal cortex's final maturation is a kind of neurological housecleaning. In its final development stage, the cortex must actually *lose* some of its prefrontal "gray matter," the clusters of nerve-cell bodies that formed transmission routes during infancy and childhood. This "synaptic pruning" peaks in late adolescence and is necessary for a regrouping of the cortical connections and routes that will orchestrate brain functions for the rest of a person's life, at least until old-age decay sets in.

It is normally during this period that a schizophrenia-inducing gene cluster will activate. The reasons that this does or does not happen remain elusive. In 1983, University of California professor of psychiatry Irwin Feinberg suggested that schizophrenia could be triggered by "excessive" pruning of the cortical synapses, especially if it is accompanied by a reciprocal failure to prune certain subcortical structures. Over the years Feinberg's hypothesis became the basis of productive refinements. In 2011, psychiatric researchers Gabor Faludi and Karoly Mirnics published a review that cited sixty references to Feinberg's "radical new theory," as they called it, and endorsed the growing consensus that schizophrenia is "a mental disorder with a complex etiology that arises as an interaction between genetic and environmental factors."

As should be evident by now, the most implacable barrier to conquering schizophrenia (besides public apathy and governmental disinvolvement) has been the almost inexhaustible complexities of the brain, with its billions of electrochemically stimulated neurons and its labyrinth of interconnecting conduits—one hundred thousand miles of axons *in each human being*, submicroscopically separated by up to one quadrillion (fifteen zeros) synaptic connections, or spaces between neurons.

We can focus on just one example of these complexities and the conceptual halls of mirrors they can produce. The MRI, which affords a "look" through the brain's gnarly protective barriers via magnetism and radio waves, has generated a wealth of new peripheral understanding—and new scientific debate—around mental illness. Scanning the brain can illuminate structural abnormalities—disconnections, say, in the pathways through which brain chemicals flow. These chemicals include the widely versatile neurotransmitter dopamine, which regulates cognition, motor control, and emotional functions. They include another vital neurotransmitter, serotonin, a mainstay of the central nervous system that governs social behavior, memory, and sexual function. MRIs are also helpful in tracking the entire trajectory of synapse and circuit formation that can damage the wiring of the brain.

Yet our illuminations often lead only to new questions. There are simply too many variables. In September 2013, the National Institutes of Health announced a list of nine neuroscience goals, in response to President Obama's BRAIN Initiative (Brain Research through Advancing Innovative Neurotechnologies), which by that point had drawn public and private pledges of more than $300 million toward developing new tools and research on schizophrenia. The research psychologist Gary Marcus at New York University, analyzing these goals in the *New Yorker*, noted that the report itself acknowledged the core challenge: that "brains—even small ones—are vastly complex." He continued:

> The most important goal, in my view, is buried in the middle of the list at No. 5, which seeks to link human behavior with the activity of neurons. This is more daunting than it seems: scientists have yet to even figure out how the relatively simple, three-hundred-and-two-neuron circuitry of the C. Elegans worm works, in part because there are so many possible interactions that can take place between sets of neurons. A human brain, by contrast, contains approximately eighty-six billion neurons.[9]

When sophisticated tools and techniques do manage to lead neuroscientists to evidence of abnormality in the brain, they are often stymied by yet another of the disease's exasperating enigmas: Is the "abnormality" they are looking at a *result* of schizophrenia? Or is it a *cause*?

This quandary is well expressed in an essay titled "The Aetiology of Schizophrenia":

> That structural brain abnormalities exist in schizophrenia is generally accepted to be established…beyond dispute. However, the *meaning* of these abnormalities, in understanding the pathogenesis of the illness, is far less clear. Questions remain as to whether structural abnormalities *predispose* to the development of schizophrenia, [or] whether acute schizophrenic psychosis can actually damage the brain, *causing* altered structure…The presence of structural brain abnormalities in [unaffected] relatives of patients

with schizophrenia suggests that "schizophrenia genes" are likely to be involved in (abnormal) brain development, but that the expression of the structural brain correlate of the genes is not enough, in itself, to "cause" schizophrenia.[10]

The genes that underpin schizophrenia may have been favored by natural selection, according to a survey of human and primate genetic sequences. The discovery suggests that genes linked to the debilitating brain condition conferred some advantage that allowed them to persist in the population—although it is far from clear what this advantage might have been.[11]

Despite these complexities, the centrality of congenital factors to the disease was resoundingly ratified in 2014 by the Schizophrenia Working Group of the Psychiatric Genomics Consortium, a collaboration among some three hundred scientists from thirty-five countries. After examining the genomes of some 37,000 people with schizophrenia and comparing them with those of more than 113,000 healthy subjects, the group claimed to have identified an astounding 128 gene variants connected with schizophrenia. These genes occupied 108 locations on the genome, with most of them having never before been associated with the affliction.[12]

It's true that contemporary research has unlocked many secrets about how the brain works. Advances have been spectacular in neuropsychology (which is, briefly, the psychiatry-based study of how reasoning works and why/how people experience impairment); in technology (such as magnetic resonance imaging, or MRI, to facilitate the study of the brain); and in the development of "psychotropic" medications, from the anxiolytic Valium to the antipsychotic Haldol and beyond.

These techniques and findings have helped alleviate a range of relatively minor discontents. They have also shed light on electrical and chemical impulses as they move through the brain; on the nature of receptors; and on the functions of the cerebrum, cerebellum, diencephalon, and brain stem. Yet, when applied to the task of conquering the most feared and devastating mental disorder of them all, our cutting-edge tools have scarcely begun to cut the edge.

3

Regulars

We arrived on the mountain-meadow grounds of the Bread Loaf Writers' Conference in August 1988 and never went home again.

Honoree and her mother, Honora, drove back to our Yonkers house to supervise the movers who were shoving our furniture and bulging cardboard boxes into the big van for the long haul up to Middlebury. The boys and I stayed on at the Homer Noble farmhouse for two or three days, taking our meals down in the town. The conference had ended. Everyone else had departed. Dean and Kevin, who were six and four then, had been on the campus only during the days when the conference was in session and teeming with writers and poets. This was the first time they had ever seen it empty. We walked the grounds, and I could tell that the stillness, and the vacant dorm buildings and Adirondack chairs, disoriented them a little.

Our nights in the farmhouse, the three of us the only human beings within pitch-black miles, conjured the aura of an older, Gothic New England. I was proud of my sons for being courageous enough to sleep in their accustomed second-floor cot beds, secure in knowing that I was in the adjoining bedroom. I was not so proud of myself for awakening from a dream at about 3 a.m. on the first night: a dream in which someone was pressing a finger down on an organ key, sustaining a high, eerie note. I sat up in bed. Then I realized that the keening sound was no organ key but a coyote wailing in the woods outside. My skin went clammy and my heart thumped for a few minutes. If my sons heard the howl (or my heart), they gave no sign. Out of respect for their bravery, I restrained myself from moving into their room to get over the jitters.

"It's all right, Dad," they might have told me if they'd awakened. "It's safe. We're in Vermont."

Honoree, Honora, and the movers arrived in Middlebury on the third day. The kids and I locked up the farmhouse, left the key for the care-taker, and drove down the mountain to meet them at our new house. Honoree had been told of its availability. She believed that it was per-fect. It was perfect. We lived there for seventeen years.

Concealed by trees and hedges, the house sat at the end of a curving cul-de-sac on the last neighborhood street in Middlebury before horse farms took over and the rolling fields reached toward the mountains. Built of gray-painted hardwood some thirty years earlier, it appeared low-slung despite its two stories. Behind it was a small kidney-shaped swimming pool, with woods on the far side of the fence. The front was crowned by a yard lamp atop a pole at the crest of the steeply terraced lawn (nice to look at, hell to mow). Years later, in a time of turmoil for him, Dean planted a Japanese maple tree near the yard lamp. As far as I know, it is still there.

When the boys and I pulled in, the moving men were unloading canvas-draped furniture from the van. I remember the exact spot in the driveway, the apex of the turn left toward the garage, where I stopped the car and the boys spilled out. Inside the echo-y house, look-ing through the front-door window, we sighted a rainbow arcing into the mountains where Bread Loaf lay. Rainbows would become familiar presences above the low-hanging tendrils of mountain fog.

We were in Vermont to stay.

Middlebury proved an ideal town for raising young children. In the fall Honoree began teaching biochemistry at the graystone college on the opposite end of the town, which had opened its doors in 1800. She was placed on a tenure track the following year. It was not exactly a guarantee of permanence: the first woman to have attained tenure there was only in mid-career when we arrived.

My adjunct appointment in creative writing would commence the following year. I wrote a little, and transported Dean and Kevin to school and sports and community theater rehearsal, and then drove to Steve's Park Diner, across the street from the town green, where I became a regular. Pretty soon, Dean and Kevin were regulars, too.

Early on, the concept of being a "regular" caught Dean's and Kevin's fancies. They quickly grasped the protocol of New England diner-talk: when the waitress—let's call her "Pauline"—approached the table, order pad in hand, and said, "Are you all set?" she was understood to mean, "Are you ready to order?" When she brought the plates and began to distribute them and said, "Are you all set?" she meant, "Is there anything else you want?" When she came back at the end of the meal and said, "Are you all set?" she meant, "Can I clear these dishes?" And when she returned shortly after that and said, "Are you all set?" she meant, "Are you ready for the check?"

Kevin was especially proud on the day he tried out some diner-talk of his own and it worked. To Pauline's "You all set?" he replied, "I'll have the usual." Only a regular would have dared order "the usual." Pauline understood. She brought him a bagel and cream cheese. Kevin was in.

As for Dean, he soon grew to regard Middlebury entire as his "regular" domain. One day, as the two of us walked along the sidewalk past the local Mexican restaurant, whose gaudy colors had been freshly repainted, I heard my son grouse: "Before long, *you won't be able to recognize this town!*"

I stopped in my tracks and stared at him. Grousing is not normally a skill acquired in childhood. Dean was either doing a shrewd imitation of me grousing, or he'd been richly endowed with my grousing genes. I didn't ask him which. After a moment, we walked on.

Honoree, the classic city girl, started a vegetable garden and planted brilliant dahlias and day lilies and purple coneflowers along the backyard fence. At the same time, she was rapidly converting herself from a career urban research scientist specializing in cultured human endometrial cells (her twenty-three publications include "Estrogen Receptors in Epithelial and Stromal Cells of Human Endometrium in Culture," which I could explain if I had time) into an academic teacher of science.

Dean spent happy hours inside his imagination, enraptured by gorgeous things the rest of us could not see. (The relationship of dreamy, artistically gifted children, a trait Dean shared with Kevin, to a propensity for mental illness, was unsuspected by us then; we simply enjoyed the richness of their ideas and talents.) Dean was quieter than Kevin, but once in a while he would briefly reveal the universes whirling inside his head.

I recall a walk with Dean at Bread Loaf in the summer before we moved to Vermont. I had stolen an hour away from the workshops and manuscript conferences to be alone with him, and we strolled out along the Robert Frost Trail. The trail, half a mile down the road from the campus, is just opposite the dirt road that leads to the Homer Noble Farm. It winds through wildflowers and along a creekbed. A wooden footbridge crosses the creek near the beginning. Every few yards a signpost greets the hiker with a few lines from a Frost poem. I was reading these snippets aloud as we walked, all caught up in the sound of my rich timbre, when I heard Dean's voice behind me:

"I heard the wind and the water rustling."

I stopped and turned around and looked at him. He looked at me.

"Go on," I said.

Dean shifted his gaze and thought for a bit. Then he looked at me again and said:

"While birds were flying and squirrels were running around."

"That's really good," I told him. "Can you keep going?"

Dean shrugged and fell silent. We walked on. Then:

"And the trees were shaking around the wild forest."

We stopped again. This time I didn't speak, for fear of breaking the spell. But I nodded at him. And he continued:

"When I was crossing the bridge,

"I heard the splashes..."

I waited again. This time it took awhile; but finally:

"...Of two sticks that fell from one tree."

When my gooseflesh had settled, I said, "Hey, are you about ready to head back to the farmhouse?" He nodded. I tried not to hurry him beyond the capacity of his six-year-old legs. I wanted to write those lines down while they were fresh in my mind.

We made it in time.

I read Dean's poem to the Bread Loafers that evening before I gave my own scheduled reading. The audience gave a kind of low gasping thrum when I'd finished. His stuff was better than my stuff that night.

At age ten, he switched from poetry to prose and produced this little fragment from his daydreams:

10 Million Dollar Mansion

Plans for Disign

The 10 Milion Dollar Mansion will be 8 stories high. Surrounded by acres of beautiful green garden, and a iron wall you can see through. After you pay your fee, you will be treated like a rich person the rest of the day. First you will be picked up by a limousine, and a shofer will come out and open up the doors for you then drive you through the road and to the mansion itslef. When you are driveing to the mansion there will be soda pop and a T.V. that will explain the park. When you get there the shofer will open the door for you and someone will lead you to the two huge doors on the mansion, then he will buzz and the butler will greet and say, "welcome to the 10 Million Dollar Mansion."

I read this as an expression both of Dean's security in the embrace of our family "mansion" and of his familiar hunger to reach higher, to magically make his world more wondrous still. Dean lived dreamily in the expectation that he could transport himself to ever-greener gardens, ever-more-shimmering mansions.

At around age thirteen, Dean got interested in sports. He played outfield in a spring-and-summer league. Commitment to the game varied among the players. The third-base person could be counted on to be tracing artistic spirals in the mud with her finger when a ground ball came wobbling toward her. Everybody knew everybody else—players and their parents. The parents sat on the aluminum slats behind the home-plate screen regardless of loyalty. And yet they were loyal. Sometimes this produced awkward moments. I remember being pressed into service as an umpire one time when the regular guy didn't show up. I called balls and strikes from behind the pitcher because the throws back to the mound from the catcher, which the pitcher generally missed, didn't have quite as much mustard on them as did the pitcher's pitches to the catcher, which the catcher generally missed.

One of the teams that day was Dean's. The other team was coached by my dentist, who just a day earlier had removed a decaying rear molar from my mouth and stanched the bleeding with a tight wad of cotton. The dentist's team was at bat, and I could see that the dentist, a rather large and florid man, had his eyes trained on me. He appeared to be scowling. Maybe he didn't like the fact that the opposing nine had a parent calling the pitches. Maybe he was one of *those* guys. With two swinging strikes in the count, my son's team's pitcher hurled, and I bawled *"Strike three!"* The dentist rose and came to the mound on a fast trot. I spread my hands in the timeless "Chill out!" gesture.

"Jeez, John," I said. "I gotta call a strike *sometime*. The zone is about three inches high!"

"Open your mouth," John said. He peered inside. "I thought I saw some bleeding from that pack. But I think it's gonna hold."

Vermont.

A season or so after that, Dean, by then a slim and growing preteen, found himself on the mound in a league for slightly older kids. He loved the uniforms, snazzy royal-blue jerseys with gold trim. We'd worked on his pitching many hours in the driveway, and he had developed a decent fastball. The problem was that no one knew where it was going once it left his hand. The patch of woods on the far edge of the drive-way remains, to this day, chockablock with former fastballs. But Dean looked great in his blue cap and jersey with bright gold lettering. I liked watching him from the sidelines in my new capacity as umpire emeri-tus. Dean's hazel-green eyes, a genetic gift from his mother, blazed as he looked down for the sign. This kid was going to be handsome.

Handsome, maybe, but just a tad scatter-armed. It was true that the batters' strike zones had grown by now; I would have put the average height at five inches. An additional five, or twenty, would have helped. In about the fourth inning, after Dean had walked something like five munchkins in a row on something like twenty pitches, the coach strolled out and gently suggested to my son that he might want to trade places with the right fielder. Dean left the mound, but not for right field. He crossed the foul line near first base. Head down, he kept on walking, in the general direction of the parking lot.

I jumped to my feet and caught up with him near the end pole of a chain-link fence.

"Where are you going?" I asked him.

"I can't play baseball. I want to go home."

"You can *too* play baseball. You know you can. You're a great out-fielder. You catch every fly ball I hit to you."

Nothing from Dean.

"Now come on. Those guys need you. We need this game."

"We're way behind."

"We can catch up. Don't let your team down. They need you."

It didn't occur to me that I was piling great responsibility and potential blame on his young shoulders. He would have been justified in saying that was not his problem and to leave him alone.

He didn't. He thought it over for a moment and then without a word turned around and walked—not ran, *walked*, with purposeful dignity—out to right field. I thought that this was an incredible act of courage, given his embarrassment just moments earlier in full view of his friends on both teams and their parents scattered in the three rows of seats.

I can't remember whether Dean caught any fly balls for the remainder of that game. But I do remember what happened in the bottom of the seventh and final inning, with his team at bat, having clawed their way to a three-run deficit. The bases were loaded and I believe there was one out. And Dean was coming to the plate with a bat in his hand.

He looked at the first pitch, if memory serves, and swung at the next one and missed. On the ensuing pitch, Dean put his aluminum on the ball and hit a smart chopper back to the pitcher. The pitcher stooped a little as it headed between his legs. The shortstop and second baseman converged, but the ball skipped merrily past them as well. It went hoppity-hopping onto the outfield's hard dirt surface like the White Rabbit late for tea. The center fielder, well coached, charged it, hoping for a dramatic throw to the plate. The outfielder came up with his glove empty and the ball, now taking on the aspect of a communications satellite, continued its trajectory toward the curve of the earth.

Dean touched them all. As he crossed home plate his teammates stormed out to high-five him. He had hit a game-winning ground-ball grand-slam home run—likely not the first one stroked in that league, but the most beautiful hit I have ever seen, or hope to see.

On the way home in the car, Dean wanted to know what was for dinner.

Kevin found his bliss within weeks of our arrival in Middlebury.

One Sunday morning I brought home the *Burlington Free Press*, along with the obligatory sack of bagels, and flipped idly through the entertainment section as I finished my coffee. A one-inch ad caught my eye:

WOODS TEA COMPANY
FOLK MUSIC
BOATHOUSE
2 p.m.

Kevin, freshly five years old, had been carrying around a little white plastic guitar that Honoree had bought for him about a year earlier.

He'd been fascinated by guitars since he'd stood and watched an Irish novelist strumming away on the Bread Loaf lawn the previous summer. Kevin had begged the man to teach him how. The writer had obligingly tried to show him a couple of chords, but Kevin's fingers were not big enough or strong enough to replicate them. Interestingly, though, he accurately placed his fingers exactly where the man's had been on the fretboard.

Back home in New York, the new stringless toy had seemed to satisfy him, and he carried it with him almost everywhere.

He had it in his grip as he, Honoree, and I piled into our van and headed for Burlington, thirty miles to the north. Dean had decided to stay at home with his grandmother. The Boathouse was a restaurant with a performance space on the second floor, anchored at the end of a pier on the Lake Champlain waterfront south of the town.

The Woods Tea Company was a much bigger deal than we'd anticipated: a legendary trio in Vermont and New England who enjoyed a fan base across America. The second-floor venue was crammed to the walls. Not a seat was left. Sold out.

We were about to leave when the second-generation-hippie woman selling tickets came to our rescue in a patently Vermont way. She gave our son the once-over, and he looked up at her with his bright blue eyes. She shifted her glance to the toy guitar. And then she said: "You can put him up here on the table if you want to. You two'll have to stand."

That particular surface was an old folding-leg card table doubling as a stand for the cash box and the red roll of tickets. I wondered whether it could support the added weight of two or three more quarters, much less a thirty-five-pound kid, give or take. We boosted him up, and the table held, and Kevin got his first look at the Boathouse concert stage. At any concert stage. He saw an array of polished guitars, banjos, mandolins, and a fiddle leaning against metal stands. The instruments gleamed orange and brown and silver beneath the overhead lights. He saw three microphones. He saw, though we couldn't have known it then, his future.

Someone climbed up onto the stage, lifted a mic from its holder, and said words to the effect of, "Ladies and gentlemen—the Woods Tea Company!" The audience sent up a vigorous round of applause, and three middle-aged men in rumpled jeans filed onstage. One of them was wearing an oversized watch cap and a vest and sported a disheveled orange beard. Another was darkly handsome under his piratical black facial hair. The third had on a battered fedora and suspenders and glasses. And a beard. They could have been regulars at Steve's Park Diner.

Without preamble, the trio launched into a thundering rendition of "The Wild Rover." The fedoraed banjo player's notes skittered around the room and trilled through the audience and bounced off the windowpanes. The savvy fans clapped in sync after the lines "No nay never" and "No nay never no more" and "No never no more." A big finish, and another big hand from the audience.

The Woods Tea Company played some more Irish drinking songs and some "sea chanteys" and some bluegrass and some of their own compositions. They played some of the great folk ballads of the '60s. They played with their own style and musicianship, and passion. They were very good, and they were playing my personal coming-of-age music, the first kind of music I loved, the kind of music I yearned to play, and *did* play—on the strings of my tennis racket in front of my bathroom mirror until I'd reached an age that would be mortifying to specify.

Kevin was hypnotized. He strummed the nonexistent strings of his own guitar and gazed over the audience at the players on the stage. What never crossed our minds was the fact that the players on the stage could look back over the audience and see Kevin.

At intermission, as Honoree and I were debating whether to get an early start back to Middlebury, we noticed a woman shouldering her way through the crowd toward us. She was perhaps in her forties, with long, straight blond hair, and wearing faded blue jeans like nearly every other woman in the place. Good nature radiated from her eyes. She wasted no time on preliminaries. "There'll be a few empty seats for the second set," she informed us. "If you can get him down to the front row, we'll put him up onstage for the last number." She was the wife of the piratical band member.

"What's his name?" she asked.

My wife and I looked at each other. For a few moments we became New Yorkers again. I picked my son up and cradled him against my shoulder like a football. With Honoree running interference, we charged down the center aisle to the stage, knocking bodies left and right, and seized two empty chairs just below the mics. Whether the chairs had been abandoned temporarily or permanently didn't matter. Show business is not always pretty.

The Woods Tea Company returned to the stage, and Kevin, nestled in my lap, suddenly was almost within touching distance of them. He gripped the white guitar. The band played another rousing set and walked off the stage to great applause. End of concert.

Then they walked back on: an encore. The piratical musician gave me a subtle nod and casually informed the audience—as if everyone had been expecting it—"Well, Kevin will be joining us now…"

I rose up and boosted him onstage. Kevin had not expected this. He turned around and surveyed the audience, his blue eyes made brighter by the overhead lights, and lifted his toy guitar to the ready.

The band exploded into a rip-roaring rendition of Woody Guthrie's "This Land Is Your Land." Halfway through, the audience was clapping along in time. The banjo and the guitar traded robust solos. The trio's hearty male voices boomed out lustily. *As I was walkin' that ribbon of highway*…In the crowd, feet were stomping. Kevin looked straight ahead, deadpan, his blue eyes catching the light, and strummed along mightily on his invisible strings.

…*This land belongs to you and* meeeeee, *eeeeee,* EEEEEE!

The audience rose and clapped and whistled. Kevin stood there taking it in. His poker face held, but inside him, volcanoes were erupting and winds were blowing one life out and a new one in. In those moments Kevin became a musician. The ovation went on.

When it all finally died down and people started to file out of the Boathouse, we joined Kevin onstage and shook hands with the band.

Each player offered a kind remark to our son, who turned his face up and accepted their praise speechlessly. Honoree and I finally headed for the exit. We had walked all the way down the curving sidewalk to the parking lot before we realized that Kevin was not with us.

We looked around in a bit of panic. It took a minute or two before one of us spotted him. He was maybe twenty yards back up the walkway, seated by himself on a wooden bench near the gangplank to the Boathouse, his legs swinging. We ran to him and told him how he'd scared us by getting separated, and how he shouldn't do that, and how glad we were to see him. What was he doing on that bench?

Kevin explained it to us patiently, as only a child can explain a concept difficult for adults to understand.

He was waiting for the Woods Tea Company to come out so that he could resume his career with them.

After that, there was no stopping him. He begged for lessons. We tracked down a college kid who gave them. Kevin met with him for a few Saturdays until the young mentor confessed that he had run out of things to teach our son.

But luckily for Kevin, we'd fetched up in a state that boasts more than its share of musicians, good ones, especially stringed-instrument players. These are the inheritors of a tradition picked up by members of the counterculture invasion of half a century ago. Among the more accomplished guitar players and teachers in this tradition was a gentle and whimsical man named Michael, who lived with his partner on a farm outside Middlebury. Michael's studio was only a couple of miles from our house, in a tiny converted bungalow down an alley and behind a family-owned bagel bakery, shaded by a pair of scrawny trees. The view was to other people's backyards and scrawny trees. I grew to savor this little hive. Unplanned, improbable, distinct in all the universe, it held a funky integrity of the sort that made neighborhoods neighborhoods and towns towns before the engineers arrived with their theodolites and power optical transit level systems and elevating tripods, and replaced our Narnias with grid.

Michael's business card was thumbtacked to bulletin boards in stores around town. We called the number and asked the voice on the other end if he had room in his schedule for our five-year-old son. Michael politely refused us. He did not give lessons to small children. We should get in touch with him in a few years, when Kevin's fingers had grown.

I think it was Honoree who called him back. And perhaps back one more time. Michael gave in and agreed to pay a visit to our house to see what the kid had.

I will always remember the moment several months later, at one of Michael's student recitals, when he drew Honoree and me aside and whispered: "*We've created a monster.*"

Some of the happiest interludes of my life were spent in that little studio behind the bagel bakery. Strictly speaking, no one except the student was allowed inside the space until Michael had finished his lesson, but I fudged. I timed my arrivals to pick Kevin up so that I was earlier each week by finely calibrated increments. After a few months, I was showing up midway through the half-hour lesson. The midpoint marked the end of the formal instruction and the onset of the jamming.

I would let myself in quietly, closing the door so that it didn't make a sound, and fold myself down onto the floor that was covered by a linty carpet, and rest my back against the wall. After a period, neither of them bothered to acknowledge my presence, which was the way I liked it. If I could've made myself invisible I would have hovered there the entire time, my daily writing quota be damned. As it was, I enjoyed the sublime pleasure of immersing myself in a long and increasingly rich series of conversations spoken entirely in guitar. Kevin's fingers were a blur but a precise blur, and the riffs, the call-and-responses, the "trading eights," deepened in technique and in passion. Michael insisted on rigorous technique, and Kevin was happy to oblige him: bend the elbow of the fretboard hand; keep the wrist straight. One finger per fret, except when not, as with the case of finger-four. Learn to use the pinky; it increases your range. Learn the several alternate ways to play the same chord. And on and on. And on.

In a short time, Kevin gained expertise in acoustic and electric guitar. Later, he would learn the essentials of classical guitar and flamenco. He mastered the electric bass and the mandolin. He learned piano and drums. He became expert in drumming the knife and the fork on the edges of the dinner plate until Honoree or I would ask him politely to please knock it off.

Kevin was never a demonstrative musician, or a demonstrative anything. Modesty, a vague shyness, and a quiet antic wit governed his personality. He never raised a fist in the air in performance, never strutted, never mugged to an audience. If you wanted to grasp his essential relationship to music, you needed only to watch him pick up his guitar. He didn't pick it up so much as absorb it into his being, swiftly and fluidly: one instant it was on its stand, or on a table or sofa, and the next it was a part of him, cradled gently in his large hands. (As he grew, his hands and feet grew ahead of the rest of him, and he exercised his fingers to keep them strong.)

Kevin and Michael were playing out of each other's souls. The music that resulted, and then vanished forever, at times reached a level of spellbinding unity and beauty, as if the notes had been composed on paper. Every Thursday I was an audience of one for duets that could have sent chills through any audience in a New England town hall, or anywhere.

Kevin did not fit any stereotypes of the pale, alienated guitar-poet. Everything in his world fascinated him. He was what certain hearty men like to trumpet as "an all-round boy." He grew up slim and not especially muscular, except for those big guitar-picking hands and wiry forearms. He was never a kid you would mistake for an athlete, yet this didn't bother him. Kevin was the catcher on his summer baseball teams; a midfielder in soccer; a guard in junior basketball (mostly dribbling around center court in private Ferdinand-the-Bull bliss until someone relieved him of the ball); a competitive swimmer. He even tried ice hockey, until Honoree and I grew tired of lacing up his high bladed shoes. His shyness gave way in time to a love of affable horseplay and a frequent lopsided grin, and he could be a charming self-satirist. A passage from a Kevin grade school essay about a family trip to Ireland:

> We went to bars a lot and I liked ther disgusting grill cheeze's and I played dart's, but Iwas really bad and I kep breaking the darts. I think that socker for us is called football for them and we did play a lot of sock...I mean football.

At the same time, Kevin inhabited an inner world that remained inaccessible to anyone else in his life, except perhaps those who shared his gifts and his passion. This became evident early on. In grade school, one of Kevin's teachers—perhaps probing the class's appreciation for life's essential things, such as food and water and shelter—asked the class to make a list of the things they needed. Kevin wrote: "I *need* music."

He needed *expression*. He drew. He asked for sketch pads and I bought him big ones, 11-by-14 Sketch Bond, which he filled with fast spare pencil strokes. Some of these were fully wrought drawings, such as the portrait of a grinning Spiky with upright witch's-hat ears, which Kevin garnished with crayon colors to make the sedate Maine coon cat look like a cartoon rock star. He drew a recurring figure, a kid with a nose that resembled the tab of a jigsaw-puzzle piece: a ski-boarder gliding above a city skyline, a denizen of a surging landscape understood only by Kevin. Maybe this *was* Kevin: he loved velocity. Sometimes the drawings spun out of coherence and became a series of back-and-forth strokes, as if the underlying vision were too urgent for careful development.

As he grew older he became a wicked little mimic of people. In just a couple of words, with dead-on inflection, he could pierce through to the essence of someone's personality. The intonation he lent to his utterance of the word *flute* became a devastating commentary on the instrument.

We admonished both our sons against using profanity, and they kept their language clean, at least around us. But the unwritten rule,

conceived by Kevin and followed by Dean, was that whenever someone dropped, say, the F-bomb in their hearing, the word was in play.
At the Rock & Roll Hall of Fame in Cleveland one summer day, when
the boys were about eight and eleven, one of them pushed a button that
brought up a video of Pete Townshend telling an interviewer: "Look at
my generation. How did that work? Jimi Hendrix. Brian Jones. Janis
Joplin. Keith Moon. The list is fucking endless. My life is full of dead
people. My friends are dead. *My friends.* They might be *your* fucking
icons. They're my *fucking* friends."

Kevin obviously considered the word to be in play. Looking up at
me with a show of earnest confusion, he asked, with perfect deadpan:
"Did he say '*my* fucking icons' and '*your* fucking friends'?"

I could not help myself. "No, Kevin," I explained with fatherly
exactitude. He said, '*your* fucking icons' and '*my* fucking friends.'"

"Wait," Dean put in. "*I* think he said 'my fucking icons' *and* 'my
fucking friends.'"

I didn't let myself look in Honoree's direction. "Dean, he couldn't
have said that," I rejoined, struggling to keep my voice academic and
meditative. "How could they be both his fucking friends *and* his fucking icons?"

"I think that if they were his fucking friends they could be his fucking icons, too," Kevin ventured. "And if they were his fucking icons,
they could still be his fucking friends."

People began looking at us. Honoree finally broke in and told us to
stop it and behave ourselves.

A quality in Kevin that I admired perhaps even more than I admired
his musical gifts can be summed up in a story I heard about him at his
memorial service.

The story was told to me by a classmate of his, a beautiful young
woman with long, thick, curly dark tresses and dark eyes. In sixth
grade she had experienced one of those rare kidhood growth spurts
that almost overnight set her apart from everybody else. She topped out
at six feet. Her height and beauty, neither of which she could understand, much less control, put her in the crosshairs of certain boys in the

class. She never invited this: her family was poor, her mother single, and she came to school in faded jeans and flannel shirts, or T-shirts with "cool" slogans. Just a kid in grade school.

One boy in particular seemed to take her innocently stunning appearance as some kind of personal reflection on him, or a challenge. The boy was built thick and tough; he was on a track to star as a college ice-hockey player. His method for dealing with her daring to be tall was to swagger up to her on the school grounds before classes or at lunch hour, and punch her. Repeatedly. Hard. On her shoulders. On her chest. Sometimes in her face. She bruised, and she bled, but she didn't know what to do. She stood there and took it. Sometimes the pain and humiliation made her cry silently. Other kids watched from a distance. No kid made an effort to intervene. No teacher, apparently, was aware of what was happening. And the girl never told anyone.

This all stopped when Kevin walked up to the two of them one day while the punching was going on and said: "Thomas, you're being a dick," and walked away. Thomas did not go after him. It was as if he said to himself, *Yeah—I guess I'm a dick*. He grew up to be a pretty good guy. And a college hockey star.

It's not for me to say, but I think the tall girl loved Kevin. Who didn't?

4

Bedlam, Before and Beyond

Through the millennia before civilizations grew sufficiently debonair to decide that mad people must be routed off city streets and hustled into prisonlike asylums, where the fashionably "sane" often could pay a few coins to come and see them howl and beg and writhe and pull at their chains, the demarcations between normal and aberrant behavior were more ambiguously drawn, and with far less fear and loathing. An archetypal figure stood between the normative community or tribe and the misfit at its margins. Sometimes the figure magically drew the misfit's fevered mental pain into himself, in a healing way. Sometimes the figure was the misfit, healing the tribe.

A typical name for that figure, drawn from seventeenth-century Cossacks who intruded into the herding societies of eastern Siberia, is shaman.[1] The descriptor's variants—schamane, saman, babalawo, sheripiari, magi, wu, baal shem, prophet, and hundreds of others—date from the earliest sentient tribes and ethnic groups, however separated by oceans, mountains, or distance. The terms denote those who can achieve excited, trancelike states and who claim access to an invisible realm of mystical presences powerful enough to intervene in the affairs of men.

Such charismatic figures in history are plentiful. Socrates hallucinated. He heard at least one disembodied voice, which he affectionately called "my daemon." He valued it. It gave him wise advice—advice that invariably warned him away from some contemplated action, as opposed to suggesting one. He went so far as to speak of "divine madness."

In one famous formulation, citing the work of ethnologists, the French philosopher Michel Foucault proposed that it is possible to recognize primitive societies' different attitudes toward madness. The key is to examine the status assigned a given community's members in each of several essential groupings: labor and economic production; family and sexuality; language and speech; and "ludic," or lighthearted, activities: games and festivals. Not every tribal member would fit comfortably into all these categories, yet "madness has *always* been excluded," Foucault wrote.[2] Those defined as "mad" (retroactively, by modern social researchers) were simply unable to fit in. They couldn't or wouldn't work, were celibate, spoke incomprehensibly, or posed a danger or disruption during festivals. The society's attitude toward them might or might not have been based on fear or the impulse to punish. It might have been based on reverence. "Depending on the case, [the madman] is given a religious, magical, ludic or pathological status," Foucault wrote. The role of madness in society is to reveal the limit between the Same and the Other, he says, and through this to reveal the truth in both of them.

Both the benevolent Greeks and their conquerors, the crueler and more bloodthirsty Romans, seem generally to have understood that madness was indeed an aberration, often a punishment from the gods, and not a divine state. It was most notably the Greek physician Hippocrates (about 460–377 BC) who initiated the glacial movement of thought away from supernatural beings as deliverers of insanity. His replacement theory, an imbalance of the four bodily "humours" (blood, phlegm, and black and yellow biles), was hardly more productive, though it held sway in the practices of some doctors for two thousand years.

Psychiatric researchers have increasingly agreed that while the *causes* of insanity resist definitive diagnosis, its *severity* can be correlated with degrees of stress. Among the most common stimulants of human stress (other than childhood life within dysfunctional families) has been urban living, especially since the Industrial Age. This correlation has convinced leading investigators such as E. Fuller Torrey that the intensity of urban living largely accounts for the acute rise in indicators of schizophrenia and related diseases. Torrey has described this rise as a "plague."* The science and medical journalist Robert Whitaker, for differing reasons, has described it as an "epidemic."†

Among the earliest of cities is London. Its origins trace to AD 50. By the Middle Ages its merchants, growing plump on the bounties of a vigorous sea trade, had firmly transplanted the ancient "guild system"—economic alliances of tradesmen and companies—within its rapidly growing borders. By 1600, its population had reached two hundred thousand people, a twentyfold increase in fifty years. By the beginning of the nineteenth century, London surpassed Paris and then Constantinople as Europe's largest city. All of this was good news for just about everybody except the dispossessed and the mentally ill, two populations that often seemed one and the same.

One might ask: Why did people then, and people today, continue to live in cities if the effects on sanity are so toxic? In 1969, the French-born biochemist René Dubos won the Pulitzer Prize for his book *So Human an Animal*, in which he postulated that humankind's essential nature has not significantly changed since the Stone Age. A key component of human nature is adaptability, and herein lies trouble:

---

* Torrey, the research psychiatrist who has covered nearly every aspect of mental illness in his books, is among those who believe that psychosis is on the rise and has been for more than three centuries. His 2001 book *The Invisible Plague: The Rise of Mental Illness from 1750 to the Present*, written with Judy Miller (New Brunswick, NJ: Rutgers University Press), will be discussed later in some detail.

† Whitaker is a leading critic of the profusion of antipsychotic drugs, which, he points out, are highly profitable to the pharmaceutics industry. (In this and other arguments, he differs from Torrey.) His 2010 book *Anatomy of an Epidemic: Magic Bullets, Psychiatric Drugs and the Astonishing Rise of Mental Illness* (New York: Random House) offers statistical evidence that instances of schizophrenia are on a dramatic rise, and speculates that "psychiatric drugs are…*fueling* the epidemic of disabling mental illness." (See chapters 13 and 15 for further discussion.)

"The greatest dangers of overpopulation [which dangers include stress] come paradoxically from the fact that human beings can make adjustments to almost anything."[3] Based on this ability, Dubos asserted, "modern man could readily return to primitive life, and indeed he does to some extent whenever he needs to." But that is far from the greatest penalty for human adaptability. In a provocative passage near the end of his book, Dubos declares:

> Most of man's problems in the modern world arise from the constant... exposure to the stimuli of urban and industrial civilization... the physiological disturbances associated with sudden changes in ways of life, the estrangement from... the natural cycles under which human evolution took place, the emotional trauma and the paradoxical solitude in congested cities, the monotony, boredom... in brief all the environmental conditions that undisciplined technology creates.[4]

If all this is true, early London, with its crooked streets and foul gutters, its cheek-by-jowl living conditions among poor immigrants from mutually incomprehensible language systems, its ambient diseases and long unlit winter nights in which thieves and cutthroats preyed—this early London was a petri dish for human stress. And madness.

This London had little time for either mad people or shamans—one and the same, to those who bothered to think at all about them. They got in the way, they contributed nothing, their speech and behavior were incomprehensible—the damned demons inside their heads, like as not!—and they very often stank.

To paraphrase Ebenezer Scrooge: "Are there no madhouses?"

Well, yes.

The flagship accommodation was Bedlam.

"Bedlam" was the vernacular name assigned to the first and most infamous madhouse of them all. The institution has occupied four sites since its origin in 1247 as a small religious sanctuary, the Priory of St. Mary of Bethlehem, near Bishopsgate. "Bethlehem" was quickly contracted in usage to "Bethlem," and, later, to "Bedlam." In time the retreat was converted into a hospital, more or less. It functioned mainly as an almshouse. Around 1403, the hospital began to accept a handful of "lunaticks" for care, and employed a few monks to look after and try to cure them. The monks were happy to oblige, and they set about beating their charges. (They probably believed that they were striking at the evil spirits.) The inmates fared better than their brethren in Spain, where Torquemada and his legions of the Inquisition were piously burning them alive.

A sewer that preexisted Bethlem's construction drew in more and more of London's growing waste until it overflowed. The sewer couldn't be fixed, and so Bethlem moved from the fetid grounds as soon as it was able, which was after 420 years. Over that time, its lineage of administrators dumped some three thousand corpses of former patients into the soft rank ground. Finally, in 1676, the facilities were relocated a short distance west to some newly constructed buildings in Moorfields. In 1547, King Henry VIII seized control of Bethlem and granted the City of London a charter to administer the desolate cluster of buildings as a sanctuary for the insane.

Moorfields epitomized the rebuilding of London after the Great Fire of 1666—outside its walls. Its dark and sinister interior came to symbolize something quite the reverse. The architect was one Robert Hooke, a contemporary of Christopher Wren. Hooke designed it specifically *as* a mental institution—the first such building in Britain. Two stories tall, with accommodations for 120 patients, it loomed grand and imposing: "a long, single-pile building with an elaborate central block connected by flanking wings to two pavilions," in the description of one architectural scholar.[5]

Two heavy stone gargoyles, one atop each interior entrance gate, mocked any possible doubt about the business inside. The fiends were carved by the Danish sculptor Caius Gabriel Cibber. One, staring out in lifeless vacuity, was called *Melancholy Madness*. The other, a grimacing man-beast raising a chained arm, was called *Raving*. Past the gates, in the cells along the impervious stone corridors, the tumultuous "Bedlam" of folklore reached its awful zenith.

For a long period, the City of London Court of Aldermen chose Bedlam's supervisors on a patronage basis from the same mercantile society that recoiled at the sight of the mad. The supervisors—unable to imagine any sort of mandate for mollycoddling these wretches—hired their cell-keepers from the same societal sublevels as those of many "patients" themselves. The keepers, delighted to have control over a mass of humanity even more godforsaken than they, took pains—as it were—to make sure that everyone within screaming range could tell the difference.

Now the beating began in earnest. The poor, uneducated, and embittered jailers unleashed levels and varieties of cruelty both physical and psychological upon their "patients" that have not been surpassed in history. Not quite, anyway. Added to this misery was the administration's lack of interest in sanitation or upkeep, either structural or human. The roof sagged and later caved in; human waste glutted the drains. The cruelty was occasionally leavened by scientific inquiry. The first experiment in blood transfusion as therapy occurred at Bethlem in 1667. The donor was a sheep.[6]

More importantly, the Bedlam keepers created a dark, enduring paradigm. Even as the asylum became infamous through the city, then the kingdom, and then throughout Europe and the American colonies for the beating, shackling, taunting, starving, hygienic neglect, and even the occasional murdering of the people on the other side of the bars—even as these depravities sickened the pious (some, at least) and caused the timorously decent to turn away—these tactics were being adopted with varying degrees of intensity in the newer asylums including the York Lunatic Asylum, built in 1777.

"Charitable" asylums were opened in the eighteenth century in eight English towns: Norwich (1713); London (1751); Manchester (1766); Newcastle (1767); York (1777); Liverpool (1792); Leicester (1794); and Hereford (1797). The ninth opened in Exeter in 1801.

The abuses continued.

And there were no shamans to intervene. Not for miles, not for decades and centuries. No schamanes, no samans, no babalawos, no sheripiaris, no magi, no wu, no baal shems. Just jailers with glittering eyes and truncheons in their hands; just bars and piss-soaked bedding and dry food scraps and chains bolted to cold stone walls. No healing here, no higher ecstasy. Just pain and ever-deepening psychosis. And for most, no exit, save death.

Here was the true dawn of the epoch in which no one cared about crazy people. The epoch, as we will see, has not ended.

Bethlem patients were "treated," occasionally and haphazardly—and always, of course, by physicians with no grasp of how the brain worked. More often they were punished. Treatment and punishment could be hard to tell apart. So could the sane and the insane: depressives and drunks and the homeless poor languished among the true psychotics, as did, for instance, wives who talked back to their husbands. Administrators did try to keep the "criminally insane" sequestered from the others. Bethlem inmates who made trouble were doused in icy water or strapped inside chairs that spun rapidly, or both. These procedures were popular partly because they delivered a double benefit: they also answered as therapy. Some inmates (to use a more accurate term than "patients") were chained to walls—sometimes for months, occasionally for years, their ankles and wrists festering with gangrene. One inmate, named James Norris, remained enshackled for fourteen years. They were stripped of clothing, kept alive on subsistence levels of food and water, and they screamed into the darkness for mercy and release. Women incarcerated there were often raped by their keepers; at least one was impregnated twice, and miscarried.

To give credit where it is due, Bethlem pioneered in the use of antipsychotic medication—that is, if you define opium, morphine, murky tonics and cathartics, or laxatives as "antipsychotic medication."

In 1818 a former patient at Bethlem at Moorfields, Owen Metcalf, unspooled to an investigative Parliamentary Select Committee a long string of abuses. In one instance, "[a] patient named Harris, for the trifling offence of wanting to remain in his room a little longer one morning than usual, was dragged by Blackburn [keeper manager], assisted by Allen, the basement keeper, from No. 18, to Blackburn's room, and there beaten by them unmercifully; when he came out his head was streaming with blood, and Allen in his civil way wished him good morning."[7]

A new apothecary named John Haslam arrived at Bethlem in 1795. Haslam fancied himself an expert in matters of the deranged mind, and he published several monographs on the subject. He professed to know exactly how to cure mental illness. First, he believed, the patients' wills had to be broken. So Haslam obligingly beat a lot of them bloody. Or bloodier.

Funding was always a source of concern to those who ran the institutions, as it is today. Societies and governments have never favored spending money to sustain their mad people. The mad don't vote; the mad don't do anything to generate wealth. Many don't even know who they are. Why toss good money at them, beyond the costs of keeping them alive? (This attitude largely explains the urine-saturated straw bedding.) In England the pauperized insane—those who had not been caught and thrown into prison—depended on the Poor Law, a scattershot welfare system that provided subsistence-level food and shelter for those wandering the streets, or at least a portion of them.

As public institutions governed by the City of London, Bethlem and its imitators could not even require admission fees from prospective patients. And indeed, Bethlem Moorfields did not habitually turn away the indigent insane, though waiting lists soon developed. The administrators were virtually obliged to be artful.

Their most benign strategy was to negotiate discreetly with, say, a wealthy family that wanted to rid its household of an inconvenient relative. After all, the masters of Bethlem were part of the elite society they dickered with. The Monros, a high-bourgeois family of Londoners with Scottish origins, supplied four generations of shrewd physician-administrators at Bethlem; well-connected and deeply scheming men. James, the first, arrived in 1728, and he immediately banned medical students from the premises, no doubt on the theory that they would see more than was healthy for the management. He began the family's cultivation of the wealthy. And he turned madness into a spectator sport.

Visitors had occasionally handed over a bit of coin, even to the monks back in the Priory days, for the pleasure of watching their fellow human beings jabber, cavort, fight, howl, copulate, and otherwise act out primal impulses.

The grounds around Bedlam's walls afforded far more expansive views. Visitors were not only welcomed but encouraged, at a price. Sometimes they arrived by the horse-drawn busload, wearing waistcoats and top hats or twirling parasols, fashionable promenaders at the Ascot of lunacy. They paid a penny; later, two, and no exceptions. The ladies and gentlemen—and their children—were allowed to mingle with the entertainment, and to scoff and jest in the inmates' faces.

In 1815, the City of London moved Bethlem asylum again, to a new building in St. George's Fields in Southwark. Moorfields had fallen into physical decay surpassing even that of the old sewage-besotted Priory. The last Monro to administer Bedlam, Edward Thomas, assumed control the following year. Edward was forced to resign in 1852, after the Lunacy Commission was shocked to find that he, too, lacked human respect for his patients.

The late eighteenth century saw the formation of the first movement to rebuke the Bedlam template for dealing with society's "lunaticks" and "mad" people. (Not until 1930, 683 years after its founding, was Bethlem's theater of sanctioned state depravity reestablished as Bethlem Royal Hospital, and its era of modern professionalism launched.) As this movement spread through western Europe and the United States, its principles became known as "moral treatment." Some psychiatric scholars maintain that it remains the most effective of all history's treatments for the mentally ill.

Moral care took shape as a concept almost simultaneously in the minds of two men who did not know each other. One was a French doctor; the other, a British Quaker businessman.

The doctor was a Parisian named Philippe Pinel, a smallish country doctor with a hunger for ideas that caught the temper of the Enlightenment. In 1773, Pinel enrolled at the University of Montpellier, France's oldest medical academy and the source of medical science's freshest thought. There, he encountered refinements on an ancient concept known as "vitalism."

Vitalism's tenets would be largely refuted by advances in biophysical understandings of how the mind and the body interacted. Genetic theory would virtually extinguish what remained. Yet vitalism's core tenets—the necessity of balance between mind and body; the power of nature to heal all sorts of human diseases—led Pinel to a historic approach toward the mentally ill.

It took a rather convincing demonstration of mass psychosis—the French Revolution—to supply Philippe Pinel with the entrée he needed to put that approach into practice.

Pinel was living the modest life of a medical journalist and translator when the French Revolution swept the country with its antiaristocratic ideals. The new government, aware of his interest in the insane, appointed him in 1793 as physician-in-chief of the infamous Bicêtre Hospital for men. This converted orphanage, later a prison, was classic in its casual barbarity. Its jailers habitually kept patients confined in shackles, often for the better part of their lives. The chains were bolted to the walls so tightly that those confined by them were obliged to sleep standing up.

Pinel commenced his reforms at once. He mandated improvement in the quality of food, ordered regular replacement of the feces-and-urine-besotted straw that served as beds, and created exercise regimens for the inmates.[8]

The reform that secured Pinel's place in history was a decision to strike off the shackles of forty-nine Bicêtre inmates. The idea might have originated with the doctor's assistant, one Jean-Baptiste Pussin, though it is entirely consistent with Pinel's vision. The directive shocked even the revolutionary Paris Commune, which summoned Pinel to justify it at a hearing. Yet the directive almost immediately justified itself: not one of the newly unchained men bolted from his cell and ran out on a violent spree.

At about the time Pinel was pioneering his reforms in France, a six-tyish Yorkshire coffee merchant named William Tuke III was mourning the death of a fellow Quaker, a young woman named Hannah Mills. Mills had expired in the darkness of York Lunatic Asylum, built in 1777 in Tuke's hometown of York, the medieval walled city in northern England.

Quakerism, the Society of Friends, had originated in Britain the century before, one of many restless Christian groups to break with the Church of England over perceived false doctrine and overweening Puritanism. The Friends gathered adherents to their tenets of pacifism, philanthropy, and social justice. They began to emigrate from England and the Netherlands to America, where William Penn would found a great city, and where the Society of Friends would leave a great legacy of stewardship toward the mentally ill.

Hannah Mills's death stunned and galvanized Tuke. A recent widow, Mills had been admitted to York Asylum less than two months before her passing—probably for depression caused by her husband's death. Whatever was wrong with her, York Asylum deepened it. The young widow lasted forty-five days. Her death was recorded on April 29, 1790. Whether she was a suicide, or perhaps a victim of lethal abuse, or both, has not been documented.

William Tuke was incredulous that the asylum administrators refused to offer an explanation for the woman's abrupt passing. Tuke did not fulminate or try to run the York Asylum out of business. That was not the Quaker way. Instead, he commissioned his own asylum and opened it in 1796.

He did not call it an asylum. Nor did he or his family refer to those who stayed there as "lunatics." Tuke designed the facility in collaboration with a London architect named John Bevans. Bevans shared Tuke's hopeful but mistaken belief, nearly identical to Pinel's, that an open, healthful environment and respectful treatment by caretakers could lead, virtually of themselves, to the restoration of an afflicted mind.

York's architecture—a compact, homey three-story brick

building—and its placement atop a hill offering views of woods, meadows, and streams, were central to Tuke's therapeutic vision.[9] So was the personal stewardship of the patients administered by him and his kindhearted wife and sons. So were the hearty, healthful meals the Tukes provided.

William Tuke's York Retreat was a success, if one discounts the matter of curing mental illness. Tuke never lost his conviction that the "lunatic" condition *could* be cured. Nor did he ever lose his determination to penetrate the secretive walls of York Asylum, which he believed iniquitous. He pursued this goal for twenty-three years. Eventually he found an ally in the town magistrate, Godfrey Higgins. In 1813, Higgins learned that a man whom he himself had decreed to be "insane" and sentenced to York had managed to get word out that he was being mistreated. Higgins decided to investigate. He used his authority under common law to command entry. What he saw—and heard, and smelled—there repelled him:

> When the door was opened, I went into the passage and found four cells…in a very horrid and filthy situation. The straw appeared to be almost saturated with urine and excrement… the walls were daubed with excrement…I then went upstairs and [the keeper] showed me a room…the size of which he told me was twelve feet by seven feet and ten inches, and in there were thirteen women.[10]

Tuke's fellow Quakers, meanwhile, had seen their humane influence flow westward across the Atlantic. America's first incorporated hospital of any kind, Philadelphia Hospital, opened its doors to patients in the prerevolutionary year of 1753. Its cofounders were Dr. Thomas Bond, a Quaker, and Benjamin Franklin. It accommodated a handful of insane patients in a few basement rooms.

Dr. Benjamin Rush, a signer of the Declaration of Independence and one of several figures celebrated as "the father of American psychiatry," joined the medical staff in 1783 and served until his death in 1813. Rush was the first man of science in this country to publicly reject the idea that insanity was caused by demons or witches. In the spirit of Pinel, he joined the argument against the use of those shackles. An eyewitness to the steady expansion of cities on the eastern seaboard, he also was the first American to identify stress as a powerful contributor to madness, if not its cause.

Philadelphia Hospital retained one noxious legacy of Bedlam: it charged visitors a shilling apiece to visit the hospital basement on Sunday afternoons and gape at the thrashing, screeching crazy people inside. This practice disgusted the newly arrived Quakers and stirred them to action. As William Tuke had in York, they financed and built their own sanctuary for the insane. The Friends Asylum for the Relief of Persons Deprived of the Use of Their Reason opened in Philadelphia in 1813, the young nation's first private psychiatric hospital. Moral treatment had established a beachhead in America.

It spread outward from Philadelphia. One of its most prestigious havens was the State Hospital, opened in 1833 as the first state-financed sanctuary, in Worcester, Massachusetts.

The hospital's first commission chairman, the future education visionary Horace Mann, supervised the planning stages. Mann got involved in creating the hospital in part because he subscribed to the growing concern that madness was rising rampantly in the young nation. One of his first acts as commission chairman was to oversee a committee that took a census of mad people, the first such survey in Massachusetts. The committee declared that at least five hundred mentally ill people were without protection.[11]

Worcester State's first superintendent was Dr. Samuel Woodward, who at six feet six inches literally towered some thirteen inches above his countrymen of average height. Once the people of Worcester recovered from their first sight of him, they were won over by his kindness and gentle nature. He greeted each arriving patient personally. If they had been transported from another asylum or prison, he would use his own large hands to free theirs from confinement. He assured the forty-two hundred citizens of Worcester that the new sanctuary posed no danger to them, and that "the law of kindness" was an essential tool in restoring the mad to sanity.

Woodward's thirteen-year stewardship was marked by a combination of his extreme personal decency, his excusable yet limiting innocence of neurobiology, and by the nature and volume of patients that came to his asylum. He rejected any notion that "madness" was a factor of low character or evidence of internal demons. He sought to reamplify the humane credos of Pinel and Tuke. On the other hand he was attracted to the new pseudoscience of phrenology, the belief that human behavior could be anticipated—and manipulated—by a study of the brain's physical features. A century later, of course, phrenology was among the baseless theories summoned to justify some of the most immoral treatment the world has ever witnessed.

The urgency that spurred the proliferation of asylums in this period was prompted by fear. Doctors, city fathers, and ordinary citizens throughout America came to believe with Horace Mann that madness was on the rise. Woodward shared this perception. As had others, they blamed city life, still a new experience in much of the new nation. "Insanity," summarized one Massachusetts psychiatrist in a paper presented in 1851, "is then a part of the price which we pay for civilization."[12]

Yet perhaps people, including the founders of Worcester, did not pay enough attention to the most plausible source of "epidemic" concerns: the phenomenal rise in the American population as a whole. Immigration and new births had already increased the number of United States citizens from 9.5 million in 1820 to 13 million in 1833. The population boom found its way into America's young cities. As they grew, it began to seem as though their streets were unaccountably filling up with "mad" people. The fact was, they were filling up with *people*, and the mad among them, by virtue of their concentration, were more visible than ever before.

Whatever the cause, the nation's first generation of public asylums such as Worcester was soon overwhelmed. Before Worcester's inaugural year ended, Samuel Woodward had yielded to a heartbreaking necessity: set aside his law of kindness and discharge as many nonviolent patients, and even some with criminal pasts, as he could to make room for newer, more violent ones—"the lunatics and furiously mad," as the term of art had it. These were the kinds of patients the state was sending to the facility from jails and prisons; and Worcester, a state-financed institution, had no choice but to accept them. In fact, Massachusetts law *required* that all dangerous "lunatics" already in jail be transferred to Worcester. This practical but unforeseen necessity soon began to erode Worcester's agenda of moral treatment therapy, diminishing the time and space its practitioners needed to do their work. Here was an ominous regression toward the asylum as jail: the very condition that moral treatment had been designed to extinguish.

Still, largely through Woodward's efforts, his asylum's national reputation as a "model" of its kind held up. Goodwill persisted among the city fathers—but was now modified by a fear for public safety.

In 1836, state appropriations funded two new wings, bringing the maximum patient capacity to 229. Still the numbers of applicants—and supplicants—surged higher. Overcrowding, another curse of the older days, continued.

Five years later, reinforcement of a different kind arrived.

It arrived in the person of a tiny, sickly woman of devout Unitarian faith, her dark hair parted severely in the middle and tied in a bun behind, which made her ears stick out, and the resolve of a Rottweiler with its teeth sunk into flesh. Dorothea Dix was on the case.

Dix had lived in the town of Worcester during her childhood. She had lived in a lot of New England places: Hampden, Maine, where she was born (later a part of Massachusetts); then Barnard, Vermont, after her boozy father and migraine-addled mother had fled from Hampden and the path of British infantry in the War of 1812. Then Boston, where she ran a private school; then to the industrialized fogs of England—perhaps not the ideal destination for a four-year sojourn to recover from what is now known as tuberculosis. The disease would recur through her long life and make her an invalid. Yet the overcrowded, sickly, and anxious hordes of London factory workers contributed to one of her most firm beliefs, which until then only Benjamin Rush was known to share: that urban turmoil correlated with vulnerability to insanity. In this, she anticipated René Dubos by eighty years.

In England Dix had been swept into a cohort of British reformers, many of them Quaker, who introduced her to the madhouse netherworld. Dix came home bristling with the determination to be of use to such incarcerated souls. One day in March 1841, she volunteered to teach Sunday school to some women confined at the East Cambridge (Massachusetts) jail. Afterward, a jailer escorted her around the facility. As she gazed into the cells she heard a scream and demanded to see the source. The jailer reluctantly escorted her to a heavy locked door. He opened it and the chilly air inside blew a heavy stench into their faces. The scream had come from within a group of huddling, half-naked "lunatics" who had been encaged in the hovel for years— in the company of convicted violent criminals, as was still common. She asked the jailer how this could be. He comfortably (and, as things turned out, famously) assured the small lady that she should not bother herself; the insane could not feel heat or cold.

That encounter settled her life's course.

Against the warnings of friends who were aware of her health problems, Dorothea Dix embarked upon an eighteen-month itinerary that took her to jails and asylums throughout Massachusetts, barging past guards to interview patient-inmates and their keepers. At the end of her journey, she was convinced that the moral treatment asylums were in fact benefiting patients, but that the jailing of excess "mad" people was rampant and their plight an affront to humanity. She returned to Worcester and in 1843 joined forces with Woodward, Mann, and a well-born reformer named Samuel Gridley Howe to inspire or shame the legislature into action. (Howe had run for and won a seat in the state House of Representatives as a Whig just so he could speak for Dix from the inside.)[13] In January she prepared a "Memorial to the Legislature of Massachusetts" (women were not allowed to address the legislature in person back then; they had to submit their thoughts in writing). Her words ring in the pantheon of American oratory—or as oratory-that-might-have-been.

> I come to place before the Legislature of Massachusetts the condition of the miserable, the desolate, the outcast. I come as the advocate of helpless, forgotten, insane, idiotic men and women; of beings sunk to a condition from which the most unconcerned would start with real horror; of beings wretched in our prisons, and more wretched in our almshouses. I...arrest and fix attention upon a subject only the more strongly pressing in its claims because it is revolting and disgusting in its details.[14]

Mann, Howe, and the others were thrilled. Representative Samuel Gridley Howe introduced the Memorial in the legislature. It was sent to the Committee on Public Charitable Institutions, then shaped into a bill by committee chairman Howe. After debates and modifications, the bill passed both houses, and Samuel Woodward was granted authority to build new housing at the asylum for 150 patients.

Dorothea Dix expanded her inspection tours to the entire country, and then to Europe, traveling thirty thousand miles by some estimates, via railroad, steamship, stagecoach, and buggy, and whatever else was available, which was not much. She cultivated the friendship and support of President Fillmore and the great Massachusetts senator Charles Sumner. She gave speeches, cajoled legislators, and talked wealthy people into funding asylum building and improvement. She took a detour through the Civil War to serve as superintendent of the Army of Nurses for the Union (where she and her nurses also treated wounded Confederates, including many from the five thousand lying maimed at Gettysburg). And then she went to work for the insane again.

She is credited with direct roles in the founding of thirty-two asylums by 1880, including the New Jersey State Lunatic Asylum at Trenton in 1848. She died in her guest apartment there in July 1887 at age eighty-five. She was having tea.

Even as Dorothea Dix's reputation and accomplishments grew through the 1840s and 1850s, Worcester's prestige declined. Another baleful law, that of diminishing returns, was beginning to catch up with the asylum and all those that shared its Enlightenment-fired ideals. America's population kept swelling: to seventeen million in 1840, then to twenty-three million by 1860, near the outbreak of the Civil War. This growth and other factors, evident even at the outset of moral care in America, kept on pushing against the founders' idealism. There were simply too many more patients, too many more criminals, and too many other kinds of hard cases among those patients. More time was needed for administrative duties and less time for supervisors' personal visitation; less time for healthful activities; less space—far less space—per patient than the early dreamers had deemed necessary. The righteous fervor and dedication of the early supervisors and staff and caretakers inevitably cooled with their replacements, and the replacements of those replacements.

Samuel B. Woodward died in Northampton, Massachusetts, in 1850, at age sixty-three. Fully twenty-three years elapsed between his death and the next—and last—effort to rejuvenate his generation's vision: twenty-three years of policy wars, scrambles for space; the replacement of passion with bureaucracy and systemized procedure. The times also brought societal changes that imposed tough choices unforeseen a half-century earlier—necessities of segregation, for instance: not just racially, but segregation of the violent from the nonviolent, pauper from affluent, immigrant from native-born. A new breed of less idealistic staff members took these distinctions as criteria for the amount of kindness and attention they were willing to confer.

A national air of pessimism was enveloping the mental health world—certainly on the question of whether insanity could be widely cured. Still, in 1873, Massachusetts pushed ahead to finance construction of a new and larger replacement for Worcester State Hospital. The cost exceeded $1 million. Its administration building virtually announced that moral treatment was here to stay. The signal proved false.

Kirkbride Hall was the new Worcester asylum's most prominent structure, crowned by a high Gothic clock tower that could be seen well beyond the borders of the city of 146,000. The tower soared above the five granite stories of the administration hall. It overlooked the nearby Lake Quinsigamond, with its eight graceful islands, to the east, and pointed heavenward in the manner of a church steeple.

It was named for its designer, the physician-turned-architectural-planner Thomas Kirkbride, who in 1840 had become superintendent of the Pennsylvania Hospital for the Insane. A Quaker like William Tuke, Kirkbride fastened on the Yorkshireman's espousal of a harmonious environment. He devoured Tuke's 1815 book *Practical Hints on the Construction and Economy of Pauper Lunatic Asylums*, and later published his own similar and influential treatise. He created concepts for siting, landscaping, and building design that found nationwide favor and determined the general look of insane asylums for the rest of the nineteenth century.

Kirkbride asylums were designed as antidungeons, ornate and elegant, incorporating features from the Queen Anne, Second Empire, and Gothic Revival styles: spires and cupolas and gabled roofs, and construction from fine timber or heavy stone. (Kirkbride provided the essential interior plans for his buildings, but construction and landscaping were jobbed out to a number of artisans around the country.)

No one expressed the vision of an ideal physical layout with greater lyricism or tenderness than Kirkbride himself:

> Great care should be taken in locating the building, that every possible advantage may be derived from the views and scenery adjacent, and especially as seen from the parlors and other rooms occupied during the day. The prevailing winds of summer and the genial influence of the sun's rays at all seasons,

may also be made to minister to the comfort of the inmates, and the grounds immediately adjacent to the hospital should have a gradual descent in all directions, to secure a good surface drainage.[15]

Few asylum-building committees cared to deviate from the master's vision: besides its utilitarian logic, a domed or spired "Kirkbride" on the edge of town (never inside!) lent an aura of elegance to the whole area. More than a few thoughtful observers, though, detected something quite apart from elegance: an indefinable brooding, an opaque heaviness, less elegant than Gothic. Others who were more informed about prevailing trends in mental health care could see even beyond the Gothic, into a gathering void. Kirkbride had meant to endorse and enhance moral treatment with his buildings, but he was enhancing a phantom. In post–Civil War America, urban industry, not the rural cycles, dictated the pace of life. Philosophies of care were changing as well, in sync with the times. Psychiatrists had grown impatient with the notion of therapy that led to cure; they'd seen precious little empirical evidence. What role was left to them, then?

It was the role of custodianship: basic supervisory care and feeding of those unfortunates whose reason was maimed by fate, yet who lived on.

This shrunken agenda for moral treatment began to lose its moorings even as the number of public and private asylums, a great many of them "Kirkbrides," swelled to nearly three hundred over the decades.

The horrid systematic cruelty of Bedlam never returned. Not completely. But it never completely went away, either. This fact is documented by almost weekly news accounts from the human disposal systems that our large urban prisons and hospitals have become.

Time has not been kind to the old moral care asylums' appearance. Broken windows and support beams left unrepaired, lawns and flower beds unmanicured, damaged furniture on the inside unreplaced—all this left the mansions exposed in their decrepitude.

Increasingly, these asylums were simply abandoned as larger, centralized (and impersonal) hospitals were built to warehouse the mentally ill. The elderly insane especially suffered the transition, as supervisors nudged reluctant families to accept them back into the home. When families refused, these people stayed in the system but endured the usual indignity of indifference, magnified by contempt and revulsion.

Some asylums burned down; some were (and continue to be) demolished for newer facilities or housing developments or shopping malls. A surprising number of them remain standing on their patches of prairie, but under conditions of decrepitude and debasement that conjure images of the inmates at Bedlam, helpless before the smirks and taunts of strolling visitors. In an inversion that would have devastated the Kirkbrides and Woodwards and Manns and Dixes, and the Tukes and Pinels before them, the remains of these buildings now represent not hope but evil. Mass-marketed commercial evil.

Many have been purchased by entrepreneurs attuned to the American appetite for the macabre, especially in the computer-generated forms of garroting, throat-slashing, and torture. These businessmen and -women, rejoicing in the caricature presented by the old sanctuaries, have made it pay: by refurbishing the cells and apartments with stage-set spooks and sorcerers and sinister scientists with bloody smocks, and splashing fake blood on the walls. The classic sanctuaries for haunted human beings are thus transformed into haunted houses. They draw attraction-seeking Americans who travel great distances, stand in line, sometimes for hours, and pay dearly for tickets that allow them to step inside and squeal as computerized mad scientists perform bloody atrocities upon shrieking "inmates" strapped to their beds. "These are the places where physicians cut into their brains with ice picks and robbed them of their personalities," exults one attraction website. "They are places where they were raped, medicated, abused, murdered."[16]

No definitive theories have explained why this haunted attractions boom (or "BOO-oom," as TV news websites merrily put it) has become, by some calculations, a billion-dollar business. America

Haunts, a trade association, estimates that there are twelve hundred large-scale, for-profit haunted attractions in the United States, not to mention another three thousand haunted houses that open for the Halloween season.

Some suggest that the haunted-house experience offers a cathartic release in our anxiety-saturated times. (A kind of therapy, as it were.) Some say it offers just another roadside attraction.

As for shamans, they have persisted, counter to all expectation. Persisted, and proliferated. The contemporary urban world has seen a resurgence in the number of self-described shamans and of shamanistic thought, expressed partly in the New Age revolution of the 1970s. And the affinities between their ecstasies, and epiphanies, remain as strong as ever—as often acknowledged by the believers themselves. Except that the believers seldom if ever describe their experiences as mental illness.

The author and self-described shaman Paul Levy has recalled insisting to psychiatrists years ago, regarding his involuntary hospitalization after an "ecstatic" episode, that he had simply been trying to express the "good news" of what was being revealed to him about the nature of reality: "I tried to explain to the psychiatrists that I WAS sick," Levy wrote, "but just not in the way they were imagining. I had a creative, psychological illness, which is to say that my seeming madness was an expression of my creative self."

He was not clinically ill, Levy insisted; he was "perturbed," suffering from a "shamanic illness"—in trauma from recalling the abuse he had endured at the hands of his "desperately sick, sociopathic father." His father had connected Levy "as a link in a chain to an unbroken lineage of violence...extending far back in time and throughout space."

Thus his "seeming madness," Levy insisted, "was an expression of my creative self, alchemically transforming an underlying perturbance in the field of consciousness so as to heal itself."[17]

These insistences from Paul Levy, and what I've learned about shamanism in general, have put me in mind of my son Kevin.

Like Levy, Kevin refused—as I've said—to define himself as mentally ill. He had a *condition*; that was as far as he would go. I have thought, as well, of the time in the schoolyard in which Kevin admonished the burly ice-hockey athlete for striking the tall young girl—and did not draw a challenge of fisticuffs himself from the bully. I thought of other such moments. Nothing really dramatic or revelatory, but moments in which (in retrospect) Kevin conferred a measure of peace, even laughter, upon a situation, armed only with directness, honesty, and his crooked grin.

I don't believe in shamanism as an extrasensory phenomenon. I don't believe that shamans have, or ever have had, a connection to the divine.

But if I did believe...

Are you listening, Kevin?

5

Eugenics: Weeding Out the Mad

Moral treatment represented a pinnacle of society's humanitarian impulses toward the mentally ill. Diagnosis and medical treatment, however, remained primitive, circumscribed by ignorance. By the first decades of the nineteenth century, "mad science" had not advanced beyond clumsy attempts to drive out demons and bad "humours."

All this was about to change—with implications both hopeful and nearly catastrophic for the mentally ill. An accidental chain of discovery, historic in its proportions, was imminent. Even as moral treatment was enjoying the height of its brief prestige, the raw materials for these discoveries, packed in cargo containers, were bobbing northward from the South Atlantic and home to England aboard an obscure two-masted brig sloop, the *Beagle*. In the early autumn of 1836, *Beagle* was on its final leg of the most transformative voyage of discovery ever made, Columbus's accidental collision with the New World perhaps excepted.

The sloop carried the seeds—metaphoric and literal—of overwhelming evidence that plant and animal species have not existed through history in an unchanging state. They have evolved by variations in inherited traits. This capacity to change, even in minute ways, enables living things to overcome deadly environmental challenges and reproduce themselves as the "fittest" survivors.

The implications for biologically damaged human brains—a subject not imagined at first even by the ship's young botanist, Charles

Darwin—were to prove momentous and beneficial in the long run. Yet these positive results could happen only after Darwin's theories were drastically misunderstood and misapplied, threatening mad people with attempted extinction. A prime source of the trouble was that word *fittest*. As ambiguous in its way as "schizophrenia," "fittest" proved ripe for misunderstanding and monstrous abuse.

The cargo containers carried some ten thousand plants, birds, small animals, and fossils gathered from exotic locales around the world by Darwin. The theory that Darwin constructed from this cargo over the next two decades of meticulous study would transform human thought. It would embolden open skepticism about the divine origins of humankind, the first mass Western questioning of Scripture since Scripture was written. It would point the way for breakthroughs in agriculture, medicine, economics, and many fields of learning. But in the hands of biased theorists, scheming industrialists, outright fools, and—inevitably—totalitarian tyrants, the revolutionary theory put forward by Darwin would be perverted into the basis of remorseless experiments upon the human brain and reproductive organs, toward the goal of creating a white master race liberated from any sort of genetic "impurity": including skin pigmentation, physical imperfection, low intelligence, and homosexuality.

And madness.

The discovery of linkage between madness and a person's genetic makeup figured among the massive chain reaction of breakthroughs in the years and decades after the *Beagle* docked.

How strange, almost uncanny, it is, then, to consider the central influence that madness exerted on the *Beagle*'s and Darwin's destinies.

On October 2, 1836, *Beagle* put in at Falmouth Harbor in a light rain. It had been at sea for nearly five years, surveying the remote coastlines of the world for mapmaking purposes. *Beagle*'s troubled captain and chief surveyor, Robert FitzRoy, just twenty-three when the voyage began, had sought someone of equal social status to come along and keep him company. Intermediaries recommended a young scion of

British intellectuals and aristocrats, a bright but restless scholar named Charles Darwin.

Darwin, a year younger than FitzRoy, had completed studies at Christ's College in Cambridge for the Anglican priesthood just before embarkation. His attention lately had swung toward beetles.

His grandfather Erasmus was an accomplished botanist. Charles may have felt Erasmus's influence when, wandering beside the River Cam one day, he spotted two rare beetles scurrying under the bark of a log. Darwin ripped the bark open, grabbed one beetle in each fist; then he noticed a third, popped one of the first two into his mouth so he could capture the third as well, and lost two of the three in a paroxysm of gagging and spitting when the beetle on his tongue shot acid down his throat.[1]

After that, he took to using a net. He'd evolved.

Madness hung about the *Beagle* and was a factor in the voyage's great destiny. FitzRoy had been given command of the sloop after the captain on its previous voyage lost his mind and shot himself amid the thundering seas around Tierra del Fuego. FitzRoy himself suffered from mood swings that whipsawed him from rages of temper into depression. His uncle, the paranoiac Viscount Castlereagh, had fatally stabbed himself in the neck in 1822.

British naval protocol, an extension of the British class system, forbade ships' officers from socializing with the crew. The ship already had a naturalist, so FitzRoy could not offer the young Cambridge man a commission. Darwin paid his own way. The official naturalist soon felt upstaged by Darwin's prowess and abandoned the expedition in Rio de Janeiro. Now Darwin had an excuse for doing what he'd wanted to do: forage for specimens when the *Beagle* put in off some remote coast.

Darwin's skills as a raconteur could not cure Robert FitzRoy of the blues. While Darwin was collecting bugs and bird skins in the Chilean Andes forests, FitzRoy grew overwhelmed with his duties and suffered a nervous breakdown. He resigned his captaincy, telling his second-in-command, one Lt. John Wickham, that he could take over the ship. Wickham told FitzRoy that he would be damned if he'd try to guide *Beagle* around the deadly Cape Horn. FitzRoy thought about that for a moment and changed his mind. Had he continued to pout, Darwin would have missed the Galápagos, and a finch, to paraphrase Freud, would have remained just a finch.

As for Captain FitzRoy, early in the morning of April 30, 1865, at his home in Norwood, Surrey, he walked into his dressing room, found a knife, and emulated his uncle by slitting his throat with it.[2] He died not knowing that he would be remembered in history for his choice of a shipboard conversation-mate who is ranked, with Einstein and Freud, among the greatest thinkers of the past two hundred years.

It is nearly impossible to make sense of the furious arguments that to this day energize and often impede the interests of the mentally ill without understanding eugenics. This in turn requires a brief review of the genesis, so to speak, of Charles Darwin's theory.

Twenty-two years elapsed between *Beagle*'s docking and the publication of his first and most historic book: years of studying his Galápagos species and specimens and annotating his meticulous journals, then coming to grips with the staggering paradigm shift that they implied, and then struggling with his reluctance to publish his discovery because the Church might (and did) get mad at him. But in 1859, the first edition of Darwin's *On the Origin of Species* appeared, sold out instantly, went through several more printings, and was followed by an equally seminal work, *The Descent of Man*, in 1871.

His studies had convinced Darwin of the validity of common descent for the multitude of species roaming the earth, particularly obvious in geographically isolated communities such as the Galápagos Islands, and resulting from small variations occurring over decades and centuries. These small variations led to such attributes as the different lengths and shapes of the beaks on the finches of the Galápagos Islands. And, compounded over time, these variations led to large differences—for example, when a common ancestor is discovered between two seemingly disparate species (such as the American buffalo, whose neck is quite overwhelmed by an enormous head extending down toward the sustenance of grasslands, and contrasts sharply with the small head of its relative the giraffe, which reaches up into the trees with its very long and slender neck).

Darwin's theory needed no conjectural leaps to support itself. (Interestingly, in the first edition of *Origin*, he did not include human beings in the evolutionary chain, though later he repaired that omission.) His theories of natural selection generated great advances for mankind. They opened gateways that led scientists to integrate and unify the multiform strands of biology. From that achievement came breakthroughs in medicine (polio vaccines, resistance to pests and pestilence, the treatments for bacterial infections and HIV). The study of natural selection energized the science of linguistics (based upon a common grounding in variability). It led to the introduction, in the 1970s, of "theory of mind" studies that traced human beings' remarkable adaptability to increasingly complex environments to the gregariousness and "excess" cognitive capacities of primates.[3] Evolutionary theory opened up new corridors of argumentation into human uniqueness and the basis of human morality, given the implied possibility of a godless universe.

The theory of common descent, and the resulting unifying "tree of life" relating man to monkey, generated anger, horror, and discord within Western Christian faith. Church leaders saw the theory as an attack on the Genesis creation story and thus a refutation of the Christian God, though none of Darwin's works argued for the absence of divine agency. Darwin himself adhered to his faith, and, by the 1890s, the Church of England had accommodated itself to his evolutionary principles. Catholicism also coexists with evolution, as represented most recently in the statement by Pope Francis in 2014 that "evolution is not opposed to the notion of Creation, because evolution presupposes the creation of beings that evolve." Yet fundamentalist Christians, for whom the literal interpretation of the Bible is essential, continue to deny that evolution occurs. Although 60 percent of American adults believe that living creatures evolved over time, 33 percent actively reject evolution and 42 percent believe that God created human beings in a form that has not changed.

The affront to Christian doctrine aside, significant misuses soon compromised Darwin's evolutionary revolution. In 1905, thirteen years after the naturalist's death, the British biologist William Bateson gave a name to his countryman's field: "genetics," a coinage of Greek derivation that means "pertaining to origins." By that time, another new term similar in sound to "genetics" had become in vogue in Britain and the United States. Soon it would find its true home in Nazi Germany. The term was "eugenics."

Bluntly put, "eugenics" referred to genocidal solutions for a monstrously illegitimate "problem": the "problem" of negative attitudes, culturally fostered, toward those perceived to differ significantly from the "norm." Most people familiar with eugenics—the practice of manipulating biological systems to refine reproduction—believe it to have been a passing atrocity of years long past, a tool of Nazi experimentation that became obsolete with the demise of the Third Reich. This is wrong in many ways. Eugenics was a gift to Hitler's scientists from American naturalist-entrepreneurs, who had picked up on it from the British. And far from being obsolete, eugenics remains very much alive in the world today. Many of its post-Holocaust refinements have been shaped to benefit mankind—conquering diseases, enhancing the yield and nutritional quality of crops. More recent refinements, while dedicated to the noble cause of combating mental illness, have indisputably crossed into the morally ambiguous territory of physically altering components of the brain. Gene-editing, to be discussed later, is the current paramount example.

And at the darker extremes, eugenics techniques are still occasionally used for their original purpose: population control; the elimination of the unwanted.

History is often whimsical when it is not brutal, and sometimes even when it is.

A central argument of *On the Origin of Species*, reviled by the pious as apostasy, was ironically inspired by a Church of England priest, also an eminent economist. To deepen this irony, the Darwinian argument in question was an error: a misreading of the cleric's point (shaky enough in itself) that human population growth was outrunning the growth of food supplies. And to turn the irony into travesty, Darwin's skewed amplification of the cleric's ambiguous point helped propel mankind into the foothills of genocide, not only of Jewry, but of any grouping deemed unfit or "surplus." Homosexuals, for example. And lunatics, idiots, morons, imbeciles, nuts. And of course the ever-shunned and vulnerable mentally ill.

The economist and priest was Thomas Malthus, who made his fuzzy argument in a widely read 1798 pamphlet, *Essay on the Principle of Population*. Malthus warned that the human population was expanding at a "geometrical" rate; that is, in quantities far higher than the simple replacement number of two; while the food supply—plants and animals—was slogging along at a much slower pace—incremental, or "arithmetical." These dynamics, Malthus predicted, would escalate under the "laws of nature" into famine and brutal competition for food.

Thomas Malthus did not really believe that man would exhaust his resources and die out, though Malthus shared (and reinforced) a belief of his time that there were getting to be too many people. It was the economist in him that researched the statistics, but it was the servant of God who drew the conclusions. He saw the burgeoning population as a sign of man's overweening sexuality, and he saw potential food shortages as a warning from God that man should—well, scale it back a little. Marry later, and spend more time being productive in the fields than being productive in the bedroom. (True to his piety, Malthus could not accept even marital contraception as a corrective.)

Charles Darwin read Malthus's treatise in 1838, when he was twenty-nine and the economist was four years dead. He was electrified to find in *Principle of Population* a missing link regarding his own theories. The link was *competition*. "Competition" lent dynamism, and supreme consequence, to what had been, despite the protean vastness and variety of evidence the young botanist had collected, a mere description of natural-world processes. Now Darwin had a tool for making his observation predictive.

"It at once struck me," Darwin later wrote regarding Malthus's impact upon his thought, "that under these circumstances favourable variations [or species] would tend to be preserved, and unfavourable ones to be destroyed. The results of this would be the formation of a new species."[4]

And, later:

This is the doctrine of Malthus, applied to the whole animal and vegetable kingdoms. As many more individuals of each species are born than can possibly survive; and as, consequently, there is a frequently recurring struggle for existence, it follows that any being, if it vary however slightly in any manner profitable to itself, under the complex and sometimes varying conditions of life, will have a better chance of surviving, and thus be naturally selected.[5]

Darwin's theories would be roundly misinterpreted in his lifetime and afterward, but this reading of Malthus was itself a misinterpretation: a small misinterpretation and an understandable one, yet one that led to a great deal of trouble. Darwin salted the first edition of *Origin of Species* with Malthus's "scarcity" arguments, and he took them more literally than his source intended them. According to the scholar Abdul Ahad, Darwin cited Malthus's notion of "geometrical increase of population" eleven times, "struggle" eighty-four times, and "competition" forty-four times—a lot more frequently, in each case, than had Malthus himself.[6] Before long, educated Britons were talking even more nervously than before about the coming nightmare of too many people and too little food.

Charles Dickens, alert as always to the zeitgeist, picked up on this anxiety and used it to satirize the comfortable classes in his 1843 classic *A Christmas Carol*. His immortal skinflint Ebenezer Scrooge, irritated at two charity solicitors, wonders why the poor don't simply go to prison or the workhouses: " 'The establishments I have mentioned: they cost enough: and those who are badly off must go there.' [One of the solicitors replied,] 'Many can't go there; and many would rather die.' 'If they would rather die,' said Scrooge, 'they had better do it, and decrease the surplus population.' "[7]

And there it was: a buzz-phrase that would soon mushroom into an illusion of self-evident truth. Malthus himself had never uttered or written "surplus population." But now, uncritically reinforced by Darwin and then enshrined by Dickens, the concept spread and soon brought into the sunlight all sorts of unworthy social bigotries that until then had remained politely covered in euphemism.

The sixth British edition of *On the Origin of Species*, published in 1869, featured another freighted phrase not conceived by Darwin yet inspired by his work. The phrase was "survival of the fittest."

"Survival of the fittest" was a coinage of the eminent British philosopher Herbert Spencer. Spencer had read the first edition of *Origin* and decided that Charles Darwin was talking not about species in general but about the human race, whether Darwin realized this or not. Spencer's overriding passion was economics; he inherited some of Malthus's ideas and ran them to the logical breaking point. Laissez-faire was his game, in economics and everything else. He had already formed some dogmas of his own about evolution by the time he picked up *Origin of the Species* not long after its first printing and found in its pages the face of Herbert Spencer looking back. He promptly wrote *Principles of Biology*, published in 1864, incorporating some of Darwin's sedate "natural selection" ideas and rebranding them with the manly tag "survival of the fittest."

Darwin, with his typical deference toward peers in his field, was happy to slip the term into the fifth edition of *Origin of Species*, which came out in 1869. "This preservation of favourable variations, and the destruction of injurious variations, I call Natural Selection, or the Survival of the Fittest," he wrote.[8]

"Survival of the fittest" was a term that boiled, for men of certain temperaments, with intimations that the mild botanist would never have arrived at on his own. Herbert Spencer was a near zealot in his promotion of unrestrained competition among men for resources and capital gain. He fanned Malthus's spark into open flame. American captains of industry, notably the ruthless steel magnate Andrew Carnegie, saw in Spencer—and, no doubt squinting very closely, in Darwin—predatory selfishness revealed as a higher law.

"I remember that light came as in a flood and all was clear," Carnegie wrote, describing the transformative effect that the "survival" trope had had on him. "Not only had I got rid of theology and the supernatural, but I had found the truth of evolution. 'All is well since all grows better' became my motto, my true source of comfort."[9]

The flame spread. In 1869, the same year as Darwin's fifth edition, another bold new stepchild of *Origin of Species* appeared. *Hereditary Genius: Its Laws and Consequences* instructed the world that a person's intelligence was immutably fixed by his or her bloodlines. The "consequences" were happy for people born into smart families, and not so great at all for everyone else.

The author was Darwin's second cousin, Francis Galton, an amateur scientist of great range and staggering intellectual gifts, and the common sense of a trilobite. He pursued geography and anthropology, traveling the Nile and the Jordan and the wilds of tropical South Africa. He studied meteorology and invented the weather map as we know it. His gift to criminology was the forensic significance of the fingerprint.

Galton's true genius lay in the mastery of numbers as keys to unlocking scientific truth. He was a tabulator and classifier, a counter- and comparison-maker; a proto-statistician. He gave the world psychometrics and quantitative differential psychology.

As if to prove that brilliance and good judgment do not necessarily go hand in hand—as eugenics itself was to prove—Galton once wrote a letter to the London *Times* proposing that it would be a good idea if the Chinese, whom he considered adequately civilized, were to relocate to Africa and shoo away all the dark savages who lived there. Where the dark savages would go, or what their take on the idea might be, Galton was not prepared to say. He apparently did not poll the Chinese, either, who, in the event, elected to stay in China. It was just a thought.

He was interested for a while in "quantifying" the beauty of women's bodies; but whereas other men might content themselves with furtive glances at female buttocks, only Galton (while in South Africa) tried to measure their bottom-line appeal by applying a sextant.

> The sub-interpreter was married to a charming person...a Venus among Hottentots. I was perfectly aghast at her development, and made enquiries upon that delicate point as far as I dared among my missionary friends...The result is, that I believe Mrs. Petrus to be the lady who ranks second in all the Hottentots for the beautiful outline that her back affords, Jonker's wife ranking as the first...I, profess to be a scientific man, and was exceedingly anxious to obtain accurate measurements of her shape...my eye fell upon my sextant; and I took a series of observations upon her figure in every direction, up and down, crossways, diagonally, and so forth...this being done, I boldly pulled out my measuring tape, and measured the distance from where I was to the place she stood, and having thus obtained both base and angles, I worked out the results by trigonometry and logarithms.[10]

With that accomplishment, Galton put the "hot" in Hottentot and the "sex" in sextant.

Such was the sexist, racist, white supremacist makeup of the man who presumed to build upon his great cousin's discoveries to tweak the human brain toward perfection.

Like Spencer, Galton concluded that Darwin's method could foretell the evolutionary traits of human beings as well as plants, fish, and animals, based on inherited characteristics, or what would be called genes. And like others to follow, he overestimated and oversimplified wildly, erring into faulty research and coarse determinism. The tools of neurobiology, for instance, which would have revealed the nearly infinite volition of the brain and its capacity to override many supposed limitations, remained far in the future. That did not stop Galton from making staggering suppositions.

What Galton had in mind, unnamed as yet, was human engineering. He began with the premise, based on his fatally parochial research, that "talent," by which he meant intelligence and productive innovation, was clustered within certain families. He employed questionnaires, studies of twins, biometrics, an analysis of bodily traits (a field that he invented), and other statistical tools. From these methods, he concluded that all human physical and mental levels were determined solely by heredity. Further—and what a coincidence!—the families favored by fate formed parts of Francis Galton's own social milieu. They were well-off, well-educated, industrious sorts, and (Galton being Galton) not hard to look at, either—unlike the greasy, swarthy wogs against whose grubby shoulders Galton and other imperialists found themselves increasingly rubbing. The beautiful and "talented" proceeded from classic Anglo-Saxon stock, tribes of blond, blue-eyed Angles and Saxons and Jutes who immigrated to the British Isles from northern Europe in the fifth century in search of open farmland and whose descendants now went to the same churches, universities, and clubs that Galton frequented. The others, those inconvenient wogs, amounted to a deadly snake coiled in the garden of his Eden. The snake was poisoning the purity of the noblest human strain, the hope of history. The serpent was embodied by the misguided champions of social reform, the philanthropists, the charitable folk. Didn't they realize that they were accomplishing nothing but the artificial propagation of the unfit, who did nothing of note but bear more unfit children? The *surplus population*? Their efforts only impeded the natural correctives that cousin Charles had identified.

It seemed to Francis Galton that natural selection needed a boost from unnatural selection.

The remedies proposed in the first edition of *Hereditary Genius* were mild in comparison to those offered by Galton's more hot-blooded adherents, and later by Galton himself. The book suggested that the human race could be improved via arranged marriages between bright, accomplished men and comely women. This solution brings to mind nothing so much as the riposte that George Bernard Shaw is said to have offered a woman who proposed marriage, given that Shaw had a brilliant mind and she had beautiful looks: "What if the child inherits your mind and my looks?"* Later, Galton fastidiously subdivided his concept into "positive" eugenics (pairing fit and intelligent and sane sorts of men and women and, incidentally, Nordic sorts of men and women) and "negative" eugenics (preventing the "unfit" from having children).

Hereditary Genius rushed to popularity amid the "evolution" mania. Fourteen years after the book first appeared, as Galton's new system grew toward international fame as an icon of the age of progress, he came up with a suitably pretentious name for it: "eugenics." His recourse to the ancient Greek was shrewd. "Eu" is a word-forming syllable meaning "goodly" or "well," as educated Victorians would know. "Gen" expresses coming into being. Thus "eugenics": a goodly birth. Galton might better have called it "pláni tou eniaíou aitía," the fallacy of the single cause.

Galton did not live to see eugenics applied to justify the mass extermination of Jews and the smaller-scale attempts to wipe out the mentally ill in the Holocaust. Common supposition has it that the practice died out with the defeat of the Third Reich in 1945, yet Galton's spawn did no such thing. Eugenics flourished in the postwar years, in subtler forms than attempted genocide, sterilization of reproductive organs, lobotomy, castration, and murder by neglect. Eugenics would constitute the preeminent indignity directed at the insane and the presumed insane for most of the ensuing hundred years after Galton's treatise. As mentioned, it is practiced today and, in some cases, practiced in the name of useful medical research. Now, for the first time in history, man was not an unquestioned creature of God but could be seen as an exponent of blind deterministic forces. And those same forces, confronted with shortages of food and water, could make part of humanity "surplus." And once mankind had internalized that utilitarian formulation...

---

* Similar exchanges have been attributed to Albert Einstein and Marilyn Monroe, Monroe and Arthur Miller, George Bernard Shaw and Isadora Duncan, Winston Churchill and Lady Astor.

"I think that stern compulsion ought to be exerted to prevent the free propagation of the stock of those who are seriously afflicted by lunacy, feeble-mindedness, habitual criminality, and pauperism," Galton wrote in his 1908 autobiography.[11] He was knighted in 1909.

The list of European and American public figures who joined the eugenics crusade under Galton's banner is stunning.

The German philosopher Friedrich Nietzsche saw in it a validation of his argument that man was not a creation of the divine, but an organism like all others, without moral purpose, part of the universal chaos. Short decades later, the Nazis would read Nietszche's thoughts as a literal call for the restoration of the master race. They appropriated, in effect, Francis Galton's ideal social class, added some myth, and claimed it as their own as they sought to propagate a fantasy population: blond blue-eyed Aryans who, in folk belief, had disappeared with the lost continent of Atlantis. The former president Theodore Roosevelt thought eugenics was a damned good means of getting rid of all those damned degenerates who were just interested in reproducing more degenerates. "Society has no business to permit degenerates to reproduce their kind. It is really extraordinary that our people refuse to apply to human beings such elementary knowledge as every successful farmer is obliged to apply to his own stock breeding," grumbled the architect of the Square Deal for the common man in a 1913 letter to the eugenics pioneer Charles Benedict Davenport.[12] Roosevelt was drawn to eugenics via his manly friendship with one of the most incandescent hero-villains of the early twentieth century.

Madison Grant, nearly forgotten today, was a titan in his time, an enduring icon of American conservation and, at the same time, as intelligent and cold-blooded an avatar of scientific racism as anyone on the western side of the Atlantic.

Grant was born into the Long Island upper class in 1865. Photographs of him in his fifties show a lean, imperious aristocrat with a silvery wide-swept mustache. His skull and clean-shaven jaw were long, in the approved Nordic fashion. His passion for the natural world grew from his boyhood ramblings among the exotic trees and flowers on his grandfather's estate. As for animals, "I began by collecting turtles as a boy and have never recovered from this predilection."[13]

A well-tutored young international traveler even before he entered Yale in 1884, Grant emerged in the late nineteenth century as a fierce champion of the natural world. His profession was the law; his avocation was saving nature. He led successful drives to prevent the destruction of California's redwood trees and the depletion of the bison. He founded the Bronx Zoo and designed the scenic Bronx River Parkway, and his visionary efforts guided the creation of Glacier (Montana) and Denali (Alaska) National Parks. A hunter himself, he pressed for stronger gun laws and for limits on a hunter's bounty. He became an expert in wildlife management, perceiving, à la Malthus, that the oversupply of stocks—their "surplus"—guaranteed their descent from perfection and nudged them toward extinction.

It was exactly within Grant's visionary genius that malignity festered like a deformed gene. The same mastery of biological process that enabled him to anticipate threats to natural perfection activated his abhorrence of "inferior" human strains—and his wish to get rid of them. He loathed not only Negroes and Jews, but any specimen of the sweating, reeking, and jostling immigrant nationalities that were invading his pristine Anglo-Saxon precincts on the immigration tide. They deserved the same fate as all surplus livestock.

Madison Grant did not bring eugenics to the United States, but Davenport, his best friend, did. And then the two of them worked for years to make eugenics theory as American as apple pie. For a time, they succeeded.

Davenport, the recipient of Roosevelt's harrumphing fan letter, was another in the unending supply of patricians/outdoorsmen/naturalists/intellectuals and future eugenicists such as Grant, and about the same age. Davenport met Francis Galton in London in 1902 and found himself transformed. A few years later, he described the encounter to Grant, whom he knew from an interlocking circle of clubs. Grant was just then expanding his interests from protecting the natural world to protecting human purity. Davenport lacked the zealotry of his friend, but Grant had more than enough for both of them. He pounced on Galton's ideas and devoured them like so many plump gazelles at a watering hole. Then he went to work.

Abetted by Davenport, Grant raced to institutionalize the eugenics movement in America. He founded the American chapter of the Galton Society in 1918 and was among the founders of the American Eugenics Society in 1926. These organizations gained funding and support on the ballast of Madison's incendiary 1916 book *The Passing of the Great Race*. Like eugenics itself, this manifesto profited from the nativist hysteria inflamed by a new swell of emigration from eastern European countries, compounded by the steady northward flow of Negroes from the agrarian South who were looking for industrial jobs that white workers had considered their birthright.

Because of these incursions into America's economic and social sanctuaries, not to mention the steely absolutism of the book's tone, *The Passing of the Great Race* proved as consequential in its way as Hitler's *Mein Kampf*.

Grant declared, in a foundational paragraph:

Mistaken regard for what are believed to be divine laws and a sentimental belief in the sanctity of human life tend to prevent both the elimination of defective infants and the sterilization of such adults as are themselves of no value to the community. The laws of nature require the obliteration of the unfit and human life is valuable only when it is of use to the community or race.[14]

And just in case anyone missed that subtle point:

A rigid system of selection through the elimination of those who are weak or unfit—in other words social failures—would solve the whole question in one hundred years, as well as enable us to get rid of the undesirables who crowd our jails, hospitals, and *insane asylums* [my emphasis]...This is a practical, merciful, and inevitable solution of the whole problem, and can be applied to an ever widening circle of social discards, beginning always with the criminal, the diseased, and the insane.[15]

It was passages such as these that led Grant's indefatigable* biographer, Jonathan Peter Spiro, to sum up his subject's imprint on history in one damning sentence: "Madison Grant's major contribution to eugenics…was to advance it from a skirmish against individuals who were socially unfit into a war against groups who were *racially* unfit."[16]

The spark was a bonfire now. Its flames soared higher on the fuels added to it by the captains of American philanthropy, the very sorts that Francis Galton had denounced as standing in the way of evolutionary progress. Now the benefactors had switched sides. Their enthusiasm was not based on ethnic genocide. It was the "unfit" of the world, most prominently those same "degenerates," "imbeciles," and "morons" Galton had denounced—the mentally ill—that had these titans spoiling for a cleansing.

Spurred by Madison Grant's evangelizing, some of the country's most esteemed people and institutions came up with fistfuls of dollars, millions in today's money, which they flung into genetics research. Those contributors included the Rockefeller Foundation, the Carnegie Institution, and Mary Harriman, daughter of the massively wealthy railroad baron E.H. and sister of the American statesman Averill. Soon great universities such as Harvard, Princeton, Yale, and Stanford, and eventually many others, were folding eugenics studies into their scientific curricula, overt racial assumptions and all.

The next and most catastrophic stage in the spread of eugenics was probably inevitable from the moment of its first Malthusian spark. *The Passing of the Great Race* saw its first German publication in 1925, the same year that Hitler's *Mein Kampf* appeared. It could not have happened at a worse time—or, as Grant and his publisher Charles Scribner

---

* "Indefatigable" in part because, as Spiro reports, Grant's relatives destroyed all his personal papers after his death in 1937. Nearly all of the hundreds of thousands of letters he wrote to prominent people are missing. Grant himself remained aloof from reporters, rarely granting interviews. He rejected the idea of an autobiography; Spiro quotes him writing, in a 1927 letter, that "the things of real interest and importance would have to be omitted."

were concerned, at a better time. Scribner was a Princeton man and one of the three sons of Charles Scribner's Sons. Charles was as racially benighted as most educated men of his time. As Jonathan Spiro reveals, Scribner took pride in having brought out *The Passing of the Great Race* because it had elevated "the race question to the fore."[17] Charles Scribner hadn't seen anything yet.

Weimar Germany seethed. Its young men and its economy vitiated in the Great War, its prideful populace humiliated, its stature among nations laid low by the ruinous Treaty of Versailles, the nation thirsted to reclaim its ancient mythic greatness. The blueprint came from a bespectacled and sickly reservist in the Great War, a weak-chinned social wallflower with a lifelong stomachache, an agronomist by education, a virulent anti-Semite by temperament, whose name was Heinrich Himmler. Himmler joined the Nazi Party in 1923 and within two years was commanding the spectral SS, bodyguards to Hitler and eventual overseers of the death camps.

Himmler was a member of the Thule Society, a shadowy group that fetishized the myth of ancient Teutonic supremacy—the "Aryans." Tall, muscular, with blue eyes and pale skin, the Aryans were thought by some to be a race stronger than God. They were the "*Übermenschen*." In myth, their forebears had emerged from the lost undersea continent of Atlantis (itself a version of Eden) to enter history and consummate an earthly paradise that would last through eternity. They sounded distinctly like Francis Galton's own idealized perfect Brits.

In the German version, the *Übermenschen* genetic line had thinned over the millennia as its carriers mated with inferior races. (Though why an *Übermenschen* would want to mate with anyone except another *Übermenschen* is an interesting question.) At any rate, as Germany's mortification in the Great War's aftermath stoked fantasies of epic vengeance in the shattered Fatherland, Heinrich Himmler was on hand to show how it could happen. And he had Hitler's ear. In 1925 Hitler was released from a year in prison and began rebuilding the dormant Nazi Party into a national movement, championing Aryan racial supremacy and the credo "Might makes right." The führer became aware of Madison Grant's book-length polemic and wrote a letter to Grant exclaiming that "the book is my Bible."[18]

Adolf Hitler's rise over a few short years is part of world folklore. He gained the German chancellorship in January 1933. Immediately his Third Reich legalized involuntary sterilization of "congenital mental deficiency," schizophrenia, manic-depressive "insanity," epilepsy, and a list of hereditary physical deformities. More than 62,000 people were relieved of reproductive capacity in that first year; and 360,000 through 1939, when more efficient and deadly measures replaced sterilization.

Hitler's euthanasia program coincided with his invasion of Poland in September 1939, the move that touched off World War II. Its first targets were children: disabled, diseased, mentally incapacitated children: "lives unworthy of life," as a Nazi phrase had it, whose existence cost the Reich good money. Agents posing as social workers coaxed families of such excess baggage to give them over to one of seven newly established "pediatric clinics," where they were gassed, shot, or simply allowed to starve to death—ammunition, after all, did not grow on trees.

The next victims were to be the mentally ill in toto.

In the autumn of 1939, Nazi soldiers overran a psychiatric hospital at Poznan, in freshly occupied Poland. They ordered some thousand patients out of their quarters, placed them on the flatbeds of transport trucks, drove them to a nearby forest, and killed them with carbon monoxide gas. The Nazis called these murders and the thousands that followed them "disinfection."

Hitler maintained a policy of never signing orders that decreed murder. The single known time that he broke this policy involved mental patients. Doctors enlisted to expand "disinfection" activities feared that they might someday be held to account by authorities who did not consider "disinfection" a legal defense for murder. In August 1940, Hitler signed a life-taking "authorization" for physicians "so that patients who, on the basis of human judgment, are considered incurable, can be granted mercy death after a discerning diagnosis." Even Hitler must have choked briefly on the word *mercy*.

By this time, at least some American foundations were starting to comprehend the macabre applications of their generosity. The Carnegie Institution withdrew its funding of Nazi eugenics research in 1939. By then, the Third Reich knew all it needed to know.

Four hundred mental patients were rounded up and shot at Chelm, in eastern Poland, in January 1940. Then the killing of the mad went industrial-scale. At Hartheim Castle, near Linz in Austria, 18,269 "disinfections" were carried out between January 1940 and August 1941. By the time Hitler ended the program in 1941, it had "granted mercy" to nearly one hundred thousand people. He halted it because some impossibly brave German Catholic clergymen had begun to denounce it. Somehow, they had not been fooled by the führer's name for the murder apparatus: the Charitable Foundation for Curative and Institutional Care. At any rate, by this time Hitler had turned his attention toward exterminating Jews and invading the Soviet Union.[19]

Historians have estimated that the Nazis sterilized up to 375,000 people in all—many of them homosexual, most of them insane. This is a small number when compared to the estimated 5,933,900 Jews exterminated in the name of Aryan purity.[20] Yet it is a pathetic marker of how far, "moral treatment" aside, the world had progressed in its care for "crazy people" between medieval Bedlam and the twentieth century.

Europe was not alone in its murderousness and abuse of the mentally ill. In America, sterilization and more invasive measures flourished before and after the war. Indiana enacted the country's first compulsory sterilization law for the mentally ill in 1909. Washington and California quickly followed. California's sunshine and sparkling beaches were drawing many newcomers to the state, and "race scientists" were just as keen as Britons and Germans to keep their paradise pristine. The Golden State became the national leader in the practice, neutering twenty thousand mental patients between the onset and 1979. It was not until September 2014 that the practice was prohibited in a bill signed into law by Gov. Jerry Brown, following revelations that the state cleansed the ovaries of 148 women between 2006 and

2010. California claimed half of all coercive sterilizations before the war; unaccountably, this percentage dipped to only a third afterward.

By 1931, sterilization laws had been enacted in twenty-seven states.

One may summon persuasive and well-intentioned arguments in support of abortion, such as preserving the health and bodily autonomy of a pregnant woman. Yet the stubborn fact remains that Margaret Sanger, still revered as the enlightened pioneer crusader for abortion and founder of the group that became Planned Parenthood, unapologetically declared her wish to head off "objectionable" babies even before they were conceived. In 1932, she proclaimed in a public speech: "[We should] apply a stern and rigid policy of sterilization and segregation to that grade of population whose progeny is tainted, or whose inheritance is such that objectionable traits may be transmitted to offspring."[21] She could be even more blunt. On August 5, 1926, she told an audience at Vassar College: "The American public is taxed, heavily taxed, to maintain an increasing race of morons."[22] Also in 1932, just a year before Adolf Hitler established himself as chancellor of the Third Reich, she proclaimed: "Knowledge of birth control is essentially moral. Its general, though prudent practice must lead to a higher individually and ultimately to a cleaner race."[23]

Among the groups obstructing that "cleaner race," Sanger listed "morons, mental defectives, epileptics."[24]

Of all the estimated sixty thousand sterilizations carried out in America before the twentieth century ended, one case in particular testifies how the specter of the Other—meaning, in most instances, the mad—is a primal menace that strips the membrane of reason from even the most enlightened men and women.

Oliver Wendell Holmes Jr. stood above the great family legacies of his generation, above even the Cabots and the Lodges, as a descendant of American secular sainthood. His namesake father was a central figure among the New England transcendentalists, the small core of Harvard-centered men and women who had epitomized learning and moral rigor in the fragile early years of the Republic. Oliver Wendell

Holmes Sr., the "Autocrat of the Breakfast Table," was a fixture at the Saturday Club at the Parker House in Boston, the monthly gatherings of these eminences. It was he who nicknamed Boston the "Hub City"—"hub" signifying the center of the universe.

Oliver Jr. proved a noble steward of his father's ideals. A lean Yankee patrician, Harvard man, legal scholar, abolitionist, thrice-wounded officer for the Union side in a cause that rejected the right of white people to use "inferior" Africans as chattel, appointed to the Supreme Court by Theodore Roosevelt, Holmes was practically an incarnation of the Declaration of Independence. And yet here is part of what Oliver Wendell Holmes had to say in 1927 regarding involuntary sterilization as a tool of eugenics: "It is better for all the world, if instead of waiting to execute degenerate offspring for crime, or to let them starve for their imbecility, society can prevent those who are manifestly unfit from continuing their kind. The principle that sustains <u>compulsory vaccination</u> is broad enough to cover <u>cutting the Fallopian tubes</u>... Three generations of imbeciles are enough."

Holmes's words were not muttered over brandy and cigars at the Harvard Club. They were part of the 8-to-1 majority opinion that he wrote for the United States Supreme Court upholding the Virginia Sterilization Act of 1924, a statute that authorized sterilization of "the unfit" regardless of consent.* The case was the despicably tainted *Buck v. Bell*, a paradigm of fabrication and tortured argument that legitimized State intrusion into the reproduction rights of individuals—in the name of a "pure" (and "sane") national gene pool.

Carrie Buck was seventeen years old and poor when her adoptive parents, a couple named Dobbs, bundled her off to the Virginia State Colony for Epileptics and Feebleminded. Her natural mother, Emma, herself a "feebleminded" inmate at Virginia State, had given the child over to the Dobbses upon entering the institution years earlier. Now

---

* Associate justices who joined Holmes in the majority were such progressive eminences as former president William Howard Taft and the great Louis Brandeis, the "people's lawyer" who had helped pioneer the principle enshrined in law as "the right to privacy."

the Dobbses claimed that the girl herself was incorrigible, stupid, and, most unforgivably of all, the unwed mother of a child.

The State Colony's superintendent, Albert Priddy, generously awarded the new inmate a mental age (nine) higher than he'd estimated for her mother (eight), but soon averred that being shut up in an asylum was not protection enough against the likes of Carrie Buck. After all, she had already polluted America's precious supply of gametes and zygotes. Her fallopian rampage must be stopped once and for all. She would have to be sterilized.

Priddy in fact wanted to use Buck as a legal prophylactic, in a manner of speaking. He was a tireless sexual moralist and a sterilization buff (he tended to conflate promiscuous women with "morons"), and he had already been sued by previous victims of his remedy, which he had no intention of abandoning. He wanted to make sure the new statute would withstand review by the highest court in the land, so that he could legally sterilize naughty morons to his heart's content. To represent Carrie Buck, Priddy hired a lawyer, one Irving Whitehead, a former director of the Colony and a friend of Priddy. Another friend was Aubrey Strode, a lawyer who actually *wrote* the new Virginia statute and whom Priddy chose to represent the Colony. Thus all the "adversaries" were on the same side, the Colony's. (Whitehead was no Clarence Darrow and had no interest in trying to be one here.) There was little question of whose interests would prevail.

Dr. John Hendren Bell, who became superintendent of Virginia State when Priddy suddenly died, steered the case to the Supreme Court by securing writs of certiorari—consent of a higher court to review the findings of a lower one. The "findings" in *Buck v. Bell* were spectacularly bogus. Whitehead called no witnesses who were of any help to the girl or who could refute the crude "science" that diagnosed her intelligence and character. Most witnesses against her had never met her; their testimony had been coached and shaped by Priddy. Carrie Buck's school records, never produced by Whitehead but revealed later, showed her to be a competent and promising student.

As for her degenerate promiscuity, the real centerpiece of the case:

Irving Whitehead did not subpoena the Dobbs couple. Had he done so, they would have been obliged to testify that Carrie Buck had borne a daughter out of wedlock because she'd been raped—by a nephew of the Dobbses while the Dobbses were out of town.

Carrie Buck eventually was allowed to leave the Virginia State Colony for Epileptics and Feebleminded. She lived in poverty or near poverty until 1983, but she proved to be neither epileptic nor feebleminded. She was said to be a wide reader. Her daughter, Vivian, who represented the third generation of "imbeciles" in Oliver Wendell Holmes's phrasing, did well in school, making the honor roll once, before she died of measles in 1932.

Buck v. Bell remains on the books, and the science of eugenics remains in the annals.

6

"A More Normal World"

Our family traveled a lot in those last carefree years before the disasters commenced: To Washington. To the Rock & Roll Hall of Fame in Cleveland, as mentioned, where I boosted Kevin up so that he could touch Jimi Hendrix's guitar. (Kev had long since mastered the electrifying opening riff of "Johnny B. Goode.") We spent a week horseback riding and watersliding near Kalispell, Montana, where we ran into a Middlebury family whose sons were close friends of the boys. We spent a week on the island of St. John in the Caribbean, where we encountered what seemed the entire town of Middlebury. We divided a week between London and Austria, where I had been invited to speak at the Salzburg Global Seminar. The theme for the gathering was "America in Our Time." My appearance was a patronage gig all the way: Olin Robison, the president of Middlebury College and of the seminar then, invited me. I recall grinding through my remarks in a conference room inside the august and historic Schloss Leopoldskron. I had constructed my talk around the hopeful metaphor of green grass sprouting through the cracks in urban sidewalks, a metaphor that had seemed resoundingly brilliant when I'd hit upon it back in Middlebury. In the event, I mostly recall the eminent historian Alan Brinkley glowering at me from the front row, trying to suppress the steam coming from his ears. I recall how perfectly the subtle plaids of his shirt matched his sweater.

I recall wanting to go home.

But Honoree and the kids had fun.

And we visited Ireland with Honoree's mother, Honora, in tow, her final visit to the realm of her girlhood. Honora tracked down the gravesite of her mother. The tombstone is visible on a steep hillside above a bay—just visible above spears of grass that have not been mowed for decades. We watched as Honora, who was then in her eighties, climbed the hill on her hands and knees to the gravesite.

Through these years, Kevin played his guitars with abandon, with passion, and, when the music called for it, with palpable buoyancy and delight. Yet he never mocked the music, or kidded it (or his audience), or tried to subsume it with theatrics. He was never a fist-pumper or a jumper or a strutter onstage. His blazing rock and blues and jazz riffs could make his instrument seem almost alive, and Kevin let that instrument speak for itself. From his solemn expression as the notes leaped and danced, you might have thought he was playing a game of chess. And perhaps he was.

Certainly he lived deep inside the world of music, and he was a grand master at producing a tune to match a situation. On our return from County Mayo to Shannon Airport, our jam-packed little red car bumping along through the second or third hour of the narrow two-lane, goose-crowded route, the silence inside the car was broken by musical notes. I thought at first that someone had switched on the radio, though I could not recall seeing a rear speaker. The tune was "Wild Mountain Thyme." It was being played by the small golden-haired musician in the backseat—played the way it was meant to be played: slowly, meditatively, one perfect heartbreaking note at a time.

Played on a small ukulele that Kevin had packed at the last minute. And played now, with the blooming heather all around us.

I taught writing at the college, or tried to, pacing back and forth in front of my impeccably disheveled students as I had seen movie professors do, scrawling words and sentences from their essays on the chalkboard, then whirling around dramatically to demand: "What's wrong with this sentence?! *Why is it up here?!*"

On balance, I don't think I did my students too much damage. I persuaded most of them that no law of literature stipulated that every essay had to begin with, "I woke up from my sleep. My eyeballs told me it was morning and my stomach told me I was hungry for breakfast." I persuaded many that a sentence such as "While I was walking to the movies with my friend..." could use an extra touch of character description, given that "my friend" might be a soccer buddy, a hot babe, or an eight-foot rabbit visible to no one except the narrator.

Honoree did much better. She managed the transition from "bench" research scientist to teaching biochemistry to ambitious and bright students at a high-ranking institution. She took advantage of the college's science laboratories to continue the endometrial cell research she had begun years earlier at Mount Sinai in New York (which Dean, in his grade school essays, always spelled "Mt. Cyanide").

Honoree's students loved her; loved her passion for science and the pains she took to relate its principles to their own lives; loved her keen understanding of them as individuals—she invariably had memorized the names of her students each semester—sometimes numbering as many as seventy—and the extra time she took with them on concepts they found difficult. Her favorite class was "Chemistry for Citizens," a course designed to integrate the principles of chemistry into everyday life. (One moss-backed colleague dismissed the course as "Chemistry for Turnips.") She cherished her young women students especially, recalling the skepticism she'd herself faced as a female science major decades earlier. Her best students came alive to her; they joyously wore T-shirts begging "Speak Slowly—I'm a Blonde." She would be up for tenure in just a few years, and we would live out our lives in our own moss-backed contentment.

Kevin brought home good grades, risked his guitar-picking fingers as a catcher in summer baseball—luckily, most pitches got by him— and formed a kids' rock band. Dean maintained an honor's student grade level through his middle school years. His auburn hair, darker than his mother's, grew thick. He was a slim boy, but we'd added a trampoline and a swing set to our small backyard, and these marked the beginning of Dean's physical transformation. He started using the top bar of the swing set for chin-ups. The results were quick and striking. Dean remained slim, but his back and shoulders took on muscle.

He made the backstroke his specialty on the summer swim team, and his relay team set several records in district competition and then won the Vermont championship.

In the fall of that transitional year, 1992, we got him involved in the town's community theater. He played the young Michael in *Auntie Mame*. He got to wear a turban and carry a scimitar, and, best of all, he (once again) got to break the family taboo on "swears," without getting lectured, by belting out the scripted line: "Life is a banquet, and most poor sons-of-bitches are starving to death!" Just to be sure her son wouldn't feel out of place among strangers (though she needn't have worried), Honoree auditioned and won a small part as Mrs. Upson.

Kevin joined Dean and the community troupe the following year for the kids' musical *Really Rosie*. He played Alligator, wearing his green cloth alligator-snout cap backward, the way he wore all his caps. And the two played Town Hill Boys in *A Child's Christmas in Wales* the following season, singing their Welsh carols in mufflers and oversized newsboy caps. By that time, I'd yielded to the town's overwhelming supplications and taken on some small parts as well.

This was how life was going to be. A road to heaven, paved with good student evaluations.

Yet fissures were starting to form in our family; hairline fissures, shifts in Dean's behavior that were nearly invisible at first. Honoree and I told each other they were "phases," the inevitable symptoms of a child's transition into adolescence. Walking from our car to the venue of a folk concert one summer night, we noticed that Kevin was with us, but not Dean. We spotted him sauntering along on the other side of the street, aloof, apart. The apartness became a motif: He found another part of the woods on hikes. He took a seat off to himself at school games. He showed gruffness in moments where no gruffness seemed necessary. Car trips became volatile: the family, confined in close quarters, produced in our eldest son an edginess that could explode into angry argument, the exact cause of which we could never recall afterward.

He continued to show curiosity and imagination in his schoolwork.

His prickliness did not seem to damage his relations with Kevin; the two remained close, and he developed a casual charm that seemed authentic. He was unusually at ease with adults, looking them in the eye and asking them questions about themselves. As he moved into mid-adolescence, his good looks and his easy manner—outside the family—made him attractive to females, including females a few years older than he. Within minutes of our arrival at our campsite on the island of St. John in the Caribbean when Dean was fifteen, we spotted him chatting up a fellow tourist in her mid-twenties who seemed pleased by his attention.

Back at home, the bad times were closing in. Honoree and I kept the reversals of fortune as far from the boys' sense of anxiety as we reasonably could, but we did not deny that they had happened.

I lost a book that had consumed three years of my working life when people associated with the project rebelled against its content and persuaded the publisher to cancel the contract. Honoree's setback arrived in a letter that she picked up at the president's office on Mother's Day in 1994. She had been denied tenure. This came as a shock. She had passed two previous reviews without a problem, her department recommended her for tenure, she'd obtained grants, and had involved her students in her published research. A professor in another department, risking bad feeling among the faculty, soon wrote a denunciation of the turndown in the *Chronicle of Higher Education*.

Honoree appealed the decision. Her appeal was rejected. I immediately resigned my adjunct appointment as a gesture of contempt for the college's blindness toward promising women professors. My furious gesture was expensive. Our household was now without an income.

Despite the risk and Honoree's misgivings, I never regretted that decision to stand with my wife. Not then, not now. Not ever.

It was in this family climate of financial uncertainty, and the resulting tension that we could not conceal from our sons, that Dean, at age fourteen, composed one of the most beautiful and psychologically freighted essays he ever wrote—though two years later he was to write an even more powerful one. Bearing almost uncanny echoes of James Agee's numinous description of the Gudger family's bedroom in *Let Us*

Now Praise Famous Men, Dean's "My Room" invites the reader into a sacred chamber. As with Agee, Dean confers holiness upon the room's objects by the simple scrupulous act of naming them. And he allows the reader to associate these objects with the tapestry of his mind.

My Room

You turn the corner, and see the door to my room. Brilliant colors meshed together formed from years of sticker collections. Marker lines stray and then cross again. Glues colored red, green and blue, are splatter painted across the once white door frame.

As your hand clasps the door knob you feel the masking tape which is wrapped around 3 or 4 times. The tape is slightly stained from the oils from hands past. As the doorknob turns you feel two clicks from inside the metal mechanism, the door is a bit sticky at first, and a little hard to open, but it finally gives way.

As it opens perhaps the first thing you notice are the ski pictures, which have been plastered to my also once white walls, giving the room a sort of bluish tint. To your left as you step on the wooden floor, covered 2/3 of the way with a free standing carpet kind of in the middle of the room, you see a 2x3' tack board. On it is a calendar held by 3 different tacks a red, a blue and a silver. A photo above the month of September shows tall slim trees rising to the sky…Adjacent to the tack board, a long narrow mirror hangs from a nail in the wall…

Along the wall the mirror hangs on, there is a box like cubical cut in to the wall. Inside this space is my bed. My bed consists of a mattress on top of the wooden bottom of the cubical. On top of the mattress is a sheet covered by a blanket and then by a white feather down comforter. The pillow is also feather down, covered by a blue pillow case…In the far corner there is a large lamp, which is controlled by a switch at the door and a switch in the bed's cubical. Along the left side of the bed there is an alarm clock/radio, a couple of books and a small reading lamp. A map of the USA is on the ceiling above the bed.

To the right of the wall the bed is in, is my desk. It is a wooden desk with no drawers...An IBM computer in good shape sits in the middle. To the left is a fan placed carefully on the end of the table facing my bed. Behind the desk are several Jimi Hendrix posters and a Duke Ellington poster. On the desk beside the computer are magazines old papers, a hammer, a tie, computer games, cards, tapes, disks and some books. Scattered about is loose change; and lying underneath the desk is a fuse box...

If you turn 90 degrees to the right, you see a wooden shelf nailed to the wall with three wooden planks. On the middle plank is a black stereo CD player, nothing big just something to play music on when I'm doing homework, reading or hanging out...

Turning to the last wall you see a dresser on top of which is a souvenir shelf. Placed in one of the three white wicker racks there are...concert tickets a couple of small flags, miniature statues, plane tickets, brochures, a Powder magazine and other odds and ends from places I've traveled to...

Opening the door one last time you'll see what I'm using as a temporary lock, a hole in the wall on the left of the door right next to the entrance, reinforced by nails which I put a screwdriver in flush with the door. You move past the doorway stepping out and away from the familiar sight and smell of my room into a more normal world.

A more normal world.

We recovered our financial footing, but slowly. Honoree found a teaching position at Trinity College in Burlington, a small institution for women administered by the Sisters of Mercy order, and commuted the seventy miles there and back for a few years until the college was forced to close for lack of funding. I eventually found a book project that restored us to solvency.

"When They Were Young"

In his conclusion to *The Adventures of Tom Sawyer*, Mark Twain wrote: "It being strictly a history of a *boy*, it must stop here; the story could not go much further without becoming the history of a *man*."[1]

Not many people—not Mark Twain himself—ever claimed to have witnessed the moment when a boyhood ended and the boy entered a new stage of life. I have witnessed such a moment. The boy was Dean, nearing his eleventh birthday then; and the "moment" was a balmy, sunlit Sunday afternoon, August 23, 1992; and the setting was a sublimely cockeyed old amusement park in the Lake George region of New York called the Great Escape.

Our family had made a ritual of visiting the Great Escape every year on the Sunday that marked the closing of the Bread Loaf Writers' Conference. Dean and Kevin had grown more attached to Bread Loaf with each passing summer. I had come to love the conference as much through their eyes and imaginations as through my own. None of us had ever quite overcome the rustic spell cast by the nineteenth-century campus with its right-angled yellow wood-framed Inn and dormitory buildings, all clustered in a mountain meadow and cordoned off from the world by pine forests and the Green Mountains rising behind them. But to the boys, their twelve days and nights there had almost become their normative lives, with the other fifty weeks of the year a prolonged hiatus. Thus the Great Escape, sixty-five miles southwest of Middlebury on the eastern border of the vast Adirondack Park, was an ideal midway point in our transition from an even greater escape back to our daily lives.

The park was and is a small nonesuch—as much amusement-park museum as amusement park. A little "graveyard" on the grounds is festooned with markers commemorating attractions that have passed on: Jungleland, Danny the Dragon, the Nightmare at Crack Axle Canyon.[2] It dates to 1954, when it opened as an attraction for small children under the name Storytown USA. The name change occurred in 1983. The Great Escape grew over the years, and thrill rides went up and then gave way to even more thrilling rides. Yet the Escape never seemed to lose touch with its own childhood. Artifacts of its early era lay scattered on the grounds. Amid the flashy Steamin' Demon roller coaster and the Rotor and the Spider, one could find remnants of its rustic origins like fossils in geologic strata: chipping wrought-iron playing cards from the old Alice in Wonderland walk-through; the petting zoo; the western-themed Ghost Town with its blacksmith shop and saloon and daily quick-draw shoot-outs on Main Street.

It seemed to us that all visitors checked their habitual American edginess at the ticket window in favor of a smoothie and wandered around in caloric bliss. I once looked up to see, striding directly at me, a heavily muscled bald guy with a cage fighter's mustache, wearing a skintight EVERLAST T-shirt and laced-up boxing gloves. He was throwing shadow punches as he bowled along. But he politely stepped around me at the last moment.

On this Sunday afternoon in orange-tinted early fall, Dean and Kevin grabbed their tickets at the booth and exploded into the park ahead of us. They knew the layout by heart. (Kevin had just turned nine.) They scampered side by side, brothers and pals, waiting up for us every time they reached a ride that interested them: the bumper cars. The pendulum-swinging Sea Dragon. The ninety-foot-high Ferris wheel. The Raging River waterslide. And as a capstone to the day, a gut-wrenching turn on the massive throwback wooden roller coaster, the Comet.

We stayed the whole afternoon at the Great Escape on that Sunday.

The sun descended, and it silhouetted our boys, and fired their bouncing hair—Kevin's gold, Dean's auburn. I had left my camera at home, but I made mental snapshots of them as they larked and ran, and with each one, I silently repeated a mantra that had come into my head once, as if to freeze the image in time: *Dean and Kevin. When they were young.*

A few days later, Dean entered middle school, his boyhood behind him, frozen in my incantation. Within five years all vestiges of his forever-young days would be forever gone.

Dean's behavioral shift toward truculence slowly continued, and by his mid-adolescence it was impossible to ignore. Honoree and I still attributed it to "phases," to "hormones," to "parental rebellion" triggered by the normal psychological need to "separate" from the parents. We assumed that if we rode it out and kept confrontation with him to a minimum, it would "go away."

It did not "go away." Not for a long time. Then it came back again. By the time it went away for the last time, or so we have hoped, things had happened that were terrible beyond our imaginations.

Dean's rebellion was not total. He asked us whether he could take guitar lessons, and we enrolled him with Kevin's teacher. He learned quickly. His guitar tastes ran to folk and rock. He played saxophone in the middle school's jazz band.

I could still take Dean to the field beside the grade school and fungo fly balls to him. We still shot buckets in the college field house, and we played catch in the backyard. The yard canted upward near the woods' tree line, and Dean liked me to throw him football passes just beyond his fingertips (not an easy task, though certain pro quarterbacks on teams that I follow seem to have mastered it) so that he could dive dramatically and land softly on the bank, whether he caught or missed the ball.

In the August before his sophomore year of high school, Dean flabbergasted all of us by going out for football. Granted that his shoulders were developing, he was still a five-foot-ten kid who weighed about 145 pounds. He played halfback on offense and defensive end—second and third teams. He took his shots from the big beefy linemen and runners.

Once he was hit so hard that he rolled backward several times like a runaway Hula-hoop. But he got up again. And he had his moments. One of them involved the first time his number, 36, was called to join the varsity huddle on the field. I don't think he ever forgot, and I know I haven't. I asked him what it felt like later, as we all sat eating hot dogs at the A&W. His emotional chilliness thawed for a moment.

"It was beautiful. I couldn't hear a sound. I just felt myself running. I've never run so fast in my life as I did running out there to the huddle."

The following season, Dean took a handoff, made a sharp pivot to the right, and burst forty-five yards up the middle for a touchdown. The head coach, who was standing near the end zone when my son crossed the goal line, told me later that Dean was grinning all the way.

His creative life expanded: He played the role of Peter, Anne Frank's doomed sweetheart, in the high school production of *The Diary of Anne Frank*. He joined Kevin for two weeklong sessions of the National Guitar Summer Workshop in Connecticut.

Yet Dean did not like being asked questions, especially about his life outside the house, or about his friends. Honoree and I made it clear to him, and to Kevin, that we expected them not to drink, not even beer, and to stay utterly away from cigarettes and drugs. This was conceivably not the first time that parents have issued such directives to their teenage children. Our ground rules brought nods of assent from the boys, while they were within our sight. And then a car would appear in the driveway, and the driver would honk his pipes of Pan, and our sons would go trotting off into the night and the mercies of an unmerciful world. We watched them leave with a sense of helplessness. There was nothing we could do, short of imprisoning them in the house. (We were soon to learn the horrors of house imprisonment.) We hoped each night that—well, we hoped. Each night.

One of my most bittersweet memories from those years is of the Ping-Pong table that dear Honoree bought for our basement. She thought that Ping-Pong would be a fun thing for the kids and their friends to do, and something that would keep them safe. The fragility of this hope still makes my throat tighten. The Ping-Pong table went unused. The night was far more interesting.

In the fall of 1997, when Kevin was freshly fourteen, his guitar mentor suggested that we enter him in some competitions, just so he could get used to that world. Application forms for *DownBeat* magazine's annual student music awards were due before the end of the year. Eighty categories were available. Kevin recorded three tunes in each of two genres, jazz and rock. His choices were challenging and sophisticated. In the jazz category he tackled "Blue Monk" by Thelonius Monk, "Ain't Misbehavin'" by Fats Waller, and "Satin Doll" by Billy Strayhorn. In blues, he submitted "Stormy Monday" by T-Bone Walker, "The Thrill Is Gone" by B. B. King, and "Tore Down" by Sonny Thompson. The submissions were multitrack dubs, in which Kevin performed lead, rhythm, and, on some of the tunes, harmony and a bass line off his electric guitar.

We sent the submissions in, and then we began to worry that we had asked too much from our young adolescent son.

The following June, *DownBeat* announced its winners. Kevin had won for his age-group in both his categories.

We made a big deal of it, naturally—in retrospect, probably a bigger deal than we should have. We made sure the town biweekly knew about the dual awards, and the editor published a photograph of Kevin with his teacher. And we spread the word to friends and relatives.

Our euphoria was not destined to last. Within a few days of the announcement, the "Before" in the Powers family saga ended with a crash, and the "After" began.

8

Madness and Genius

Among the many mysteries that enshroud the nature of schizophrenia is that of whether it is causally linked to artistic genius and to extraordinary cognitive levels in general. These questions are of more than academic interest to me, of course, and to Honoree as well.

Creativity and mental illness have been conjoined in cultural myth beyond the point of stereotype. A great deal of received opinion has it that one cannot be creative, or extremely bright, without being at least a little insane.

The mad scientist of the movies has done his test-tube-tipping best to reinforce and exploit this supposition. Though a subset of the larger horror-movie genre, mad-science films are distinctive in that they express primal human anxieties toward, say, man's tampering with the will of the gods, or God. (You'd have to be *crazy* to try anything like that, they seem to be screaming to their doomed wild-eyed protagonists.) They offer lurid morality plays on the evils wrought by eugenics, lobotomy, the transplantation of limbs and organs, robotics, weaponry and man-made pestilences, and the quest for eternal life. And, of course, they invoke the invisible but always-proximate border, which, overstepped by the genius, lands her or him in the lair of lunacy.

Current-day loathing of scientists is fed by the great tides of anti-intellectual sentiment in general and, in particular, by blindered resistance to such ideas as global warming, abortion and sex education, and certain bedrock economic realities. The resistance, a staple of news headlines and Internet memes, is absolutist, and it is fed by a variety of converging sources: from evangelical Christians citing biblical absolutism; from political candidates who believe these citations or claim to, and thus scorn the "reality-based" community as laughably naive; from great systems of commerce and education that do not see compatibility with their self-interests, and a populace trained to suspect madness as a by-product of hyperrational thought.

Yet just beneath the surface of these topical rationalizations lies strong evidence of a far more ancient, and more pervasive, source of the skepticism directed toward science and scientists, and toward intellectualism in general—to say nothing of the mentally ill. This source is *the Other*, a spectral figure that generates fear and loathing, and that will reappear in these pages.

The scientist bears oppressive historical baggage. The calling has evolved from deep roots in alchemy and even sorcery. The annals of fable are saturated with tales of the sorcerer who misuses his arcane insights for evil, or who corrupts himself in pursuit of transcendent knowledge. It is a testimony to the grip that these myths exert upon the imagination that the masterwork of German literature, Goethe's tragic play *Faust*, portrays the fate of a doctor who sells his soul to an agent of the devil, Mephistopheles (or Mephistophilis), who promises Faust, in return, the knowledge of "what holds the world together in its innermost self."*

The Faust/Mephistopheles theme (which in fact predates Goethe) spilled over from the dramatic stage and into opera, ballet, novels, and, inevitably, the movies with their keen attention to the temper of the times—the *zeitgeist*. The Faust-like Dr. Frankenstein and his monster first appeared on-screen in a silent sixteen-minute film in 1910, made at Edison Studios and possibly directed by Thomas Edison. From there, indirect cinematic treatment flourished: In the silent 1920 film *Dr.*

---

* *Faust* had its full part 1 premiere in Braunschweig in 1829. The wild and chaotic part 2, which brings the play's onstage time to twenty-one hours, has never been produced in full.

Caligari's Cabinet, made in post–World War I Germany, the evil doctor stood in for a mesmerizing yet warmongering national government. In 1933, during the dawn of eugenics as a perverse Nazi experiment in racial purification, Paramount released *The Island of Lost Souls*. Along with two its remakes as *The Island of Dr. Moreau*,* this movie features a deranged scientist who has developed an operation that turns human beings into feral animals. In 1927, liberal Germanic fears of a demonic, science-engineered future emerged again, this time with breathtaking sets and towering iconic images. Fritz Lang's phantasmagoric *Metropolis*, the progenitor of modern dystopian science-fiction films (*Blade Runner* prominently among them), delivers a barrage of murky allegorical foreboding. It hints at Christian ideals in retreat before columns of poor, subjugated workers under the thumb of a cynical elite, whose leader commands a bug-eyed scientist, Rotwang, to build a destructive robot. The robot breaks free from all control and destroys the city.

Following World War II and its hellscape of technology-driven destruction, the movie mad scientist began to share thematic billing with mad science itself, a force of apocalyptic intent spawned by a collective mad world. (It was only some fifteen years later that the former British army psychiatrist, the Scottish R. D. Laing, began to popularize his belief that the world was *in fact* mad, and that those who bore the label "schizophrenic" were its sane exceptions. People in the distant future—if there is one—Laing wrote, "will see that what we call 'schizophrenia' was one of the forms in which, often through quite ordinary people, the light began to break through the cracks in our all-too-closed minds.")[1]

A rational question far more central to the mysteries of the brain, and far more pertinent to both my sons' vulnerability to madness, is one both ancient and current: Do neural links exist between creativity and mental illness? Or, to put it in a couple of other ways: Did Kevin's and

---

* All three films are adaptations of the 1895 novel *The Island of Dr. Moreau*, by the literary science-fiction writer H. G. Wells.

Dean's artistic gifts put them on the path to schizophrenia? Or, perhaps, vice versa?

Archetype in many lands tends toward the affirmative. The intuitive-affirmative might be more accurate. The crazy artist, along with his relatives the mad scientist, the nutty professor, and the pointy-headed intellectual—all these are enduring staples of biography, entertainment, even political scorn. And of course admiration: Plato, anticipating R. D. Laing, implied that insanity was one with artistic achievement: "There is a...kind of madness which is possession by the Muses...the sane man is nowhere at all when he enters into rivalry with the madman."[2] Among artists, it has been the musician, the writer, and the painter who have been most susceptible: Beethoven, Liszt, Tchaikovsky, Charlie Parker, William Styron, Sylvia Plath, Robert Lowell, Ernest Hemingway, Vincent van Gogh, not to mention the famous clinical depressive Sigmund Freud—the list is at once familiar and seemingly inexhaustible.

In this instance, modern neuroscience tends to agree with ageless archetype, though only tentatively—the tentative-affirmative, you might say—with many caveats in the way of a definitive link.

One obstacle lies in pinning down exactly what creativity *is*. Its neurological origins and processes are as amorphous as those of chronic madness itself. Where does creativity come from? What are its functions? Why would anyone even think to link it with mental illness?

At the level of everyday conversation, creativity is almost self-defining. It involves "novel approaches requiring cognitive processes that are different from prevailing modes of thought or expression." It is "the ability to produce something that is novel or original and useful or adaptive." Creative people "are better at recognizing relationships, making associations and connections, and seeing things that others cannot see."[3]

Educational psychologists and others have taken the question to higher ground, proposing that creativity is an essential tool for human development and survival. Among them is Sandra Bruno, a researcher and associate professor at the University of Paris. Bruno has argued that creativity at its origins in the human child is not creation, in the sense of creating something entirely new, but rather an act of imitation: the infant experiences reflexes—instinctual responses to activity in the world. The first creative leap occurs when the child begins to adapt these reflexes into a *scheme*, one that is useful to new situations. This process is, among other things, the route to language acquisition. "Habits, imitation, language acquisition may seem in opposition to creativity," Bruno writes, "but they are actually rooted in [the impulse] to go beyond the present set of competencies. The issue is, for the child, to find equilibrium between repetition, stereotypy, and norm on the one side (which avoids creativity) and uniqueness on the other side." She concludes her paper by noting provocatively, "In a pragmatic consideration, these two extremes may lead to various types of neurosis."[4]

Which leads us to the threshold of creativity and madness.

As with most of the secrets still locked away in the labyrinths of mental illness, the question of this relationship yields no settled answers. Under study for more than half a century, it ranks as a top-tier enigma for neuroscientists, and among the most acute thinkers on this subject is Gordon Claridge, emeritus professor of abnormal psychology at Oxford University.

In 1997 Claridge introduced the concept of "schizotypy," which argued—controversially, as Claridge himself acknowledged—that personality traits lie along a spectrum, inherited yet different in each individual, that range from "normal" and temporary dissociative states (nonconformity, superstition, occasional disorganized thoughts, a withdrawal from the pleasures of life) to full-blown psychotic disorders. Every brain contains a measure of schizotypy. Not every brain degenerates into madness.

What is it, then, about schizotypy that links it to creativity—and from there to mental illness?

The social psychologist Susan K. Perry has written that "looseness and the ability to cross mental boundaries are aspects of both schizophrenic thinking and creative thinking."[5] The point, or circumstances, at or under which schizotypy transforms into full-blown schizophrenia or bipolar disorder—which it resembles in milder form—is yet to be discovered. Yet the notion of a "spectrum" supports the views of Eugen Bleuler, who believed that no clear line separated "sane" and "insane" behavior.

If true—and the distinguished Claridge claims strong experimental and clinical evidence—the implications are enormous and revisive. They would overturn, for instance, the long-held doctrine that schizophrenia can originate only from a genetic flaw, though damaging external, environmental factors must stimulate it to form the dreaded disease. No, says Claridge: schizotypy reveals that *everyone* is born with the potential for schizophrenia. The potential may be actualized into mental illness, depending on circumstances. Or it may result in enhanced creativity, or even spiritual ecstasy.

Other researchers have gone so far as to propose that schizophrenia is more than a tragic risk for creative people: Its persistence in the gene pool is *essential.* It is there "because of shared genetic linkages to creativity."

This is the view of a paper published in 2014 as a chapter in the book *Creativity and Mental Illness.*[6] Its authors, a five-person team of PhDs specializing in psychiatric research, report that 103 studies in recent years suggest a genetic connection between creativity and psychosis. "Moreover, schizotypal thinking is often viewed as sharing features with creative thought, such as cognitive flexibility and divergent thinking via unusual but meaningful associations. These commonalities, coupled with the observed heritability of both constructs, suggest that there may be genetic factors common to both creativity and schizophrenia."

A fearless and profound early-modern searcher into the dark wilderness where madness and creativity might be found intertwined was Carl Jung. Jung held a lifelong fascination for thought and images that lay beyond the restrictive borders erected by his former mentor and later antagonist Sigmund Freud. He believed that without an unfettered immersion in them, the mind would forever keep its secrets locked, and human awareness would remain only partial, stunted at best. His explorations included Eastern religions with their lavish and often terrifying imagery; an "unconscious" universally shared and stocked with bizarre totems of human experience; devils; gods; tricksters; the mother; the child; the shadow.

Jung, in part at least, was coursing through the mind via the vehicle of art.

"In order to do justice to a work of art," he wrote in *The Spirit in Man, Art, and Literature,* "analytical psychology must rid itself entirely of medical prejudice; for a work of art is not a disease, and consequently requires a different approach from the medical one."[7] A doctor's aim, he continued, is to pull disease out by its roots, but a psychologist must take the opposite point of view: he must inquire into the work's *meaning,* irrespective of an individual artist's intentions. Perhaps the artist in his conception was more like Icarus, privileged and damned to fly too close to the source of all light, risking, even sacrificing his life in exchange for a glimpse of infinite truth.

I think of Kevin reaching for and becoming one with his guitar.

Relatively few people have the opportunity to compare the temperament and goals of an actual scientist with the lurid fantasies just described. I am one of the lucky few. Honoree fits the mold of the actual, working scientist far better than any white-coated cinematic eccentric who throws a switch and screams, "It's alive! IT'S ALIVE!" After earning her PhD in 1975 at the University of Chicago, Honoree developed a line of investigation into a largely unanswered central question in cell biology that surrounds the roughly seven trillion cells in the human body, containing nearly identical genomes: How is it that they differentiate into so many different cell *types,* such as muscle, blood, nerve, and skin cells? At this writing, forty years later, she at last is well along in synthesizing and organizing her notes, papers, and six hundred-odd cell photographs into a sophisticated, unified consummation of her patient, painstaking work, which has broadened quietly but considerably. I have yet to hear her scream "Eureka!" or see her dash from the house with a beaker of mysterious boiling gases; and I will assert that academic science-department Christmas parties are a lot more convivial and laced with good conversation than are the Christmas parties thrown by English departments, where the celebrants tend to brood.

Conjoined, Janus-like, with the pop-mythological face of the mad scientist is the mad artist. Vincent van Gogh may or may not have sliced off his own right earlobe in 1888—some scholars now believe that the painter Paul Gauguin clipped it with the tip of a sword during an argument. In any case, the injury, and its devastating coda two years later, when Van Gogh fatally shot himself in a wheat field that he was painting, made him an icon of genius-and-death romanticism.

The necrology of renowned artist suicides in the twentieth century reinforced this sentimental view of the Artist as tragically insane: among them, Virginia Woolf walking into the Ouse in 1941, her coat pockets filled with stones; Ernest Hemingway turning a favored shotgun on himself in 1961 (his widow, Mary, insisted that it was an accident); the poet Sylvia Plath gassing herself in 1963 after several failed attempts on her own life; the painter Mark Rothko slashing his wrists in 1970; the poet John Berryman jumping from a bridge in Minnesota in 1972; the grunge guitarist Kurt Cobain shooting himself in 1994; the monologist Spalding Gray leaping from the Staten Island Ferry in 2004.

Curiously, the (mad) scientist and artist are diametric opposites as measured by the goals that damn each as mad: eternal life in the scientist's typic quest; eternal death for the artist. This is a little counterintuitive when one thinks about it: the scientist (who, after all, is only pursuing what most people crave) is generally assigned the villain's role in popular morality plays, while the artist (whose madness is confirmed exclusively by her suicide) is generally mourned and venerated—in retrospect, of course.

So: Does neuroscience support the myth of mental illness as a concomitant of high intelligence, scientific genius, artistic creativity? Is madness the price that humans must pay for being exceptional?

Sadly, the answers appear to be yes—but only a dubious and deeply qualified yes, and only to a limited extent. Which is to say, not really. Not conclusively. Certainly not always: the same answers that one encounters at the end of nearly every inquiry into the origins, constituent properties, and cognitive effects of schizophrenia.

Among the most eminent recent investigators who argue that creativity and madness share common origins in the brain are Nancy Coover Andreasen of the University of Iowa; Kay Redfield Jamison, professor of psychiatry at the Johns Hopkins University School of Medicine; and Arnold M. Ludwig, a professor of psychiatry at the University of Kentucky.

Andreasen, unique among neuroscientists, claims expertise in both brain science and the creative arts. After earning a doctorate in literature in 1963, she was appointed to the English department at the University of Iowa as an instructor in Renaissance literature. There, she found herself in close proximity with the faculty and students of the renowned Iowa Writers' Workshop. She grew curious about the mental stability of writers as a class. She reenrolled in the university's medical school and completed a residency in psychiatry in 1973. Then she plunged into a field she had virtually invented: an empirical investigation into creativity as it might intertwine with mental illness, specifically bipolar disorder.

In 1974 Andreasen and the psychiatrist Arthur Canter, a colleague at the university, copublished a journal paper announcing that creative writers "differed significantly" from a group of fifteen "non–creative control" volunteers when examined for symptoms of psychiatric disorder.[8] Their methodology was "a structured interview and specifically defined diagnostic criteria." The two researchers found that "seventy-three percent of the writers suffered from some form of psychiatric disorder, as compared with 20 percent of the controls. The most common illness was affective disorder."

"Affective disorder" might strike the ear as a close relative of schizo-affective disorder, the severest form of schizophrenia. But it is a synonym for "mood disorder," which in some cases might include bipolarity, a mental illness similar in many of its symptoms to schizophrenia, but which normally does not involve psychosis. As for "some form of psychiatric disorder," this is self-evidently a catchall term that includes alcoholism and depression, which are not chronic. The very nature of the writing life—isolated, incremental, intense, inherently frustrating as the writer searches for coherence and an elevation of language—can be viewed as an invitation to alcoholism and depression. Those who invest their lives in other art forms may make the same claim.

The Andreasen-Canter study has been criticized for advancing (however unintentionally) a false picture, by drawing upon a small, narrow, homogeneous field, as well as for the compromising ambiguity mentioned above. At least some of their subjects might have been showing signs not of actual mental illness, but of the aforementioned schizotypy. This condition, as the cognitive psychologist Scott Barry Kaufman has written, "consists of a constellation of personality traits that are evident in some degree in *everyone*."[9] It can produce traits similar to those of schizophrenia, as Kaufman points out, including "unusual perceptual experiences, thin mental boundaries between self and other, impulsive nonconformity, and magical beliefs."

A similar explanation, recently advanced, is that such traits are not signs of mental illness but rather expressions of extreme yet normal human behavior, imposed in part by the very nature of the creative project.

This view is acknowledged by Robert A. Power, a genetic psychiatrist at the Institute of Psychiatry, King's College London. Yet Power believes that he and his team have discovered a true genetic link. For a period ending in 2015, Power led a group of psychiatric researchers who computed the genetic risk scores in some eighty-six thousand citizens of Iceland for predictors of mental illness. Power concluded, "Our findings suggest that creative people may have a genetic predisposition towards thinking differently which, when combined with harmful biological or environmental factors, could lead to mental illness."[10]

The study was conducted in Iceland because it was funded by a genetics company called deCODE, based in Reykjavik. Its CEO, the neurologist Kari Stefansson, echoed Power, claiming that "what we have shown is basically that schizophrenia and creativity share biology."[11]

But the Icelandic study, as with the University of Iowa investigation, has been criticized on methodological grounds—and for its underlying assumptions as well. Albert Rothenberg, a professor of psychiatry at Harvard, has held it up as an example of "creativity's" elusiveness as a concept. "The problem is that the criteria for being creative is never anything very creative," Rothenberg told an interviewer. "Belonging to an artistic society, or working in art or literature, does not prove a person is creative. But the fact is that many people who have mental illness do try to work in jobs that have to do with art and literature, not because they are good at it, but because they're attracted to it. And that can skew the data."[12]

Working in art or literature not only fails to prove madness; it is widely seen as its antidote. "Nearly all mental hospitals use art therapy," Rothenberg points out, "and so when patients come out, many are attracted to artistic positions and artistic pursuits."[13]

The enduring power of the "mad" stereotypes over people's perceptions suggests that certain anxieties might be at play, anxieties that may not spring exclusively from fear of mental illness, and yet exert tremendous inhibiting influence upon society's ways of dealing with it. An important generator of these anxieties might be our friend the Other.

The alienation scientists experience is strikingly at odds with their centrality in creating the dynamics of the modern world, dynamics of convenience, health care, and communications, among others, that their detractors tend to take for granted as the natural, given condition of human life. The great naturalist and philosopher Loren Eisley virtually defined the Other in this context when he wrote, "It is frequently the tragedy of the great artist, as it is of the great scientist, that he frightens the ordinary man."[14]

I frankly acknowledge that my lack of expertise in medicine, neuroscience, and even statistical analysis makes me an unreliable narrator in the areas I have attempted to explicate above. The fact that most neuroscientists remain, to a large extent, at odds with one another is cold comfort. Something terrible happened to my sons, and I want to know what and why.

I think, of course, of Kevin and his joyful virtuosity. I think of him near the end of his life, when he was deeply schizo-affective, yet (if *yet* is the right word) playing with an intensity and abandon—and *playfulness*—that went almost beyond musicianship. In the autumn of 2004, after a series of psychotic breaks made it clear that he could no longer cope with the demands of living away from home, we secured an enrollment for him at nearby Castleton College, where Honoree was then an associate academic dean, so that he could play with the jazz band. A common exercise for jazz musicians is "trading eights": a horn player, say, will blow out a series of notes, and another member of the ensemble must immediately answer, note for note. The back-and-forth escalates in speed and complexity. Kevin's bandmates told us later of watching, transfixed, as Kevin dueled with the instructor, an accomplished saxophonist. As the "stairstepping" of difficulty progressed, Kevin would continue to replicate the notes flawlessly on his guitar, until he grew bored with the drill and began to replicate them in reverse order.

I think of this, and the statistics and correlations begin to dance in front of me.

And I think of Dean, the storyteller who might have been a writer. He seemed always convinced that fabulous realms, peopled with beings very much like himself, stretched just beyond the curve of the mundane earth where he was obliged to live. He wanted to get to those realms. This could seem at times like ordinary petulance, a restless belief that the grass was always greener—somewhere. If he and I were successful at getting a kite into the air (which we rarely were), Dean immediately longed for a larger kite, a higher altitude, stronger winds. If I rounded a curve a bit too fast on one of Vermont's many country roads, making the car veer a little, Dean, belted into his car seat, would crow: "Let's do that *again*!" (And I did it "again," more times than I care to admit.)

If enhancement of ordinary experience was not available via

repetition or a larger kite, Dean could make it available in his mind. He could reach for that fabulous realm and pull it toward him, imposing it upon the mundane.

A couple of years after we'd settled in Middlebury, Dean began to explore the terrain near our neighborhood—largely wildflower meadows and pastures. One day he discovered the remains of an abandoned house foundation. It lay half-buried under weeds and vines at the edge of a rise on the far side of the blacktop road that led into town. It was just an old cracked cement rectangle, fortified by a couple of rusted beams. The spookiness of it grabbed his attention at once, but not in the way it might grab other children's. For Dean, the remains weren't spooky *enough*. They needed some mystery imposed upon them; a few ghosts, maybe. So he summoned the realm. And he asked me if I would enter it with him.

("I shan't be gone long," Robert Frost wrote. "You come, too.")

It was an enchanting invitation.

He wanted the two of us to write a story about the secret place he'd found. A mystery. I said sure. For several nights that summer we sat together at a table under a lamp in our screened-in back porch. With invisible crickets chirping in the darkness beyond the patio, we tossed around ideas for characters and plot and jotted notes on our yellow legal pads.

Collaborating in a fantasy with one's child is a sublime pleasure, rarely given; but in the end it was not fully a collaboration. Nearly all the story is Dean's. I think he liked me sitting there beside him in the tamed and terrible semidarkness. I think that for both of us it re-created nights already vanished, when Dean and Kevin were both small, and I would lie between them on the top bunk of their beds, an arm around the warmth of each, telling them my improvised stories as they floated to sleep. On the ceiling above us glowed the adhesive moons and stars I had bought at Woolworth's. The fabulous realm had never seemed closer.

But now Dean had taken over the story—he'd taken over *story*. He'd fashioned the characters in his tale from himself and a neighborhood pal. And he fashioned those ruins into a realm that might have expanded into the cosmos as he grew older and more adept, had things gone differently.

9

"If Only, If Only, If Only..."

My life was fairly normal before June 12, 1998. I had ordinary friends that I could hang out with and laugh with, and talk to between classes. I was in a clique of friends I guess I would say. I went to regular classes, and some were even advanced for my grade. I was an average student who dreamed about the freedom and journey I would soon discover after high school. I, like many kids had a dream about what senior year would be like. I would be with the kings of the school, I would probably have a steady girlfriend, and I would go to the prom, and graduate with my class another guy with a smile in a black robe. None of this was meant for me.

—*The beginning of an essay
by Dean Powers, written on June 25, 1999*

June 12, 1998, was a Friday night in full Vermont spring, the end of Dean's junior year of high school. The temperature had languished in the seventies through the middle of the day and the air smelled of wet cut grass. Kevin and his band had a gig that night in the gymnasium of a grade school a few miles south of Middlebury. By 6:30 I had the van packed with the equipment, which was usually stored in our basement—drum set, amps, mics, and cords. Kevin, Honoree, and I left the house and rounded up the other band members and drove them to the school. I helped them haul their stuff into the gym and set up. We stayed until things ended, at around 9 p.m.

Dean had other plans for the evening. He wanted to visit a girl—I will call her Amy—who lived about thirteen miles southwest of Middlebury, in rolling farm country. Honoree lent Dean her car, a 1997 Volvo. She asked him to promise her that he wouldn't drink and would drive carefully, and reminded him of his usual 11 p.m. curfew. Dean had owned his driver's license for seven months, since his sixteenth birthday the previous November. He had not yet mastered all the skills and disciplines of driving. He tended to drive fast, a sadly commonplace tendency among sixteen-year-olds. A week earlier, we had restored his driving privileges after someone had told us that he had seen Dean speeding.

Amy was fifteen. At her house, out of earshot of her father, Amy's older half brother told them about a party nearby, a gathering of softball teammates a few years older than Dean, and offered to lead them to it. Later in the evening, a young man of legal drinking age would help purchase beer for the two of them.

We distributed Kevin's fellow musicians and returned to our house not long before 10 p.m. Honoree and I stayed up for a while and talked, and then we went to bed.

The ringing telephone awakened us some time after midnight. This was the sound and the time of night that all parents dread. Honoree answered the call, and she soon told me that Dean had been in an accident. He and Amy were at the hospital in Middlebury. She hadn't learned the extent of any injuries.

We agreed that Honoree would go to the hospital and I would remain at home with Kevin. While she was en route, Amy was transported to a larger facility in Burlington, thirty-five miles to the north. She'd suffered serious head injuries when Dean took a curve at too much speed on a two-lane blacktop road strewn with wet leaves.

In the span of a few seconds around 11:15 that night, I would lose control of my mom's Volvo beige 350 GLT, and forever remove myself and Amy from the lives we once had. But like Otter creek the night drifted by like any other night in any other town or city and the wreckage was cleaned, Amy was brought to the hospital in Burlington.

Dean had been hurrying to bring Amy home from the party. She was already past her curfew. Earlier she'd called home, hoping to get an extension. Her father had refused it. This refusal placed pressure upon Dean—or so Dean saw it—to trim as many minutes from Amy's tardiness as he could.

In the car with them were two other high school classmates who had jumped into the backseat, uninvited, at the last minute. Dean lost control of the car on a curve in the dark rural macadam. The rear wheels fishtailed to the right, and the car's right side slammed hard into a tree. Amy, sitting next to Dean, absorbed most of the impact. Her head crashed against the window. The force knocked her unconscious and into a coma that would last for several weeks. Dean was unhurt, and one of the young men in the backseat suffered a broken leg.

An ambulance and a Vermont State Police car arrived on the scene. The ambulance rushed the girl to the hospital at Middlebury. Soon she was transferred to the larger hospital in Burlington for surgery. The state policeman administered a Breathalyzer test to Dean. The test showed that Dean's blood did contain traces of alcohol, but that the content was well under the minimum for an intoxication charge. The policeman charged him with a misdemeanor for negligence in operating a motor vehicle, but he did not charge him with driving under the influence. This is a critical fact to bear in mind given the years of conflict that lay ahead for my son.

Honoree picked up Dean and drove on to Burlington. At the hospital there, she told me that she didn't yet know the extent of Amy's injuries, and she would call me when she had more information. The information was slow in coming. I sat beside the telephone for three hours, dreading the worst, hardly moving, not daring to leave the room, not able to distract myself with reading, crosswords, the computer— anything—until Honoree returned home at 4 a.m. Dean had insisted on staying behind at the hospital, along with the injured girl's parents and stepbrother. He stayed at the hospital the next day, too, when Honoree and I drove up together. He wanted to be in the room with Amy, but was forbidden by her parents, so he came home with us.

Honoree thought to hire a lawyer, and we did. At some point the state's attorney elevated the charges against Dean from a misdemeanor to a felony count: grossly negligent operation of a vehicle resulting in serious bodily injury. We never learned the reason for this. Dean had not joined several others in getting drunk at the party. He admitted to possessing alcohol and to passing a beer to a minor.

Dean insisted on making a daily trip up to Burlington for a few days after that. At length, the nursing staff allowed him inside Amy's room, and he sat beside the bed of the motionless girl for hours. One day he asked his mother to stop at a jewelry store so that he could buy a present for his friend, who was still in a coma.

Minutes of waiting slipped into hours slipped into days slipped into months. With every day those first two weeks or so after the accident, I felt the anticipation of a change in Amy's condition. She would wake up hopefully this afternoon if not this morning and it might take a few weeks for her to learn to walk again, but either way in a little while I can tell her how sorry I am, and I would be right there to support her and talk to her a million times about the whole thing.

At the jewelry store, Dean purchased a necklace and brought it to the hospital in a small gift box. He left the box on a tray near her bedside.

But I would not be allowed to see her for a long time after that.

This was because not long after he arrived with the necklace, Amy's parents barred him permanently from her hospital room.

After three weeks of torturous anxiety for everyone, Amy began to emerge from her coma.

My friends would come back to me and say that they saw her and that she recognized them and smiled and waved to them. My heart sank every time I silently realized that she would never smile and wave to me again. I was confined to my house. Not because of the legal system, yet, not because of my parents so much, but rather because of the impact the accident made on me and the guilt that I carry to this day. I was scared of what others thought of me, who was mad at me, who my real friends still were, and what would eventually happen to Amy.

I smoked cigarettes on my porch and began to silently learn a lot about the world and myself.

In those early weeks, even after she had regained consciousness, no one could predict how thorough the young girl's recovery would be, or even whether she would recover further. For Honoree and me, our racing thoughts ricocheted back and forth between her physical and mental prospects and Dean's psychological state, which had him pacing the house, head down.

I called Amy's household weekly to find out how she was progressing. Her father's tone was never welcoming, and on the day his voice fairly vibrated with iron, I stopped calling. Several months later I wrote a letter to Amy's parents, in which I restated our regret for what had happened and expressed our hope for a meeting, reconciliation. It went unanswered.

We eventually learned some details of Amy's ordeal.[1] While in her coma, and for days and weeks after emerging from it, she breathed with the aid of a ventilator, a mechanical form of artificial respiration. She was fed through a feeding tube and spent months in a wheelchair. Assisted daily by her parents, she underwent five months of painful rehabilitative therapy to recover her movements.

Amy's parents purchased Honoree's wrecked Volvo from a salvage company. We never learned the full extent of their intentions, but one of them, expressed in a request, was to place the car on the Middlebury town green and oblige Dean to stand beside it and be photographed and videotaped by the regional media.

Nor did we ever learn, for sure, the reason for the flawed reports on the crash that quickly appeared in Vermont newspapers and on the state's sole network-affiliated commercial TV station (CBS), WCAX. The papers and the TV station uniformly identified Dean as the "drunk driver" in an accident that seriously injured a fifteen-year-old girl. Clearly, none of the news outlets had bothered to check the primary source, the on-scene patrolman's record of the Breathalyzer test. Either they had defaulted to a standard supposition without checking the facts or someone had supplied them with the false information.

Dean would be described as a "drunk driver" in the press for years, as litigation proceeded through the courts. The misrepresentation infuriated us as it became settled truth in the state. We wanted to demand corrections from the newspapers and TV stations. But our lawyer cautioned against it. He worried that any sort of protest from us—as "flatlanders" living in a tony college town—might arouse resentment in the region, along with accusations of trying to influence the media. We let it go. This was a bad mistake, in retrospect. As the news outlets kept finding ways to renew the story, frequently by examining and reexamining the topic of adolescent drivers and "booze," Dean became Vermont's Public Enemy No. 1.

At a hearing a few weeks after the accident, the court imposed a house arrest ruling on Dean pending the hearing that would follow several weeks later. Now his isolation was obligatory. Most of his friends deserted him. Only one, a football teammate, continued to drop by. The effects of the order reached deeply into our household. Until it went into effect, Honoree and I could legitimately assure Dean that we were his allies, his advocates and protectors. Now we were his jailers.

I did a lot of thinking that summer. When I was at work, the only other place I spent the majority of my time at, I could take my mind off of it, but back home it consumed me. Time is what I thought about most. The seconds in which my life changed, the days before the accident, how I had gotten from point A to point B without choosing to get there. This was a new experience, and why couldn't I go back, it was so easy to avoid if only I hadn't called her, if only I had been sick that day, if only the Volvo had a flat tire, if only, if only, if only…

Dean's daily reprieve from house arrest, and the only interruption in his obsessive despair, was his early-morning job helping to make bagels and serving customers at the Middlebury Bagel & Deli shop. The owner, Jim Rubright, an industrious and good-hearted family man, had hired my son some months earlier. Dean wanted to hold on to that job after the accident, and the judge allowed it, and Jim Rubright welcomed him back, a gesture of humanity and respect that our family never forgot. So every morning Dean continued to rise before dawn, put on his white apron and join Jim, his wife, and grown children making breakfast for the town. Of course things were different now. Greeting customers had always been part of the job's fun for Dean. These were mostly people he knew: friends and parents of friends from swim team, football, church, school.

But now the routine exchange of eye contact, the taking of a customer's order, was freighted with the unspoken. Many of the patrons, Dean was certain, now looked back at him with silent contempt. Here was the notorious "drunk driver" in the flesh. Dean dreaded this exposure. Yet he performed his job without complaint and with what I can only describe as gallantry. (Gallantry was and remains a part of Dean's nature. Late one night, years later, as he and I crossed Kearny Street near San Francisco's Tenderloin district in a knot of pedestrians, Dean trained his attention on a man in front of us who'd abruptly separated from the crowd, walked up to a young woman, and begun yelling into her ear. Without hesitating, Dean bellowed: "LEAVE HER ALONE!" Everyone around us suddenly looked as though they were trying to will themselves somewhere else. The man left the woman alone.)

And so returning to his job was a mixed blessing. Yet the work hours broke up the tedium of his house arrest, and, more importantly, the job pieced back together some of his shredded self-esteem. When his workday was done, he would come home and resume his thoughts. Inevitably those thoughts settled on the girl in the hospital in Burlington.

But it couldn't have been avoided, and that is fate, which I have spent days wondering about. What I didn't know back then though, was just how much of Amy's life and my life could be ruined by the gigantic blaze that grew from a spark I created that night in a matter of seconds. I have a good feeling of how hard this was on Amy and [her] family, I can only try to imagine how hard it would be to live Amy's life, all she knows is that things got really tough after the black haze that sits in the corridors of her memory from that time. So I can't tell anyone what she went through, except it was worse than me, and what I can tell about myself was hard for me.

I cut myself off from a lot of my old friends that summer, I didn't hang out with them at night, I didn't go out on the town and do fun things, and at the bakery I didn't want to wait on customers, I just wanted to work in back so I didn't risk seeing anyone I knew, or who knew of me. I was worried about anyone seeing me have a good time anywhere, ever. I wasn't supposed to. Not until I had paid for what I had done and Amy was all right again and I apologized to her. I strongly felt that, and never let anyone tell me, "shit happens" or something along those lines, because of how that cut me off the hook of responsibility, and basically said, "Well, you know, your right. How was I to know that would happen, its not really my fault, it could happen to anyone." No. I was determined to stand and face the music, and own up to my doings. I am not a stupid person, and I can see right through a person who shrinks away from responsibility, and so through that image I had of what responsibility was, I made a sharp turn in the path of life I traveled.

Nowhere in this essay does Dean deny his accountability in the accident. Nowhere does he cast an aspersion at Amy, or try to lessen his culpability in any way. Nowhere does he try to refute the slander that he was driving drunk. His empathy for his friend, and her parents, permeates the lines: in his insistence, for example, that Amy's ordeal was worse than his own.

Even though the police had not found him to be intoxicated after the car accident, the sad fact is that our son *had* become an underage drinker. Whether his use had made him a habitual "underage drunk" we never found out. The signs, or the lack of them, gave us hope. We had never seen him intoxicated after a night out, and at the party on the night of his accident he had clearly shown restraint—although even one beer was against our rules and against the law. Our lack of information on these matters may sound like indifference or parental incompetence, but if some means exists of monitoring a young teenager outside the home at night in the company of his or her friends, a means that doesn't require shadowing the child or relying on his or her friends to act as snitches—either of which seems freighted with ethical and practical obstacles—then we have not heard of it. The alternative, as I have said—keeping a child under lock and key through the end of adolescence (however *that* might be determined)—didn't seem like such a hot idea either.

We understood the lethal hazards that awaited any child crossing the threshold into adolescence and out the front door. We understood that we had little choice but to sit and wait until the child got home, if he got home, and that the following night, that child's departure and his parents' vigil would all begin again.

We knew of several strategies adopted by parents in our town and in the country. Home drinking was one: An underage child could drink, and even hold drinking parties, in the household, on the lesser-evil theory that the son or daughter at least would not be out on the road then or later. Whose responsibility it was to get the buzzed partygoers home safely was presumably worked out among the families.

Clueless though we were about alternative solutions, home drinking had never struck Honoree and me as a realistic option, although we could sympathize with the parents who allowed it. It was the unstated messages of this strategy that bothered us—that forbidden behavior was okay as long as you weren't caught, and that liquor had no bad effects on the developing brain.

Our own zero-tolerance strategy was hardly foolproof. We talked to Dean and Kevin about the dangers of drinking and bore in on our simple but absolute rule: Not a sip. Anywhere. At any time. Not until they had reached the legal age.

Parents across time and space, of course, have marveled at how devoutly their children, otherwise programmed to rebel, obey such moral sermons and unenforceable rules. Policy established, we trusted. And sat at home, clenched and distracted, praying that one more night would pass without delivering catastrophe.

Dean himself shattered our recourse to fantasy. Weeks before the accident, he had told us, with an adolescent male's typical defiance—but with the honesty intrinsic to him—that he and his friends had used alcohol. And would continue to use it.

What to do with that? Lock him in the basement? We protested his decision, and pleaded with him to be aware of limits. We even enrolled him in a weekly counseling session with a local psychologist. He joined several of his friends whose parents already had signed them up. Dean attended, but he gave no sign that his habits had changed.

Through all of this, there was Kevin. Our younger son graduated from middle school less than a week after the accident, and he turned fourteen that July of 1998. He remained a silent, absorbed witness to all that was happening. We watched him for signs of his own distress, but he concealed whatever feelings he might have been harboring. His trademark ebullience did seem to be lacking.

I believe that this was the summer the brothers began to forge their true friendship, a mutual understanding that elevated them to a level beyond that of childhood siblings. The process was subtly closed off to Honoree and me, and it probably proceeded without too many words between them. But there are other forms of communication. This was the summer that Dean mastered the guitar with Kevin's help and began to play duets with Kevin. He had learned the basics over the past couple of years from sessions with Kevin's teacher and then the guitar workshops. Now, increasingly, instead of sitting and smoking, he would disappear upstairs into his room when Kevin was gone and play for hours on end. Often he howled as he played, howled out his pain and his rage, making music that was angry but to me sounded coherent. Within a few years he and Kevin would be appearing together in coffeehouses around Vermont and later in Colorado.

It wasn't long after the accident before the posters began to appear around town.

They showed up in the windows of some of the stores on the main street downtown that crossed Otter Creek. One of them was taped inside a window, facing the street, of the bank where we had our account. We closed the account and reopened it at another bank.

The posters showed a black-and-white photograph of Amy. The caption below quoted her as advising adolescents to avoid getting into cars with drunk drivers—excellent and important advice, in itself. The poster went on to state that Amy was speaking from experience, having survived an auto crash with a "drinking" driver (unnamed) at the wheel. Hardly anyone in the town, county, or state who saw the poster had any doubt as to the driver's identity—or to his condition when he had driven his mother's car that night.

Still hoping for a breakthrough with Amy's parents, we again decided to let the matter go. We also decided not to challenge the felony indictment. We wanted to spare both Dean and the young victim the ordeal of a jury trial. We would accept whatever penalties the court handed down. We never disputed, nor did Dean, that he had been guilty of reckless driving that resulted in the crash. We were prepared to accept a fine, probation, conditions of release, community service.

Amy's parents requested that Dean be sentenced to three to eight years in prison.

Three to eight years in prison. Dean lived for a year with that grotesque possibility burdening his thoughts and dreams. *Three to eight years.* Three to eight years in confinement, out of the sunlight, out of the world, out of the company of anyone other than convicted criminals and cynical guards, older, tougher, life-hardened men. *Three to eight years* without freedom. Without variety. Or discovery. Or laughter. Or love. Or music. Or dignity. Or reassurance of his worth. Or anything he cherished. Three to eight years: a black tunnel of forever to an adolescent.

It was a possibility only in his mind, of course. No court in America could conceivably be barbaric enough to impose such a nightmare of a sentence on a boy, a new driver scarcely out of childhood, for a car accident in which no one was killed and for which no charge of intoxication was imposed.

Or, hell, could it? Sometimes the newspaper headlines told, and tell, a different story.

As if the sentence request might not make their level of hostility clear enough, the parents added a further rebuke to any hope of personal conciliation. It happened at a court hearing a few weeks later. As we sat waiting for the judge to appear, the girl's father, who was seated a couple of rows ahead of us, stood up, turned, and stepped toward us. I recall for some reason that he was wearing Bermuda shorts. He was holding a small gift box. He held the box toward us. "Amy wanted Dean to have this," he whispered.

We did not have to open the little box to know what lay coiled inside it.

We shielded our son from the knowledge of this gesture. But we could not shield him from the new round of persecution that greeted him that autumn.

Dean was arraigned on September 28, 1998.

When school came, so did the legal aspect of the aftermath. I was arraigned into court. I trembled I was so scared, and to top it off, Channel 3 news was there. I got terms and conditions of release, a curfew, an alcohol restriction, and a restriction from talking to Amy.

In fact, a court order prohibited Dean from being in the same area of the high school with Amy at any given time. He was banned from both lunch periods, lest he cross her path, and as a result ate alone, outdoors. He was obliged to walk along separate corridors from the ones she took.

I also knew that I was under a magnifying glass, so to speak. School was hard and I felt like an outsider. The friends I once felt comfortable talking to and hanging out with I made little or no attempt to acknowledge, nor did they to me which scared me more. When I realized that what was troubling me almost more than the accident itself was the school environment, also the most dangerous, I dropped out of regular school and began getting tutored.

More accurately, at the end of that hideous semester—the first of his senior year—Honoree and I arranged for Dean to be released from the high school's malignant climate and allowed instead to meet with a tutor at the public library.

To this day I am still learning with [the tutor,] *who has never seemed judgmental about me after the accident. And with whom I am very comfortable, and inspired to complete all my assignments with.*

Dean suited up for every Middlebury football game, home and

away, in that autumn of his senior year. But the coach did not once put him in, and from our vantage point in the stands, it did not seem as though his teammates noticed him. In the final game of the season, on the road in southern Vermont and with the score settled, the coach at last turned to Dean and offered him a chance to go onto the field.

I was watching at field level, just on the other side of the chain-link fence from the Middlebury bench, and I could plainly hear Dean's response. He said, "No, thanks."

Still I am a dropout from society with only one and a half close friends the one being my brother, the other is still not complete because he chooses a somewhat risky lifestyle which I can't have any part of. I don't call anyone, I don't go anywhere, and I worry constantly now, that if I don't get out of Middlebury soon, I will never go anywhere, ever. I am quite ready to leave this town, and the horrible memories it has, but I am now tied down, by legal restrictions. There are less than a dozen people I think that actually care about me, so why should I stay? And I am afraid that because of certain factors Amy and I will not have the intimate chance to confess to each other the things we have needed to hear and say to each other for almost a year. So I might have to wait a few years for that step of the healing process anyway.

That brings me to today, I have been in a blur at work with [the overflow of customers during] Middlebury College graduation week, and this last month or two has been quite busy in general. In a week I will find out where my life goes next. I wish I could take control of it again but like I said, my life is like a river and I am being swept away helplessly. I know that I am close to the end, and what happened brought tragic results. However it helped a seventeen year old see just how precious life really is, and how your life can slip away from you if you're not careful. I sometimes feel like an old man who had the chance to go back and live his life over again. Maybe it's because I've had so much therapy, and from AA I heard men who were like me and ended up dying for years or decades, in an alcohol haze. So here I am, and I was given a second chance to see the light and change my life. And so I did.

The high school principal contributed his own final gesture of gratuitous punitive humiliation. This factotum forbade Dean the dignity of participating in his class's graduation ceremony, although Dean had completed his requirements. And he banned Dean's senior photograph from the 1998 school yearbook.

The dreaded date of Dean's sentencing neared. His days of confinement in our house began to seem as though they might last forever—or be replaced by the foreverness of prison.

These were the days and months and events, I am convinced, that launched my eldest son into his rendezvous with schizophrenia.

"…my life is like a river and I am being swept away helplessly."

10

Chaos and Heartbreak

As I've researched and written this book, I have kept files of news reports that illustrate the daily "chaos and heartbreak" of mental illness and the treatment of mad people in law enforcement, in the courts, in the jails and prisons, and in efforts at psychiatric intervention. I have drawn upon these files for use in my narratives—such as the killing by a police officer of young Keith Vidal in North Carolina in 2014, the incident that appears in chapter 1.

These files have long since over-spilled the book's capacity to contain all of them. Yet like the Keith Vidal story, they yield near-unthinkable examples of atrocity and malfeasance and systemic callousness toward the insane. Their litany of "civilized" society's failure to protect its most helpless members is itself a narrative of atrocity on a grand scale. Yet the stories result in no sustained collective sense of affront to personal or civic decency on a scale necessary for reform. The stories flare and vanish into the maw of other atrocities: mass shootings, terrorist attacks, apocalyptic political candidates. Any possible interconnections are mentioned, perhaps, then forgotten or ignored.

I have retrieved a small sampling of these stories from my files and laid them out below, in roughly chronological order but in no special "order of importance." They are all important.

I have excluded accounts of atrocities, mostly mass shootings perpetrated *by* people suspected of being in psychotic states: at Tucson, Aurora, Sandy Hook Elementary School, the Washington Navy Yard, the Emanuel African Methodist Episcopal Church in Charleston, Colorado Springs, San Bernardino, Orlando, Dallas, other venues. These have burned into the national memory and need no fresh review here. While it seems clear almost by definition that these shooters were mentally ill in most if not all these incidents, they were unavailable for diagnoses—in most cases, due to their suicides.

Some readers will probably recognize a few of the incidents described below. Yet to read or re-read them sequentially is to be bombarded anew with evidence that something is wrong at the foundations of our society.

Among stories of mentally ill people shot or beaten to death by police on the streets—or, in this case, in the foothills—the vile fate of James "Abba" Boyd ranks as one of the most excruciating in my files. The deadly confrontation occurred about six weeks after the Keith Vidal killing.

I am able to describe this act of defilement in detail because the defilement was recorded: recorded, with the deadpan surreality that marks so much of "sane" American life, by one of the assaulting officers. The officer had been issued a small digital recording device, attached to his helmet, and dutifully kept it active through Abba Boyd's long ordeal. This was a variation of the "body cam," which this incident helped transform from a marginal law enforcement tool into a central artifact of our culture. Less than three years after its dramatic emergence, the body cam is spreading not only through police organizations; it is a hot item among civilian consumers, a deus ex machina on the half-shell. The body cam (along with its cousin the cell phone camera) has managed the dubious achievement of obliterating the taboo against witnessing a human death on the screen.

More importantly, though, these devices have served to provide society's most defenseless and preyed-upon members—the insane, urban minorities—with the most effective counterweight yet invented to the tyranny of the gun.

Both these functions were on display in the killing of James "Abba" Boyd.

Boyd was a thirty-eight-year-old homeless man with a history of paranoid schizophrenia. At the time of his mountainside execution he had been wandering for several days along the Amya foothills outside Albuquerque, sleeping amid the rocks and sagebrush with little covering except what he carried in a knapsack. Boyd was an outlaw: he had not obtained a camping permit from the city, thus violating an ordinance.

Boyd did not carry a gun, but he had a couple of knives and a history of punching police officers who tried to remove him from places where he didn't belong. Those who knew him said he was not a violent man except when confronted while in the midst of a "break"—a virtually universal reaction among those in psychosis. Boyd suffered from delusions, believing himself at times to be, variously, a one-man federal agency, and God. He had no wife or children. He'd spent short periods in jails and psychiatric hospitals, but no apparatus existed for keeping him under treatment or from injuring others or himself.

In early 2014 Boyd had provoked the annoyance of a man who lived in the open country where Boyd often roamed. This man had called the police several times to complain about Boyd. The afternoon of March 14, 2014, a squad of officers, armed with assault rifles, pistols, flash grenades, and an attack dog, tracked Boyd down in the foothills near a boulder where he had been camping. As reinforcements made their way to the scene, these early responders ordered him to "surrender."

"Don't attempt to give me, the Department of Defense, another directive!" Boyd shouted. He was clutching a pair of knives. The team, assault weapons at the ready, edged toward him. One team member, a thirty-year-old officer named Mikal Monette, who'd had some training in crisis intervention, tried to talk Boyd into a peaceful surrender. (The department did not send out a full crisis-intervention team. Budget cuts—another pandemic form of maltreatment toward the mentally ill—had reduced the number of available specialists.) As the journalist Colleen Heild reported in the April 16 *Albuquerque Journal*, the two talked for about an hour as the number of police slowly increased. Their topics ranged from PlayStation games to whether Boyd could have a meal at Denny's. A still photograph accompanying Heild's article shows Boyd, near the left of the frame, looking through dark glasses at the men who would shortly shoot him to death. He stands slightly slumped, a big man in a faded blue shirt. The lower half of his body is concealed by a boulder, but his right hand, nearer to the camera, holds a small object that gleams in the fading sunlight. He faces five men in police blue, about ten yards from him. Two are aiming rifles at him and one a pistol. The officers' postures recall nothing so much as a group of Union infantry preparing to fire upon an advancing Confederate brigade.

The helmet cam recorded what happened. At length, on the recording, James Boyd raises his hands, palms upward in a kind of shrug, and turns to his right to pick up his knapsack. There is yelling. One of the officers fires a flash grenade that lands at Boyd's feet with a loud pop and a burst of white smoke. Such grenades are nonlethal, designed (cluelessly) to startle the target. At the same moment a police attack dog, a Belgian Malinois, is released to rush at the man.

Boyd, curiously, doesn't seem to panic. He extends his hands down toward the dog. He half shoulders his backpack and turns to his left in an apparent decision to walk away. Three officers, two of them aiming rifles, close on him, yelling, *"Down! Get down on the ground! Down now!"* The nearest gunman is barely four feet from Boyd when the shooting starts: about eight bursts in rapid succession. Boyd falls on his face in the opposite direction of his assailants. His heels spasm a little. The officers shout more commands. Then they fire more rounds into the prone man. One bullet rips through his shirt, and a shred of it flaps briefly. Another catches him in the small of his back, causing a similar flapping in his trousers near the belt. Boyd's right hand is on the ground near his head and his left arm is under his torso, but the officers scream for him to "drop" the knife. The police release the dog again, and he worries at Boyd's backside with his teeth. The helmet cam captures it all.

The shooting stops, and the police chat among themselves for a few moments, striking attitudes of disengagement weirdly typical of officers—and perpetrators as well—in the seconds following use of lethal force. Then an officer leans down to the mortally wounded man and tugs harshly at his left arm. At length he yanks it free, and everyone crowds around to see what is in Boyd's hand. From the video it is not clear what, if anything, he had been holding.

At length, the officers transported Boyd to the University of New Mexico Hospital, about half an hour distant. He died there the next morning after surgeons had amputated his shattered right arm and removed a lung in their efforts to save him. The helmet-cam video was released to the media on lawyers' demands. It unleashed days of street protests and some violence by Albuquerque citizens who had seen thirty-seven people shot down by their police department since 2010 alone, twenty-three of them fatally. Three-fourths of these were mentally ill.[1]

All this attracted the attention of the Justice Department, which launched an investigation that lasted sixteen months. In April 2014 the department accused the Albuquerque police of "a pattern...of use of excessive force" against suspects that often violated their constitutional rights. "Force" included, besides gunfire, kicking, punching, and violent restraint. Many of these victims, the department stated, were mentally ill and often nonthreatening.[2]

A district attorney for Bernalillo County indicted two of the officers, Keith Sandy and Dominique Perez, for murder. Their trial was scheduled for the fall of 2016; as of this writing, it has not begun. In July 2015 the city agreed to settle a civil lawsuit brought by Boyd's brother Andrew for $5 million.[3]

Should a mentally ill suspect (or any suspect) survive an encounter with police, their next stop, quite often, is the modern-day equivalent of Bedlam. The American prison system is an archipelago of barbarity. In many important ways its assumptions and practices bespeak the Middle Ages. This is to some extent inherent in the very fact of a prison system and of the timeless callousness, either inborn or inculcated, of its wardens and guards. In any case, the consequences of imprisonment, to the human mind and body, are incalculably more debilitating than most people care to imagine. Or than an ethical society should tolerate. Or than is necessary.

Contrary to public perception fed in part by incendiary political rhetoric, crime rates have been consistently declining since reaching a peak in the 1980s, and now resemble figures from the mid-'70s. In 2014, violent crime alone declined by 4.6 percent from the previous period.[4]

Prison populations have been declining as well, but at a slower rate than crime. The year since 2009 saw the first reversal in population size since the mid-1970s, when draconian sentencing, galvanized by the "War on Drugs," led to an increase of inmates from 300,000 to a peak of nearly 1.6 million. State and federal populations, by standard consensus, totaled just under 1.4 million in 2016, though some advocacy groups have put the number as high as 2.3 million.[5] In fiscal year 2014, overcrowding in federal prisons was at 39 percent above capacity in medium-security facilities and 52 percent above in high-security ones.[6]

The most repugnant reason for prison overcrowding can be found within the bureaucratic wisdom that "no one cares about crazy people." It lies in the effects of the carelessly bungled experiment in deinstitutionalization.

Since that era, the American system has been "criminalizing mental illness," Thomas Dart, then Cook County sheriff, remarked to Nicholas Kristof of the *New York Times* in 2014.[7] Kristof described the Cook County Jail as "the largest mental-health center in America," and cited a 2006 Department of Justice study announcing that more than half of prisoners in the United States had a mental health problem of one form or another.

For many among the incarcerated, a mental health "problem" leads not to treatment, but to problems that might cause Hieronymus Bosch to cover his eyes.

Among the most gruesome and least forgivable forms of sanctioned torture by prison factotums is "punitive segregation," as the delicate euphemism has it. The more familiar term is "solitary confinement."

Solitary confinement, even for brief periods—several days, say, with an hour's respite each day—is known to trigger hallucinations and paranoia among sane and insane prisoners alike. For people already mad, it is a quick route to deep and lasting psychosis. The human psyche is essentially social and abhors isolation; enforced separation from others thus amounts to an act of sanctioned depravity.

Solitary confinement has been used as a short-duration measure in the past. In recent decades, overwhelmed wardens increasingly have turned to it in a hair-trigger way, popping prisoners into tiny, badly ventilated cells, often restricting food, water, and medications as part of the bargain.

Solitary confinement is a petri dish for the suicide impulse. Yet attempted suicide is a violation of prison rules. If an inmate is caught trying, or is discovered after having failed, he is often beaten within an inch of his just-rescued life, or worse.

Solitary confinement ranks with batons and boot-tips as the punishment of choice at the most dreaded detention facility in America. Rikers Island opened in 1932—like Bedlam, on a fetid landfill of the same name in the East River, just north of what is now LaGuardia Airport. Its fifteen low-slung buildings command more than four hundred acres. Their cinderblock walls trap and exacerbate frigid air in winter and 100-degree heat in summer. Upkeep is minimal; the floors show large cracks that flood during rains. Unswept broken window glass provides handy shards for slashing faces and necks.

Rikers's designated holding capacity is fifteen thousand. Virtually none of the inmates are serving sentences for a crime. Mostly poor, overwhelmingly black and Latino, they are awaiting trial on one charge or another, their families too poor to supply bail money. It is widely estimated that about 40 percent of these inmates have some form of mental illness. Crazy people, historically, have proved irresistible targets for sadistic guards. Mayor Bill de Blasio, who has faced criticism for helplessness in the face of the near-daily brutalities at Rikers, announced in 2016 that the city will triple the number of PACE staffers (Program to Accelerate Clinical Effectiveness) under a program that by 2020 is estimated to cost more than $24 million.

In the meantime, the ordained enforcers at Rikers continue to dole out "punitive segregation" when it suits them, which is often. News coverage does not seem to dissuade them, and there is virtually no public outcry. This may be what inspired the *Times* reporter Jim Dwyer to write, in 2013, that Rikers "is the basket into which society drops the disruptive mentally ill."[8]

In September 2013, as later reported by New York newspapers and television news groups and investigated by Jake Pearson of the Associated Press, a thirty-seven-year-old inmate at Rikers Island and schizophrenia sufferer named Bradley Ballard made an obscene gesture to a woman guard. Other guards locked Ballard in his cell and left him there. The guards withheld some of the man's antipsychotic medication, as well as insulin injections that he needed for his diabetes. They also denied him many of his meals. They checked him through the cell door's small window "dozens of times," according to the AP report, but did nothing to intervene as Ballard grew progressively agitated, clogged his toilet so that it overflowed, stripped himself naked, and wound a rubber band tightly around his genitals. On the seventh day, a guard noticed that the inmate was motionless on the floor, smeared with his own feces, his genitals swollen and red. He died in a hospital a few hours afterward.

One year later, Ballard's mother, Beverly Ann Griffin, filed a wrongful death lawsuit against the city. The amount of the suit was not made public, and the suit has not been resolved at this writing. Ballard had been brought to Rikers from Texas in 2013 for the crime of changing his address without notifying his parole officer. He had been arrested for assault.

In February 2014, careless mistreatment by Rikers staff resulted in the grotesque death of another inmate. New York City police had arrested Jerome Murdough, a fifty-six-year-old Marine with a history of schizo-affective disorder, for trespassing in a Harlem public-housing building. The AP's Pearson, among others, reported that Murdough told the officers that he had been trying to escape the bitter cold. Unable to pay the twenty-five-hundred-dollar bail assessed for the misdemeanor, Murdough was placed in a six-by-ten cinderblock cell, in a unit designated for mentally ill inmates. Temperatures in the cell-block hovered around 100 degrees. Despite loud complaints, no one came to fix the heating system. Nor did the guards pay much attention to the Marine. It took a week for Murdough to bake to death. Before his family's intended $25 million wrongful death lawsuit could be filed, the city quickly settled with them for a payment of $2.5 million.

Kalief Browder did not commit suicide at Rikers Island, but it was there that he learned the technique he used to take his own life in 2015 at his home in the Bronx at age twenty-two. That is the conclusion reached by writer Jennifer Gonnerman in a *New Yorker* essay dated June 2, 2016.[9] She also obtained documents of Browder's deposition conducted by lawyers for the city. Gonnerman had interviewed Browder in 2014, after the charges against him had been dropped and he had been released from Rikers.

Browder's persecution began when he was arrested for robbery in 2010, at age sixteen. Browder and a friend had been falsely identified on a nighttime Bronx street by a man who said the boys accosted him. Police found no evidence on either of the two; yet, after a day of confinement, Browder found himself charged with robbery, grand larceny, and assault. Because he was on probation for a previous, nonviolent offense, the youth was ordered held over; his bail was set at three thousand dollars. The family, as is so typical in such cases, could not afford to pay. So a terrified Kalief Browder was placed on a police bus to Rikers Island.

There he spent three years, nearly two of them in solitary confinement, in a seven-by-twelve-foot cell. He insisted on his innocence all the while. And he attempted suicide at least five times. He formed the idea of hanging himself after seeing a fellow inmate removed from his cell after a failed effort, the remains of a bedsheet still fastened around his neck.

On one of his attempts, Browder told the lawyers deposing him, corrections officers walked into his cell as he was about to jump from the rim of a lavatory sink with a bedsheet threaded through holes in a ceiling vent and tied around his neck. Instead of lifting him down, the guards taunted him: "Go ahead and jump!" Browder, by now frightened of death, refused—at which point the guards cut the bedsheet, then threw the young man onto his bed and began beating him.

(Jennifer Gonnerman cited the results of an investigation by the *Times*, published on July 14, 2014, which revealed "scores" of "brutal attacks by corrections officers on inmates—particularly those with mental health issues" inside Rikers.[10] Among the facts revealed by the investigation: that 129 inmates had suffered serious injuries over an eleven-month period; that 77 percent of those injured had been diagnosed as mentally ill; that in 80 percent of the cases, the inmate-victims reported having been handcuffed; that none of the officers involved in the cases had been prosecuted or been brought up on formal charges as of the article's publication date.)

After his release, Browder—who'd shown no previous symptoms of mental illness—enrolled at Bronx Community College and achieved a 3.5 grade point average. His achievements there included a scholarly research article on the dangers posed by solitary confinement to the human mind. "Instead of solitary confinement rehabilitating inmates there is evidence of it actually causing severe mental problems for inmates and in the long run leaving the mental disorders for their families to deal with," Browder wrote.[11] By that time, his own mind had been infected. He suffered from delusions and paranoia; tried again to kill himself; made three enforced visits to psychiatric wards. After enduring three depositions, one of them a five-hour grilling in May 2015 that probed his suicide attempts, Browder decided to try the bedsheet approach once again, less than a month later, and succeeded.

Urban jails and prisons are not the only settings for the lethal abuse of the mentally ill, just as cities are not the only venues for police shootings of the mad. Atrocities by wardens and inmates can, and do, occur around the country, including in the Heartland.

In October 2014, a thirty-nine-year-old man, Josh Francisco, the father of two children, hanged himself while in solitary confinement at the Farmington, Missouri, Correctional Center. As Blythe Bernhard reported in the November 8 *St. Louis Post-Dispatch*, Francisco suffered from a bipolar affliction, and "for four years, his family desperately tried to get the help he needed."[12] His mother, Anne Francisco, filled in the details of Josh's life and of the reprehensible yet familiar bureaucratic cluelessness that dragged him inexorably beyond the reach of his loving and desperate family and into that cell. She composed those details on the day of her son's suicide, in an essay of remarkable clarity and eloquence—and universality. She sent it to the blog[13] of the distinguished journalist Pete Earley, himself the father of a mentally ill son and the author of *Crazy: A Father's Search Through America's Mental Health Madness*, a finalist for the 2007 Pulitzer Prize in nonfiction. Below are some edited excerpts, which Earley republished in 2015:

> My husband and I knew little about mental illness until four years ago, when we received a call from our daughter-in-law telling us that Josh's behavior had changed and she needed our help to convince him that he should enter a hospital for psychiatric treatment. She explained that Josh . . . had become hyper-vigilant about national/government affairs and hyper-religious, praying in strange tongues.[14]

Josh refused to seek treatment, believing he was sane—the classic symptom of anosognosia. His wife, alarmed at his behavior, obtained a restraining order against him. Josh persisted in trying to contact her. He was arrested for stalking. Arriving in Missouri from California, his parents "learned Josh was living in a storage locker." They found a psychiatric facility. Josh balked. "The hospital admitted him only after I exaggerated his symptoms. It was the beginning of his resentment toward me."[15]

The divorce papers arrived while Josh was in the hospital. "He used a telephone there to call his wife and apologize." He was released, and then immediately rearrested for making the call.

Deprived of his medications for four days in a cell, Josh had an outburst when he was taken into the courtroom and his defense attorney wasn't there. We later were told that outburst had angered the prosecutor. Josh's bail was raised, and we were told that he couldn't be released or return with us to California. We suddenly found ourselves fighting the criminal justice system as well as our son's mental illness and our badly broken mental health system. It cost us upwards of $40,000 in legal and other fees to get Josh released and finally bring him home with us. My husband, a retired minister, and I would have preferred to spend our savings for Josh's treatment.[16]

Josh's troubles were only beginning. In California, he himself aborted his first suicide attempt—by asphyxiation, in his mother's car—and agreed to hospitalization. His older brother invited him to live with him and his family in Southern California. There, he found a new psychiatrist and got a job at a retail home improvement store. A photograph shows him posing proudly, a confident-looking young man in glasses, wearing the franchise store's red vest, the fingers of one hand spread jauntily on his hip.

Yet Josh continued to resist the notion that he was mentally ill, and he continued to suffer the consequences. He quit his job after four months. "Two days later," his mother wrote, "his brother found him delusional in a hotel conference room, where he was waiting for people who he'd invited to sit on the board of directors of an international foundation he was forming."[17]

Not long after that, Josh hit the streets. "Soon he was stuck in a vicious cycle. He would be hospitalized and become stable, but would suffer horrible side effects from the medication and ditch the medications when he left the hospital. He would decompensate until he was hospitalized again." Back with his parents in Northern California, he again tried a recovery regimen, but the anosognosia returned to delude him with the idea that he was well. He proclaimed that without his medication, he felt better than he had in years. He believed that the United States was about to fall under martial law.

His mother found a respite and temporary hope in a local chapter of NAMI (National Alliance on Mental Illness). Yet Josh continued to refuse medication. In March 2013, his probation officer in Missouri directed him back to St. Louis, where, she believed, "he would get the help he needed." Instead, he was talked into waiving his right to a preliminary hearing, and he embarked upon another ordeal common to sufferers in his situation: he spent two months, unmedicated, in the St. Louis County jail, awaiting an empty bed in a state psychiatric hospital. Six weeks later, he was issued a court order to resume medication because he had failed a mental competency exam. One night, he tried to contact his ex-wife, using the patients' telephone. In doing so, he violated the terms of his probation. He spent nine more months in the hospital. "In January of this year," Anne Francisco wrote in 2014, "we flew to visit him. He blamed us for his circumstances. The heartbreak we felt was indescribable."[18]

More jail time. Another hearing, delayed for months, resulted in his probation being revoked. A new, sustained refusal to take medications. Then, felony charges for using that patient telephone at the state hospital. He was sent to prison in early July to fulfill his original three-year sentence.

Josh himself requested solitary confinement. He was paranoid about living amid the general jail population, his mother wrote. He remained in solitary for part of July into late October, without psychiatric supervision. HIPAA laws* forbade the authorities to give his parents any information about his condition—yet another source of anguish for relatives of the mentally ill.

On October 22, a warden from the correctional center called to

---

* The Health Insurance Portability and Accountability Act was created in 1996 to protect the privacy of hospital patients and jail/prison inmates by withholding their medical records from anyone outside their institutional caretakers, such as private investigators and predatory insurance companies. Critics have charged that its unintended consequences include shutting family members off from knowing the condition of their loved ones in hospital or jail, and from allowing clergy access to their parishioners.

report that Josh Francisco had hanged himself in his cell. Apparently the HIPAA laws permit this sort of information.

These stories make up but a small fraction of all reported and recorded accounts of murderous mayhem directed at the mentally ill in America by police officers and prison officials. They are drawn exclusively from the second decade of the twenty-first century, long after such encounters had drawn the vociferous interest of the press, television, sociologists, psychiatrists, clergy, coalitions of bereaved relatives, and even some politicians.

Despite occasional promises of "reform" and actual initiatives such as New York City mayor de Blasio's PACE plan for more psychiatrists at Rikers mentioned above, these patterns of mayhem by agents of the state against the state's most abject citizens continue as though the perpetrators are convinced that they are acting with impunity. Thus far, this assumption is largely correct.

It seems fitting to conclude this tour of atrocity with a stop in California, where the deinstitutionalization fiasco of the early '60s begat the scourge of homeless and vulnerable mentally ill people, which in turn begat prisons as "the basket into which society drops the disruptive mentally ill."

In April 2014, the Federal District Court judge Lawrence K. Karlton reviewed the policies and practices employed by the state's Department of Corrections and Rehabilitation in dealing with mentally ill inmates, who make up 28 percent of the system's population. The policies and practices included a profligate overuse of Tasers, pepper spray, forcible extraction from cells, and recourse to solitary confinement.

Judge Karlton issued an order ruling that these practices were unconstitutional.

11

The Great Unraveler

The 1960s, a decade of political explosion and social splintering, witnessed one masterful engineering project that has not received its due respect. That project involved the road to hell, which was thoroughly repaved with good intentions.

If America's social fabric was frayed by the idealistic revolutions of the '60s, the subnation of the mentally ill was virtually dismembered. Its self-assured "rescuers" arrived in three distinct yet interrelated waves. One wave, actually a one-man tsunami, delivered a lingering wash of denunciation against psychiatry. Another wave, a joint production of laboratory science and marketing, drenched society with "wonder" medications guaranteed to make the mentally ill tractable and sociable, whose manufacturers and advocates promised would spell the obsolescence of traditional psychiatry—and nearly did. The merits and menace contained within these drugs remain under fierce debate to this day.

The third wave, its crest ridden by myopic politicians and cynical bureaucrats, achieved a bungled liberation of the mentally ill. It sent hundreds of thousands of patients streaming from the imperfect custody of state-run asylums and into the fickle mercies of the nation at large with wonder-drug prescriptions in their pockets and purses, on the complacent assumption that small care centers and the new meds would make everything just fine. The small care centers and the new meds didn't. Instead, and counter to the American myth of "progress," the three waves combined to touch off more than a half-century of crisis in American mental health care, a crisis unimaginable even in the dark days of lobotomy and genetic experimentation.

The first wave stepped off a steamship in Hoboken, New Jersey, in 1938, with his brother at his side.

Thomas Szasz was one among a scattering of Eastern European Jews who had managed to get out of Hungary ahead of the Nazi *Wehrmacht* and the eruption of World War II. Adolf Hitler's regime was just then pulling tiny Hungary into an alliance with the Axis powers. In 1944 the Nazis would violate this alliance via occupation. German soldiers rounded up some 440,000 Jews and sent them away on trains—most of them to Auschwitz, the remainder to dig trenches on the Austrian border.

Hungary was trapped in a pincers of totalitarianism—a fact that left an imprint on the mind of Thomas Szasz. To its northeast, on the far side of Ukraine, sprawled the vast Soviet Union. And indeed, following its liberation from the Nazis, Hungary suffered occupations by the Russians in 1949 and again in 1956, when the Red Army invaded to crush a revolution. The last Soviet troops left in 1991.

Neither Thomas nor his brother George spoke English when they disembarked at Hoboken. Each was small and lean, with wavy hair, a high forehead, and an air of continental assurance. Their father, Julius, a lawyer and businessman, had secured emigration visas for the family. Julius and his wife, Livy, would shortly join their sons in exile. The family would make its way to Cincinnati, Ohio, where the boys' expatriate uncle Otto was a research professor in mathematics at the University of Cincinnati. George Szasz would attain a PhD in chemistry at the university and live a quietly productive life.

Thomas Szasz taught English to himself in less than a year. He mastered the new and complex language to such a high degree of sophistication and nuance—and occasional sophistry—that intellectuals who had been speaking English all their lives would, in later and more contentious years, shy from engaging him in debate. He read deeply into European and American history, philosophy, psychology, medicine, religion, political science, literature, and linguistics. He remembered what he'd read. He took a degree in physics at the University of Cincinnati and graduated from the medical school in 1944. In his spare time, he refined his grander ambitions until they comprised what would become an assault on American psychiatry and the very notion of mental illness. Thomas Szasz saw in psychiatry the same coercive will to power that fueled the annihilating threats to his native country. He planned to expose its adherents, from Sigmund Freud onward, as mere poseurs—as profit-driven opportunists at best, and, at worst, as para-agents of a governmental state bent on shrinking the civil liberties of its citizens. He intended to mock and proselytize the field of psychiatry out of existence.

Szasz earned a diploma at the Chicago Institute for Psychoanalysis in 1950, at age twenty-nine, and joined its staff. He enlisted in the Navy and was assigned as a psychiatrist at the US Naval Hospital in Bethesda, Maryland, where he found himself repelled by "the dehumanized language of psychiatry and psychoanalysis," as he told his close friend and acolyte, the psychologist Jeffrey Schaler. He took a position as a professor of psychiatry at the Upstate Medical Center of the State University of New York in Syracuse, where he remained until he retired in 1990. He taught psychiatry, he told Schaler, as an atheist might teach theology.

Szasz was to churn out thirty-five books before his death in 2012 at age ninety-two, but none matched the bombastic influence of *The Myth of Mental Illness*, published in 1961. The book, which nearly cost him his tenured position at Syracuse, declared that what people called "mental illness" was simply a range of behavioral choices that others found annoying or threatening. Mental illness was the stuff of metaphor, given that "the mind" was itself a metaphor. Therapeutic psychiatry was nothing more than "an arm of the coercive apparatus of the state."[1]

He challenged the very psychomedical establishment—just then emerging from the dark ages of asylums, lobotomies, and the wholesale application of electroshock therapy—and avowed that "all of medicine threatens to become transformed from personal therapy into political tyranny."[2] Hospitalizing a person in the midst of psychosis against his or her will, said Szasz, was a gross violation of civil and human rights, and amounted to a crime against humanity. In fact, it was worse than that: "Involuntary mental hospitalization is like slavery. Refining the standards for commitment is like prettifying the slave plantation. The problem is not how to improve commitment, but how to abolish it." Ditto for medicating a psychotic patient without consent. Hysteria (an important early subject of Freud's interest) was for Szasz hardly a symptom of madness; it was merely a form of communication, a "non-discursive language," and need not be diagnosed. The unconscious, a cornerstone of Freud's great fame, did not exist: Freud and his disciples invented it as a metaphoric explanation for why people could not remember traumatic events in their lives. Nor did the United States government have a right to prohibit illegal drugs, according to Szasz. It was prescription "psychotropic" medications that needed banishing; as Szasz expounded in a later book, *The Medicalization of Everyday Life*, "The dogmatic view that mental diseases are brain diseases, treatable with chemicals, dehumanizes the…patients."

Regardless of our evaluation of Szasz's assertions—and evaluations have been legion, both pro and con—it remains impossible to dismiss them, even nearly sixty years after they first appeared. In spite of the persistence of the mental illness establishment and the evidence that people get depressed or manic or suffer delusions and cannot connect with others in a consistent and loving way, Szasz's indictments of psychiatry and of the definitions of mental illness have knocked over pillar after pillar of received truth, as well as some pillars of actual truth. They have worked their way into public policy and into the fabric of mental health opinion and mental health care debate. A United States Supreme Court decision in 1975 established that involuntary hospitalization and treatment violate an individual's civil rights. It now generally requires a court order—and a waiting period of days or weeks, and sometimes months—before doctors can enforce the treatment of a patient in psychosis who resists receiving care. As recently as the summer of 2015, the governor of Texas vetoed a bill passed with bipartisan support that would have allowed hospitals to detain a patient in psychosis for a brief period, until law enforcement officers could arrive and determine whether the patient was a danger to himself or others. The governor acted on the advice of several lobbying groups dedicated to the conviction that mental illness does not exist, and he explained that his veto was an effort to protect patients' civil liberties.

The most powerful group among the advisers was the Citizens Commission on Human Rights (CCHR), formed in 1969 by Szasz and L. Ron Hubbard, another mental illness denier and the founder of the Church of Scientology. Hubbard was a science-fiction writer and a believer that when human beings die, flying saucers transport them to Venus, where the locals retool them like so many extraterrestrial Mr. Goodwrenches and send them packing back to earth, where they are dumped into the Pacific Ocean, wading ashore on the California coast to go looking for new human bodies. Hubbard's theory has yet to undergo peer review so far as it is known, but if it is true, it might explain a few things about Californians.

In the 1950s and 1960s, Szasz's ideas gave form and substance to a crystallizing "antipsychiatry" movement, a loose yet enduring affiliation of citizen groups in every state dedicated to the abolition of involuntary mental health care. CCHR quickly formed international branches as well as associations. These groups included many former and current schizophrenia patients who found in Szasz a rare voice that explained to the world how they felt about themselves and the crushing diagnoses imposed upon them. Small in absolute numbers, over the last fifty years these groups have been highly effective in legislative hearings around bills such as the Texas measure—and often influence their outcome.

Besides promising to curb the "abuse" of psychiatric patients and offer them "consumer protection," the CCHR in recent years has pushed the claim that a category of high-selling "second-generation" psychotropic drugs—such as Abilify, Risperdal, and Zyprexa, all marketed for the treatment of schizophrenia and bipolar disorder—is partly responsible for the depravities of school shooters, mass murderers, and terrorists. Rather than ameliorating the symptoms of mental patients who might become violent, these drugs impel people into violent acts—at least according to the latest generation of Szasz's acolytes. This position, to say the least, seems inconsistent with the Szaszian notion that mind-altering drugs of other sorts—hallucinogens, for example—should be freely available to everyone. But then, Thomas Szasz was an elusive thinker.

Much of the support for the antipsychiatry movement has come from people who have been themselves diagnosed with schizophrenia—or who have not been diagnosed but might have symptoms of the disease—and found in the movement a ratification of their own beliefs, which had previously been hard for them to articulate. They got further reinforcement from disaffected members of the psychiatric profession, such as the charismatic New Age Scotsman R. D. Laing, who had been a psychiatrist in the British army when he developed a fascination for talking with disturbed patients. This led him to a philosophy expressed in his most famous work, *The Divided Self*, written when he was thirty and published in 1960, just a year before Szasz's *Myth of Mental Illness*. Laing famously proclaimed that what society calls psychosis is in fact a bursting-free from the "false self" that individuals construct in order to survive under the world's coercive, repressive norms. He had a gift for provocative, often gnomic aphorisms ("Insanity: a perfectly rational adjustment to an insane world"; "Life is a sexually transmitted disease, and the mortality rate is one hundred percent").

As the 1960s progressed, a coalescing counterculture greeted Laing's emergence with unquestioning glee; it is possible that had he not been swept up in the adulation, his supple intellect might have produced deeper, more profound works. Young refugees from the 1950s avid for any ideas that attacked settled wisdom and authority also lionized the French philosopher and "militant intellectual" Michel Foucault. Foucault had already published *Madness and Civilization*, which challenged the social construction of madness and posited "rationality" as a pretext for confining and punishing undesirable people.

It was soon clear that Szasz had drilled into a gusher. Though his early groundswell of endorsements came mostly from the ideological left, Szasz himself was anything but a bleeding heart. "I'm as far right as you can go," he remarked. He dismissed Laing as "a preacher of and for the soft underbelly of the New Left." Before his death, Szasz had supplanted Karl Menninger, the Kansas-born doctor who had Americanized psychiatry in the 1950s and made it safe for the home folks, as the most famous psychiatrist in the world.

Szasz was perfectly equipped to spearhead a one-man revolt against the orthodoxies of psychiatry, which by the 1950s (and in spite of much American suspicion that it was either pointy-headed European hogwash or just an excuse for having as much sex as you want) had finally struggled to the legitimacy and status—and power—that it had craved since Freud's visit to the United States in 1909. Psychiatry's prestige was never quite the same after Szasz's insurrection. "Mental illness" never again went unchallenged as an explanation for human behavior.

A solicitous friend to those in his circle, scrupulous and polite in responding to readers who wrote to him, Szasz transformed himself into a stinging force of nature in debate or at the keys of a typewriter. No barrage of argumentation could sway him from his adamantly crafted line of reasoning, which again and again equated efforts to reach people in psychosis, particularly government-supported efforts, with the menace of state-sponsored coercion.

He had a whimsical side, and he enjoyed constructing aphorisms, as did Laing. Szasz's were deadlier. "If you talk to God, you are praying. If God talks to you, you have schizophrenia," he famously quipped. And, "Formerly, when religion was strong and science weak, men mistook magic for medicine; now, when science is strong and religion weak, men mistake medicine for magic."

Szasz's analogies were equally caustic, and effective. He used analogy in ways that too often substituted for proof. He likened psychiatry to alchemy and astrology. The Inquisition was to heresy as psychiatry is to mental illness. Therapeutism recapitulates paternalism. Psychiatry is medicalization. Psychoanalysis is medicalization squared.

And then there was his reliance on pronunciamento: the flat assertion, delivered without expectation of rebuttal, and usually without substantiation, that

> suicide is a fundamental human right. This does not mean that it is desirable. It only means that society does not have the moral right to interfere, by force, with a person's decision to commit this act. The result is a far-reaching infantilization and dehumanization of the suicidal person.

And: "Psychiatry is probably the single most destructive force that has affected the society within the last sixty years." World War II apparently had slipped his mind.

And, most descriptively of his abiding philosophy:

> The more aggressively I reminded psychiatrists that individuals incarcerated in mental hospitals are deprived of liberty, the more zealously they insisted that "mental illnesses are like other illnesses" and that psychiatric institutions are bona fide medical hospitals. The psychiatric establishment's defense of coercions and excuses thus reinforced my argument about the metaphorical nature of mental illness and importance of the distinction between coerced and consensual psychiatry.[3]

Declarations such as these carry the whiff of absolutism, a hallmark of the same totalitarian political regimes that Szasz abhorred—and apparently feared might prevail in the United States. His untiring attacks on psychiatry—books, papers, lectures—are peppered with phrases and terms such as "coercive" (a favorite), "violent," "wicked" (to describe the aims of the medical ethicist Peter Singer, for instance), "agents of the state" (to describe medical doctors), and "therapeutic ideology," which seems to imply that Szasz himself was a neutral broker, not beholden to ideology. He was beholden, and the ideology was libertarian.

His adherents worshipped him, and the surviving ones still do.

Jeffrey Schaler, a gray-bearded, burly, and soulful man, a psychologist and teacher himself, has spent the last thirty-odd years of his life upholding his mentor's ideas in talks, books, and websites. If Szasz were Don Quixote, the gentle Schaler was his Sancho Panza.

For Schaler and others, qualifying one's understanding of Szasz, or merely attempting to explain him, seems always to require a line of reasoning that can strike the layperson as convoluted. "Thomas Szasz is not opposed to psychiatry," Schaler has said. "He is opposed to what is done to people in the name of psychiatry. He has always differentiated between crazy persons and those labeled by psychiatrists and politicians as 'mentally ill.' He does not deny that people do very strange things for even stranger reasons: He refutes that people do strange things because they are sick. He denies they lack free will."[4] This statement starts off on solid ground—Szasz is opposed to what is done to people in the name of psychiatry—but then veers into the marshlands of vagueness, seeming self-contradiction, and unanswered questions. What, exactly, is a "crazy person" if mental illness does not exist? What are some of those "stranger reasons" for strange behavior? And why do those "stranger reasons" categorically exclude "sickness"? And why is "free will" an issue if the psychotic person, by her own compass, is acting in free will?

Or consider this statement by another of Szasz's adherents:

Many psychiatrists to this day believe that Szasz denies that mental illness exists and even denies that mental suffering and disturbance exist. On the contrary, Szasz does not deny the existence of suffering. How foolish for anyone to think so. Szasz acknowledges the existence of mental illness, but differs from the conventional view of it. The critical point is that mental illness is not a disease that exists in people, as pneumonia exists in lung tissue. Mental illness is, rather, a name, a label, a socially useful fiction, which is ascribed to certain people who suffer or whose behavior is disturbing to themselves or others.[5]

So, Szasz "acknowledges the existence of mental illness," but only as "a socially useful fiction." That seems a long way from acknowledging "the existence of mental illness" but simply differing "from the conventional view of it." If certain people "suffer," and they're not suffering from insanity, then what *are* they suffering from?

Early in his career, Szasz relied heavily on his "lesion" argument for discrediting attacks: while illness and injuries left their traces on or in the body—scars, organ enlargement or shrinkage, cysts, blindness, and so forth—no such irregularities could be ascribed to so-called "mental illness," despite Emil Kraepelin's and Eugen Bleuler's visionary predictions from a century earlier. This was because, for Szasz, mental illness was a metaphor, and an illegitimate one at that. As for lesions in the brain—well, that was called "brain injury," and was in the province of neurosurgery, not "mind-healers."

But from the 1980s onward, a series of dramatic advances—various types of magnetic resonance imaging (the MRI scan); positron-emission tomography (the PET scan); and computerized axial tomography (the CAT scan)—did make it possible for researchers to identify, in living human bodies, such persuasive lesion evidence as enlarged ventricles in the brains of schizophrenic patients. As Paul Harrison, professor of psychiatry, editor, writer, and head of the Translational Neurobiology Group at the University of Oxford, wrote in 2015:

> Despite the many controversies and contradictions, there are now established facts about the neuropathology of schizophrenia. The disorder is associated with ventricular enlargement and decreased cortical volume. The pathology is neither focal nor uniform, being most convincingly demonstrated in the hippocampus, prefrontal cortex and dorsal thalamus. The pattern of abnormalities is suggestive of a disturbance of connectivity within and between these regions, most likely originating during brain development.[6]

A trio of researchers at the Harvard Medical School reported in 2010:

Between 1984 and the present there has been a burgeoning of MRI studies in schizophrenia. Further, during this 26-year time period there are more definitive findings with respect to brain abnormalities in schizophrenia than have been documented in any previous time period in the history of schizophrenia research.[7]

So, did the advent of brain-scanning technology and its findings move Szasz to concede that schizophrenia lesions did in fact exist—and thus, so did mental illness? Not really. "The evidence is not scientifically compelling," he insisted late in his life. "And if it were, then these patients should be described as having brain diseases, not 'mental illnesses,' and should be treated accordingly. Neurologists don't accept the 'mental illness' model"—though they do, as Harrison and the others quoted above affirm, by their use of the very term "schizophrenia"—"so psychiatrists try to invent 'neuropsychiatry.' Most of the brain correlates of psychopathology are descriptive, not explanatory, and give no evidence of causation. There is also much inconsistency entailing false positives and false negatives."

Among the most unsparing critics of Szasz has been Rael Jean Isaac, who herself has written for many libertarian publications and a number of books both supportive and critical of libertarian ideas. Writing several days after the psychiatrist's death, Isaac rebuked Szasz's contributions with cold-eyed clarity: "Szasz serves as a powerful testament to the proposition that ideas have consequences—and that terrible ideas, no matter how demonstrably false and even absurd, can not only survive, but shape our institutions, in the process doing untold damage to human lives and the social fabric."[8]

But what if Isaac and every other detractor has been misinterpreting Szasz? And what if that universal misinterpretation has been a key to his extraordinary legacy?

The American literary critic Alfred Kazin once wrote of Ralph Waldo Emerson that he "was always to have a positive effect on people who did not know what he was talking about."[9] Change the word *positive* to *powerful*, and you just might have Thomas Szasz. As one reads through the voluminous inventory of Szaszian criticism, it can begin to seem that no one understood him—not his detractors, and not his admirers. It can further seem that this very opacity of his fed a great deal of the intellectual clashes over his work.

History has certainly provided other examples of how people can project their own meanings onto abstruse texts. Reading his works, I sometimes felt that Szasz was attacking not psychiatry, or even "mental illness," so much as he was attacking language itself. Viewed from this angle, Szasz might have had less in common with the diagnostics of mental illness than he did with the approaching era (roughly, the 1980s) of post-structuralism and deconstructionism.*

Szasz himself made several statements during his career that seem to bear this out. He offered a couple of them early on, as brief asides, in his introduction to *The Myth of Mental Illness*:

A psychiatry based on and using the methods of communication analysis has actually much in common with the disciplines concerned with the study of languages and communicative behavior, such as symbolic logic, semiotics [the science of signs], semantics, and philosophy.

And, even more explicitly:

My writings form no part of either psychiatry or antipsychiatry, and belong to neither. They belong to conceptual analysis, social-political criticism, civil liberties, and common sense.[10]

---

* Post-structuralism, among its many other applications, interrogates language for its inability to convey truth, and for its concealment of power hierarchies. Deconstructionism, actually conceived in the 1960s by Jacques Derrida but not influential in the United States until the 1980s, seeks to discover ideological biases in traditional language.

What comfort is this, then, to the countless sufferers of mental illness, most of whom in the acute stages of their disorder are demonstrably bereft of self-awareness and self-control, who have been left to survive as best they can on their own, their symptoms untreated and their blurry impulses unchecked by the courts, hospitals, psychiatrists, or law enforcement officers? What of the lengthening list of sufferers who have been shot dead by officers who saw their movements as threatening and had no training in the restraint of people in psychosis—in part because such training has been deemed unnecessary, given that "psychosis" is a "myth"?

Szasz's impact was well and bitterly recognized by those in the profession he despised. Lawrence Hartmann, a former president of the American Psychiatric Association, remarked in 1992, after Szasz's retirement: "He gave patients the opportunity to deny they were sick, and he gave legislators the opportunity to deny they were responsible."[11] And writing in 2001, the psychiatric researcher and author E. Fuller Torrey declared:

> The major reason...why increasing insanity became a non-issue in the latter half of the twentieth century was the emergence of historical theories that appeared to negate it. If there had been any hope of seriously examining the question of epidemic insanity, that hope died in 1961 with the publication of three books: Michel Foucault's... *Madness and Civilization*, Thomas Szasz's *The Myth of Mental Illness*, and Erving Goffman's *Asylums*.[12]

It is true enough (as we have seen, and will see again) that the mental institutions of Szasz's early career—and many throughout his life—were hardly the answer to the care of the mentally ill, shot through as they were with filth, neglect, starvation, ignorance, and outright sadism. No one, not even Szasz himself, drove these truthful images into the nation's perception as forcefully as did a novel published a year after *The Myth of Mental Illness* and the movie adaptation of it that followed thirteen years later.

One Flew Over the Cuckoo's Nest, Ken Kesey's scathing novel of sadistic abuse and brutalization inside an Oregon insane asylum, became an international best seller when it appeared in 1962. (Kesey had not read *The Myth of Mental Illness* before writing his novel, but he and Szasz later corresponded with mutual admiration.) The book's effect grew exponentially with the film version released in 1975, in which Jack Nicholson gave a virtuoso performance as "Mac" McMurphy, an inmate who throws himself between his fellow patients and the totalitarian cruelty of Nurse Ratched, played by Louise Fletcher. *One Flew Over the Cuckoo's Nest* swept the major Academy Awards, winning Best Picture, Best Director (Milos Forman), Best Actor, Best Actress, and Best Adapted Screenplay— only the third American film ever to claim that array of awards.

Thus the potent cocktail of Szasz's denunciatory book, Forman's cinematic fireworks display, and the fiery antiauthoritarian mood of the culture in general succeeded in damning psychiatry to a hell from which it has never entirely emerged. The new antipsychiatry movement also powerfully reinforced the conviction held, especially but not exclusively by the political right, that imposing medications or restraints on anyone going through a psychotic episode was a categorical violation of civil rights.

And now consider the story of a couple I know personally, Livy and Frank McClellan and their son Martin, a rare victim of pediatric, or "child-onset," schizophrenia. (I have changed their names, and I have not met Martin.)

Livy is a slim, handsome woman in her sixties who wears her graying red hair piled atop her head. Three decades of virtually nonstop anxiety over her son have given her a hyperintense manner. She speaks rapidly yet in perfectly formed sentences. Her husband, Frank, a husky businessman, is agreeable and more laid back, yet clearly depleted by the recurring crises surrounding Martin since his childhood.

Martin, who turned thirty-one the summer of 2016, is a walking casebook of nearly everything that can go wrong for a person with schizophrenia in this country. Since childhood, Martin has suffered from the failure of child psychiatrists to recognize certain subtle but critical symptoms in early-phase schizophrenia; the rigidities of a misguided legal system; the helplessness of legally and financially compromised care systems on the level of the US state; the catch-22 legal idiocy that prevents people from receiving medical care until they become "an imminent danger" to themselves or others (a condition they frequently demonstrate via actualizing some imminent danger or another); prolonged waits for treatment in hospitals without medication; and, ultimately, being prosecuted as a criminal. Any of these blows would be enough to aggravate, rather than heal, the cruelty of schizophrenia itself. In their aggregate, these systemic failures embody the continuing, jumbled, post-Szaszian atrocity that our society calls "mental health care."

As is the case with countless parents of children with schizophrenia, Livy's life in many ways has merged with Martin's. Her waking and sleeping hours, often jumbled together, are filled with thoughts for his safety and fears of his possible actions, with accompanying visits to courtrooms and hospitals, legal advocacy at various hearings, and her volunteer work for the National Alliance on Mental Illness.

None of Livy's efforts on behalf of her son have produced improvement in Martin's condition beyond the medical prescriptions she and his inpatient psychiatrists have wrung from hospitals in the state, which Martin can be convinced to take only sporadically, and the safe harbor she and Frank have created for him, thanks to a small apartment on the farmhouse grounds. His future remains devoid of much possibility beyond just existing.

Yet Livy's efforts have produced results in one respect: they have made her enemies. Because of her intensity and her untiring advocacy, Livy has often felt the sting of harsh criticism and vituperation from people associated with antipsychiatry, and the pointed, supercilious indifference of most state political figures from whom she has sought help for her son and others with mental illness.

"Martin's signs and symptoms, in retrospect, became manifest in his early childhood," Livy told me on one of my visits to the McClellan house. "He showed physical aggression toward other children by age one. He'd hit them for no reason—though he was never spanked or hit by either of us." The young child was irritable; worse, he progressively lost empathy toward other people. (However, he was uncommonly tender toward animals and even insects.) He grew paranoid, blaming others for his problems and things that went wrong. "For example, if he couldn't find something, he'd say that another family member took it," Livy said. "By mid–elementary school he thought teachers and other children and family were trying to harm him. He was verbally hostile and unkind to others, including my mother. He called her a murderer when she killed an ant."

Terrifyingly for his parents, the child developed what his mother at first called "the Evil Eye." (When she and Frank came to understand his affliction, Livy changed that designation to "the Stare.") She later learned that such a gaze is a common symptom for those with schizophrenia. From around age six on, Martin rarely seemed happy. In the years leading up to his eighteenth birthday, he was verbally fluent, "but he would rant on and on, often not making sense, and usually angry and hostile." He hated loud noise and the scratch of tags on shirt collars. He could not perceive extreme cold, and he went outside in winter without a coat or gloves. He slept through the day and was active at night.

When Martin began exhibiting these reactions and behaviors, Livy took him to a child psychiatrist and recounted his symptoms to her. The woman listened, then asked Martin's mother whether her son had reported hallucinations. When Livy said no, the doctor concluded that he was not schizophrenic. Livy's next visit was to a child psychologist, who agreed that "something is terribly wrong," and wondered about Asperger's syndrome, an autism-spectrum disorder that afflicts children. This consultant tried to get the first psychiatrist to see Martin again, but she refused, insisting he did not need to see a psychiatrist.

Livy took it upon herself to add a working knowledge of schizophrenia to her already thorough physician's education. She believes that her son was negligently or at least imperfectly diagnosed for many crucial years. On his eighteenth birthday, Martin suffered a severe psychotic break and entered the early stages of catatonia. The irony was that this birthday established Martin as a legal adult. Thus, on the same day he finally showed irrefutable evidence that he was in dire need of treatment, he gained the legal status to decide whether any-thing should be done about it, from medications to a hospital stay for treatment. Martin predictably ruled out each option.

"There is no flexibility in the system whatsoever," Livy said. "The eigh-teenth birthday is seen as a definitive line of demarcation between a child brain and an adult brain. This cutoff was intended, I suspect, to allow for the drafting of males" into the military, "as soon as they are of full adult physical stature regardless of mental development. We could not get him appropriate medical care until he became 'an imminent danger,'" Livy repeated bitterly. "By the time he proved it, he'd been psychotic for about three years at a minimum. There is evidence that duration of untreated psychosis [DUP] does have a bad effect on long-term outcomes." To risk oversimplification, the schizophrenia entrenches itself ever more deeply.

"So Martin is an example of how care is in essence denied for years to someone so brain-diseased they don't even know they're diseased— denied for years under the guise of 'civil liberties.'" Livy paused to take a deep breath before continuing, "Our system has failed to face the fact that when schizophrenia has done this to a person's brain, it has *already robbed him* of that liberty. Our society needs more adult pro-fessionals to help these people, and protect them, not let them roam 'free' until they are jailed for their behavior."

Martin's catatonia was contained, but he was far from healed. In 2006, at age twenty, his mother said, the affliction caused him to commit crimes, including felonies. "He broke through glass into the office of a former employer and did thousands of dollars of damage," Livy said. "Then he left, bleeding from several lacerations, and tried to hijack a car by trying to strangle the driver, who mercifully escaped. I think this was during an 'excited' phase of his catatonic state."

Police arrested Martin and transported him to the emergency room at a nearby hospital that was associated with a medical school. At first he was combative, but shortly he fell into a catatonic stupor. When he regained consciousness after a few hours, he could barely speak or move. His parents gave him water and he was put in a wheelchair and transferred to the local jail without treatment. Livy called the jail several times and provided the relevant medical history. Only when he attacked a guard did the jail transfer him to the state psychiatric hospital. After several criminal hearings, which added to Martin's psychic agonies, Livy was able to find a private lawyer who convinced the prosecutor that because of his insanity, Martin was not guilty of the charges leveled against him.

The lawyer was able to keep Livy's son out of jail. But nothing, Livy feels, could undo the damage to his brain that resulted from his long stretches without medication. "The literature indicating that there can be toxic effects of protracted untreated psychosis on the brain concerns me," Livy said.* "For the most part Martin has barely been able to

---

* One study appeared as an editorial in the *American Journal of Psychiatry* in November 2000. It was written by Jeffrey A. Lieberman, who is director of the New York State Psychiatric Institute among many other affiliations, and the late Wayne S. Fenton, who was an associate director of the National Institute for Mental Health, and a psychiatrist well known for his courage in dealing with severely psychotic and often dangerous patients. On September 3, 2006, Dr. Fenton, fifty-three, was found dead in his suburban Washington office, having been fatally beaten by a nineteen-year-old patient whom the doctor had been counseling to resume his antipsychotic medications.

Lieberman and Fenton's study had drawn the following conclusions, among others: "If patients are treated promptly and effectively, good outcomes can be achieved. However, these same studies have revealed that throughout the world, individuals suffering a first episode of psychosis experience an alarming delay between the onset of psychotic symptoms and the initiation of treatment. More than 10 studies conducted on several continents have described typical durations of untreated psychosis that average 1–2 years."

While acknowledging new studies that cast doubt upon a prevailing belief that prolonged untreated psychosis inevitably results in "measurable neurotoxicity and lifelong disability," the authors continued:

Undiagnosed and untreated psychosis imposes a significant burden of terror, suffering, and bewilderment on patients and their families. Impairments in functioning that accompany untreated psychosis wreak havoc on the normative processes of young adult development. The maturational tasks of establishing and maintaining a peer group, achieving independence from family, cultivating romantic interests, acquiring independent living skills, and preparing for productive work may all be disrupted at a most critical stage of development. These disruptions too often alter the trajectory of a young person's life in a way that is not easily repaired. In addition, an untreated person with psychosis is at risk for episodes of behavioral dyscontrol, including violence, with the potential for long-lasting consequences for himself or herself and others.

mutter for years. He cannot advocate for himself. We must do that for him." Martin has been hospitalized seventeen times as of this writing. In several of those admissions, he waited from sixty to eighty-eight days for involuntary treatment. The hospitalization that started with the eighty-eight-day wait lasted a year and a half.

To judge from Livy's account, the network of courts, psychiatric hospitals, and law enforcement agencies that dealt with her son has done its collective best to keep Martin in full possession of his rights since his affliction was first diagnosed. Livy and Frank live with the galling belief that their son's protracted suffering, and worsening condition, is due in part to a court system that for decades has been buffeted by the conflicting claims of psychiatric professionals on the one hand and, on the other, the hypervigilant mental health deniers and civil libertarians who often seem more concerned with sustaining an ideology than with relieving the suffering of those in psychosis.

Martin remained mired in a catatonic state for several months, enjoying his rights somewhere in the deep woods around his rural home. His physician mother fears that he is approaching malignant, or lethal, catatonia.

Thomas Szasz's personal life and relationships, while undoubtedly circumspect, are generally not discussed by surviving friends. It is easy to assume that he scarcely had a private life apart from his writing, teaching, talks, debates, and interviews.

In 1951 he had married a Lebanese woman named Rosine Loshkajan, whom he mentioned once in his autobiographical writings. She bore him two daughters. Szasz and Rosine were divorced in 1970. Rosine died by suicide in a motel the following year. Schaler believes that it was Szasz's skyrocketing notoriety that "pushed Rosine over the edge."

Thomas Szasz died in 2012 after a fall down a staircase. The coroner ruled it a result of a severe injury to his spine. The direct cause of his death, according to the Kaddish delivered by Jeffrey Schaler, was suicide.

12

Surcease

The prodromal stage of Dean's schizophrenia, I believe, was triggered by the sustained trauma of the accident and the pressures he absorbed in its brutal aftermath. Prodromal investigation has a relatively short history in studies of chronic mental illness, dating for the most part to the early 1990s. *Prodrome* is from the Greek meaning "running ahead of"; and in neuroscience it bespeaks a shift from focusing exclusively on a cure for schizophrenia—still a hope, yet far from imminent—and toward identifying the early, "subclinical" behavioral signs that psychotic illness lies in a person's future. This identification could lead to early intervention in the disease's progress toward "frank" psychosis and a lessening of the patient's lifelong struggles. As a paper published in 2010 by the National Center for Biotechnology Information explained:

> The prodromal period can last from weeks to several years, and comorbid disorders are very common during this period. The prodrome of schizophrenia and other psychotic disorders is characterized as a process of changes or deterioration in heterogeneous subjective and behavioral symptoms that precede the onset of clinical psychotic symptoms.[1]

On the sunny Tuesday of June 1, 1999, Dean, Honoree, and I climbed the steps of Middlebury's new district courthouse. The bricks of its Queen Anne exterior had retained their bright red sheen three years after its completion, contrasting with the purplish old facades of the surviving nineteenth-century buildings facing Court Street to its west. We entered one of the small hearing rooms and seated ourselves around one of two polished counselor's tables. Above the tables was the judge's elevated desk.

We were there to attend the hearing that would determine, after twelve anxious months, whether our son was to be incarcerated for the rest of his adolescence and the first half of his twenties.

Amy and her family were already seated at the other table. The lawyers for each family were unzipping their briefcases and placing documents on the surface before them.

We all rose as the judge entered the room. He offered a few preliminary remarks and then invited Dean to make a statement. Dean rose from his chair at the counselor's table. His new, forlorn, de rigueur white business shirt was already showing some perspiration stains, and his de rigueur necktie was a bit askew. He leaned forward, balancing his weight on the table with his knuckles. I was loathing this moment: the potted pomp of the judicial seal on the wall and the American flag and of my son's absurd and pointless shirt and tie and of the judge's impassive face; and the scowls from the other table. All of it.

Dean's knuckles trembled on the polished hardwood. I had rarely seen my son afraid, and never this afraid. I wondered whether he could pull himself together. He did. He pushed himself erect, composed his thoughts, and made a brief, dignified speech of regret for his responsibility in the accident and of sympathy for what Amy had gone through. Amy's parents sat with their scowls in place.

Dean finished, and a silence overtook the hearing room. At the other end of that silence—I am sure that Dean understood this—lay his path for the next eight years, which could define the path he would travel for the remainder of his life.

Then I stood up and asked the Court's permission to put my foot in my mouth.

Actually, I asked permission to speak, which amounted to the same thing.

Sanctimonious bloviator that I so often was—am—I thought it would be a good idea to talk about forgiveness. Specifically, I wanted to talk about the healing benefits that forgiving can confer upon the person doing the forgiving. My clarity, or lack of it, didn't matter. As soon as the word *forgiveness* passed my lips, I was interrupted from the family's table with the sharp remonstration: How dare I talk about forgiveness? Dean did not deserve forgiveness! Dean's recklessness had nearly killed...

I sat back down again, wondering if hell was going to be anything like this.

In the seconds of silence that followed, I also wondered whether I had poisoned my son's prospects for a favorable ruling.

The judge interlaced his fingers and studied Dean through his rimless glasses. He was an intense jurist, unreadable as most good judges are, a gaunt man in a black robe, his combed black hair whitening at the sides. He seemed to embody the timeless Yankee moral figure.

"I see hope for this young man," the judge said at length. These were the first words of human respect that any adult with power outside our family had spoken to or about Dean for more than twelve months. I think that the blackness surrounding my son began to crack apart a little just then, although I have never asked him about it. It certainly cracked for Honoree and me.

The judge handed down a sentence of three to eight years in prison for Dean: suspended.

Our son was placed on probation, with conditions that included a fine of twenty-five hundred dollars, five hundred hours of community service, a suspension of driving privileges for one year, the completion of five weekends on the Addison County work crew by the end of the summer, the continuation of his house arrest for a year, and various smaller fines.

And so Dean's long road back from perdition commenced.

Case closed.

But not Dean's sense of being swept away helplessly in the river of his life.

It was Honoree who pulled Dean out of that river and saved him from being swept away forever.

Honoree never gave up on her faith that eventually the Vermont justice system would listen to a plea that her son's punishment be tempered by mercy, or at least by common sense. Never one to be rattled in a crisis, she understood the importance of timing and patience. She believed that it would not be in Dean's interests to make the request she had in mind when the community's opinion might still be tilted against him by the shamefully misleading posters around town and by the predatory interest of WCAX TV news, with its blinding censorious lights in the courtroom and its mulish insistence on referring to Dean as a "drunk" (on his "own booze," which, as hearing transcripts show, was one bottle of beer). She waited until the WCAX TV news reporters and crews lost interest in the case and went off to find other stories that would allow them to broadcast the same kind of insinuating questions they'd posed in Dean's case, such as "If you hold a party and someone gets drunk—on their own booze—are you responsible for any harm they may cause?"

Honoree waited as long as possible, given that the school year would soon commence, and then went quietly back to work on Dean's behalf. She insisted to our lawyer that he petition the judge with a plea that our son be allowed to enroll that fall for a postgraduate year at a college preparatory school, instead of remaining confined for the duration of his house arrest sentence. Amy's parents were present at the hearing on this petition. Her father argued vigorously against lifting Dean's restraints and giving him a new chance in a new place. "He can find plenty of opportunities right in his own backyard!" this man declared to the judge. Several times I have often wondered whether he heard the irony in his words. Dean had paced in his backyard for nearly a year as opportunities in the larger world floated past, out of his reach.

The judge set aside the parents' objections. He granted our petition that he terminate Dean's house arrest and allow him to enroll in school in Maine.

And so our son resumed the life of his young, battered, and overstressed mind.

* * *

Dean's case may have been resolved, with the hope of starting over, but our own trials were to continue. Back in March, in an attempt at reconciliation before Dean's sentencing, I'd written a letter to the family, asking for a meeting, perhaps mediated by a counselor, where all of us could begin the work of healing. I thought a meeting like this would help both Amy and Dean recover from the physical and psychic trials. Dean spoke many times of his wish to "atone" to Amy, her mother, and her father. The family did not respond to my letter. Instead, on a hot summer afternoon shortly after the judge altered the terms of our son's sentence, I was mowing the steep bank of lawn in front of our house when I turned to see a white sheriff's car crawling up our driveway. The sheriff was staring out the window at me through his sunglasses. I killed the lawn mower, wiped the sweat off my forehead, and stutter-stepped down the bank to the patrol car. The sweet aroma of the wet cut grass trailed me.

I had a feeling of what this was about. We'd picked up on the possibility from our lawyer, although—naive to the end—I refused to believe that this would really happen. More than a year of criminal court penalties and out-of-court maneuvering from Amy's family surely were enough—especially given the psychological toll extracted from both young people.

The sheriff stretched his arm through the open window. He was holding a thick envelope.

"I'm sorry." He seemed genuinely embarrassed.

"I understand," I said. "You're doing your job."

He nodded and backed down the driveway.

I opened the packet. Inside was the notice of a civil suit filed against Honoree and me by Amy's parents. The suit sought to establish criminal negligence on our part, for allowing our "reckless"-driving son to have Honoree's car that night. The suit would consume three more years of our lives.

Amy's parents' lawyer hired an investigator who canvassed households in neighborhoods inhabited by the parents of Dean's friends, interviewing them for evidence and testimony that Honoree and I had been negligent parents. After the interviews came the depositions. The lawyer deposed roughly the same pool of people, many of whom were or had been social friends of ours.

And then the lawyer deposed Honoree and me.

In November 2003, the family withdrew its suit, citing lack of evidence. Yet the case never disappeared. Traces of it have lingered in cyberspace ever since. When anyone seeking information on Honoree's scientific career types her name into Google, the first link that appears is to a document bearing her name. The document has nothing to do with her nearly half century of scientific accomplishments. It is a Vermont Supreme Court judgment on some procedural fine points in the misbegotten civil suit that bears this good woman's name.

Amy recovered from her injuries. We understood that her restoration to health required weeks upon weeks of painful, disciplined rehabilitation, encouraged and supervised by her parents. Amy had been a promising school basketball player, and her conditioning surely worked in her favor. By all accounts, she remained courageous and cheerful through her ordeal. A few years later, she married and started a family.

Founded in 1835, the Gould Academy is a small, redbricked, right-angled school in Bethel, a town of two thousand people and as many maple trees in western Maine, near the Androscoggin River and the White Mountain National Forest. Its academic standards are high, and so are its tuition and board. The administrators at Gould were dubious about Dean's application because of the felony conviction on his record. (I'd glimpsed Dean's application letter as he wrote it, just long enough to read the poignant sentence "I am not aggressive.") Again, Honoree refused to surrender the field. She telephoned the academy's headmaster, William P. Clough III, and talked him into a meeting in his office with herself and Dean. They drove the nearly four-hour route due east to Bethel. Like the judge, Headmaster Clough heard and saw gravitas, intelligence, and sincerity in the young man seated opposite him, and in the young man's mother. He welcomed Dean into the student body.

A couple of emails from me to Dean that fall give a suggestion of how things were going for him:

Subject: **your great grades**
Date: Thu, 02 Dec 1999 12:05:45 -0500
From: Ron Powers <ropo@sover.net>
To: Dean Powers <junior_304@hotmail.com>
Dean,

Mom just guided me into the Gould page that lists your tremendous grades and your Honors Student status. The physics and calculus scores are stupendous, but then everything is. Congratulations and keep up the outstanding work. With this on your record, there is no limit to what you can accomplish in college. If you don't watch out, you might even turn into a goddam intellectual. If you feel that coming on, head for the woods.*

Dad

Subject: **more congratulations**
Date: Thu, 02 Dec 1999 20:01:20 -0500
From: Ron Powers <ropo@sover.net>
To: Dean Powers <junior_304@hotmail.com>
Dean,

Mom figured how to code into your personal evaluations for each of your classes. She brought them home tonight and we read them (and re-read them) over dinner. Beyond spectacular. They really appreciate you there, and their praise is stunning. I never heard anything like that during the whole time I was getting educated. Couldn't be prouder of you.

Dad

---

* Dean had earlier confessed to me his regret that he probably would "never be an intellectual." It was an insight into the damage done to his self-esteem.

Kevin, meanwhile, was scheduled to enter high school that same fall of 1999. He was just fifteen and vulnerable to any gossip about his brother that might have swirled around town. The previous year, just six months after the car accident, Amy's parents unaccountably had invited Kevin to her sixteenth-birthday party at a local restaurant. Equally unaccountably, we allowed him to go. Maybe we saw the invitation as a gesture toward reconciliation and took the bait. After an hour or so, the telephone rang. It was Kevin, who told Honoree that he was feeling uncomfortable at the party and asked that we come and pick him up. We did.

After that incident, we understood that we needed to get Kevin out of town as well.

A positive motivation was our younger son's progress on the guitar. Over the summer of 1999, he had matured in his passion for the instrument and extended his understanding of what it could do. Besides jamming with Dean and continuing his sessions with his teacher, Michael—by now his fast friend, who'd rather sadly confided to us, "I've taught him everything I know"—he had been taking weekly lessons in Burlington from a legendary player and teacher named Paul Asbell. As a young musician in Chicago, Asbell had played and recorded with Muddy Waters, John Lee Hooker, Howlin' Wolf, Lightnin' Hopkins, and Otis Rush. He had resettled in Vermont, from where he'd traveled to various studios to record with Paul Butterfield, Joshua Redman, and Julian Lage. His tutoring pupils had included Trey Anastasio of Phish.

But Kevin had reached a stage where instruction was not enough. He needed performance experience. In addition to his *DownBeat* awards, he had appeared onstage by now with his heroes, the Woods Tea Company, and at Middlebury's Festival on the Green. Yet these were rare, episodic events. He was ready for regular ensemble playing and soloing, and for instruction across the full range of guitar genres. Vermont, as rich in music as it is, was not able to provide this.

We began looking for music schools. Our first foray had been in early spring, to a prep-level arts academy southwest of Boston. We scheduled a midday appointment with an administration member and arrived in the town the night before. We shared a spectacular pizza, and the next morning we shopped at a mall, where I bought my son a nifty sweater-vest, white with yellow and blue trim, for his interview.

An hour or so later we found ourselves sitting on folding chairs in the center of an immense, dim, and empty performance room, awaiting the admissions official. Kevin wore his new sweater, and he balanced his acoustic guitar on his lap. At length, the metronomic, echoing clomp of her power shoes announced her arrival. She bolted herself into a seat facing us and glowered at her clipboard. She glanced up at us without introducing herself or offering a welcome and launched into a list of reasons why this academy probably would not be "a right fit" for Kevin. It was as though she had no memory of speaking with Kevin's mother and arranging our interview appointment. It was, in fact, as though she suspected us of breaking into the building by picking a lock.

After making it clear that Kevin would enjoy the approximate status of a biblical leper if by some miracle his application were accepted, she invited him to play a demonstration piece.

I turned to look at my son. We were far enough apart that I could see his entire body hunched in his metal chair, a rabbit in the sights of a blunderbuss. His hands were folded on top of his guitar and his feet were locked tightly beneath him, and he was looking at her with his head slightly cocked, as if trying to fathom why this person was being so unfriendly.

As for me, I wanted to grab Kevin and walk out. I wanted to read her out at a decibel level the entire campus would be able to hear, on the matter of her unconscionable assault on a child's nerves and self-respect.

I held back. A confrontation would only serve to mortify Kevin and probably ruin his willingness to risk any more encounters with people from music academies, and thus any opportunity for further training and encouragement.

It hurt me physically, in my stomach, but I kept silent and let it go. Kevin, I noticed, was pale. But he absorbed his guitar into position with that beautiful fluid motion of his, and he began to play.

His brief performance was flawless. It may have lacked the passion and some of the inventiveness and deep interpretation that he routinely poured into his playing, but technically, it was beyond reproach. Kevin seemed to be saying, *There is a level below which you will not intimidate me. You will not violate my dignity.* And it's possible that Kevin was also saying to the woman: *You can't have my passion, either. You're not worthy of it.*

We walked out of that dim building into the early-spring snow and mud, and drove away from that campus knowing we would never go back there, not even if invited, not if it turned out to be our only option. I assured Kevin of that during our rather subdued drive back to Middlebury. My sole concern remained whether Kevin would ever again risk the hostility and the humiliation of another audition with someone from a music academy. I needn't have worried.

A few weeks later the phone rang at our house and a man with a genial voice asked if he could speak to Kevin Powers. After learning who the caller was, I handed the receiver to my younger son, who glanced at me curiously before taking it. Within a few seconds his lopsided grin had broken out. The caller was a guitar instructor at the Interlochen Arts Academy in Traverse City, Michigan, and he had called to tell Kevin that he had been accepted there.

Earlier in the year, Kevin had filled out the Interlochen application we'd obtained for him and sent it back, along with the required two videotapes we had made of him performing solos "of contrasting style." Now he glowed as he told us that the instructor had been very complimentary about his solo work.

Interlochen accepted about 440 students for the 1999–2000 year. Of these, only eleven were guitarists.

We didn't have to ask Kevin whether he wanted to go off to this arts boarding school a third of the way across the country. The answer was all over his face.

That September, I drove Kevin the nine hundred miles to Interlochen. It was a memorable ride. He and I chose a route that took us north to Montreal, then westward on Highway 17 for six hundred miles, skirting Ottawa and then the vast and pristine Algonquin Provincial Park, its primitive interior saturated with lakes and moose. We ate hamburgers at a log-built restaurant and gift shop along the route, which would become our traditional stopping-place on future trips. Traditions were important to both boys, but especially to Kevin. We stopped for the night in a motel in Sudbury, Ontario. At Sault Ste. Marie, we turned south into Michigan along Interstate 75. We crossed the Straits of Mackinac, linking Lakes Michigan and Huron, on the majestic suspended arc of the Mackinac Bridge that stretched five miles.

Kevin was upbeat during the long drive, but he admitted to me that he was worried about meeting new people at the academy. For one thing, he said, he didn't know any good jokes. I told him that jokes could be overrated, and the best way to make new friends was to ask them a lot of questions about themselves. This went for girls, too, I added. Girls especially.

In our Sudbury motel room in Ontario, as I was unpacking toiletries from my suitcase, Kevin was sitting behind me on one of the twin beds. I heard acoustic guitar notes and turned around.

The lamplight brought out the gold in Kevin's hair, and he was in his usual playing position, bent forward a little, head down, the sole of one messy sneaker planted on the arch of the other.

The piece was short, but lyric, and haunting, like a medieval ballad, and as it went on I stopped unpacking and sat down on the bed beside Kevin and listened. When he had finished, and when the quotidian sounds resumed—traffic horns, voices in the hall, TV sounds in other rooms—I asked Kevin where he'd learned it and how long it had taken him to memorize it. He shrugged and said that he'd made it up as he went along. He was just doing some finger exercises.

Some weeks later, walking with him around the Interlochen campus during a visit, I brought it up again. I asked my son if he could reconstruct that piece from memory. He gave an absent shake of his head, his attention on a pretty girl riding a bicycle in and out of the sunlight. A temporary, beautiful, golden thing had passed through that motel room in Ontario that evening, and then vanished, a presence to be experienced only once, and briefly, and then never again.

We reached Traverse City in the sunlit afternoon of the following day. We made our way around the lip of the small city's sparkling harbor dotted with sailboats, and then on a two-lane road out of town past cherry orchards and scrub-pine woods, toward Interlochen. The campus shares its twelve hundred acres with a forest of virgin pine and maple trees about fifteen miles southwest of Traverse City. It is situated between Green and Duck Lakes. Most of its buildings—dormitories; studios; rustic visitors' cabins; adminis- tration buildings; dance, art, concert, and theater performance spaces—are concentrated on a quarter of the acreage. The students walk among the pine and maple trees to get almost anywhere on the campus.

The day was sunny, Green Lake shimmered behind the trees, and children—the young artists—walked and jogged and bicycled the paths, friends halting to squeal and hug one another after a summer away. I worried that Kevin might feel excluded as he watched them, and again, I was wrong: Kevin gave himself at once to Interlochen. He was cheerful as we registered him, met some faculty, and found his room in a trim, low-slung residence hall amid the aromatic pines, and met his new roommate, a simpatico pianist named Jesse. They hit it off right away. I heard no more anxious concerns about telling jokes.

I hugged him close for our good-bye until he gave me a subtle nudge with his hip, and then I turned and got into the van for the journey home. As I shifted out of reverse, I put my arm out the window to give him a final wave, but he didn't see me. He was standing in a cluster of Interlochen boys and girls, and he wore his lopsided grin. He was already commencing the happiest three years of his life.

13

Debacle

On Halloween Day, 1963, President John F. Kennedy signed into law the last bill that would come before him: the Community Mental Health Act. Designed to solve, once and for all, the malingering scourge of decrepit mental asylums and barbarous care, the act provided $150 million over four and a half years to finance a massive experiment in human relocation. The money would be spent on grants to the states for establishing, via new construction or adaptation of existing facilities, community centers for treatment of the mentally ill.

This marked the first attempt by the federal government to take an active role in the care of the insane. The various states would administer their local mental health centers largely autonomous of the federal government, whose role was to lessen the financial burden imposed on the states by providing periodic infusions of money.

That was the plan to which Thomas Szasz's antipsychiatric teachings lent some false legitimacy. It became one of the century's most enduringly disastrous policy experiments for the mentally ill. The program that Kennedy had signed into action came to be known as "deinstitutionalization," a name that carried the lilting harmony of silverware spilling from a cleanup tray. The very sound of the name, with all its bureaucratic syllables, suggested what would be the vast project's overall record of shoddy planning and repeated bungling. The unintended consequences of deinstitutionalization have expanded seemingly beyond restraint. They reverberate strongly into our own time.

The Community Mental Health Act—CMHA—was crafted by a group of psychiatrists and hospital executives brought together by Congress in 1955 as the Joint Commission on Mental Illness and Health. Its members, selected by the American Psychiatric Association and the American Medical Association, were well-meaning professionals, well informed for their time. As history has shown, their time was lacking in critical information and understanding about the nature of the mentally ill and the support they required. As the new law took effect, government-employed psychiatric workers commenced several years of moving about 560,000 patients out of the nation's 279 mostly dingy and overcrowded state-run psychiatric warehouses. The corrections-system bureaucrats fortified most of them with a farewell jolt of the new potion Thorazine, which they seemed to assume would act on the damaged brains the way spinach acted upon Popeye's forearms. Nearly half of the departing patients had been jammed into asylums glutted with more than three thousand patients each. In such conditions, as President Kennedy observed in something of an understatement, "individual care and consideration are almost impossible."

The patients' destination was intended, by contrast, to be a sunlit archipelago: fifteen hundred small, freshly constructed "community health centers" (CHCs) scattered about the country. There, the previously institutionalized mentally ill would flourish (it was confidently imagined) in small-scale environments of clean, well-lighted rooms, healthy food, and the care of trained and sympathetic staff. Most of these patients would be near enough to their homes that they could sleep in a family environment. Their benevolent day care would be a modern iteration of the days of moral treatment, which had propounded psychic equilibrium as essential to mental health.

President Kennedy had recognized the dire state of psychiatric hospitals as an opportunity to extend his agenda of New Frontier accomplishments. His sensitivity toward the mentally ill had almost certainly been sharpened by the plight of his sister Rosemary, who in 1941 became a victim of the Walter Freeman–James Watts lobotomy circus (see chapter 17). Kennedy took the unusual step of folding the two hundred thousand patients suffering "mental retardation" into his announced total of eight hundred thousand mental patients in state institutions whose relocation the act would finance. Many of these, Rosemary perhaps among them, were undiagnosed schizophrenics.

Most decisively, perhaps, the optimistic president and the Joint Commission as well were prodded to action by the supposed curative power of Thorazine. The drug and its successors would transform mental health care, for better and worse, through the decades.

Thorazine made its debut in 1954, a year before the Joint Commission came into being. It is critically important to reiterate that neither this so-called "wonder drug" nor any of its successors "cure" patients of schizophrenia or its kindred afflictions. Their mission is to *stabilize* certain chemical processes in the brain, the regulation of serotonin and dopamine balances, for example, and thus modify the symptoms of the illness. The symptoms stay modified only as long as patients renew their intake of the drugs—stay modified in most cases. As we will see, this fundamental distinction between cure and stabilization was seldom spelled out in the early marketing of the wonder drugs. This obfuscation led a great many mentally ill patients of the period, not to mention their underinformed prescribing psychiatrists (who relied upon salesmen for the products to explain how they worked), to vastly overestimate the drugs' functions and power. It is conceivable that deinstitutionalization might never have taken place had Thorazine not been misperceived as a cure.

Among those who bought into the myth that the wonder drugs were cure-alls was President Kennedy:

I am convinced that, if we apply our medical knowledge and social insights fully, all but a small portion of the mentally ill can eventually achieve a wholesome and constructive social adjustment. It has been demonstrated that 2 out of 3 schizophrenics— our largest category of mentally ill—can be treated and released within 6 months, but under the conditions that prevail today the average stay for schizophrenia is 11 years...It is clear that a concerted national attack on mental disorders is now both possible and practical…We can save public funds and we can conserve our manpower resources.[1]

Three weeks later, John F. Kennedy flew to Dallas, where he was shot dead by a sniper.

What can explain the monumental chain of blunders and miscalculations that ensued?

The Joint Commission set about its work in the gentle twilight of one age of cultural misapprehensions about mental illness and the fiery dawn of another. In the twilight years, most people, including psychiatrists, still believed that Sigmund Freud had the discontents of the "mind" all figured out; believed in the existence of the "schizophrenogenic mother," that mythical Meanie Mama whose coldness and rejection of her offspring literally drove them mad; believed (in complacent thrall to the Menninger brothers) that schizophrenia could be cured. And after 1955, as mentioned, almost *literally* everyone believed that Thorazine and its progeny could do the job. No muss, no fuss.

And so it was just before the fiery dawn that the Joint Commission got busy building its bridges to nowhere.

The first ray of merciless reality materialized in the form of the escalating Vietnam War. The number of US "advisers" multiplied after the president's death until they gave way to a full-fledged fighting force, one that required constant, constantly increasing, and constantly more expensive infusions from the national treasuries of money and young men. The booming post–World War II economy absorbed much of this drain until 1973, when a global oil crisis and the severe stock-market plunge drove the country into recession. These crises largely account for the slashes in the CHC operating budget, freezing construction at fewer than 650 community centers, less than half the intended figure. This resulted in the stranding of about half of the 560,000 patients who were released or scheduled for release.

Yet the great enforced exodus of mental patients did not stop when the money ran low. Like a charging rhino that had taken a bullet to its head, it rambled forward, dead on its feet and without the cognitive means to reverse its course. The outflow gained numerical momentum. Nor were there beds for those patients new to the system who needed inpatient care. "By 1980," as Olga Loraine Kofman of Claremont McKenna College has written, "United States mental asylum populations plummeted from 560,000 to just over 130,000, leaving many of the chronically mentally ill homeless or incarcerated because of a lack of community follow-up care and housing. One-third of homeless people were believed to be seriously mentally ill."[2]

And the road to hell continued to receive the pavement of good intentions. In July 1965 President Lyndon Johnson, hurrying to consolidate his Great Society agenda in the lingering national sorrow over John F. Kennedy's assassination, signed two companion pieces of landmark progressive legislation: the Medicare and Medicaid acts. (He had steered the historic but inflammatory Civil Rights bill into law the year before, invoking the late president's vision for it; the following month, he would sign the Voting Rights bill into law.) Medicare proved its worth as a great and lasting benefit to American citizens. As, to a lesser extent, did Medicaid—with one crushing exception.

Medicaid prohibited federal reimbursement to the states for psychiatric patients in state hospitals and any public facility that treated mental illness. The (good) intention was to speed deinstitutionalization along, and to hold the states responsible for care and treatment costs. But in fact, the states proved not interested in that kind of responsibility. Instead of welcoming this helpless horde of mental patients and finding the means to shelter and treat them, as the CMHA envisioned, the states—leery of spending an extra taxpayer dollar—whisked large numbers of them right along into private nursing homes and into—well, into the *community*. The nursing homes and the *community* would take care of them, and receive Medicaid reimbursement in return.

Unfortunately, "the community" came to mean "the streets." Most of the state-hospital refugees lacked the sophistication and the reasoning skills to proceed to the nearest private facility or community haven.

Unless family members, friends, or kindhearted strangers took them in, they wandered at large. For thousands of them, the most severely incapacitated, their wandering led to jail or prison, where the taxpayer dollar covered the cost of hopelessness.

The state most tragically influential in modeling the national approach to treatment (or lack of treatment) for the insane was California. With its population the size of a small nation (around 20 million people in 1969, nearly a tenth of the United States' 205 million citizens) and its magnet pull for the wealthy and ambitious, the state has long reigned as a national bellwether. Its political, social, and cultural innovations drift eastward.

Deinstitutionalization was no exception. The program enjoyed its most explosive implementation in the Golden State. It cross-fertilized with the Szaszian wave of dissent against the very notion of insanity that rose to greater prominence in the '60s and '70s counterculture and also with the Church of Scientology.

Eight years after publishing *The Myth of Mental Illness*, Szasz, as mentioned, crossed the continent and, with the Scientologists, coestablished the Citizens Commission on Human Rights in Los Angeles. By then he had published two more books and given dozens of talks and broadcasts and written a steady flow of papers and articles. He was a worldwide celebrity, respected in many academic circles.

His Scientology funding partner for the commission was the quasi-mystical former science-fiction writer L. Ron Hubbard. Hubbard had founded Scientology in 1953. Hubbard was respected in no academic circles at all, yet he had carved out an image as a kind of prophet among millions of people around the globe.

Hubbard wore his red hair in a high pompadour. His lips were voluptuous, the lower one curling over his small dimpled chin. He'd served as a naval intelligence officer during World War II. He liked to wear ascots and often sported a cowboy hat. He cut some albums featuring himself crooning to his own jazzy compositions. They never made the charts.

That was all right. His several books over the years, according to Scientology's unverified claim, have sold more than 250 million copies.

Like Szasz, Hubbard was fueled by near-obsessive antipsychiatry and insanity-denying convictions. ("PSYCHIATRY KILLS," suggested a banner in one Scientology parade.) He had in fact preceded Szasz as a mental illness denier, though his publications did not receive serious discussion in the academic world, perhaps because they advanced a somewhat unacademic argument: that thetans (billion-year-old human beings, except for the terrestrial body, which the phantasmal thetan must replace now and then, combing hospital nurseries as if shopping for a new wardrobe; it's complicated) are immortal and that their lives are ruled by aliens from outer space. His 1950 book *Dianetics: The Modern Science of Mental Health*, self-published and a breakaway best seller, explained this and other principles overlooked by conventional science: for instance, that people not fortunate enough to have found Scientology risk having false ideas implanted into their minds by "implant stations" located on Mars or Venus.

In 1969, Hubbard was expanding his "church" and propagating its doctrines with monomaniacal energy. In its sixteenth year of existence, the church already had gathered considerable wealth—all of it from individual donors, many of them politically conservative rich men and women in Southern California. Yet when Hubbard joined forces with Szasz, his holdings were pocket change compared to what was to come.

Szasz by then was a worldwide celebrity of another sort: a rare intellectual celebrity. He had produced three more books and dozens of papers, articles, and speeches since *The Myth of Mental Illness*. His partnership with Hubbard was thus a marriage of convenience: Szasz had the legitimizing cachet, and CCHR had the necessary money. Szasz found kindred cause in CCHR's mission: to "eradicate abuses committed under the guise of mental health and enact patient and consumer protections."

Szasz served on the commission's board of advisers for forty-three years, until his death. Delivering the keynote at its twenty-fifth anniversary in 1974, he declared, "We should all honor CCHR because it is really the only organization that for the first time in human history has organized a politically, socially, internationally significant voice to combat psychiatry. This has never been done in human history before."[3] Yet his feelings about his involvement were mixed. He always made it clear that he had no organizational ties with Scientology and no affinity with their mystical beliefs.

There is no evidence that either the libertarian-leaning Szasz or the flamboyantly right-wing Hubbard ever attempted to influence the California legislature regarding their beliefs and causes. They really didn't need to. Southern California was heavily predisposed to agree. The region's massive population, politically diverse and disengaged in decades past, had been coalescing toward the right since at least the early '60s, and that suited Szasz and Hubbard just fine.

"Southern California's" borders are imprecisely defined. With its eight large metropolitan areas, including Orange County, on the southern rim of the Los Angeles city limits, it makes up two-thirds of the state's population. Thus it was an extremely potent political trend-maker, in the state and in the nation. In the 1960s and '70s, thanks in part to the vexations of the insane, the area began to harness and use that power and became a cradle of right-wing thought.

CCHR enjoyed a reception perhaps beyond its expectations when it opened its doors in Los Angeles and started mailing and broadcasting and speechifying its fiery screeds. Southern Californians were predisposed to Szasz's and Hubbard's combined message that "mental illness" was a fraud, cooked up by phony "psychiatrists," and that involuntary hospitalization and forced drug treatments were but devices for advancing a statist, totalitarian agenda if not an explicitly Marxist one. Many of the predisposed were state legislators, set a-quivering by the Red Scare.

In 1966, Orange County Republicans spearheaded a drive to elect a right-thinking hero as governor of the state. Their man was the born-again Southern Californian and born-again conservative Ronald Reagan. (The former Midwestern baseball announcer had come to Hollywood to get into the movies in 1937, and stayed.) Reagan neither understood nor cared much about mental illness, but he liked to save a buck or two when he could. Among Reagan's first acts as governor was to order the firing of 237 psychiatric technicians from the staff of the Patton State forensic hospital. The following year he ordered the canning of 212 more.

That was for practice. Then Reagan signed the Lanterman-Petris-Short (LPS) Act.

The chief author of this legislation was Assemblyman Frank Lanterman, a powerful Republican who represented Pasadena, which Fuller Torrey has called "the heartland of California's anti–mental health movement." Lanterman's constituency, and allies, included such reactionary forces as the Minute Women of the U.S.A., the Daughters of the American Revolution, and the John Birch Society, which thought of mental health treatment as a "Marxist weapon" aimed at controlling people's minds. As one scholar concluded, "This politically conservative culture made it natural for Lanterman to distrust psychiatry and especially involuntary commitment."[4]

LPS's good intentions included providing "individualized treatment, supervision, and placement services by a conservatorship program for gravely disabled persons." This aim proved a pipe dream. Over the next two years, tens of thousands of patients from the big asylums streamed out across the state, overwhelming the unprepared county and private treatment agencies and flooding the streets and the criminal justice system.

The Lanterman-Petris-Short Act "set the precedent for modern mental health commitment procedures in the United States," according to the published opinion of the Superior Court of California, County of Los Angeles. To paraphrase Henry Kissinger, this had the added misfortune of being true.

Nevertheless, LPS became the national gold standard for clueless, destructive government interference in the interests of mentally ill people. Intended to accelerate deinstitutionalization, it instead served to barricade state hospital doors against the admittance of stubbornly resisting patients—at least until a hearing was held. Not a medical hearing, with psychiatrists, but a judicial hearing, with a judge and lawyers. Because stubbornly resisting patients almost always were patients in psychotic states who almost always were in the collateral grip of anosognosia, the legislation meant that the most desperately vulnerable of all sufferers were the ones least likely to get help.

The act included other requirements almost guaranteed to inhibit necessary funding and to encourage the manipulation of both finances and patients. It stipulated, for instance, that California counties with more than one hundred thousand residents establish mental health treatment programs, with a 90 percent funding match from the state.

Good luck with that. LPS found the states in no more a mood to cooperate than had the previous agencies been with CMHA. The states now were signalmen on Highway Good Intentions, rerouting the helpless insane to the hells of shoddy private nursing homes and board-and-care houses—and to the streets—and to the jails. No one, it seemed, cared about crazy people.

Governor Reagan and his successors eventually closed nine of the fourteen state hospitals. In terms of financing, the federal government was in the clear.

Politician Frank Lanterman himself later expressed regret at what became of his good intentions. "I wanted the law to help the mentally ill," he told a reporter years later. "I never meant for it to prevent those who need care from receiving it."[5]

And a new category of American citizen was crystallizing: "the homeless."

The flow of the mentally ill out into the community was irreversible. Most of the new arrivals in communities found their sudden freedom terrifying. Most could not find Realtors willing to rent to them, or business owners willing to hire them. The new federal antidiscrimination laws prohibited this sort of thing; but how many of Dr. Szasz's "mythically" insane could summon the wherewithal to report the injustices? Afflicted children were taunted by their new schoolmates and peers. Bias against "crazy people" among "respectable" residents of these communities quickly formed and hardened. More and more former state hospital patients found bleak refuge in the streets, and many of these became prison inmates.

The criminalization of mental illness was in full swing.

In 1970, with half of California's mental asylum population

already gone (its peak was 37,500 in 1959), Governor Reagan decided to get serious about deinstitutionalization. On the ballast of LPS, he ordered the release of thousands more mental patients from California's large asylums into the community. The policy gained momentum and scope as the decade went on. In June 1972, for example, the governor approved the release of thirty-eight hundred mentally ill people from Agnews State Hospital, then in San Jose. This effectively closed down the mental health operations of the institution founded in 1885 and known as the "Great Asylum for the Insane."

And it contributed to the unofficial transformation of the Los Angeles County Jail into "the largest mental health provider in the county," in the words of the former official in charge of the facility.

And then, miraculously, things began to look up—or appeared to begin to look up. For a brief shining hour in the mid-1970s, it was possible to think that if this question could never be decided, its implications could at least be minimized to society's satisfaction.

Deinstitutionalization was fifteen years along when Jimmy Carter ascended to the presidency in 1976. A year after his inauguration, Carter created the first President's Commission on Mental Health. First Lady Rosalynn Carter, a longtime advocate for the insane who had organized the annual Rosalynn Carter Symposium on Mental Health Policy in Georgia, served as the commission's active chair, and she helped draft what might have been a landmark federal policy: the Mental Health Systems Act, which her husband submitted to Congress on May 15, 1979. MHSA was designed to streamline and coordinate the federal-state effort in combating mental illness, especially in the country's drastically underserved small towns and rural areas. It guaranteed badly needed new funding for those financially imperiled community centers, provided for a sophisticated partnership to replace the disheveled and adversarial relationships between federal and state governments, and promised "special emphasis" on the needs of the chronically mentally ill: sufferers of schizophrenia, schizo-affective disorder, and bipolarity.

After many months of hearings, debate, and revision, the act was signed into law on October 7, 1980. It offered an array of "categorical" federal health programs that had not been tried before. Funding for categorical programs arrives with strict rules that limit how the funds are spent. Carter's programs included an emphasis on the treatment of *chronic* mental illness—schizophrenia and its allied diseases—which had not previously been dealt with via federal funds at the community level. They also introduced federal grants for preventive projects and education in mental health care, and other grants to organize advocacy initiatives to protect the legal and social rights of the mentally ill.

Years of continued innovation and civilized management—and hope for the mad—seemed to lie ahead.

The Mental Health Systems Act survived for 310 days. On August 13, 1981, an old nemesis of mental health care struck again. Ronald Reagan, who the previous November had defeated Jimmy Carter to become the fortieth president, got Congress to effectively rescind the act.

MHSA's funding was among seventy-seven categorical grants obliterated by Congress at Reagan's urging, to be supplanted by nine "block grants." A block grant contains far fewer rules than a categorical one, giving expansive discretion to state and local governments as to its funding use—and also giving expansive new meaning to the phrase "in good faith." The new president had in fact targeted eighty-five programs, hoping to squeeze them into seven, far less pricey, block grants.

Congress instead consolidated seventy-seven categorical grants into nine block grants. With those changes, block grants came to make up 17 percent of total federal aid to state and local governments. They reduced funding by about 25 percent.

MHSA vanished into the maw of Reagan's Economic Recovery Tax Act of 1981, a stunning across-the-board measure intended to put an end to years of economic "stagflation," as it was known—an economic miasma of anemic growth, high unemployment, and high inflation. On the theory that if taxes were cut for rich people and corporations, the saved wealth would be invested in growth and production ("supply-side" economics), the economic recovery act increased estate tax exemptions in phases from $175,625 to $600,000 by 1987,

cut marginal tax rates by 23 percent over three years, and relieved corporations of $150 billion in tax obligations over five years. The cumu-
lative reduction in taxes from 1982 to 1986 has been estimated at $749
billion, or about the same figure as the gross national product in 1966.
Not every agency dependent on federal spending suffered, of course.
Some were even enhanced. Defense spending increased 12.5 percent a
year from the fiscal years 1981 to 1985, a total of 60 percent.

Of course the government had to find some spending trim of its own
to offset its historic tax reductions. So it vitiated nearly every domestic
program available to cuts. It struck where resistance was weakest: at
people and groups ill-suited to the demands of lobbying, or even the
demands of voting, most of them, and therefore without political influence. It struck at the federally funded school lunch program, at Aid
to Families with Dependent Children, at the food stamp program, at
unemployment insurance, at low-income housing, at the mentally ill. It
repealed all existing legislation covering these programs and replaced
them with the austere "block grants."

Ronald Reagan seemed never to have thought much about mental
illness beyond the political, social, and fiscal impressions he'd picked up
as governor of California back during the years of L. Ron Hubbard's
and Thomas Szasz's public-education efforts, and the general hatred
toward the mentally ill then at large. In March 1981 he picked up some
field experience in the phenomenon. He was shot in his left armpit at
near-point-blank range, and nearly killed, outside a Washington hotel by
the schizophrenic gunman John Hinckley Jr. From his hospital bed, the
president disclosed to his visiting wife the sum of his soul-searching on
the implications of the incident, and untreated psychosis on the streets,
and the avalanche of available handguns, and the nation's narrow escape
from the trauma of enduring the second presidential assassination in
barely more than seventeen years: "Honey, I forgot to duck."

The nation's state and federal lawmakers did not forget to duck. Successive legislatures and congresses resiliently avoided the question of enlightened reform—for instance, overhauling the Lanterman-Petris-Short Act
to allow evaluation and treatment against the will of people in psychosis,

while honoring due process. And so in California and all around America hundreds of thousands of the untreated were "free" to continue along that tragic and at least partly preventable course.

Deinstitutionalization (and California) did produce, however unintentionally, one group that grew into an institution of great benefit to the mentally ill. This was the National Alliance on Mental Illness, or NAMI.

It began in 1974, with a small circle of Oakland and San Mateo parents whose children were victims of chronic mental illness. The parents became exasperated with the hostility directed at their sons and daughters, and with the ignorance that fed much of it, including ignorance within the hospitals. They began meeting around one another's kitchen tables to plan some sort of coordinated response. Attendance grew, and so did the stories of helplessness and anger.

In October 1977, the group calculated that they had enough support to form a state organization, which they called Parents of Adult Schizophrenics. One of its organizers was Eve Oliphant, a small, intense mother with long, dark hair and outsize glasses. She was already a growing celebrity in these circles, celebrated for her sharp, admonitory talks to psychiatric groups around the nation. A naturally buoyant woman—photographs of her as a young mother show her with a goofy grin, head tilted, radiating optimism—she, too, had been wounded into activism. One of her two sons had been diagnosed as schizophrenic and placed in the Napa State Hospital. Adding to her wash of torment, the doctors decided that she could not visit him. She would only make things worse, given that her son's illness was all her fault: she was a by-god "schizophrenogenic mother"!

Eve Oliphant and her allies launched a grassroots blitzkrieg around the state that quickly galvanized a community that had not even known it was a community. Heads of stricken families heard the rumblings, discovered one another, and formed affiliated groups. Following the classic trajectory of California-born ideas, the movement sped eastward through America.

Eve Oliphant drew media coverage, some of which inadvertently revealed the complacency and condescension toward the disease and toward its new activists, especially the female ones. A writer for Oliphant's local newspaper, the *Times* from San Mateo—a woman writer—trumpeted her as the "Peninsula's 'Little Lady'" who was going to "let the psychiatric community have it," when she addressed the World Congress of Psychiatry. "She's a little lady, but she's packing an increasing wallop, and when she talks people listen," the paper crowed.[6]

The "little lady" did deliver her wallop. Oliphant blistered the learned, Freud-marinated attendees with her attack on their "schizophrenogenic mother" myth and other complacencies of the profession. At one point she laid out the reasons that the grassroots organizations had been formed. "We failed to understand," she declared in a widely reprinted burst, "why parents of a child with leukemia were treated with sympathy and understanding, while parents of a child with schizophrenia were treated with scorn and condemnation."[7]

At a 1979 meeting in Madison, Wisconsin, the groups formally unified as the National Alliance on Mental Illness—NAMI. Eve Oliphant became the organization's star and most persistent advocate—a kind of twentieth-century Dorothea Dix, presenting the strong claims of suffering humanity to hospitals, elected officials, newspapers, and anyone else who would, or wouldn't, listen. She persisted, though progressively slowed by age, until she died in California in June 2010, two weeks before her ninetieth birthday.

NAMI's record of education, advice, and engagement in mental health issues is hardly free from criticism. Journalist and author Robert Whitaker, for example, has castigated the group for its unquestioning endorsement of antipsychotic medications and for accepting donations from drug companies such as Eli Lilly.[8] Still, NAMI's outreach has remained vigorous through the years.

But by 2015, the nation's prison system was so overstuffed with people whose reasoning capacities were impaired that a study published by the normally sedate Stanford Law School bristled with outrage: "When Did Prisons Become Acceptable Mental Health Care Facilities?" It was written and copublished by state senate pro tempore Darrell Steinberg, the Stanford law professor David Mills, and the Stanford Law School special projects director Michael Romano.

Among its particulars: insane people in America "are far more likely to be treated in jail or prison than in any healthcare facility." The mentally ill account for more than 350,000 inmates in US prisons, more than ten times those in psychiatric hospitals.

"Although litigation-related reforms have resulted in a significant overhaul of prison mental health services...mental health care in prison still falls well below minimal constitutional standards, not to mention medical standards, in many important respects."[9]

Among the study's many damning assessments, this one rings with particular eloquence:

> We have created conditions that make criminal behavior all but inevitable for many of our brothers and sisters who are mentally ill. Instead of treating them, we are imprisoning them. And then, when they have completed their sentences, we release them with minimal or no support system in place, just counting the days until they are behind bars once again. This practice of seeking to save money on the backs of this population comes with huge moral and fiscal cost. It is ineffective because we spend far more on imprisonment of the mentally ill than we would otherwise spend on treatment and support. It is immoral because writing off another human being's life is utterly contrary to our collective values and principles.[10]

A 2015 report issued by the Vera Institute of Justice pointed out that the mentally ill are put at further risk by the very design, operation, and resources of most jails. "Characterized by constant noise, bright lights, an ever-changing population, and an atmosphere of threat and violence," the report points out, "jails are unlikely to offer any respite for people with mental illness. Coupled with the near-absence of mental health treatment, time in jail is likely to mean further deterioration in their illness."[11]

The institute added that when lack of treatment—the plight of 83 percent of jail inmates—is factored in with a "chaotic environment," the illness typically deepens, and such inmates "are more likely to be placed in solitary confinement, either as punishment for breaking rules or for their own protection since they are also more likely to be victimized." Of course, these "chaotic environments" also describe those at state hospitals shut down for abuses. These disgraceful human-storage barns also featured patients in rags or naked; twenty-four-hour-a-day lights; neglect; and victimization including rape by other inmates—and by staff.

The institute might have added that solitary confinement is among the most soul-destroying, desolate, madness-inducing, and morally barren of punishments that can be visited upon an insane person. Or any person.

On January 21, 2013, six weeks after the massacre of schoolchildren and staff members at an elementary school at Newtown, Connecticut, by a deranged and suicidal young man, *Forbes* magazine editor Steve Forbes seemed to come within an eyelash of demanding that the big public hospitals be filled once again with the insane and presumed insane. "Instead of...accepting the commonsense notion that people with serious mental problems can't rationally decide what is best for themselves, we have largely emptied our public psychiatric hospitals," wrote the normally reliable proponent of free-market solutions.[12]

Two years later, three ethicists at the Perelman School of Medicine at the University of Pennsylvania proposed exactly that.

Acknowledging that President Kennedy's bold experiment had proceeded from legitimate concerns about genuine problems—overcrowded hospitals, the protection of the civil rights of patients, the prospects of more efficient economics—the three academics declared that time had shown the remedies had failed. And they pointed out how drastically the times, and the demographics, have changed in the past fifty years: a doubling of the United States population since 1955 and a mentally ill population of ten million (not all of them chronic), yet a shrinkage of inpatient psychiatric beds to forty-five thousand (a 95 percent loss) to create "a wholly inadequate equation."

They declared that "deinstitutionalization has really been transinstitutionalization. U.S. jails and prisons have become the nation's largest mental health care facilities. Half of all inmates have a mental illness or substance abuse disorder; 15 percent of state inmates are diagnosed with a psychotic disorder...This results in a vicious cycle whereby mentally ill patients move between crisis hospitalization, homelessness and incarceration." They called for a return of medical facilities that would house the mentally ill in a "safe, modern and humane" way, and proposed that "the term 'asylum' should be understood in its original sense—a place of safety, sanctuary and healing."[13]

Perhaps a return to large-asylum care is indeed a feasible means to end the outsize costs of criminalization and social disruption, not to mention the countless individual and family catastrophes fueled by our present broken system of mental health care. Yet any visionary or movement that seriously proposes launching such a gigantic and complex countermigration—such a towering payload of good intentions—must be equipped with a detailed map for avoiding the road to hell.

Any such enterprise would have to be founded upon a thoroughgoing program of public/private planning and agreements: on design and construction and upkeep of new hospitals; on screening and surveillance procedures for doctors and staff; on nutrition, cleanliness, and counseling ensured by vigilant oversight and enforceable (and enforced) by bipartisan law. It would have to find ways to bring together the "abolitionists" and the "paternalists," whose entrenched mutual opposition has shown, at this writing, no sign of willingness to abandon absolutism and seek compromise. This could be brought about only by a public leader or leaders blessed with wisdom, deep knowledge of psychiatric and technological theory, and the capacity to inspire people toward a greater good. Such leaders have not been conspicuous on the American scene in recent years.

All this of course would require an ongoing public and private investment of tremendous proportions. Which, in turn, would require an equally historic mobilization of unified public will, perhaps on a scale equal to that of preparing for war.

Can such an all-encompassing and permanent reformation of mental health care be expected to happen?

It hasn't happened yet.

14

"Hey Fam—"

Kevin emailed us after his first performance on the Interlochen campus. He played a guitar-piano duo with his roommate at a coffeehouse, an informal evening venue. His message was filled with exuberance and wonder at all that was unfolding in his life.

Subject: !!
Date: Tue, 28 Sep 1999 08:50:55 PDT
From: "Kevin Powers" <hoist@hotmail.com>
To: ropo@sover.net
Hey fam—

Well heres how the coffee house went. The Interlochen Jazz Combo went first and of course they were smokin' and everyone went nuts, me and jesse [his roommate] went about 10th and played Equinox and a lot of people said we stole the show which is supposedly incredible since even having enough courage to play the first Interlochen Coffe House was in and of itself pretty amazing, not to mention being sophmores. There was pretty impressive talent and i guess even though I was not thrilled with my performance everyone loved it. I am still getting compliments so I'm pretty excited. Also the other big news is last night I met my girlfriend and her name is Ali, so theres another one of my missions accomplished. Whats new with you all? Everything is great here obviously. Talk to you later

Kevin

He had less than two years of sanity left.

Honoree's message to Dean several weeks later, on the birthday that he and I share, offered a rare insight into the anxiety that she had kept under tight control throughout Dean's ordeals. The anxiety, it seems, did not end with the judge's decision.

Subject: Happy Birthday
Date: Thu, 18 Nov 1999 05:50:37 -0500
From: Honoree Fleming <ropo@sover.net>
To: Dean Powers <junior_304@hotmail.com>
Well dear,

> *I woke up in the middle of the night again so I thought I'd get up and send you happy birthday wishes. I hope it's a great one for you. Someday I suppose I will get beyond this dread and insomnia that I've been feeling. It will be nice when you and Kevin are home and I know that you are safe.*

> *I love you—happy birthday.*

MOM

As for Dean, his intellectual development, interrupted by the pariah status he'd suffered at Middlebury Union High School, flowered again at the Gould Academy. He had composed several perceptive, vigorously written school assignments on topics including Shakespeare, the Constitution, Thomas Jefferson, and—with bittersweet innocence—mental health:

Good mental health is important in anyone's life if they hope to enjoy it. Someone who is mentally healthy can maintain a more positive outlook on things... People who maintain a balance of good mental and physical health seek intellectual stimulation, and human interaction, and make creative use of their time through work and volunteer activities. This promotes self confidence and an overall good feeling about themselves.

Stress is the punishing our bodies experience as we adjust to our continually changing environment... [It] can result in feelings of distrust, rejection, anger, and depression, which in turn can lead to health problems... With the death of a loved one, the birth of a child, a job promotion, or a new relationship, we experience stress as we readjust our lives.

Identify the causes of stress in your life. Sharing your thoughts and feelings with a family member, friend, co-worker or counselor can help you see your problems in a different way. Try not to get depressed. Depression can make you feel miserable...

Set short-term and life goals for yourself... Realize that drugs and alcohol don't solve life's problems. Develop a sense of humor and make time for fun. Schedule time for play and become involved in activities that make you laugh.

Near the end of his first semester, Kevin wrote to us about the breakup of his second romance. (We hadn't known there had been a first romance.) But he wrote with his usual optimism, coupled with a sense of eagerness to get home for the holidays. He asked, as he always did, after his grandmother. In my response, I reminded him that he, Dean, and I had tickets to see the musical *Rent* in New York during their winter breaks in January.

Old Vermont and Old Maine, decked out for the holidays, enveloped Honoree and me as we headed east to Bethel along two-lane roads on the Friday before Christmas. In the early twilight, the farmhouses and large cedar trees came ablaze with colored lights, many of them surely preserved in newspaper wrappings and stored in cardboard boxes over the decades until the season. Styrofoam candy canes and giant plastic candles festooned the telephone poles of the small towns. Merchants had set up miniature manger scenes in their display windows. Wreaths decorated the lighted doors of the Congregational and the Catholic churches.

Arriving on campus, we were greeted by a smiling Dean. He led us to the auditorium and then disappeared backstage, and we settled in amid the other parents to watch the evening's program. It included, besides Dean and some other instrumentalists, a robed boys' choir that sang hymns and holiday songs. They sang with the timeless cherubic, O-lipped earnestness that seems the hallmark of school choirs everywhere.

Then the parents and their children filed out of the auditorium and got into their cars for the holiday drive home. Two nights later, one of the robed young carolers, an earnest and intelligent boy with soft round cheeks, walked out of the darkness into his parents' farmhouse kitchen, raised and aimed a shotgun, and decapitated his mother. The boy later explained to a tutor who had befriended him in a Vermont jail, "I *love* my mother. If you saw what I did, you'd understand."*

The four of us enjoyed a warm Christmas, and I took my sons down to New York by train for the early-January performance of *Rent*, as I'd promised them.

Dean had grown intensely interested in politics and the news in general:

Subject: Re: (no subject)
Date: Wed, 01 Mar 2000 05:28:32 PST

---

* The boy's name was Laird Stanard. In 2015 he was furloughed, with restrictions, from a Vermont correctional facility after serving fifteen years of a twenty-five-years-to-life sentence. As closely as I can determine, he was never given a psychiatric evaluation. His jailhouse tutor, the writer Theo Padnos, included Laird's story in his underrated 2004 book about adolescent murderers, *My Life Had Stood a Loaded Gun: Adolescents at the Apocalypse* (Miramax). Laird told Padnos that he had developed a fantasy reinforced by the film *American Beauty*, which he had watched several times. The movie offered a vision of murder as a gift of transcendence, because a character who is killed—an adolescent's tormented father—does not seem to really die: he narrates the film, commenting on the plot. He is serene, still sensate, hardly inconvenienced by his own demise.

From: "Dean Powers" <junior_304@hotmail.com>
To: ropo@sover.net

How's it going Dad? You wouldn't believe what Ive been doing the last few days, reading the newspaper. Ive been keeping up with the primary rhetoric and it looks like a religious race lately huh? Did you hear about all the Bob Jones U. stuff? Also there was another school shooting, in Michagan. I wonder how close Kevin was. did I tell you I been out riding snowmobile trails, Ive been out five times. I also have been ravin! RAves are a blast (techno music) I want to go to one in NYC or Boston. I got a band now and we're jamming to alice in chains, and singing it sounds pretty good. I got exams this week then IM out I will see you this weekend. see ya - jr.

Several weeks later, an anguishing motif resurfaced: a renewal of the estrangement that had been growing between Dean and myself. The tensions seldom had an understandable cause. Dean would erupt in fierce anger, for example, over nothing that I could perceive. In hindsight, I believe that his edginess was being fed by the long prodromal stage of the disease that was slowly overtaking him.

In early April 2000, Kevin flew home from Michigan for spring break, and the two of us drove to Bethel, where Dean had lined up a gig on the Gould campus. It was the boys' first performance together in front of a sizable audience, and it was a smashing success: hard-driving gutbucket rock 'n' roll, with the amps all the way up to eleven. Dean had long dreamed of kicking it onstage with his phenomenal brother. He was almost giddy at the chance to show off Kevin's gifts, and his own. The performance room was filled, and the boys did not disappoint. Kevin played with his usual intense, fiery brilliance, but kept his trademark poker face. Not so Dean. He laughed and shouted and his eyes sparkled and his dark mop of hair bounced and he leaped into the air as he hit his chords. I had not seen him in such a state of wild pure joy for years. The prolonged cheers and whistles and applause at the end would have awakened the Grateful Dead.

The joy did not survive the rest of our day together. The tension overtook it shortly before Kevin and I departed the campus for Vermont. I cannot recall the cause; there probably was no cause. At any rate, both Dean and I were seething as my car pulled out of the campus.

Back in Middlebury, after having crept home through a late-winter blizzard with Kevin wide-eyed in the passenger seat, I tried to repair things via email—which succeeded only in revealing my cluelessness and perhaps giving grim satisfaction to the demons that had lodged inside my son:

Subject: the visit
Date: Sun, 09 Apr 2000 18:05:22 -0400
From: Ron Powers <ropo@sover.net>
To: Dean Powers <junior_304@hotmail.com>
Dean,

Got home about an hour ago. Brutal snowstorm the second half of the trip, nearly a whiteout between Montpelier and Burlington; mountain routes out of the question. But we are safe.

I know how frustrated you are and have been with me. I know your feelings that I have not made a connection with you.

I guess I wasn't ready for the changes that took place in you when you hit adolescence. Mom and other people have often said that you and I are a lot alike, and that's one reason why there is so much friction between us. I think that you are an extremely good kid, and at your best you are nothing short of heroic.

I don't want us to be at war forever, Dean. I look forward to us being friends sometime. There's so damn much I want to talk to you about that doesn't have anything to do with our problems. I hope that someday, when all this anguish settles down and you and I are both a little older and wiser, that we

can make peace and enjoy one another's company again. I love
you, Dean. I would stand in front of gunfire for you.
    Please believe that.

                                                   Dad

In spite of our increasing friction when we were together, I remained
determined to keep up a friendly tone in my emails to Dean. He largely
returned the gesture. Emails replaced the times together we had once
enjoyed as a mode of friendship.

By May 2000, the first phase of their time away from home was
drawing to an end. Dean had made his college choice: Fort Lewis College in Durango, a town of seventeen thousand that lay beside the Ani-
mas River and nestled in the San Juan Mountains. It boasted incredible
mountain-and-wilderness scenery and five ski areas, which may have
played a part in Dean's decision.

Meanwhile, Kevin prepared himself for leaving Interlochen, if just
for the summer, the dreamlike little universe that had embraced him
and claimed his soul.

That summer breezed along in what I recall as a mellow haze of
guitar music and dinners, grilled chicken and corn on the cob, with
friends on our screened back porch, the Woods Tea Company in concert now and then. Our sons off in the Middlebury night with their
friends and supposed friends. Someone in that group almost certainly
was sharing marijuana, a substance that, as we now know, can gravely
exacerbate the symptoms of schizophrenia. Several months afterward,
we came to believe that the equally destructive LSD had been introduced into the circle. At the time, we remained innocent. A book that
I had cowritten was published to good reviews and large sales, and the
family financial crisis, acute to the point of credit-card juggling since
Honoree and I had left the college, was over. It was the last summer of
the old millennium.

In September, Kevin and I packed up his belongings in the family
van for the long drive back to Traverse City. Honoree flew with Dean

to Albuquerque. They rented a car and drove north to Durango, where Dean began his first year of college. Kevin was ecstatic to learn that he had been invited to join both the jazz combo and the larger jazz ensemble at Interlochen. A few days after that, we learned that Kevin was not only learning at Interlochen; he was teaching: acting as a tutor for some of his fellow students. Honoree and I drove to the academy for Parents Weekend. The jazz ensemble was to perform, and our son had won the first guitar chair. On campus, we joined the early-evening flow of gussied-up parents heading toward Corson Auditorium, past the Marshall Fredericks sculpture in front of the entrance, a bronze piece that depicts two bears resting back-to-back, one large, the other small. We produced our tickets and filed into the auditorium, a bright, curving panorama of nearly a thousand red-covered seats on a polished hardwood floor that inclined downward toward the stage.

The stage was bare. No scaffolded rows for the musicians to sit on. No microphones. Nearly a thousand of us looked into the empty brightness and curled and uncurled our programs and waited.

There came a rumbling noise. Part of the stage floor slid back. We heard the ensemble before we saw it: a muffled thump of a big-band number from the depths. The ensemble levitated into view, twenty young men and women, all in black, in stacked tiers, blowing and drumming and tickling the ivories and strumming and playing the hell out of Duke Ellington's "Take the A Train." The lights made the trombones and the drum fixtures shine like gold, and there was Kevin, down low at stage right in his black tux and bow tie; the lights blazed off the gold trim on his black Martin, and turned his blond hair gold, as bright lights always did. Poker-faced, one polished black shoe resting on the arch of the other. Head bobbing just a little to the big-band beat.

He took the first solo. The band snapped quiet and Kevin's notes went skipping and dancing all alone, through the amps and up the aisles and into the audience and then out again. They somehow got through the curved beige acoustic tiling and escaped the auditorium, and headed straight up and toward the early evening stars, and then on into deep space, joining all the other music ever played, coursing to eternity. The solo ended and Kevin ducked his head in a bow, and the eruption of applause startled him and made him peek upward a little before it burst clear and followed his music into the cosmos.

Kevin's remaining years at Interlochen floated along on the ballast of that ovation, in an illusory haze of time suspended. He extended his mastery of technique and instinct until his teachers had little left to teach him. He directed a guitar ensemble in a memorable performance. He composed wondrous guitar pieces that seemed to blend rock and jazz and flamenco and other assorted artifacts of his musical memory. He and his bandmates performed at Stanford University and in Chicago. He tore his concentration from music to the classroom enough to earn reasonable grades in his studies—although he never tore away completely.

In late October I wrote to tell Kevin of an encounter Honoree and I had that reconnected us with his "creation story" as a guitarist:

> **Subject: Amazing incident!**
> *Date: Fri, 20 Oct 2000 23:47:47 -0400*
> *From: Ron Powers <ropo@sover.net>*
> *To: Kevin Powers <hoist@hotmail.com>*
> *...It happened while Mom and I were in the Volvo show-room on Wednesday. We were talking to one of the salesman, a nice guy who has helped Mom in the past, when I noticed another salesman was looking at us. When there was a pause in our conversation, he called over to me: "Is your name Powers?" I nodded and he asked, "Do you have a son who plays guitar?" I said yes; two sons who play, actually. He said: "I met you 10 or 12 years ago at the Boathouse. You had your little boy with you. You guys sat right next to me. I remember that he got up onstage and played with the group. He had a little toy guitar. I remember how excited he was. And I knew he was going places, right then. I've followed news items about him in the paper. Where is he now?"*

Is that not unbelievable? This guy was sitting next to us at THE pivotal day in your whole life's direction, Kevin, and he remembered it—almost as clearly as we have. Crazy world, huh? Take care of yourself. Write when you can.

Love,
Dad

When I picked him up at the Burlington airport near the end of winter break 2000, Kevin was in a frenzy to get to the parking garage. He was back home from a visit to his new Interlochen roommate, Peter, who lived in Jacksonville, Florida. Kevin had a surprise for me.

He dumped his guitar and backpack into the rear seat of the van, foraged in the backpack, then barreled into the front seat brandishing a CD in its jewel box, which he ripped open. I had hardly got the motor started when Kev shoved the disk into the car player and shouted, "I want you to hear this!"

I left the car in parking gear and we listened as the music started to play. Kevin turned up the volume and then peered at me.

The songs were punk. But what punk! Six driving pieces of blazing force and disciplined musicianship—guitar, bass, drums, and vocals. I had never been a fan of punk, but this was something else, something beyond. The songs surged forth, alternately seditious, playful, and charged with young-male defiance, typically toward a girl who'd thrown a young male over. "I won't change myself for anyone," the lyrics ran, and "Why do we pretend that we were made for each other?" and "Why did you lie to get your way?" (When Pedant Father suggested a few days later that she had lied to get her way *to get her way*, Kevin shot Pedant Father a sidelong you-are-so-out-of-it look, and Pedant Father kept himself out of advice-giving after that.) The lyrics contained the requisite quotient of alienated-youth trashmouth, yet the songs were not dark at all. The words seemed to be present mainly to provide a superstructure on which to mold the magnificent music.

The longest and best of the six pieces was an aural fireworks display titled "Epistemological Commentary." Kevin took his longest solo in that one, and it was out of this world: an intricate display of fast scale-running, up and down and up and down again, but shaped into an exhilarating musical idea. Kevin shifted chords upward near the end, and his guitar turned into a calliope, tootling away in some celestial circus of joy everlasting.

I didn't say anything when it was over and the disk slid out of its slot. I didn't want to trivialize what I'd just heard with some inane boilerplate comment. I think that I ended up just shaking my head, and putting my hand on my son's shoulder. The only sound was of the van's engine humming in the chilly parking lot.

Kevin had his lopsided grin working. He nodded. He understood.

At sixteen, he had just lived out a kid musician's fantasy: an all-night recording session in a professional studio. They invited a third musician, a young, dynamic drummer named Scott Shad. Scott was a member of Inspection Twelve, a Jacksonville band on the cusp of its national debut with a CD titled *In Recovery*.

On New Year's Eve, as Kevin told the story, the trio entered the soundproofed room, set the volume and tonal controls, and began playing. They recorded and rerecorded and edited throughout the night—a detail that richly flavored Kevin's fantasy-come-true. By morning they had nailed it. They ran off several copies of the master, with the intention of sending them out to record companies. And they awarded themselves a suitably macho punk band name: Booby.

They sent their CD off to several places including an emerging musicians' go-to website, garageband.com. It took the site about four months to begin posting the songs.

Subject: The rave reviews
Date: Sun, 06 May 2001 07:52:35 -0400
From: Ron Powers <ropo@sover.net>
To: Kevin Powers <hoist@hotmail.com>
Kev,

I assume you've been checking out the reviews of "Episte-mological Commentary" on garageband. They're mostly over the top! I love the one that says, "I've listened to a heap of songs on GB and this is the best Punk song I have heard on the site thus far! This song rocks! That guitar line is so damn cool I can barely stand it..." and on and on. It must give you a tremendous rush to read this kind of praise. I also notice that you've made the Qualifying Round and that your Punk ranking is 100. I think you're still on the way up, and next Wednesday should give you a real boost from reviewers. Pass the word to Peter—you guys are stupendous!

Love,
Dad

Kevin's voice was leaden when he called home from Interlochen in March. Scott Shad, the gifted young drummer who'd sat in on that magical recording session in Jacksonville, was dead. Scott was a diabetes sufferer. On March 6, he'd been caught without a needed dosage of insulin at the worst possible time. While driving his car, he apparently had a seizure and succumbed to a fatal crash.

Honoree and I flew to Interlochen in late March to bring Kevin home for spring break. We made an evaluation appointment with one of his teachers, who told us, "Kevin is probably the most talented musician I've come across in my time at Interlochen."

But then, in April, another death: my wife's mother, Honora, at age ninety-eight, whom both the boys had adored. Both sons were stunned with grief. Kevin was tongue-tied during our telephone conversation, and soon afterward sent this post:

Subject:
Date: Wed, 25 Apr 2001 20:19:34
From: "Kevin Powers" <hoist@hotmail.com>
To: ropo@sover.net
Hey dad
I'm sorry for my initial inability to say a lot, I probably sounded bitter but I'm still getting used to this and I'm so thankful for

you and mom allways being there for me. I almost feel hardened
though, it hasn't sunk into me what happens when someone dies.
I feel like I took advantage of people like grammy and scott allways
being there and I never fully had the chance to spend the time or
say the things I would want to before they were gone. I don't know
what it means that I can't fully become emotional when something
like this happens, I guess I realize though that for grammy this is
what she wanted. I heard her say it and I don't blame her she lived a
full life more than 90 years. Anyway, thank you, take care of mom
as I know you are and I'll see you in a few days.

Love Kevin

Subject: Re:
Date: Wed, 25 Apr 2001 16:35:53 -0400
From: Ron Powers <ropo@sover.net>
To: Kevin Powers <hoist@hotmail.com>
Kev,

Your reactions, believe me, are absolutely normal. Tears are
not the only measure of grief. You're in a kind of shock. I know
you well enough to know how intensely you feel things. Your
silence on the phone spoke worlds—you were deeply connected
to the moment and your sense of loss.

As for "taking advantage"—no. You didn't take, you gave.
With Grammy you were always the picture of sweetness and
tenderness and understanding. You always approached her in
a searching way; you looked and listened for what was going
on inside her head, and responded to that with amazing gentle-
ness and good humor. The humor you shared with her was so
wonderful. Whenever I think of the two of you together, I have
this wonderful image of Honora's face opening up, losing its
guardedness, and then that deep belly-laugh she could release
on occasion, when her whole body and shoulders would shake.
You knew how to kid her, be a little outrageous, jolly her along.
It was one of the things she lived for.

I agree with you that Grammy gave you something too. You and Dean. She gave you an understanding of the need to be tender. Living with her, adjusting to her needs and moods, helping her out when she needed it, like escorting her into the dining room or fetching her a blanket or a cup of tea—these are the little things that enrich human life and offer the deepest satisfactions. I think that the kindness she nurtured in both you and Dean is stronger than all the hatefulness and ugliness of this scary world. And I think that nothing you encounter out in that world will ever corrupt you because you will always carry a piece of Grammy in your heart.

Maybe when you wrote that lyric, "I won't change myself for anyone," that was partly Grammy speaking.

She loved you. Mom and I love you. You're a wonderful person.

I can't begin to tell you how proud I am that you are my son.

Love,
Dad

The world, which Kevin had embraced so buoyantly as a child, was by now showing its true nature to him. On the day of the attacks on the World Trade towers in September 2001, he wrote this to us:

Subject: hey
Date: Tue, 11 Sep 2001 20:29:32 -0400 (EDT)
From: Kevin B Powers <POWERSKB@INTERLOCHEN .K12.MI.US>
To: ropo <ropo@sover.net>
Dad-
What a day in history…I am beside myself with confusion as to who would do this, and why. There are no words for something like this its safe to say that this will be one of the biggest events in US history but we will see. I hope the guys fighting

for our country will make smart moves and I hope Bush takes
cautious but advancing measures whatever they might be. Do
you have any colleagues in that area? Well everything here for
the most part is fine, I think some people will be affected by this
more than others but I'm ok and I hope you and mom are doing
well. I'd love to hear your thoughts on this, and I will most likely
call later tonight or tomorrow.

Kevin

I read his message and wished that I could drive to Interlochen to hug and comfort him. I could have, of course. In retrospect I dearly wish I had. But I wrote him this reply.

Subject: Day 1 of the New World
Date: Tue, 11 Sep 2001 16:06:56 -0400
From: Ron Powers <ropo@sover.net>
To: Kevin Powers <hoist@hotmail.com>
Kevin,

I just got home from the grocery store, and Mom told me I'd
missed your call, which we both had been hoping for through-
out this sad, terrible day. (We were so gratified that Dean called
in the morning—we really wanted to make contact with both
of you.)

The funny thing is that I was thinking about you on my ride
home, probably at the same moment you and Mom were talk-
ing. Thinking about the things I'd want to say to you. The most
important of those things is to urge you to be brave, and to
keep your optimistic outlook on life. That will be important
for everyone in the country in the hard days ahead. The second
thing is to savor the preciousness of life, every moment of it—
but I think you do that already.

The third thing is to be aware of the contribution you can
make as an artist to the healing of your friends, your school and

perhaps someday even your country. Terrorists, criminals and evil people are always the ones who blow our world apart, and always it is the artists who put it back together again. We really need your music now. We need to hear the joy and power and hope that you generate with every note you pick from that beautiful guitar. We need you, and Peter, and the people in your combo, and the whole widening circle of musicians across this shattered society, to help restore our sense of humanity and the sweet flavor of life.

Play well, and with extra passion. As you always do.

With lots of love and respect,
Dad

And he did, for as long as he could.

15

Antipsychotics

Few discoveries in the history of science triggered anything like the welling of euphoria in the Western world that greeted the arrival of antipsychotic medication in 1954. Certainly none reached as deeply into the wells of human terror and desire as psychoactive drugs, with their promise of identity restored and protected, the Self insulated from demonic colonization.

Cold War–fighting, Red-Scared, bomb-shelter-digging, beatnik-averse America hungered for some good news about humanity's prospects. What better news than that madness was about to be wiped out? Newspapers, magazines, and television wolfed down the great helpings of sugary press releases served up by factotums of the once-staid, newly Delphian drug companies. They raced to trumpet the latest breakthrough, quote the most utopian promises of corporate lab scientists. The Freudian high priests with their dreary old theories of "mind-cure" found themselves blindsided at the height of their hard-won prestige—blindsided by chemicals!

The very notion—Sanity in a bottle! Peace of mind in a popped pill!—so perfectly fit postwar America's marketing-conditioned faith in E-Z solutions via consumer products that the wonder-drug blitzkrieg was complete almost as soon as it started. The companies' onslaught of grandiose claims at first paralyzed the usual gatekeepers of the public interest. Who, after all, had the scientific savvy necessary to analyze and challenge them? Not the press, that great consortium of laymen reporting to laymen. Not public officials, mostly science-illiterate and lobbyist-friendly. Not the academy, generally lethargic in shifting its sights from dusty tomes toward civic affairs (unless, as events often proved, certain monetary considerations were proffered). And not consulting psychiatrists, far too many of whom were only too happy to reinvent themselves as pill prescribers as they saw their talk-therapy clientele abandon the couch for the nearest Rexall.

As a preamble to exploring the deeply flawed rise of Big Pharma, a rise built largely upon avarice, profiteering, deceptive and even false marketing, bribery, and even—as its profits soared beyond imagination—a willingness to settle multimillion-dollar lawsuits out of court and proceed on to further perfidies as a preamble to all this, it is fair to acknowledge that the hope of the wonder drugs has not been completely misguided. Prescription antipsychotics, the good ones, anyway, have enabled millions of schizophrenic patients to experience quantum improvements in their lives. For them, the medications have restored cognition, suspended hallucinations, including "voices" inside the head, and enabled control over destructive irrational impulses. They have made it possible for mentally ill victims and their loved ones to resume communication, a gift beyond value. They have allowed uncounted sufferers to return to the workplace.

Modifications on the antipsychotic compound, known generally as psychotropics, have been effective in stabilizing the mood swings of bipolar sufferers. A host of antidepressant and antianxiety products, distinct from psychotropics* in their chemical makeup and their lesser potency, treat the complaints of "the worried well," those one-in-four patients who crowd doctors' appointment schedules with nothing especially awful to report. Whether the "worried well" actually need such sustenance is a question that has always triggered doubt. Lately, the doubt has been buttressed by new observations of mice. Laboratory

---

* "Antipsychotics," "psychotropics," "psychoactives," and similar terms are somewhat interchangeable, but with a few distinctions. "Psychoactives" and "psychotropics" both refer to any chemical mixture that reduces activity in the neuron-transmission process in the brain and spinal cord—the central nervous system. They produce tranquilizing effects and moderate thoughts and behavior. The same holds true for antipsychotics, the difference being that these compounds are far more potent than the others, designed as they are to control psychotic breaks.

mice, that is, not the other variety. Those are supervised by marketing experts.

Psychoactive drugs have impelled doctors and scientists to make their historic break with Freudian orthodoxy, shifting from "the mind" to the brain. As the new drugs were sweeping the world and turning pharmaceutical companies into financial empires, scientists remained ignorant as to what made them work. Lobbied and prodded by drug company salesmen—themselves as clueless as anyone—a great many doctors and psychiatrists dropped their initial skepticism and came to assume that antipsychotics cured chronic mental illness. They did not. They temporarily repressed its symptoms. When the patient stopped taking these meds, the symptoms came crashing back, sometimes with fatal results.

The antipsychotic revolution proved to have arrived with side effects. Within a few years of their appearance in the marketplace, and irrespective of their sustained bonanza of profits and popular prestige, these "miracle drugs" stumbled into quagmire after quagmire.

Deinstitutionalization was only the first. Antipsychotics, exuberantly sold to President Kennedy by his Joint Commission as "moral treatment in pill form," proved utterly useless—as we have seen—in stemming the catastrophe that ensued. The half-century that followed saw an ongoing morality play starring pharmaceutical corporations, the government, a cadre of outraged watchdog writers and journalists, and a grassroots oppositional movement that hardened into an ideological force. Even as they created a market valued beyond $70 billion, the corporate purveyors of antipsychotic drugs have been sued by class-action groups, found guilty in courts of cover-ups and false claims, denounced by civil libertarians, and castigated as evil by victims of schizophrenia who believe that the use of such drugs made them worse instead of better.

No one really set out to find a chemical solution for irrational human behavior. Most intellectuals of the early twentieth century, including scientists, assumed that the Viennese master and his followers had that area covered. The origins of psychopharmacology lay, as they have with so many seminal discoveries, within a search for something else—something entirely different. Scientists have a term for this kind of sublime inadvertence: "serendipity."

In the mid-1930s, certain French scientists were toiling along what they hoped was the path to a workable antihistamine. Something was needed to neutralize the problematic neurotransmitter histamine. This component in the immune system combats pathogens taken into the body via food and breathing. But the chemical can transform itself into part of the problem, a protopathogen that triggers allergies, such as hives, and damages the heart and smooth muscles. In extreme cases, it can cause the often fatal allergic reaction known as anaphylactic shock.

A series of breakthroughs that took antihistamine research into an unforeseen and revolutionary direction commenced in the late 1930s at the Pasteur Institute in Paris. Among the scientists was a brilliant young Swiss-born scientist with the bony features and intense gaze that called to mind Sherlock Holmes. His name was Daniel Bovet. In 1937, the thirty-year-old Bovet and his twenty-three-year-old colleague Anne-Marie Staub, who had been thinking about leaving biochemistry to become a nun and treat lepers, were trying to develop a "selective antagonist" of histamine that could be safely ingested by human beings. They synthesized an antihistamine with the self-explanatory name thymoxyethyldiethylamine.*

---

* The name, as is true of most synthetic compounds, is an amalgam of its components. Examining those or any synthetic's components can be an eye-opening excursion into the unexpected, usually counterintuitive range of adaptations for natural substances.

Thymox, for example, is an oil extracted from the herb thyme that has been used for cleaning dental equipment and the hooves of cattle. Ethyl is extracted from sugarcane. Its derivatives are used as an extraction solvent in pharmaceuticals, as artificial flavoring in industrial foods, in treatment for arthritis (in Chinese medicine), in varnishes and lacquers, and of course as the intoxicating ingredient in liquor. Diethyl is a distillation of ethanol and sulfuric acid and has been around since the sixteenth century. It is a component in starting fluid for diesel engines, is used in anesthetics, and is a recreational inhalant. Amine refers to an organic dye extracted from tropical plants. When modified and injected with its companion elements into the bloodstream, it (and dyes of other colors) adheres to the tissue under examination, making the tissue easy for scientists to identify. Amine's

Among the substances whose properties aroused Bovet's curiosity was a powerful chemical distilled from ergot, a fungus that grows on rye. Other scientists were examining it as well, and it was synthesized in the following year as lysergic acid—the first step along the trail toward LSD. Bovet was the first to extract from it an important truth: that even simple molecules can touch off powerful mood changes and perceptions. As a 2007 review of his career noted, his observations "exerted a marked influence in the field of psychopharmacology, and in particular psychedelic drugs...Bovet's work helped to shape scientific thought regarding psychoactive drugs that are used in therapy today."[1]

Bovet and Staub's discovery of thymoxyethyldiethylamine set the stage for the use of synthetic drugs in brain therapy. It took time. Refinements of this compound, also (and thankfully) known as 929F, would consume nearly fifteen years before the resulting wonder drug stood revealed. Bovet himself conducted more than three hundred thousand experiments in the four years after discovering 929F to find the right formula.[2] His efforts earned him recognition as the founder of psychopharmacology and, in 1957, the Nobel Prize in Medicine.

Bovet and Staub's new synthetic chemical might have pointed the way only toward a good sneeze medicine, had it not caught the attention of a hovering Parisian pharmaceutical company, Rhône-Poulenc. Rhône-Poulenc, formed just nine years earlier, was interested in the pharmaceutical uses of synthetic textiles. The company formed a collaborative partnership with Pasteur. A chemist named Paul Charpentier incorporated Bovet's findings into his research toward a usable antihistamine. Within a short time, Charpentier perfected the

---

fumes are said to stink to high heaven and to be fatally toxic when inhaled in its pure state. It has become an important ingredient in treating cancer, syphilis, and other diseases. In the 1950s it was a component in rocket fuel.

Bovet himself alluded to this, in an understated way, in his Nobel speech on December 11, 1957: "The origin of many drugs must be looked for in substances of a biological nature, and in particular in the alkaloids. The elucidation of their structure has been a starting-off point for chemists to synthesize similar compounds." (See http://www.nobelprize.org/nobel_prizes/medicine/laureates/1957/bovet-lecture.pdf.)

compound promethazine, which went on the market as Phenergan. This drug not only acted against allergies, it produced a sedative effect as well. Thus it clearly was working upon the central nervous system—changing behavior. But its side effects in some patients—convulsions, increased heartbeat, fatigue, fever—made it a risky bet.

The relay baton was passed on to Henri Laborit, a dashing, dark-pompadoured physician, artist, movie actor (as himself), and wartime man of action. This summer of 1949 found Laborit, at age thirty-five, serving as a naval neurosurgeon at the Bizerte Naval Hospital at the port in Tunis. He was searching for some new medication that would reduce postoperative shock in victims of severe war wounds. He would soon light the spark to the combustible chain of research begun by Bovet and blast the psychotropic era into existence.

Laborit opened a package one day and found samples of Charpentier's new mixture from Rhône-Poulenc. Laborit took the compound into the lab, tested its properties, and intuited that its sedative powers offered possibilities beyond curing infection and runny noses. It produced hypothermia, or what Laborit called "artificial hibernation"—a kind of drug-induced anesthesia. Returning to Paris, he asked Charpentier for additional compounds that might increase the potency and reduce the side effects. In one of those tests, on December 11, 1950, Charpentier added a chlorine atom to the promazine molecule and produced chlorpromazine (CPZ).

Laborit continued his lab tests before trying it out on a living person. In February 1952, he and others administered some trial doses at the Val-de-Grâce military hospital in Paris. The doses, he reported, did not automatically put his patients to sleep. But they did produce an indifference to what was going on around them, and to their own pain.

In that year, Laborit recommended CPZ for use on patients in emotional or mental pain, though he still saw it mainly as an anesthetic. Rhône-Poulenc made it available by prescription in France as Largactil ("large in action"). In that same year the small, flailing American firm Smith, Kline & French (SKF) took a chance on buying license rights for the substance in the United States.

The thing was that still, nobody knew exactly what to do with it. Smith Kline invited Laborit to come to America and show off its "artificial hibernation" capacities to surgeons. This time, his magic went missing. His experimental dogs kept dying after their doses. Laborit went back home. He turned to writing and produced more than twenty books on science and evolutionary psychology. His ideas about free will and memory attracted the attention of Alain Resnais, a pioneer in the French school of New Wave filmmaking. He played himself in Resnais's mold-breaking 1980 movie *Mon oncle d'Amérique*, starring Gérard Depardieu. He faced the camera at intervals in this story of three characters groping for their destiny yet conditioned by their past, their lives implicitly compared to white rats in a lab cage. The film won the Grand Prize at Cannes. Laborit died in 1995.

As for Smith Kline, it began to think it had bought the rights to something like a failed high school chemistry experiment. Before cutting its losses, the little company decided to invite one last French scientist to come over and see what he could do. This was Pierre Deniker. Deniker was a colleague of Laborit's and one of the first to understand the true value of chlorpromazine. With his square, white crew-cut head, dark brows, and tight little grin, he called to mind a small-town police chief. Unlike Laborit, who had the appearance of a man who might at any moment don a beret and drag a woman across a cabaret stage, Deniker projected a businesslike demeanor. Like Laborit, he possessed a brilliant mind.

Deniker had already proved his knack for selling the new compound. Early in 1952, Rhône-Poulenc dispatched him to the Sainte-Anne Psychiatric Hospital in Paris, where he wowed the staff with a confident air. As recounted by the psychological historians Steve D. Brown and Paul Stenner, Deniker arrived one morning at Sainte-Anne, "from where the mentally ill, whom the Paris police have picked up the night before, are distributed. 'How many do you want for the clinic this morning?' the charge nurse asks... Normally these patients were not 'particularly welcome' on the wards... Nonetheless, Deniker... tells her he will take them all. He says to the nurse, 'We have found a trick that works.'"[3]

It did work. Not that day, but within a week or so, the "mentally ill" subjects (none of whom, of course, had been clinically diagnosed for schizophrenia; nor, for that matter, been cured of it by Deniker) had improved dramatically in their behavior. Shackles and restraints were no longer necessary. They were recognizably "normal" again. Or nearly so. Or so it seemed.

Soon after that, Deniker was taking his "trick" on the road in the United States, at hospitals and academies along the eastern seaboard. Again, he coaxed dubious professionals into listening to his claims and then witnessing the remarkable calm that descended upon their patients within several days. Demonstrating that he intuited where the real power lay, Deniker also looked into state mental institutions, dosing selected inmates and persuading their administrators that the wonder drug could radically diminish their overcrowded wards. Again, the results were amazing. The wardens, eager to impress state legislatures, sent the word along.

In 1954 CPZ appeared as an American prescription drug, approved by the FDA and licensed and distributed by Smith, Kline & French (today, GlaxoSmithKline). Its proprietary name was Thorazine.

Nothing like this could have been dreamed, or even conceptualized, by those generations of luckless inmates at Bedlam, or their keepers. "Technological solutions to mental disorders," as it has been described, was at the threshold of history.

Antipsychotics work as suppressants. Another generic name for them is "neuroleptics," because they function by producing neurolepsis in the brain through blocking certain transmissions. Neurolepsis is a condition of emotional quiescence, indifference to surroundings, and the tamping down of "psychomotor" function—that is, the effect on physical movement of thought impulses. These results are quite similar to the symptoms of negative schizophrenia.

The target of most neuroleptics is the neurotransmitter dopamine. More specifically, the target is one of dopamine's five receptors, D2, "the primary site of action for all antipsychotics," in the phrasing of one paper.[4] Receptors are proteins that bind to neurotransmitters and move chemical information along through neural pathways. Dopamine, through its receptors, influences nearly every function of the body, regulating the flow of information from anatomical areas to the brain. Its signals enable us to pay attention, to learn, and to remember. It regulates bodily movement and augments immune systems. Its release enables people to experience pleasure from food, sex, recreation, and the abstract series of vibrations known as music. Dopamine is the Self's Dr. Jekyll.

Except when it is transformed into Mr. Hyde. This can occur when its balance is disrupted—when there is either too much or too little of it. Stress is a leading cause of dopamine oversupply. Lack of sleep is another. Drugs, even prescription drugs and certainly "recreational" ones, are common causes. The consequences can be heightened anxiety, paranoia, adrenaline rushes, and hyperactivity—at its extreme, tardive dyskinesia, or uncontrollable grimacing and tongue-thrusting and other movements in the lower face. Given the right genes (that is, the wrong genes), all of this can produce schizophrenia.

Stress, a truly insidious state, can also *lower* the dopamine supply; as can obesity, a bad diet, and too much alcohol intake. Lower dopamine can result in Parkinson's disease, depression, too much sleep, a lowered libido, aggressive behavior, and a lack of concentration, among other things. Antipsychotics are aimed at oversupply; they are "antagonists" to it.

Another important neurotransmitter is serotonin, discovered in 1948 by the Italian pharmacologist Vittorio Erspamer. Serotonin is known as "the happy chemical": "Happy" because the molecule is believed to safeguard the balance of mood in much the same way as dopamine. That, and because it is the leading receptor for LSD.

Unlike dopamine, serotonin is manufactured in two distinct regions of the body, and the chemicals from each do not cross the other's boundaries. Up to 90 percent of the chemical is located in the gastrointestinal system, where it regulates bowel movements, aids the formation of blood clots that result from wounds, and hastens the expulsion of toxic food and drink via vomiting and diarrhea. Serotonin's smaller but at least equally vital production point is the hypothalamus, deep inside the limbic system of the brain—the delicate collection of many tiny structures that govern human emotion and memory. From this region, serotonin patrols the same territory as dopamine: mood, appetite, memory, sleep, and libido.

In the constantly pruning and regenerating adolescent brain, serotonin is believed to be a critical gatekeeper of thought and behavior. If there is not enough of it, the chemical is thought to be incapable of inhibiting impulses to anger, aggression, anxiety, panic, fear, and depression. Raising serotonin levels is the goal of the many antidepressant medications originally known as "mother's little helpers," the tranquilizers that arrived and proliferated on a parallel trajectory with antipsychotics. Miltown, introduced in 1955, was the first, working its way into thirty-six million prescriptions in two years. It was followed by Prozac, Zoloft, Paxil, and the rest. These medications are known collectively as SSRIs—selective serotonin reuptake inhibitors. "Reuptake" refers to the absorption of neurotransmitters by the same nerves that released them. SSRIs block this process and leave more serotonin available for action.

This summary comprises the accepted understanding of how antipsychotics work—accepted at least for a while. After all, it was only in 1975 that the Canadian researcher Philip Seeman discovered the D2 receptor. Before that, no one really knew how the new wonder drugs worked. They just worked. More or less.

And it appears that no one knows still.

Sales of Thorazine exploded on impact. Two million patients regarded as mentally disturbed ingested it by prescription in the first eight months. Smith, Kline & French, not a firm to let a single golden egg go uncracked, set an enduring pharmaceutical template by marketing its product as if it were a—product. It launched a barrage of print advertising in 1954 depicting Thorazine as the answer for just about anything that could ail a body short of dishpan hands: Arthritis. "Acute" alcoholism. "Severe" asthma. "Severe" bursitis. Behavior disorders in children. (It would be years before state and federal agencies started cracking down on indiscriminate and ethically reckless claims that psychotherapeutic drugs could help children, whose delicate neurochemistry is far more vulnerable to chemical distortion than adults'.) Menopausal anxiety. Gastrointestinal disorders. Psoriasis. Nausea and vomiting. Senile agitation. And, brushing once more against the border of ethical responsibility, even cancer.

These display advertisements set the stage for decades of charges that Big Pharma manipulated its customers' expectations via weaselly marketing techniques. Nearly all of them avoided direct claims that Thorazine would cure the complaint in question, including schizophrenia. They *insinuated* cure, but they were really selling *relief*—relief from symptoms. The modifying adjectives *acute* and *severe* served subtle notice of this, as did the small print that preceded the big scare words. The display ad for Thorazine as the enemy of cancer, for example, was presented as follows:

**relief from the suffering and
mental anguish of
CANCER**[5]

Among the small handful of ads that did make absolute claims was the one that trumpeted "*Another* dramatic use of 'Thorazine' ": in eight out of ten patients, it stopped hiccups.[6]

By 1955 the drug had rocketed around the Western world, trailing clouds of money: to Switzerland, England, Canada, Germany, Hungary, Latin America, Australia, and the USSR. Within a year Thorazine increased the company's sales volume by a third. SKF net sales increased from $53 million in 1953 to $347 million in 1970. In 1957, Deniker, Laborit, and their colleague Heinz Lehmann, who had supervised the first CPZ experiments in North America, shared the prestigious Albert Lasker Award for medical research.* The age of "miracle drugs" was under way.

Psychiatrists began to survive by transitioning from "talk therapy" with their patients to being de facto agents of the drug industry. Their classic roles as methodical counselors of troubled people, their time-consuming search to locate the *causes* of those troubles in traumas suffered earlier in

---

* Later in life Lehmann, who in fact was an admirer of Freud, expressed his dismay that psychopharmacology led to what he called "cook book" psychiatry, in which the necessary intimate relationship between therapist and patient is lost.

life—these pursuits evaporated, to be replaced by medical expertise. This was by way of prescribing proper medications to control *symptoms* of discontent by altering brain function. "Brain disease" replaced "the unconscious" as a near-consensus truth. (Or, as the pioneering child psychiatrist Leon Eisenberg joked, American psychiatry shifted from brainlessness to mindlessness.) And once that ambiguous truth was settled or at least agreed upon, commerce's doors swung open to admit the stampede of new pharma-entrepreneurs.

Haloperidol (Haldol) was synthesized in Belgium in 1958; lithium, an alkali metal with multiple adaptive uses in weapon-grade nuclear fusion, airplane-engine grease, ceramics, optics, polyester clothing, and air purification, was adapted and put on the market for use against bipolarity in 1970. The list increased steadily: Mellaril, Prolixin, Navane. The number of antipsychotics available today, in widely varying degrees of effectiveness and public awareness, approaches fifty. And then came clozapine, a watershed drug in several ways.

Clozapine appeared a few years after Haldol. It was developed in the early 1960s by the Swiss company Sandoz and promoted as a drug that succeeded with patients who seemed unreachable by Thorazine and the other early meds. Further, its developers declared it to be effective against suicidal tendencies in patients. A serotonin antagonist, clozapine could block both dopamine and serotonin receptors, which multiplied its control of overflow. But not long after its debut, clozapine disappeared. It did not reappear for a decade. It was pulled because of the problem that has bedeviled the "wonder drug" makers virtually from the outset; that has cost them millions of dollars in fines and settlements and the stigma of scandal even as their revenues soared into the billions; that has done damage to many patients, and has never been eradicated. The problem was side effects.

Clozapine's side effects, often virulent, were detected early by the corporate scientists who discovered it. These included seizures, constipation, weight gain, and, rarely, sudden death. None of those scientists or their employers said a word about these hazards. After all, the percentage of mental patients who experienced these ailments was low. And profits were high (though not as high as they soon would be). Not until researchers began linking it to a dangerous and sometimes fatal white blood cell depletion called agranulocytosis did Sandoz squeeze its corporate eyes shut and pluck it off the market.

Clozapine did not regain a place in the market until 1972, when it was sold in several European countries as Clozaril. Now—finally—it was carefully marketed as a medication to be administered only when patients' symptoms showed resistance to other antipsychotics, or when the patients began to talk seriously about suicide. It remained, and remains, a dangerous potion for many people. This problem was addressed not via adjusting its components, but via advertising—beneficial advertising, for a change: when it finally appeared in America in 1993 (as clozapine), its packaging carried five serious, or "box," warnings, including warnings for agranulocytosis.[7] The FDA pledged that its use would be carefully monitored.

Clozapine in ways good and bad was the narcoleptic drug of the future. It was the first of the "atypical" or "second-generation" antipsychotics that began to appear on psychiatrists' prescription lists in the 1970s. Drugmakers claimed that the new drugs were more versatile and bore less harmful side effects. This latter was contrary, of course, to the evidence of clozapine itself. But as we shall shortly see, exaggerated and outright false claims were already fast becoming the lingua franca of the brave new drug-world. The really ugly days lay ahead.

To open the dossier on the behavior of American and European pharmaceutical giants over the past quarter-century is to confront a fortified casino of riches and debauchery. Accounts of documented piratical atrocities gather, thicken, and expand like locusts blotting out the sun: corruption, criminality, contempt for public safety, buy-offs, payoffs, kickbacks, and the overarching pollution of medical integrity. All wrought by what seems a virulent new genetic strain of greed; a strain impervious to public disclosure, to staggering court fines, to continual calls to personal conscience and civic accountability. A sobering artifact of this scandal-beyond-scandal is the liberty that reformers feel to tar Big Pharma with analogies to the underworld, via use of such comparative terms as "organized crime" and "the Mafia."

These accusers are part of a new generation of watchdogs. They have taken up the work of those who exposed the overcrowding and inhumanity of state psychiatric hospitals more than forty years earlier. They are medical journalists and unspecialized journalists; PhDs, psychiatrists, and doctors repulsed by the malfeasance they have witnessed firsthand; they are current and former psychiatric patients. They share outrage over the mockery of public trust as it has unfolded and enlarged in plain sight—their plain sight, at least.

Their published output keeps growing. From the beginning of the twenty-first century alone, books regularly hit the stores bearing such titles as *Selling Sickness*; *Big Pharma* (2006); *Big Pharma* (2015); *The Big Pharma Conspiracy*; *Bad Pharma*; *Pharmageddon*; *Bad Science*; *The Truth About the Drug Companies*; *Overdiagnosed*; *Overdosed*; *Overdosed America*; *How We Do Harm*; *On the Take*; *Know Your Chances*; *Taking the Medicine*; *Death by Medicine*; *Our Daily Meds*; *Drugs, Power, and Politics*; *Pill Pushers*; *Poison Pills*; and others.

The sheer tonnage of all this can leave one feeling that a vital membrane in the social fabric is tearing open under pressure; a membrane that already bears the weight of big banks and finance institutions; a membrane that has held us back from decadence.

The list of companies shamed yet undeterred by stupendous fines reads like an inventory of vial labels on the shelves behind the bathroom mirror: Johnson & Johnson, Pfizer, GlaxoSmithKline, Abbott Laboratories, and several others. Many of their product names are even more familiar: among them Risperdal, Bextra, Geodon, Zyvox, Lyrica, Abilify, Wellbutrin, Paxil, Advair, Zocor, Oxycontin. Their perfidies, less so: off-label promotion (marketing a drug for uses not approved by the Food and Drug Administration), kickbacks, failure to disclose safety data, Medicare fraud, making false and misleading claims, and bribery, among others.

No category of medication, or medication user, has escaped the consequences of this collapse of medical and professional ethics. Certainly not the suffering and misinformed consumers of these products, the sick, the depressed, and the "worried well." These are the ones who have paid the price, or the ransom: paid in dollars and often in the well-being of their minds and bodies. In some cases, they paid with their lives. The most defenseless category of all the victims, as usual, has been the mentally ill.

How did it happen? How could an industry with roots so deep in the venerated healing arts have turned so feckless, so grotesque? Where have you gone, Anne-Marie Staub?

It happened via a chain of causality. The most volatile element in this chain was a December 1980 bipartisan vote in Congress. The vote went virtually unremarked in the punditry unleashed by the election of Ronald Reagan to the presidency. The vote was an amendment to the patent law.

Patents are rarely brought up in topical conversation, yet industries and state economies can rise and fall on them. The 1790 Patent Act was designed to financially protect the inventor of "any useful art" from profiteering by imitators. In 1967, the concept of "intellectual property"—roughly, the ideas of inventors that lead to new products—was given legal force by the World Intellectual Property Organization, an agency of the United Nations.* This and later patent-law refinements have led to a rapid product expansion of high technology and biomedicine, and have underscored the point of view that patent protection drives the US economy.

This particular patent act amendment was sponsored by the Democratic senator Birch Bayh and the Republican Bob Dole of Kansas. President Jimmy Carter, freshly unseated by Ronald Reagan, signed the new measure into law. Its intention, in simplest terms, was to stanch the US industrial drain to the Third World by creating new domestic industries almost from scratch. Among the most important of these would be the industries related to biotechnology.

To that end, the Bayh-Dole Act reversed decades of policy regarding ownership of inventions financed by federal funding. In a word, it

---

* A more limited understanding of "intellectual property," the international copyright protection of books and other artistic creations, was contained in the treaty created by the Berne (Switzerland) Convention in 1886.

privatized them. Previously, inventors (typically salaried research scientists from universities and nonprofit institutions) were required to turn over the rights to whatever they produced to the federal government. Now, these innovators, along with those from small businesses, could patent their own discoveries and take them to the marketplace: to the pharmaceutical companies, as a prime example. In 1979, universities secured 264 patents for research discoveries. By 2002, that number had increased to 3,291. In 2014, it stood at 42,584 in the biotechnology industry alone—an increase of almost three thousand from the previous year. In 2012, American universities earned $2.6 billion from patent royalties, according to the Association of University Technology Managers.

But holding a patent and realizing a profit from it are two different things. In recent years, this fact has begun to threaten the momentum and even the viability of the bonanza created on the good intentions of Bayh-Dole—not to mention the companies' widely known competitive "rush to the market" to be first with a new patent. Litigation costs surrounding patent deals inevitably have skyrocketed, as have so-called "transaction costs"—the various obligations one incurs in putting any patent (or product) into play. High-stakes lawsuits have challenged the legality of so-called "me-too" drugs: copies of established brands, the molecular structures of which are altered just enough to justify a new patent and new riches. As a result, patent-holders began cautiously withholding their products from licensure. The useful scientific knowledge that some of these patents hold is withheld from society—wasted. The unrealized economic value of this waste to the American economy has been estimated at $1 trillion annually, or a 5 percent reduction in potential GDP.[8*]

---

* These dynamics were studied at an October 2015 roundtable discussion among researchers and developers sponsored by the Tufts Center for the Study of Drug Development. Ken Getz, director of sponsored research at the center, told the group that "drug development cycle times have not gotten faster, costs continue to increase, and drug development has become riskier than ever with only 11.8% of products that enter clinical testing receiving regulatory approval, about half the rate of the 1990s." Adding that advantage would accrue to companies able to reduce "clinical time and cost" of this cycle time [which another Tufts study estimated at nearly nine years from the start of human testing to the marketplace],

This commodification of research had other consequences. It thrust universities and nonprofits into the hard-eyed venture-capital world. No longer would "serendipity" be permitted to work its happenstance magic, as it did with penicillin. No longer would time stand still for "pure" research—unpurposed, intuitive, trial-and-error experimentation that sometimes consumed decades of a scientist's life. From now on, *applied* science (in which the result was expected or intended at the outset) would rule.

And in the bargain, the American public would now be required to pay commercial prices for the results of this public-funded research—antipsychotic and antidepressant drugs included—having already paid, through taxes, the costs accrued by public universities and nonprofits in developing them. In vernacular, this is known as paying twice.

Bayh-Dole was just the second of two little-noticed landmark procedures in 1980 that cleared the way for legal entrée into the human brain. The previous June, the Supreme Court had ruled (by only a 5-to-4 majority) that a living microorganism, modified by man into a useful substance, is eligible for patent. That ruling marked the legal foundation for the transformational biotech industry.*

None of this is to imply that the University and Small Business Patent Procedures Act was intentionally insidious. Its sponsors saw it as a job-creator, a conduit for creative cooperation between industry and academia that would lead to proliferating new products, and that was in many other ways an unshackling of Yankee know-how for the

---

Getz offered a figure that by itself illuminates the true breadth of Big Pharma's swollen financial stakes: that the total capitalized cost of bringing a new drug to market averages out to $2.6 billion. http://csdd.tufts.edu/news/complete_story/rd_pr_october_2015.

* The case, known as *Diamond v. Chakrabarty*, pitted Ananda Mohan Chakrabarty, a microbiologist employed by General Electric, against Sidney A. Diamond, commissioner of Patents and Trademarks. Chakrabarty had developed a genetically engineered bacterium capable of disintegrating the elements of crude oil toward the goal of rapidly cleaning up oil spills by tankers in the ocean. He filed to patent the compound, but was rejected on the ground that living entities were not patentable under historic congressional understanding. The high court ruled in favor of Chakrabarty.

betterment of society. And to varying degrees, it worked. But like a narcoleptic drug rushed to market without enough testing, it carried destructive side effects.

It worked for a circumscribed sector of the American economy: the once prim-and-dutiful pharmaceutical industry that now cavorted on a permanent gusher of cash; for the university research bio- and neurochemists who suddenly discovered that they could do well by doing good, and do sensationally by doing even a little bit more good; for the tech PhDs on campus who used public funding to conceive and sell increasingly miraculous computer-enabled machines and processes: brain-computer interfaces, high-resolution microscopes, neuron-controlling optogenetics; the CRISPR gene-editor; even DNA versions of their filament-and-molded-plastic selves. It worked for the insane and disease-ridden patients who found relief in a scattering of genuinely "breakout" medications. For others, it didn't work so well. Especially those consumers of needed medications for ailments mental and physical. They, too, paid twice.

It took a few years, given the public's obliviousness to Bayh-Dole, for consumers to notice that they were paying twice (and then twicer and twicer and twicer). The consumers didn't like this. But they paid. And paid. And paid, even as prices for drugs rose and many of the elderly recipients responded by cutting down on or doing without some of the prescribed meds in their regimens. Or all of the prescribed meds in their regimens.

The consumers paid and paid, even as Big Pharma's rationale for constantly raising its prices—the "cost of research" involved in making the drugs—grew ever more hollow, given that the companies now were harvesting research from academia, or farming it out to other public entities for negotiable prices. (Their own, in-house research, as mentioned, tended increasingly toward the "me-too" micro-altering of patented compounds already on the market.)

And the consumers paid and paid, even as their anger at last rose. Some tried to develop grassroots strategies to combat the rising prices. Americans who lived a reasonable driving distance from the Canadian border, for instance, would cross that border to shop at pharmacies where they could buy their medications at a tenth of the US prices. Often they would make the trip in chartered buses. When the people on the buses were well along in years, as they usually were, a member of their state's congressional delegation would sometimes ride along as an escort. (Vermont senator Bernie Sanders pioneered this practice in 1999.)

Here is a brief index to how much they paid, and how much the government paid: In the act's first year, 1980, the government spent $55.5 billion (in 2000 dollars) for research and development. Sales of prescription drugs in that year stood at $11.8 billion.[9] In 1997 the figure was $71.8 billion in pharmaceutical sales; federal funding totaled $137 billion, but a large proportion of that went to the Strategic Defense Initiative and other military programs. In 2014, consumer spending rose to $374 billion,[10] with federal funding back down to $133.7 billion. That same year, the US Food and Drug Administration approved forty-one new pharmaceuticals, a record; and in 2015, the *Wall Street Journal*, citing research by the firm Evaluate Pharma, reported that global prescription drug sales are projected to grow by nearly 5 percent annually and reach $987 billion by 2020.[11] The reason, in the insouciant words of the *Journal* reporter, is "largely attributed to a crop of new medicines for hard-to-treat illnesses such as cancer *and fewer patents expiring on big-selling drugs*" (emphasis added). In November 2015, Intercontinental Marketing Services Health projected the sales number at $1.4 trillion.[12]

That the rising flow of riches in the pharmaceutical industry might bring trouble in its wake—trouble in the form of litigation—apparently did not trouble the giddy pharma-entrepreneurs of the Reagan years and beyond. (And as the years went on and litigation spread and court settlements and fines seemed to add zero after zero to their totals, it grew clear that the entrepreneurs didn't really care. Their sales figures were adding even more zeros.) The international catastrophe of thalidomide should have been recognized for the dreadful omen that it was, but for some reason this did not happen. The German-made drug, introduced in Europe in 1957 as a completely safe antidote to morning sickness and soon a global phenomenon, caused multiple thousands of birth defects in children of women who trustingly bought it—such as flipper-like arms and the absence of toes, legs, and ears. Roughly half the cases were fatal. Some of the litigation continues today. (Thalidomide was never approved for sale in the United States, yet the makers sent samples to American doctors, who passed them along to their unsuspecting patients, with the inevitable results.)

The first serious American-made hint of bad consequences arrived with clozapine, whose makers flirted with legal reprisal before voluntarily withdrawing their new atypical drug. But it was the debut of another "atypical" drug, Risperdal (risperidone), that introduced Big Pharma to Big Lawsuit.

Risperdal went on the market in 1994, a product of Janssen, itself a subsidiary of the pharma giant Johnson & Johnson, the largest marketer of medications in the world. The drug was sold as a treatment for bipolar disorder and schizophrenia. Its makers assured the public of its safety based on three internal trials before submitting it to the FDA for review. Somehow, the trials failed to demonstrate that the drug could result in fever, muscle stiffening, irregular heartbeat, trembling, fainting—and the dangerous disorder tardive dyskinesia.

These complaints caught the attention of consumer protection agencies in thirty-six states between 1993 and 2004.[13] The state's full catalog of complaints would have made a Gilded Age railroad baron recommend prayer and penitence. They included allegations that J&J paid kickbacks to the charmingly named Omnicare Inc., the largest nursing home pharmacy in America, to prescribe Risperdal to the generally clueless seniors—many of them suffering from dementia. (Risperdal's packaging includes a "black box" warning with this language: "Elderly patients with dementia-related psychosis treated with antipsychotic drugs are at an increased risk of death." Risperdal of course is an antipsychotic. Caveat emptor.) The kickbacks included money, offers of paid vacations for doctors' trips, and "lucrative consulting agreements" to prescribe Risperdal to more patients.[14] Johnson & Johnson decided to contest these charges and lost. Omnicare, for its part, agreed to pay $98 million to resolve claims that it accepted this booty and thus violated the False Claims Act.[15]

J&J later reached separate settlements with Texas in 2012 and

Montana in 2014 for $158 million and $5.9 million, respectively. Settlements with other states added up to $181 million.

The dollar amounts of these state trial costs and settlements might lead a reasonable observer to conclude that they taught Big Pharma a lesson it would not soon forget. The reasonable observer is invited to read on, preferably while seated or holding on to a firm object. Not long after the turn of this century, settlements and verdicts against drug companies began to roll out from federal court trials on a monetary scale that obliterated the state-level penalties and threatened to obliterate the very notion of "scale" itself.

The first and largest of these decisions did not directly involve an antipsychotic drug, though the company in question had one of those (Saphris*) on the market. It is of interest because it highlights the entry of the Department of Justice into the arena, and because it opens a view into the realm of Big Pharma as it balances its growing flood tide of revenue against its ethical responsibility to public safety.

In 2007, the global health-care company Merck, with headquarters in New Jersey, agreed to pay $4.85 billion to settle lawsuits filed in relation to its medication Vioxx. The substance had been introduced in 1999 as an antidote to pain brought on by rheumatoid arthritis, then pulled off the market in 2004. The lawsuits numbered about twenty-seven thousand and covered forty-seven thousand sets of plaintiffs.[16] They had been filed by Vioxx users or their relatives who claimed that the medication had resulted in heart attacks, many of them fatal. The Justice Department's investigations turned up documents that Merck researchers had been aware of these risks, but that the company did not report them. In 2011, Merck agreed to pay an additional $426 million to the federal government, $202 million to state Medicaid agencies, and $321 million in criminal charges, to round out the litigation.

Merck had claimed revenue of $2.5 billion in 2003. That was big money in those days.

---

* In 2011, the FDA warned that Saphris users can suffer serious allergic reactions. Merck agreed to revise the drug's label to include this information.

In September 2009, Pfizer settled with the government for $2.3 billion in a similar deal. This one involved Pfizer's painkiller Bextra, which is no longer on the market. One of the plaintiffs in the case, a former Pfizer sales representative named John Kopchinski, told the *New York Times*, "The whole culture of Pfizer is driven by sales, and if you didn't sell drugs illegally, you were not seen as a team player."

In 2010, another subsidiary of Johnson & Johnson* agreed to a settlement of more than $81 million in civil and criminal penalties to resolve allegations in a federal suit that involved its drug Topamax. Once again, the charge was "off-label" marketing. Once again, the specific wrongdoings were more impersonally amoral than legal language can communicate, and once again, the prey of the predators were the nation's mentally ill. The FDA had approved Topamax as an anticonvulsant drug. The Department of Justice charged that the makers illegally went beyond that by promoting Topamax for psychiatric problems.[17]

May of 2012 saw another stunning outlay. GlaxoSmithKline, spawn of the company that had stumbled onto Thorazine more than half a century earlier, agreed to pay $3 billion in criminal penalties for illegal promotion of its antidepressants Paxil and Wellbutrin and the diabetes drug Avandia. The FDA found that GSK had not warned that children and adolescents taking Paxil showed increased tendencies toward suicide, and that pregnant women taking Paxil were more likely to have autistic babies. Wellbutrin, approved for depressive disorder, was promoted off-label for remedies such as weight loss, the treatment of sexual dysfunction, substance addictions, and attention-deficit/hyperactivity disorder (ADHD), among other off-label uses. As for Avandia, FDA clinical studies showed that it increased the risk of heart attack by 43 percent—and double that after a year of treatment.[18]

That same year, Abbott Laboratories drew $1.5 billion in criminal and civil fines after pleading guilty to misbranding Depakote, approved by the FDA to combat epileptic seizures and bipolar mania. Abbott admitted to recruiting a specialized sales force to peddle the drug to nursing homes as

---

* Ortho-McNeil-Janssen Pharmaceuticals, Inc.

a control for agitation among the demented patients, and as a companion drug with antipsychotics to combat schizophrenia. Neither use had been shown to work in clinical tests; each was accompanied by side effects.[19]

In November 2013, Johnson & Johnson paid the federal piper for its fraudulent and dangerous marketing of Risperdal (one of Kevin's medications). The price was $2.2 billion in criminal and civil fines. The charges against J&J replicated the earlier ones raised by the states and added one or two new ones; for instance: In its original review of Risperdal, the FDA had withheld approval for Janssen, a subsidiary of Johnson & Johnson, to market the drug for children. Janssen did so anyway. In fact, Johnson & Johnson, it was alleged in court, directed its sales force to promote Risperdal to children's doctors. Parents of male children who used the drug began reporting cases of gynecomastia, a swelling of breast tissue caused by imbalances of estrogen and testosterone.

These federal court victories over Big Pharma and its depredations might not have been possible without substantial impetus from that figure of dubious reputation in popular opinion, the whistle-blower. These were not malcontented cranks, as the stereotype has it, but educated professionals, men and women who typically had held high positions within the pharmaceutical industry. John Kopchinski had been a sales representative for Pfizer. They took risks—perhaps not life-threatening, yet scary enough for people unused to cloak-and-dagger intrigue. Most of them wore hidden recorders—wires—to company meetings to capture incriminating policy conversations. The resulting transcripts proved devastating. But the potential rewards—ahh, the rewards! The rewards offer another glimpse into the surreal levels of money flowing into Big Pharma from around the world.

John Kopchinski was awarded more than $50 million in whistle-blower fees for his role in exposing Pfizer. The six former employees who testified against Johnson & Johnson and its companies shared $102 million from the Department of Justice settlement.

The whistle-blower rewards, of course, paled before the largesse that poured into federal coffers from these cases. The Department of Justice announced in 2015 that it had realized more than $3.5 billion in settlements and judgments in the fiscal year ending September 30. This marked the fourth consecutive year that the department had exceeded that figure, and it brought recoveries since 2009 to a total of $26.4 billion.[20]

It does not seem to have mattered. Not a penny. Not a word.

Not even, to give a specific example, the announcement in 2010 by the reformist group Public Citizen that Big Pharma had become the biggest defrauder of the federal government, surpassing the defense industry. This did not generate national media discussion. Certainly not on the level of vitriol aimed at the evils of Obamacare.

None of it seems to matter to Big Pharma's CEOs. Their names rarely appear in the press or on television, unless they are being honored as humanitarians by some myopic or bought civic organization. Their names appear even more rarely in news of the big settlements: corporate individuals are almost never held liable for even the worst company crimes. And the largest penalties, the ones reaching into the billions, scarcely match the value of a few weeks' revenues.

"It's just a cost of doing business," one pharmaceutical analyst remarked of the cash penalties, and added, "until a pharmaceutical executive does a perp walk."[21]

Looking back at it all from nearly forty years as a doctor and medical researcher, and, before that, a marketing manager in the pharmaceutical industry, the Danish author Peter Gotzsche voiced the inevitable analogy. "Much of what the drug industry does fulfills the criteria for organized crime in U.S. law," Dr. Gotzsche observed. "And they behave in many ways like the mafia does; they corrupt everyone they can corrupt, they have bought every type of person, even including ministers of health in some countries."[22]

The perp walk will not likely happen soon. Nor are drug barons likely to burst into tears of epiphany at being compared to dangerous criminals. They and their companies have long since risen to take their place above the clouds of true accountability, alongside the banks and financial institutions, the firearm manufacturers, the tobacco industry, and the other global denizens of Too Big to Fail, Too Big to Nail.

And why should they not? No one cares about crazy people.

16

"Something Unexplainable"

The first signs of Kevin's descent into schizophrenia came to light in January 2002, when he was seventeen and beginning his final semester at Interlochen. Kevin himself alerted us to his situation in a frantic telephone call one evening not long after he and Dean had returned to their schools from the holiday break. Based on what he told us, his mental state seemed to have been affected by his drug use. I emailed to Dean a digest of what Kevin had told us, or what I'd understood of it from the jumbled conversation:

Dean,

On Monday, Kevin admitted to us that he has a serious substance-abuse problem and wants help. His problem pretty much covers the gamut of available substances, and his craving for them is severe, and it has led to blackouts and other extreme results.

Nearly all of Kevin's specific information turned out to be wrong or exaggerated. His use had covered no gamut. He'd been caught using chewing tobacco. But what the call did reveal, unfathomable to us then, was far worse. It was a symptom. He was hallucinating.

Honoree and I agreed that one or both of us must go to him. In the meantime, we reached the dean of students at the arts academy, who was aware of Kevin's psychic disorientation and already had begun working with him. The school did not intend to expel him, as I wrote to our elder son, "but the dean made it clear to us that she feels Kevin should take a medical and emotional leave of absence."

As a condition for allowing Kevin to remain enrolled, the dean of students asked us to place our son in a psychiatric hospital or clinic somewhere for a minimum of two weeks of inpatient therapy. Symptomatic of the chronic shortage of psychiatric beds in the country, we could find nothing for our son. The Interlochen administrators proved accommodating, and we reached a backup agreement: Kevin would stay on as a day student under Honoree's supervision. She would rent living space for the two of them in a residency hotel, drive him to and from the campus, and then to daily consultations with a therapist in Traverse City. Honoree drove straight to Michigan the next day.

How and why did Kevin develop his addictive urges? Or Dean?

The past thirty years or so have seen a flourishing of research into "comorbidity"—the possible correlation between the use of illicit drugs, even some prescription ones, and the emergence of schizophrenia. This field of study has generated hundreds of papers from physicians, psychiatrists, and PhDs around the world, which have tended to be at once inconclusive and highly suggestive. They typically report a high correlation between substance abuse and bipolar disorder and schizophrenia, at least among those genetically predisposed to the affliction.[1] A paper published in 2003 by three French neuroresearchers is typical:

> The use of psychoactive substances usually leads to a general deterioration of the patients' condition. Pharmacodependent schizophrenic patients relapse more often, they are more frequently hospitalized, they show more violent behaviors, and they are more frequently homeless. In particular, the positive symptoms [hallucinations, delusions, confused thought] of these patients are generally exacerbated by the [illicit] psychoactive drugs.[2]

The team named "psychostimulants" such as cocaine and amphetamines, "anesthesic dissociatives" (PCP, ketamine), and hallucinogens (cannabis, LSD) as prominent in exerting "psychotomimetic" effects, and also listed amphetamines, cocaine, ecstasy, and heroin as causative substances.

The French psychiatric researcher P. Batel, reviewing the leading hypotheses for the high comorbidity in 2000, is among those drawn to the theory of "self-medication," which suggests that "schizophrenics may be attempting to counter the deficit linked to their disorders by using the substances they take…to cope with their emotional problems." Among the high-correlating features he lists are "very high nicotine and alcohol dependence, with a very poor prognosis."[3] There has yet been no consensus on whether the drugs enhanced the illness or the illness led to higher drug use. But there has been growing evidence that both may be true.

Batel published his paper at a time when "substances" were not generally believed to cause psychosis; their use was seen as a result of it. By around 2007, research had further focused the comorbidity searchlight. It now shone on cannabis: marijuana. In July of that year, the prestigious British medical journal *Lancet* published the results of a survey of thirty-five studies from nearly five thousand references. The evidence, its authors asserted,

> is consistent with the view that cannabis increases risk of psychotic outcomes…although evidence for affective outcomes is less strong. The uncertainty about whether cannabis causes psychosis is unlikely to be resolved by further longitudinal studies such as those reviewed here. However…there is now sufficient evidence to warn young people that using cannabis could increase their risk of developing a psychotic illness later in life.[4]

Seven years later, another study appeared that made the *Lancet* piece sound waffling. In 2014 three widely published psychiatric investigators produced "Gone to Pot: A Review of the Association Between Cannabis and Psychosis," which concluded: "At the present time, the evidence indicates that cannabis may be a component cause in the emergence of psychosis, and this warrants serious consideration from the point of view of public health policy."[5]

Noting that cannabis is the most commonly used illicit drug in the world, with an estimated five million daily users, the three cited evidence suggesting many associations between the substance and disorders that included schizophrenia. "The relationship between cannabis and schizophrenia," they assert, "fulfills many but not all of the standard criteria for causality, including temporality, biological gradient, biological plausibility, experimental evidence, consistency, and coherence."[6] One of the three, Samuel T. Wilkinson of the Yale School of Medicine, went so far as to unequivocally affirm a comorbid connection. In a 2013 *Wall Street Journal* essay that protested legalization of marijuana, Wilkinson cited articles in *Lancet* and the *British Journal of Psychiatry* to substantiate his conclusion: "As research accumulates, the emerging picture is that marijuana precipitates schizophrenia or related psychotic disorders in people whose brains are inherently vulnerable to psychosis."[7]

These studies appeared too late to trigger warnings in the Powers household that cannabis could induce mental illness, though we tried, without success, to keep our sons from using it anyway. The world at large has remained equally, willfully clueless. As of June 2015, twenty-three states and the District of Columbia had enacted laws legalizing marijuana in some form and with varying limits.[8] In Vermont, of course, cannabis is practically the unofficial state flower. The countercultural migration here in the 1970s enshrined it as the puff of choice. Organic, backyard-grown weed was a social amenity that cut across class lines. Once again, legislation on an issue with profound and toxic implications for the mentally ill was spreading across the country without attention paid to the interests of the mentally ill.

Kevin's two weeks of intensive therapy and Honoree's maternal companionship produced their desired effects. He finished out his final semester at Interlochen without further crises to blemish his three years of achievement. He began building his dreams for the life beyond the school. His dreams seemed at once fantastical and attainable. Kevin would continue his guitar training at the Berklee College of Music, a haven of contemporary music instruction and performance inside a deceptively drab brick-front on Boylston Street in Boston. Berklee's alumni includes Quincy Jones, Branford Marsalis, John Mayer, Melissa Etheridge, Donald Fagen of Steely Dan, Brad Whitford of Aerosmith, and others. His bassist comrade Peter would pursue the classical double bass at the Boston Conservatory, an elite academy that accepted fewer than 250 undergraduate students. The two of them would be studying within a five-minute walk of each other in the historic Fenway neighborhood.

Kevin's letter of application to Berklee is one of the treasures of our family memorabilia. Unembellished, humble, almost unconscious-seeming, it stands in my mind as the purest, most revelatory composition my son ever wrote, in any genre. Though he surely did not intend it as such, it is a verbal jazz piece, simple and demotic at its outset, establishing the theme, then opening up into rich, spontaneous passages of color and passion before returning to the main line for its quiet close. It is all of Kevin's music, compressed. It is all of Kevin.

Kevin Powers
Musical Experience

As a musician, one of the most profound events I experienced was getting my first Pat Metheny CD. I was in eighth grade and the CD was "Like Minds," a Christmas present from my dad. It featured Gary Burton, Chick Corea, Roy Haynes and Dave Holland. This was my first exposure to the jazz art form. Hearing that CD made me want to play jazz guitar.

From the first chord of the first song, something unexplainable made me listen more intently than I ever dreamed I would to a jazz recording. Gary Burton's solo was intense. His playing was classy and smooth but not cheesy, his melodic runs and progressive energy were all there. When Pat started his solo, this was the first time I decided to give a new player a chance. I was, up until then, a die-hard for the rock scene. I had never heard someone play jazz in a way that inspired me to. That all changed with Pat's playing.

His solo was begun in a manner that made him sound like he was in my room talking to me, telling me all the great things the guitar could offer. He started a little behind the beat with a short concise phrase and much as the title of the song would suggest, "Question and Answer," the second phrase followed the first one perfectly. It was so lyrical and melodic. I had always enjoyed Joe Pass; however, I appreciate the two for different reasons now. I had never heard improvisation that was in a sense a melody itself. Pat was doing this. I had heard over and over again from camps that I attended that "space" was important, that one's solo needs to "breathe." Now it became clear to me why. It was happening here.

As soon as I was at the next record store, I bought a Pat Metheny Group CD. I realized that what I had heard on "Like Minds" was probably a small pixel in the larger scope of this guy. For a period of about a full year, each successive CD of his that I bought was more interesting than the last. Pat's compositional ability is hard to comprehend. His songs are so expressive and the forms are so intricate. The most memorable experience I will have is attending the National Guitar Summer Workshop in New Milford, CT, where Pat came and spoke to us. It was three hours with the words from the man himself about what he has been doing, does and will be doing in the future. He is one of my biggest inspirations and I am very lucky to have been able to hear his music and see him.

Kevin and Peter would head for Boston almost immediately after graduation, where Peter had lined up summer jobs for them as waiters at a club. They would share an apartment in Roxbury before starting classes at their academies.

We applauded Kevin as he directed a guitar ensemble on the Corson stage during Festival Week leading up to graduation in June 2002. A day or two later we applauded him again as he walked across the stage of Kresge Auditorium on the shore of Green Lake to receive his Interlochen diploma. And then we packed his belongings into the van, resting his black Martin guitar on top of his bags and boxes, between protective pillows. We said our good-byes to faculty members near the spot where three years earlier I had watched my son begin to make new friends. Then we drove home to Middlebury, the Interlochen years already a memory, one that would grow, and then recede.

Kevin and Peter moved into their Roxbury apartment and commenced their summer nights waiting tables at the club. By day, they worked toward their true summer goal: to re-form Booby and book a gig at the Middle East, the iconic music-and-restaurant complex on Central Square in Cambridge. A landmark with its bright gold canopies, several dining areas, and four performance stages, the Middle East had showcased and often introduced legendary bands in rock, jazz, punk, ska, and hardcore: Aerosmith, the Mighty Mighty Bosstones, and hundreds more. Kevin and Peter wanted to make it there before they began college. They put out flyers for a drummer, wrote new songs, and rehearsed daily. They found a skinsman who suited their standards. By August they had auditioned at the Middle East and secured a September booking.

Early the following month, they moved into their separate college residences. Kevin was assigned a third-floor room with another guitarist in a Berklee student residence, a fine old graystone on Massachusetts Avenue, an easy walk to the academy. To Honoree and me, it was a wonderful building, an artifact of the Proper Bostonian Era. In fact, all of it seemed too good to be true, and it was. By then, out of our sight, Kevin's dreams and his life had begun to fall apart.

A midsummer email was our first warning. "Hey guys," Kevin began in a typical salutation, and then dropped into a tone of uncharacteristic dejection:

I'm writing partly to purely just vent about some things and partly to seek some advice from you as I value both of your wisdom equally and very strongly. I've been feeling real stressed lately here, more so than I have before. I'm not at any point of giving up or complete dispair. But as you could imagine, for me, I feel like I need something else right now that I'm not getting here.

What Kevin was not getting, he went on, was support from Peter. He felt that his friend was pulling away; losing interest in the friendship and in Booby as he immersed himself in preparing for the demands of the conservatory.

One of the harshest lessons an adolescent must learn is among the most common: things change. The childhood world falls away, and with it the childhood verities. Change often means loss, and loss can wound the adolescent heart. Among the most painful and bewildering of these losses are best-friendships and romances. The spurned generally heal over time. But not everyone heals.

Physiologically speaking, these early (metaphorical) blows to the heart often coincide with the actual and necessary severing of cortical synapses described earlier in this book: the "neurological housecleaning" of obsolescent gray matter formed early in life so that new connections can form to meet the challenges of adulthood. This pruning-away stage usually happens from age sixteen through the early twenties. It is the same period of life when the genes for schizophrenia, if they are present, come alive to help fill the vacuum.

Peter, of course, could not have known any of this, and likely had no idea of his bandmate's perceptions. Two years earlier, Kevin might not even have noticed his friend's actions, nor been upset by them. Honoree and I were likewise oblivious. We did not think to connect Kevin's distress to his January crisis, though I now believe that these were both symptoms of what was to come. We simply knew that our buoyant son had fallen into an untypical state of depression. We hoped it would pass.

Shortly before their Middle East performance, Kevin wrote, "I'm rehearsing with the band tonight and Pete and Jeff [the drummer] and I have already run the set, so it should go well. We're very excited about the show and we'll certainly tell you all about it."

The show did go well, apparently. But Kevin's message afterward was one of devastation. He expressed it in another long, almost despairing email. Peter, in his perception at least, had quickly left the stage at the end and joined a crowd of friends with hardly a word to Kevin or the drummer: "What hurt me the most," he wrote, "was that he turned his back on me after a triumph of a show." He mentioned a state of feelings that we did not recognize at the time as a four-alarm warning for those with a schizophrenia gene complex: "The last thing I want to do is move into my first Berklee year with the stress that is eating me alive."

He strove—I could almost feel him doing it—to recapture some of his characteristic optimism: "I like it here [at Berklee]. I like the kids, I like the environment, I don't feel like someone 'different' because I like rock, classical and jazz and bluegrass at the same time. This is my kind of place." He followed with an attempt at philosophical detachment: "Maybe Peter has found his place too. But OUR place is no longer a thing in my mind, our common ground is not there and I can't see it forming again." And then the close, and a sentiment that he almost never failed to include in his messages to us, yet, in this instance, might have signaled some deep foreboding about his future:

> *You guys are everything to me and thank you for all your love,*
>
> > *Sincerely,*
> > *Kevin*

As Kevin pushed on into his first semester at Berklee, Dean was navigating a new campus as well. In autumn 2002 he began classes at Colorado State University in Fort Collins. He'd transferred up there from Fort Lewis College at Durango, pursuing a girlfriend who had made the same change. He had not come back east during this transition, electing to sign up as a summer volunteer with the Colorado Trail

Crew that was clearing logs and boulders for a road through the vast Front Range.

He'd lived in the mountains on a spartan diet, played his guitar around evening campfires, and slept in a tent. The wilderness had called to Dean since boyhood, when he'd hiked and camped and skied in the tamer mountains around Middlebury. Now, the heavy lifting in the cool mountain air hardened his athletic body, and the company of his taciturn fellow volunteers made real a romantic escapist dream, the origins of which were known only to Dean. Dean and the girl broke up in the fall of 2002. How serious—or seriously wounded—were the feelings on each side was unknown to us, as was her name. But before long, Dean was sending us CDs of ballads he had written and recorded. The earliest ones were filled with raw emotion and harsh chords, but even these showed moments of tenderness: he built an entire song, in fact, around the image of a blue backpack. It seems that he was working through an ache of loss that paralleled Kevin's—an ache made worse by the same stealthy transformation of his mind.

Once again, we had no means for grasping this.

As the weeks went on and he sent us more of his songs, the pain in his lyrics softened beneath an overlay of clever irony and wordplay, and, from there, into poetry that was alternately playful, joyous, and nakedly tender.

He continued to excel as a student. "Your English scores are phenomenal!" I'd written him shortly before Kevin's crisis. He let us know that although he remained haunted by the accident with Amy and its aftermath, and suffered from anxiety, his burst of songwriting had paid off: he had booked a gig at Jon's Blue Note, a small but popular coffee shop and a stop on the Colorado independent folk circuit: "I'm gonna make fliers today."

We emailed back and forth a lot—about the national scene, Dean's music, his writing, many topics. Emails provided the unexpected benefit of letting us purge the inexplicable tension that hovered over our times together. They somehow allowed Dean to drop the monosyllabic retorts he used in our personal conversations and open up his full expressive range—funny, ironic, informed, companionable, and refreshingly profane when the situation seemed to demand it, as in this reply to some tale of political perfidy I had sent to him:

> *that is some scary shit, pardon my arab, ill check it out i told this girl whos sitting next to me, and she kind of looked back and seemed to think if she just smiled long enough i would go away, my point is nobody cares, nobody, really cool, alright take care, im going to read*

And:

> *well, my fuckin teachers a dickhead, and i put up with him every day cause of his attendance policy is so strict, you know, im going there i pay to go to school, i have to listen to his bull shit and today he says "dean powers, where are you? why are you looking so mean?" everyone turns to look at me, and i joked "i just got done with mean class im practicing my homework." silence in the class, as if we were having a moment of silence for the deceased, my humors pretty poor i guess but then i felt mean, and i wasn't before, and he went on teaching the class without responding to me either, and as if he were truely upset with me, im pissed, and im trying to let it go, ive got a lot of shit in my head, i understand hes very insecure, he wants everyone to be onboard with him in his jocularity, and i don't have to laugh i don't have to pretend im enjoying the class and worry the teacher is going to whip me into shape for not doing so, ya know?*

I admit to laughing, possibly even out loud, at that "i just got done with mean class" line.

I was oblivious then to certain other products of his imagination; a line from a song, say, that may or may not have amounted to a warning sign:

These are such good songs, Dean. Some of your lyrics are amazing. And clever as hell. I love the one about the man inside your head and you have to disagree with what he said. That's as good as anything Dylan wrote.

Perhaps I should have wondered: *What* man inside his head?

Once in a while, I did wonder. After we'd both watched a televised football game, separated by two thousand miles, he emailed:

i think that game was fixed, and probably by the government

Somehow, that remark struck me as more than a joke.

His psychic struggles resurfaced, and with them his own yearning for anesthetization via drugs and alcohol.

As for Kevin, notes of anxiety persisted as his semester went on, intruding into his attempts to be upbeat. "Wow, it can be intense here." "It's like you were saying in your email, all the tiny little things in everyday life get magnified and come to a much broader meaning than ever before." "It's almost nerve racking..."

Was he all right? We had no real evidence to assume that he wasn't all right. He must be all right. Every adolescent had a rough patch or two. Kevin was Kevin. He would be all right.

At four o'clock one October morning, the ringing telephone roused us from our sleep and into the realization that Kevin was not all right. Nothing would ever be all right with Kevin again.

Honoree got to the phone first and heard Kevin's breathless voice announce that he had been selected by a senior member of Berklee's administration, a man who himself was a renowned musician, to accompany him on a concert tour of Russia.

Honoree listened for a minute and then handed me the receiver without a word. Kevin repeated the information to me. He sounded out of breath, as well he might after learning of such an honor; but there was something else in his voice as well, a quaver, and he was talking very fast. I tried to pin him down on specifics, starting with why he was calling at this hour. He said something, in his rushed voice, about having just come from an all-night planning session. I pressed for more: When are you leaving? For how long? How did this selection process work? But I quickly realized that I was talking into a dead line. Kevin had hung up.

Honoree made coffee and we sat in the living room in our robes trying to make sense of it. Such is the power of persuasion, or the need to believe, or something, that we tried to fit his announcement into some plausible context. He was pretty damn good, after all. Had he made it through an all-night winnowing process of deserving students? But why all night? And why did he hang up? But then why would he have called to tell us this in the first place if it weren't true? There lay the rub, and neither of us could summon the will to articulate it right away. We stared at the coffee cooling in our cups until I at last spoke up, framing my suspicions in words that I have never managed to recall without wincing.

"Unless," I said, "he wigged out."

I guess I put it that way to distance myself from the ghastly chance that it was true. But then Honoree's and my eyes met, and we both knew that it was true.

Honoree picked up our landline receiver and dialed Kevin's mobile phone. No answer, just his message. Should we call his roommate? We told each other that we didn't want to wake him. It was too early, by hours, to contact anyone at the school. And so we resigned ourselves to waiting. At some point I believe we returned to bed. But we didn't sleep. We stared at the ceiling and wondered where our son was, and why, and at what point it would be necessary to call the police.

It was Kevin himself who reestablished contact, at midmorning. He had just boarded a westbound Greyhound bus, he told Honoree. He was headed to Los Angeles, where he expected to find work as a rock star.

Honoree didn't engage him on this. The tour to Russia was revealed as the vapor it was, but this new destination, if not the immediate dream behind it, was unnervingly real. Already, our instincts were sharpening, growing strategic. She ended the conversation; we found a map and determined that the bus's first stop would be Albany. We probably could get there in time to intercept him and find help. Albany was about three hours from Middlebury, and three to four hours from Boston, depending on traffic and the route. We dressed and headed right out, our mobile phones, thankfully, in tow.

At the Albany terminal we waited an hour and then exited our van as the Greyhound from Boston pulled in. Its door opened and its passengers filed out. Kevin was not among them. For some reason I had anticipated this. My wife and I returned to the van and sat there trying to think of what to do next. Honoree's mobile phone rang. It wasn't our son, but a New York state policeman. He had found her number on Kevin's phone. He told her that he had picked up Kevin and taken him to a hospital in Syracuse. I started the van and we set out on the two-hour drive west.

There we learned that Kevin had been removed from the bus at a service stop near Albany. He'd awakened, disoriented, from a sleep, and stormed up the aisle toward the driver, demanding to know where he was being taken. He'd grown belligerent—for the first and only time in his life—and a good Samaritan passenger, a powerful man, had hurried up the aisle behind him and gently enveloped Kevin in his arms. The driver ejected him from the bus at the service stop, and the state police had taken over from there.

A hospital doctor in Syracuse led us to an emergency room where we found our son sound asleep on his side, his back to us. He had been sedated. The attending doctor was not certain what had happened. He said that it might have been a drug overdose. And then he said it might have been an onset of bipolar affliction. This shocked us, as we had heard the term "bipolar" infrequently in our lives, and we instinctively believed it was a disease that happened to other people. We were typical in our clueless denial.

Then the doctor said something that unsettled us even more. He said that bipolarity was a better diagnosis "than the alternative." He did not name "the alternative." Yet, uninitiated as we were, we thought that perhaps we knew.

We spent nearly that entire afternoon not in consultation with the hospital staff, but in phone calls to and from our insurance provider. The conversations were silly, and maddening. We were told, for instance, that the provider would not offer us coverage unless Kevin were transported to Middlebury by ambulance, a distance of 230 miles and a driving time of four hours. The problem was, there were no available ambulances. We asked why we could not drive our son, given that we were going that way ourselves. The provider provided an answer of some kind. Versions of this exchange went on for perhaps three hours, until someone came to what passed for their senses and said that it was okay for us to take Kevin home. He was given another sedative, and he slept until we reached our house in Middlebury after dark, filled with apprehension over what our son's mood might be on the following morning.

He was thankfully subdued as we made an emergency appointment with a psychiatrist in Middlebury, who prescribed more tranquilizing meds and, after a few more visits, confirmed his condition as bipolarity. Perhaps this was correct at the time. The manic phase of this disease certainly features symptoms that describe our younger son's behavior: impulsiveness, irrational euphoria and grandiose hope, the loss of judgment, high energy, sleeplessness. But as I have written earlier in this book, these symptoms are almost identical to those of schizophrenia, though they involve different, yet sometimes overlapping, out-of-balance brain networks. It is possible that Kev's affliction deepened over time and crossed diagnostic boundaries. It is also possible that the similarities of symptoms may have disguised the fact that the latter, more destructive disease was already at work.

The point in writing this is not to place blame on the psychiatric physicians who examined our son in these early stages. I believe that all of them were working in good faith to isolate the precise synaptic failures from a spectrum of dauntingly similar possibilities. If anything, I write this to stress how utterly unprepared we were for grasping the overwhelming obligations that lay before us; how eager—how understandably humanly eager—to accept and cling to the least dreadful of the possibilities. We did not know what my later studies of chronic mental illness have made crystal clear: that the most useful weapon in the meager arsenal is early intervention. Early and persistent. No cures exist for mental illness, but the quicker and more accurately the early symptoms are noticed and treated, the better the prospects for minimizing the effects.

The larger point in writing this, then, is to arm other families with a sense of urgency that perhaps came to us too late: When symptoms occur in a loved one, assume the worst until a professional convinces you otherwise. Act quickly, and keep acting. If necessary, act to the limit of your means. Tough advice. Tough world.

At Middlebury, a brief hospital stay; doctor's appointments; rest. Kevin acknowledged his relapse into marijuana dependency to us. We talked about recovery strategies with him, as did his doctor. Kevin was emphatic that he intended to get over his addiction and return to Berklee. But as it turned out, the handsome old residence building on Massachusetts Avenue was among the worst possible places for Kevin to live. The air in its three stories, the air that Kevin breathed, was tinted blue each evening with marijuana smoke. We did not learn until later that Kevin had stopped going to his academic classes almost immediately and stayed in his room except to attend his music workshops. When we did learn these things, we felt no impulse to blame the Berklee School of Music. This was life in American colleges. Most students made it through. The few who carried schizophrenia genes tended to be not so lucky. We didn't know anything yet about "the few who carried schizophrenia genes," even though a teachable moment lay directly in front of us.

He seemed to need solitude, and we allowed it. We'd installed a hot tub on the small brick patio at the rear of our house, and this became his refuge; he spent long stretches there, his chin on his chest, his guitar-playing posture. Motionless, impassive in the swirling water.

The spells of giggling were still some months in the future.

Dean flew home for the holidays, and the two of them spent a lot of time together, private and contemplative. Dean's mood seemed to have lifted. He told us that he had passed the flight reading Thomas Wolfe's great first novel, *Look Homeward, Angel*, and was spellbound by its towering bursts of lyricism: *"O lost, and by the wind grieved, ghost, come back again."* When his plane landed at Burlington, Dean exited with the line of passengers, but the novel remained on his seat. *"O lost!"* he declaimed to us at intervals over the next few days, his hand over his heart. *"O lost!"*

We picked up on a subtle deepening in his relationship with Kevin. Without making a big deal of it—he kept his tender feelings tightly guarded from family view—Dean made himself available to his younger brother, just as Kevin had done for him over the summer of Dean's house arrest. They drove one night to hear a band in Burlington. They attended AA meetings together regularly for the three weeks they were home. It was a gossamer thing to watch, all but wordless, all but invisible to our eyes, yet beautiful, and full of hope.

Berklee agreed to accept Kevin's reenrollment for the spring 2003 semester, on condition that he attend regular sessions with a counselor on the academy staff. We agreed, and we also secured appointments with a psychiatrist in nearby Brookline. We located an AA chapter for him as well. We found him a small apartment on Burbank Street, four blocks south of his classes, and Kevin repacked his clothes and his black Martin and returned to school. An email in mid-February began: "Hey guys, I hope everything is going well with you!"

> *All things considered I'm doing fine right now, I've kept a consistent day to day running routine. I feel pretty good overall, some days are rather hard and I think about using drugs (not plan, just think) but those periods really don't last to long. The more I get a perspective on how irresponsible I was the more and more I want to be away from it entirely.*
>
> *On a brighter note, (and the trumpets call!) I've met a really great girl named Bianca. She's really really cute, warm, and very nice, she's great and things are going well. She seems to be very level headed and that's rare to find here!*
>
> *All the best, and thank you both for your tireless support, Love, Kevin.*

The news from Fort Collins was bright, as well:

> *thanks, i really enjoy the support from you guys, things got good yesterday, really good, i got some invitations to see music, a drummer came over and a bass player and i felt more confident in a jam than i ever remember and then i went out and listened to other musicians at an open mic, it was all good, and then i met a guitar player who wants to jam with me, so a lot seems to have happened yesterday after i wrote mom that e-mail, and i feel pretty good, so now for some reading, take care-*

Dean's avidity for classwork, American literature in particular, continued, as he playfully kept letting us know:

> *Have you ever read Mrs. Bridge? It's dreadful and quite absurd, as Mrs. Bridge would say. It was good cause I got really emotionally involved with the book, but it makes you want to shake up Mrs. Bridge. You think our family had problems? This is a stark outlook on a rich family that has no understanding or compassion or emotions at all. You almost get that feeling that housewifes used to feel in the 40s. Anyhow, I'm gonna get crackin on homework.*

I took pleasure in keeping Dean supplied with upbeat—and genuine—responses to the musical CDs he sent us. His fingering technique kept improving, and the poetry of his lyrics could be stunning. He sang of angels with suitcases. Part of a verse in one song, called "Skipping Stones," went: "Fathers and sons / Lessons shared / Don't look at the past / Don't show you cared…" At some summer lake, when Dean was a small boy, I had taught him to skip stones. He'd been delighted.

> *Dean—*
> *Your songs show a pervasive, indomitable manliness. A braveness of vision, and an insistence on taking delight in the world that you live in, never mind how close that world came to engulfing*

you. I think it's what will make you an important artist if you get the breaks you deserve. You are uncompromising, trusting of your best instincts, and at ease with wit, playfulness, tenderness and unabashed wonder at the bounties of this world. I cannot begin to tell you how much I admire you for this—both artistically and in matters of the soul. I am everlastingly proud to be your old man.

I also let him know whenever someone in town mentioned him in a favorable way, which was far from rare. Dean's probation period was set to expire in a few weeks, and he had let us know that he was anxious he would "screw it up" at the last minute. Further, both Dean and his mother suspected that the town had never forgiven Dean for his role in the accident. I didn't share that impression, though I knew that some enmity still simmered, and that sympathy for Amy remained deservedly strong. To hearten him, I wrote to him about positive encounters I had with the locals:

Guy came up to me at the Bakery about an hour ago. Leaned down and said, low voice, "I met your son at a meeting. He's really a fine young man."

I go to the health club, some guy comes up and wants to talk about you. Mom and I go to Steve's, all of a sudden some guy is sitting in our booth talking about you.

I meant every word of these messages. Yet reading them again after all the years that have passed, I can discern another intention in them, unconscious at the time. It involved the end of his probation. In praising him and relaying praise from people who knew him, I was cheerleading him as well; I was *willing* him to beat his craving for bad substances, get healthy, stay healthy, believe in himself and in his art and in the love that people felt for him.

My will wasn't strong enough.

17

"We Have Done Pitifully Little About Mental Illnesses"

War, to paraphrase Clausewitz, is the continuation of insanity by other means. The twentieth century exemplified this as no other period in history.

The century just past accelerated developments in ever-newer, ever more mechanized, ever more terrifying and destructive weaponry. It made routine the strategies of "total" warfare, which metastasized from the ancient practice of relatively small professional armies facing one another across rural fields into the spectacle of million-man juggernauts sweeping across terrain and through towns and cities, butchering, burning, and raping indiscriminately.* (Both of these profanations had been tested in the latter stages of the American Civil War.)

Infantry of the twentieth century were the first to employ poisonous gas and flamethrowers, and death camps where tens of thousands of civilians perished in gassy fumes. The century introduced programmed starvation, mass machine-gunning of noncombatant prisoners, torture, and sadistic bloody experiments on the bodies of conscious victims.

---

* By contrast, the largest Western force in history until the Imperial Russian army of six million men was the "Grande Armée" of Napoleon, organized in 1805. It reached its numerical apogee of 680,000 prior to the invasion of Russia in 1812. This thrust proved a disaster for the French general, as it would for Adolf Hitler's invasion force in June 1941. Battle attrition and the brutal Russian winter vitiated both forces. Napoleon retreated with only 120,000 men.

The century introduced the aerial bombing, and then the firebombing, of great metropolitan centers. The twentieth century introduced the atomic bomb.

One might expect to learn that the effects of these routinized atrocities upon the mental health of combatants and civilians of the twentieth and twenty-first centuries are incalculable. But that is not strictly true. They are at least roughly calculable, thanks to improvements in the sciences of tabulation and statistical sampling.

It is possible to say with assurance, as did two psychiatric researchers writing in the journal *World Psychiatry*, that "among the consequences of war, the impact on the mental health of the civilian population is one of the most significant." And that studies of general populations "show a definite increase in the incidence and prevalence of mental disorders." And that "women are more affected than men." And, of course, that the most vulnerable groups include children and the elderly.[1]

Certainly war's effects have always been keenly felt by veterans and their families. Poets, correspondents, priests, medics—all have likewise experienced the shock of battle firsthand and witnessed its power to derange the human mind. Yet before the unpopular Vietnam War, nobody said much about it beyond these tight circles. The military code of manly silence, the hard strictures of patriotism, and medical ignorance of how the brain works made it all but unthinkable for a combatant to admit that he or she had become unhinged. Any soldier foolish enough to give voice to such unmanly sniveling risked being mocked by an officer or slapped around by a three-star general, then reviled as a coward and physically kicked out of the medical tent. The veterans brought their psychic wreckage home with them, awoke screaming in the night for decades, soaked their pajamas with sweat and urine, drank themselves insensate, filled themselves with pills of all kinds, brawled with their wives or in the workplace—and, all too often, ended the torture by killing themselves.

It took a president who himself had known intense, highly mechanized combat—had known it as he screamed out artillery orders in the chaos of a massive and decisive battle—to awaken the federal government and push it, for the first time in its history, into a role of responsibility in the financing and the care of warfare's psychic casualties—and from there to a share of responsibility toward all of the nation's mentally ill.

The president who spurred Congress into action on mental health was Harry Truman. On November 19, 1945, before a joint session of Congress, Truman declared:

> There is...special need for research on mental diseases. We have done pitifully little about mental illnesses...There are at least two million persons in the United States who are mentally ill, and as many as ten million will probably need hospitalization for mental illness in the course of their lifetime. Mental cases occupy more than one-half of the hospital beds, at a cost of about 500 million dollars per year—practically all of it coming out of taxpayers' money.[2]

Truman's call to action on mental illness came as the embers of history's greatest, ghastliest war still glowed in Japan and Germany. The speech was an elaboration of a bold transitional challenge that Truman had issued two months earlier, on September 6, just four days after the United States accepted Japan's surrender that formally ended the war.

Truman's September address to Congress had been shrewdly timed. Less than a year earlier the small Missouri senator had only reluctantly accepted the summons of Franklin Delano Roosevelt to join the Democratic ticket and run for vice president. In office only three months, he'd been thunderstruck at the news of Roosevelt's death on April 12. But he had regained his combative self-assurance in time to drop two atomic bombs on Japan in early August, forcing the end of World War II. Now Truman was at his full cruising speed. He'd hammered out an ambitious peacetime domestic agenda, and he wanted it enacted sooner rather than later. Perhaps calculating that some of its items were more radical than those even of his late beloved boss, Truman chose a moment when America's patriotic exhilaration was at the flood, and when grief over the lost national father—who after twelve years in office had become "virtually the presidency itself," in the words of David McCullough[3]—was still fresh. Thus he rolled out his agenda under the title that the dying Roosevelt had introduced in his State of the Union address on January 11, 1944: a "Second Bill of Rights."

In his own version, Harry Truman ventured where not even FDR had dared to tread. His left hand chopping the air in emphasis, Truman all but dared Congress to enact a program that had already stirred up fiery partisanship, and would continue to do so for the rest of the century: compulsory, federally administered *health* care.

Truman anticipated the hornet's nest he had stirred up. And yet, instead of pouring all his energies into the idea's defense, he pivoted to another offensive on November 19: he introduced his crusade for government *mental* health funding.

Thus Truman widened the definition of *health* to encompass the brain.

If American outreach toward its insane and psychologically troubled population can be said to have experienced a golden age, it began here.

The president had little chance of seeing his larger dream realized. Universal federal health care, long since common in western European countries, had appealed to Americans as well in the years before World War I. Theodore Roosevelt had run on it in his 1912 "Bull Moose" campaign to recapture the presidency, but he lost the election. Franklin Roosevelt sent signals in 1933 that he would revive the idea as part of his Social Security bill, the centerpiece of his transformative "hundred days" of New Deal legislation. But he backed off. By then, federal health care had aroused the snarling attention of a powerful natural enemy, the American Medical Association.

The AMA had organized in 1847 in Philadelphia to rescue the public from the quackery, ignorance, and shambolic training standards that were rampant among physicians. Less than a century later, reformers were wondering whether the public needed rescuing from the AMA. The organization had hardened into an interest group: one dedicated to enriching its member-doctors and borrowing the ruthless tactics of the newly fashionable political consultants to smear those who might encroach upon its interests. "Those" included presidents. When he learned that the AMA was planning to attack his federal health-care initiative, Roosevelt withdrew it from the bill—more out of annoyance than intimidation. He would get to the issue another time. As the White House physician, Ross McIntire, told a colleague, "The president knew that the American Medical Association would stir up opposition... there is no way of appeasing that crowd." [*4]

But Roosevelt died before that "other time" arrived. And when the stubborn, defiant Truman took it up—in 1946 and again in 1950—"that crowd" hit him with all it had.

"This is *not* socialized medicine!" Truman had insisted in his September 6 oration. "The American people are the most insurance-minded people in the world! They will not be frightened off from health insurance because some people have misnamed it 'socialized medicine.' I repeat—what I am recommending is not socialized medicine! Socialized medicine means that all doctors work as employees of government. The American people want no such system. No such system is here proposed." [5]

The AMA would be the judge of that. The group bellowed that it damn well *was* "socialized medicine," and by-god "anti-American" in the bargain. As for the president and his fellow communistic-type pinkos in the administration, why, they were nothing but "followers of the Moscow party line." Before the AMA was finished, Republican senator Robert Taft of Ohio was baying that compulsory health insurance came out of the Soviet constitution, and Republicans were boycotting congressional hearings. Lest anyone was still a little hazy as

---

* The colleague was Edwin E. Witte, the executive director of Roosevelt's Committee on Economic Security. It was Witte, an economist and passionate advocate for social justice, who crafted the wording of the bill that became the Social Security Act of 1935.

to where the AMA stood on the issue, one of its members quoted Lenin himself to the effect that "socialized medicine is the keystone to the arch of the Soviet state." At any rate, all this reasoned argumentation was good enough for Congress, which voted federal health care down.

Truman seethed. "I put it to you," he railed during a campaign stop in Indianapolis during his famous come-from-behind reelection campaign in 1948. "Is it un-American to visit the sick, aid the afflicted or comfort the dying? I thought that was simple Christianity!"[6] Almost no one believed that Harry Truman stood a chance of winning that election against Thomas E. Dewey, so he might have been wise to put the issue aside and come back to it later.

But Truman had no intention of ditching his federal health-care crusade, even though it likely cost him precious votes. He squeaked through to victory anyway.

Yet he still couldn't beat the AMA. In 1950, when Truman reintroduced his federal health-care measure to Congress, the AMA counterattacked with the most vicious propaganda onslaught that money could buy. The group paid $1.5 million to the wholesome-looking California husband-and-wife team of Clem Whitaker and Leone Baxter, the founders of Campaigns, Inc., the nation's first political consultancy firm. Whitaker and Baxter struck the template for nearly all political consultants to come, flooding national and local media with relentlessly dishonest facts about federal care and playing to Americans' worst instincts. They managed, for instance, to link "the opiate of socialized medicine" to both Hitler and Stalin.[7]

Such was to be the fate of health-care reform bills and initiatives for the ensuing sixty-five years, until the association decided to support the Barack Obama administration on the Health Care and Education Reconciliation Act of 2010.

Viewed in this context, it is a tribute to Truman's bulldog willpower that he did not withdraw from the fight, but planted his two-toned shoes and launched his second, equally radical parallel campaign: federal guarantee of financial protection for treatment of the mentally ill. Here, he drew on strong allies. He had the indispensable support of many psychiatrists inside and outside the armed forces. These experts testified powerfully in Congress for the cause. The leading advocates were the two most celebrated American psychiatrists of the time, the Kansas-born Menninger brothers, Karl and Will. We will shortly examine the history-changing careers of these two forces of nature.

In 1946, Truman signed the National Mental Health Act, which provided federal funding, for the first time ever, for research into the human mind. William Menninger, who by then was the head of the neuropsychiatry division of the US Army, helped draft the act. A key argument made by Menninger and others was that an infrastructure of sound psychiatric counseling would end up saving money when measured against the tremendous costs to society of incarcerating the insane. In the words of the historian Ellen Herman, they were "advocating that mental health, rather than mental illness, be the centerpiece of federal policy."[8]

The act led to the formation of the National Institute of Mental Health in 1949. NIMH is now the world's largest research organization that is devoted to mental illness. Its annual budget is $1.5 billion.

President Truman's fight to guarantee public financing in mental health care was squarely in line with the progressive Democratic ideals of his time, and, in that sense, unsurprising. But Truman brought a special understanding to the enormous bulge in the numbers of mentally damaged Americans that World War II had produced. Truman knew about what happened to combatants in twentieth-century warfare. He'd been one of them.

First Lt. Harry Truman had arrived in France in March 1918 with the 129th Artillery Regiment. He rose to the rank of captain, took command of Battery D, and directed artillery fire from forward positions during the horrific Meuse-Argonne Offensive the following autumn. It was the largest (and most climactic) American engagement of the war, pitting twenty-two US and four French divisions against forty-seven German divisions across a twenty-mile front. The Thirty-Fifth Division, of which Battery D was a part, went into battle with 27,000 men and took 7,300 casualties, the highest rate suffered by any American division in the war.[9]

Adding to the casualties caused by bullets and shells was the unholy noise generated by the machines that fired the bullets and shells. World War I was history's first battle, the Civil War perhaps excepted, in which sound itself was a debilitating weapon—but a weapon that did not take sides. Battery D's four 75mm howitzers contributed their small part to a universe of acoustic hell that often reached decibels of 140 to 185 or more, levels that ripped men's eardrums open and could be heard in London, two hundred miles and across a sea channel to the west.[10] The maximum tolerable decibel level over a several-hour period is currently held to be about 85.[11]

In one of war's infinite little ironies, the mission of Truman's battery was to provide support for a nearby light tank brigade commanded by a captain named George S. Patton. Patton was destined for glory and an ambiguous legacy in World War II: "ambiguous" because his heroic record of lightning advances at the head of his Third Army was marred by two incidents in Sicily in which he slapped soldiers in hospital tents for their "cowardice." Patton kicked one of these men out of the tent and drew a pistol on the other. At least one of these soldiers was recovering from shell shock; the other was later diagnosed as having "malarial parasites."*

World War II increased the din and its tortures to the psyche. Its combat arms were more varied and more powerful than ever: The tank, a marginal presence in the first war, now saturated the battlefield. Its 90mm guns fired at 187 decibels. The new howitzers were even louder, at 189 decibels. Recoilless rifles reached 188 decibels, machine guns 155 decibels, and even a submachine gun could generate 160 decibels.[12]

During engagements, all or most of these battlefield Frankensteins could be in full roar at the same time, for hours, along miles of front,

---

* A barometer for public understanding of combat stress could be found in the thousands of letters to President Roosevelt inspired by the incidents. Most of the letters supported Patton. General Eisenhower, however, forced the general to apologize, then relieved him of duty for nearly a year.

on both sides of the lines. Their racket approached physical dimensions. Some soldiers believed that they could actually "see" the noise as it curled over them like a giant wave. The mere concussions of exploding shells gouged deep craters. Given all this, it seems miraculous that any combatant could survive ten minutes inside this hell with his sanity undemolished, much less an entire campaign or the war in full. (The madness, of course, was hardly generated by noise alone. Fatigue, anxiety, fear of death, grief over the loss of a comrade or the horror of shooting an enemy—these and other factors did their share in separating fighting men from their senses.) Whatever the causes, the incidence of mental flameouts proved to be double the rate of World War I.

The war's effects on the human mind produced even more insidious consequences. Like Patton, many officers assumed that twitching, convulsing, or fetally positioned men without visible wounds were faking trauma to get out of combat. The captains, majors, and generals ordered these wrecks back into the line, thus heaping humiliation on top of their jangled psyches.

The vast majority of these "fighting men" in that war, of course, as in all wars, were, and are, boys in the peak years of their susceptibility to schizophrenia.

The Nazi atrocities of human experimentation, revealed to the world in the Nuremberg "Doctors' Trials" in December 1946, abruptly revoked the popular prestige that eugenics had enjoyed since around the turn of the century. The mentally ill have mostly been spared this particular form of mass torture since the first liberating British tanks rolled into Bergen-Belsen.*

---

* This is not to say that eugenics was obliterated. No panacea that promises so much in terms of man's perfectibility, and that has proved workable even in limited degrees, could ever be uninvented. Eugenics theories continue to be refined and practiced today, in fair uses and foul. What is called "modern eugenics" seeks to identify and, if possible, repair diseased genes. Gene therapists now envision the eventual cure of cancer, as well as blindness and many childhood diseases. Genetically modified crops and foods are now commonplace on a planet that faces severe shortages in the decades ahead, but concerns about side effects cause many of these products to be banned, especially in European countries.

Yet the demise of eugenics did not spell the end of suffering under "the lights of perverted science" for America's mentally ill. Even as World War II—at long last—laid bare the simplistic assumptions of eugenics theory and the moral depravity inherent in its practice, the war pushed an even more outrageous pseudoscience into the mainstream of psychiatric "cure." That perversion of the healing arts was called the lobotomy.

The modern lobotomy—the back-alley abortion of brain surgery—had been conceived as an antidote to schizophrenia in 1935. Its inventor was a Portuguese neurosurgeon, as he styled himself, named António Egas Moniz.* Moniz called what he did "leukotomies" because he was after white matter—as in brain tissue—and *leukos* means "white" or "clear" in the ever-dignifying Greek.

Diagnosis was imprecise in those years and would remain so for a long time. No one in the 1930s, as we have seen, had as yet established a baseline for differentiating insanity from severe psychological problems. Thus there was no way to verify that Moniz's patients—twenty hospitalized and helpless men and women—were in fact insane. As for a cure, no one really had a clue. Lobotomy made as much sense as electroshock, insulin coma therapy, even "refrigeration" therapy. These and other untested methods were being rushed into operating rooms as fast as doctors and tinkerers could dream them up.

Moniz came to believe that his patients' common problem was an oversupply of emotion. Moniz did not have a lot of training in neurosurgery. In fact, his new technique helped create the concept. He knew a little about the brain's geography, just enough to theorize where the emotional "off" switch was located. He hit upon the idea that had some crude nineteenth-century provenance: drilling holes into a patient's skull, then poking inside with a long thin rod to probe the edges of the frontal lobe. The rod had a small wire attached to the business end.

---

* The first known intrusions into living human brains were performed in 1892 by a Swiss physician and insane asylum supervisor named Gottlieb Burkhardt. Burkhardt removed portions of the cerebral cortex from six patients thought to be schizophrenic. Two of the six died, and no one tried it again until Moniz.

When the doctor gave the rod a twirl, the wire would sever the long nerve fibers that link the frontal lobe with the emotion-producing parts of the brain, the limbic system.

Moniz believed this could neutralize psychosis. And he was right; it could, and did, and often neutralized the patient's memory, personality, and, sometimes, the entire patient as well. Accidents happen.

Moniz won a Nobel Prize.

It took less than a year for Moniz's brain-scraping technique to make its inevitable way to the United States, a continental seller's market for cures. Its importer and promoter was a goateed and dapper Washington doctor named Walter Freeman. Freeman was a brain surgeon in the manner that Professor Harold Hill was a marching band consultant. In fact, he wasn't a neurosurgeon at all; he was a neuropathologist, and thus no more qualified to stick things into people's heads than Moniz. So he hired a qualified sidekick named James Watts to handle the drilling and twirling.

Freeman seems to have decided that the European product was underperforming somehow; it could use some American pep and zip. He rebranded it "lobotomy," perhaps to carve out some marketplace distinction. *Lobos* means "lobe" in Greek, and is every bit as classy as "leukos." After several years of directly replicating Moniz's approach via Watts, Freeman hit upon a way to make the operation more user-friendly, plus eliminate the middleman. Why not just slide the rod in under the eye socket? No sheepskins necessary for that! Freeman saw that he needed a thinner rod than Moniz had used. He settled on an ice pick—one that he'd found in his kitchen drawer.

The pick needed a couple of knocks from a hammer to get it started, but once inside, it was as easy as one, two…what comes after two?

Freeman named this refinement "transorbital" lobotomy. Watts, now superfluous and finally repelled by it all, fled. No more middleman.

And no problem! Walter Freeman could handle everything on his own. He was a natural publicity animal. (It was he who had nominated Moniz for the Nobel Prize in the first place.) He honed a personal style that set him apart from the pack: he never washed his hands before an operation nor wore a mask during it. He disdained anesthesia for his patients. He performed up to twenty-five lobotomies a day. Sometimes he performed two simultaneously, one with each hand. Often, he would invite audiences into the operating room, including the press: an archival photograph in the *Wall Street Journal* shows him gripping an ice pick dagger-style, his head cocked in rakish preparation, as observers crowd in. Sometimes he had a bad day at the office. A couple of times the tip of the pick broke off and lodged in the patient's skull. (Oops.) Even more embarrassing, Freeman once looked up from his patient into a photographer's lens, lost his concentration, and let the pick slide too deeply into the brain. The patient died.[13] The photograph turned out well.

This unfortunate victim thus joined the estimated one-third of Freeman's patients whose cases the doctor himself admitted were "failures." Not all died; some simply lost all affect, or were bedeviled by seizures, incontinence, or emotional outbursts.[14]

Ethically conscious doctors and surgeons were appalled by Freeman's method, not to mention his style. They pointed out that no medical literature existed to verify its legitimacy or warn of its side effects. Certainly Freeman provided none.

A few thoughtful souls did step forward to excoriate him. In 1948, Nolan Lewis, director of the New York State Psychiatric Institute, demanded of his colleagues: "Is quieting a patient a cure? Perhaps all it accomplishes is to make things more convenient for those who have to nurse them. The patients become rather child-like; they are as dull as blazes. It disturbs me to see the number of zombies that these operations turn out. It should be stopped."[15] The great mathematician and social theorist Norbert Wiener took a similar line of attack that same year: "Prefrontal lobotomy...has recently been having a certain vogue, probably not unconnected with the fact that it makes the custodial care of many patients easier. Let me remark in passing that killing them makes their custodial care still easier."[16]

Such condemnations were met with the same judiciousness, compassion, and restraint that had greeted eugenics and "scientific racism": in 1949, civilian and military doctors across the United States were twirling away to the tune of an estimated five thousand lobotomies a year.[17]

What under the stars kept this P. T. Barnum of the brain propped up as a legitimate doctor for so long? (His career lasted thirty-two years before his recklessness finally caught up with him.)

The law could not touch him. No laws *existed* to prohibit lobotomy. No such laws exist today. But the larger reason for Freeman's impunity derived from need. Specifically, it derived from World War II: the war, and the unprecedented numbers of deranged veterans—both men and women—that this global charnel house was disgorging back to the United States. They had been streaming home, or directly into military hospitals, since Pearl Harbor in late 1941. By war's end, around 680,000 of them had been wounded in combat. Those were the physically wounded. What truly shocked the populace, as well as psychiatrists, was that almost three times as many veterans, some 1.8 million, had come home needing treatment for wounds to their minds.

For a while in the postwar years, the Veterans Administration hospital psychiatric chiefs tried to keep Freeman at bay. But the overwhelming stream of needy patients soon made it impossible for them to be, as it were, picky. They held their noses and allowed him and Dr. Watts over the threshold. Each man was soon raking in $50 a day—$678 and change in 2016 currency—in consulting fees; that is, fees for teaching other doctors how to tap, shove, and twirl.

When the supply of raw material in the VA hospitals around the country at last began to taper off, Walter Freeman realized that he needed to create a new market. So he purchased a van, christened it "The Lobotomobile," and went haring around the country, stopping at mental hospitals to do his specialty and, again, to demonstrate it for the resident doctors. It really wasn't all that hard. A no-brainer, so to speak.

Not until 1967 did the medical community decide that it had had about enough of Walter Freeman. Doctors informally agreed to relieve him of his operating-room privileges. This decision was reached after the woman who proved to be his last victim died from a brain hemorrhage—on Freeman's third intrusion into her skull. By the time of his own death in 1972—of cancer—Freeman had directed or performed thirty-five hundred operations.

Lobotomy did not expire with Freeman, but it became extremely rare. The antipsychotic drug revolution, which had started in the 1950s, gradually replaced it as a more humane form of mass treatment. The most eloquent eulogy was written by Stephen T. Paul, professor of psychology and social sciences at Morris University in Pittsburgh: "Lobotomy was finally seen for what it was: Not a cure, but a way of managing patients. It did not create new people; it subtracted from the old ones. It was an act of defeat, of frustration."[18]

Walter Freeman and his ghoulish fad aside, the early postwar years marked one of the few eras in which the United States seriously engaged the problem of madness amid its populace. It didn't last long, and it was abruptly supplanted by a kind of Dark Age from which the momentum of public policy has yet to recover. But for a time at least, serious professionals seemed to be on the verge of wresting the fate of mentally ill people from the control of quacks, deluded ideologues, and callous public servants.

The most legendary among them hailed from Topeka, Kansas: the above-mentioned Menninger brothers, Karl and William. These sons of an old-fashioned Presbyterian town doctor and a pious, domineering mother were big men with high domes and prominent beaks and straight-arrow values—well, mostly straight-arrow values. William, born in 1899, became a lifetime Sea Scout. Karl, older than Will by six years, liked to equate mental health with moral health, and occasionally salted his books with pious exhortations. In *Whatever Became of Sin?* he enjoined men of the cloth to "teach! Tell it like it is. Say it from the pulpit. Cry it from the housetops...Cry comfort, cry repentance, cry hope. Because recognition of our part in the world transgression is the only remaining hope."[19]

Evangelistic in their boosting of psychiatry; driven, paternalistic, and brilliant, the two accomplished something that probably no one else among their countrymen could have managed. They rescued psychiatry from the liabilities that were threatening to extinguish its early-century cachet (its taints of Europeanism and elitism on the one hand; clowns such as Freeman with his ice picks on the other). They replaced this imagery with their own stamp—then unique among US psychiatrists—of home-cooked American optimism regarding mental cure, flavored with their entrepreneurial genius. In truth, their conception of psychiatry was destined for obsolescence. Paradoxically, they accomplished this with a staff liberally stocked with German-Jewish psychiatrists who had fled the encroaching Third Reich.

It all started in 1919, when Karl Menninger returned to Topeka from the Harvard Medical School, where he'd graduated cum laude. His mission was to help his father, Dr. Charles Frederick Menninger, establish the Menninger Diagnostic Clinic. Karl was twenty-six then, and William was twenty. The clinic welcomed patients with emotional and "psychological" problems, though years would pass before the brothers could afford to include psychoanalysts on their staff.

For a while, it seemed that there might be no staff—and no clinic, either. The Wicked Witch of the West herself could not have been less welcome in this respectable Kansas town of fifty thousand people and eighty-odd churches than doctors who opened their doors to "maniacs." Even though the family was known, several upstanding citizens tried to sue their clinic out of town. It didn't work, but the Menningers' persuasive powers did, though father and son had to smuggle their patients in under fake diagnoses until everybody calmed down. It helped that Charles Frederick Menninger was a reputable physician, a homeopathy man, which suited the region's self-reliant traditions. People began to notice that his son spoke in new and fresh and reassuring ways, unlike that gloomy sex-minded Freud over there in Europe. Karl promised "a psychotherapy for the people" and a movement toward "progressive analysis" (which meant roughly the same thing).

The clinic gained popularity, local investors got interested, the father and son attracted psychiatrists who at first had been skeptical, and within five years the clinic had become the Menninger Sanitarium. Starting out in a converted farmhouse with thirteen beds on Southwest Sixth Street, it grew into a nationally known enterprise that spread to over 430 acres on two campuses. Its staff grew to nine hundred.

They cared for patients housed in thirty-nine buildings, including an administration building with a clock tower. Patients were encouraged to linger for months, even years, if they could afford it. These lengthy stays had a self-selecting effect on the clientele: movie stars, politicians, even political officeholders came for treatment. (The brothers were not in fact elitists; their aim was to get psychiatry ingrained into the nation's cultural fabric. On the other hand, a movie star was a movie star.) In time, the sanitarium became a de facto salon as well; it attracted psychiatric intellectuals and social activists from around the world for formal and informal talks and debates.

Tower, setting, and philosophy of treatment—which emphasized the humanity of the patient, her comfort, exercise, and intellectual stimulation—all of this resonated strongly with the waning moral care era. Patients and their families arriving at Topeka by train or over dusty roads, perhaps after hours or days of chugging along through a dry, blank dust-bowl landscape, were greeted by a billboard whose message stood apart from the ubiquitous Burma-Shave signs: "WELCOME TO TOPEKA, KANSAS, THE PSYCHIATRIC CAPITAL OF THE WORLD."

An important event in the rise to national fame was the publication of Karl Menninger's debut book in 1930, *The Human Mind*. The intended readership was medical students, but this was among the first books on Freudian-derived psychiatry to be written by a professional yet in language that lay readers could understand. It was a call to liberate the mentally ill from the shadows of "otherness." It advocated the inclusion of psychiatric principles into the professions, education, and everyday life. It boldly gave voice to a truth that not many people were comfortable contemplating: few if any differences existed between mental asylums and jails.

Most audaciously for that era of entrenched stigma and fear of "maniacs," *The Human Mind* maintained that the differences between mentally ill and normal were matters of degree, not of kind. Neurological science would later demonstrate that this assertion was but partially true at best, and naive. The chronic diseases—schizophrenia and its related disorders—were indeed beyond the healing power of Freudian "talk" therapy alone, the root system of Menninger's approach. Yet Karl was convinced that psychotic illness was reversible. He was a big fan of Freud, though he disagreed with the emphasis the Master placed on sex as a font of human motivation—at least publicly. Privately, he ratified it several times.

He had undergone Freudian analysis in 1930. Inspired, he'd traveled to Vienna in 1934 to meet Freud and discuss his methods. Freud kept him waiting and then treated him, as the great Ring Lardner put it in another context, like a side dish he had not ordered. Menninger went home mad. Still, Karl's message on "degree" had value that ordinary people could understand and respect, even as it assaulted their prejudices. Here at last was a point of view that demanded dignity and acceptance for those selfsame "maniacs" of the town, the state, the nation, the earth.

Karl Menninger would write eleven books in all. His first led to a long-standing advice column in the *Ladies' Home Journal*, which further cemented his rapport with middle Americans. This in turn earned him the folksy nickname Dr. Karl, an honorific that only after several decades would be bestowed (or self-bestowed) again, this time upon Dr. Phil.

He was a complicated man, and his complexities increased as he aged. While avuncular in his column and charming in his public appearances or when hobnobbing with the likes of Eleanor Roosevelt, Margaret Mead, Aldous Huxley, and Hollywood celebrities, Dr. Karl could be a dour, demanding, irascible man away from the spotlight. His Vulcan-like personality could intimidate underlings. Sometimes even dignified Viennese doctors on his staff felt his sting. "He was... quite arrogant and immensely abrasive," recalled one of them.[20]

Over the years these spells of crankiness hardened and played their part in his downfall in the institution he had created.

Karl being Karl, the role of public ambassador for the growing enterprise was left to his younger brother, and Will Menninger was born to that task. He joined the family business after graduating from Cornell College of Medicine in 1924 and studying psychiatry at St. Elizabeth's Hospital in 1927. In 1941, anticipating the imminent need that war would produce, Will assisted Karl in creating the Menninger Foundation for Psychiatric Training and Research. The following year Will was appointed director of the Psychiatry Consultants Division in the office of the Surgeon General of the United States Army. He oversaw the upgrading of the US classification of mental disorders. This document standardized the process by which Army psychiatrists evaluated the mental health of masses of new servicemen and psychically damaged veterans. It was adopted by all the armed services.

By 1944, Will had risen in the Army to brigadier general and chief of Army neuropsychiatry. He knew that the war's end would soon increase the flood of "battle fatigue" cases, as they were still called. He issued a call for federal support in an initiative to train and hire hundreds of psychiatrists and staff to process the onrush.

His next step placed him in his historic alliance with President Truman. On July 3, 1946, Truman signed the act that created the National Institute of Mental Health. Will was among the chief architects and most persuasive lobbyists for this partnership with the federal government.

The early postwar years proved as needful of their profession as the Menningers had anticipated. As the psychoanalyst and author Kate Schechter has written, "Medically oriented, psychoanalytically trained psychiatrists like William Menninger spearheaded the rapid buildup of psychiatric forces during and after the war, and they soon found themselves at the top of a pyramid of mental health manpower and resources, directing research programs, university departments, and hospitals."[21]

The Menningers symbolized psychiatry's brief golden age. Thanks largely to them, not only the armed services but the American public was embracing the mental healing professions as never before. Psychoanalysis, once scorned as arcane and fraudulent, had become a middle-class status symbol; virtually a consumer product.

In retrospect the golden age was not all that golden. The various Menninger clinics and sanitaria, justly celebrated for their professionalism and abiding decency toward their patients, presented a misleading picture of asylum life in America. It was as awful as it had always been, for the most part. In cities and towns across the country, the mentally ill continued to be mistreated, tortured, deprived of warmth and fresh air and healthy food and human sympathy. A succession of investigative journalists, both print and broadcast, was about to shine its lights into these caverns of atrocity.

The result of this scrutiny, however, would be all too glumly familiar to the universe of the insane: unintended consequences.

In their heyday, Karl and Will Menninger had performed miracles. They had been instrumental in healing, or at least easing, the suffering of tens of thousands of veterans from the psychic damage of World War II. They had resurrected and sustained, for a while, the highest principles of moral care. They had managed the unthinkable task of budging the great American middle class off its great American hindquarters and persuading it to attend to its mental health. Psychiatry for the masses at last was a respectable commodity. As for those kooky people who had to be locked up in "insane asylums"—well, somebody was doing *something* for them. Weren't they?

The early postwar years were a time as Dynaflow-driven as a Buick Roadmaster (if one could take one's mind off nuclear annihilation, at least). Psychiatric care was just as comfy as Linus's security blanket (a "transitional object," in the hep new lingo). In the words of the psychologist and scholar Jeremy Safran, the friendly neighborhood shrink "became a purveyor of conservative American middle class values rather than a culturally subversive force." Safran added acutely,

"Mental health, by extension, tended to be defined in terms of conformity to those values."[22]

As the 1960s began, some new varieties of "culturally subversive force" were abloom in the nation. Dissent against authority spread, widening its targets: the New Left's consolidation at Port Huron in 1962, the formation of the counterculture after the assassination of President Kennedy in 1963, the Free Speech movement at Berkeley in 1964, bloody race riots in Selma and Montgomery in 1965, followed by the first anti-Vietnam student march in Washington, followed by the first urban race riot (Watts). The Rev. Dr. Martin Luther King Jr. was gunned down in April 1968 and urban rioting lasted for days; Robert Kennedy was assassinated in June. The women's movement was launched with a demonstration at the Miss America pageant in Atlantic City. Antiwar crowds rioted at the 1968 Democratic Convention in Chicago. Yale University broke tradition by admitting women. The Weathermen staged their Days of Rage in Chicago. People began to wonder whether the whole world was going crazy. (And, as mentioned, Thomas Szasz arose to tell them it was *not*!) Soon, though, that fanciful question became a serious proposition, and a justification for many to celebrate individual madness.

Eclipsed by these history-changing events, nearly all of which dealt blows to traditional authority in government, race relations, education, and family—eclipsed, and virtually forgotten—lay the archipelago of the insane. And the fragile archipelago fragmented even further.

18

"Primoshadino"

It was around dinnertime on a rainy day in mid-March 2003 when the damned ringing telephone once again brought us devastating news. We were in the kitchen. Honoree was watching pasta boil in a pot while stirring some shrimp in crumbs and olive oil. I was chopping a vegetable salad. My wife reached for the phone and held it to her ear for a few moments, and then her mouth opened and I think she lost color. She listened for several moments more, and then she began to speak to Dean in a fast, whispery voice. She listened again, and then she said, "Dad is right here. I'm going to put him on." She held the phone in front of her and cradled the speaker tightly. "Dean is in trouble," she said. "He's violated his probation. He thinks he's going to be arrested and put in prison."

I didn't know how to respond. So I carefully lowered myself until I was flat on the kitchen floor, looking up at the overhead kitchen light, my hands stretched out wide. I lay like that for a little while. I wanted to lie like that for the rest of my life. But instead I got to my feet, took the phone from Honoree's hand, and put the receiver to my ear.

Dean's voice was choppy and thick with agony. A urine analysis had come back with traces that prompted his probation officer in Fort Collins to tell him her patience was at an end. She was considering placing him under arrest. Conviction would lead to a prison sentence.

Dean had remained on probation because his nolo contendere felony conviction was still on the books back in Vermont. A lawyer we'd consulted had told us we had a good chance of getting it expunged, but Dean was not up to facing another courtroom unless he had to. (His final probation hearing was scheduled for the following January.) The dread of prison, which had hung over Dean for years, had arisen again, undead, implacable. And too much a horror for our son to bear.

Dean told me what he had told his mother. He didn't know what to do. My own feverish mind supplied dreadful possibilities. From childhood, Dean had loved to figure out ways to escape tough jams. Watching a movie with us, he could predict what the hero or bad guy had up his sleeve. Often Dean's strategies involved finding tricky ways to escape.

I convinced myself that Dean was going to bolt. To flee up into the Rockies, the Front Range where he had happily worked in the previous summer's sunshine. Dean had always romanticized the wilderness, but he didn't really know it. Now (as I convinced myself) he was about to entrust it with his life, alone, in winter, supplied with God knew what meager cash, food, clothing, or protective weaponry. (Maybe a knife, maybe not. As for a gun, Dean had never owned or fired one of any kind.) The Front Range in March, where nighttime temperatures dipped below freezing, where snowstorms blew up suddenly, where human habitation was sparse (and in any case off-limits to a fugitive). Where no one alone and on the run, inexperienced in wilderness survival, could expect to last for very long. Days, perhaps.

O lost.

We held him on the phone for a long time, alternately reasoning and pleading with him through our own haze of helpless terror. His replies continued to sound desperate. Yet he did not hang up. I tried to convince him that a prison sentence was not a sure outcome, and that if he did have to serve (the thought had tortured me as well), he would be released at some point, and we would support and protect him. Dean listened.

I made a request that had come from somewhere beyond my conscious thoughts: "Stand with us, Dean." I wasn't even sure exactly what I meant. The words sounded precious as soon as I'd said them. And they drew no response. The line was quiet. Dean was listening.

"Stand with us, Dean," I said again.

"Stand with us."

He did stand with us. And we stood with him. And nobody loses all the time. His probation officer decided to give him one more chance.

A few months later, we met Dean at the Burlington airport in April for his spring break. We stood in the arrival/departure lounge and gazed through the window at his plane as it taxied to the gate. I turned to Honoree on impulse and said, "I really hope that I will live long enough to see Dean at peace with himself." The passengers, kids mostly, with stocking caps and skis, filed through the door into the lounge, and there was Dean, near the end, and he spotted us and grinned in a way that we had not seen in years, and his eyes were bright, and when he greeted us the affected deepness in his voice was gone, replaced by the softer voice we used to know. And I realized that I had lived long enough.

On the drive from the airport down to Middlebury, he told us that his near miss with a jail sentence had jolted him out of his drugs-and-alcohol torpor and he had quit both, cold turkey. He had volunteered to answer phones on an AA hotline in Fort Collins. He had rejoined the world.

"I'm making friends with people who were invisible to me when I was in the life," he told us from the backseat. "Food tastes better. I'm thinking more clearly."

He added: "I miss the highs. But I will never miss the lows."

Dean's self-willed recovery—*reprieve* is probably the better word—held benefits for his younger brother. Kevin was able to make it through his spring semester without another setback. Dean invited him to spend the summer in Fort Collins, passing up the chance to return to his beloved Front Range for road-building work. He had rented an apartment on the first floor of a modest brown wood-framed house in a residential neighborhood not far from the university campus. Kevin gratefully accepted, bringing with him his Martin and amp, and the prescription antipsychotic that was now a part of his daily obligations.

The two of them had the best time of their lives together. They

played coffeehouses and bars around Fort Collins and along the wind-
ing mountain roads above the city. Sometimes Kevin set aside his guitar
and backed Dean up on a borrowed drum set, playing as though it were
the only instrument he had ever touched. Dean wrote a new flurry of
ballads, including the two best pieces of his life, and the brothers captured them all on the TEAC recorder that Dean had used for his earlier
songs. When Honoree and I arrived for a midsummer visit, the two
were as eager to let us hear them as Kevin had been to play the Booby
pieces for me in the Burlington airport two years earlier. They tugged
us into Kevin's room and flipped on the TEAC almost before we had set
our bags down.

We listened first to "Annie Don't Wake the Day," Dean's madcap
romp about a night on the town with a frolicsome, laughing girl who
skips and dances through the revels, sits in briefly with a bar band, then
whirls on, "back out on the street with the bright lights shinin' away."
Dean sings lead vocals and alternates with Kevin in a jubilant guitar
bridge, two solos apiece, the brothers driving hard, a pair of young
musical tigers bursting loose from their cages.

"It's been a long, crazy night, but don't wake the day!"

That was for starters. The anthem that followed, the cathedral
of notes and lyrics that meditate on loss and journey and hope, on
redemption-through-letting-go, stopped our breathing and cupped us
in its guileless majesty.

Its title was—is—will always be—"The River East of Home." Dean
wrote it and sang lead; Kevin sang harmony. A bridge in the midst of
the verses brings up Kevin's guitar in a cascade of notes that seem to
fall from a high place and gather for a moment in a pool before over-
flowing and dropping again, until they find resolution in the flowing
melody at the base.

The opening image is of a figure on horseback, forging along a
western mountain path until horse and rider fetch up "at some forgotten fountain." The rider tries to push his filly on through. "But though
it wasn't wide / She buckled and she balked / She couldn't see the other
side." The rider tells us of his years of roving "between the wilds and

mountains." Sometimes he's on an Arizona highway, straight down that center line. Sometimes, crossing water, he falls, and stays down "until I'm good and ready. / When I can't fight the current no more / You'll find me in the eddy."

But always, the chorus tells us, the rider is searching. Just as Yeats's wanderer searches for the silver apples of the moon, the golden apples of the sun, the rider is on a quest for the elusive River East of Home. It sounds as though his quest will be eternal. But then, "one chipped and faded chapel shines up out of the valley." The rider ventures through the doorway, because a voice, long forgotten, calls him. "I said my life's been driftin.' / He said that there's an answer. / And if I just believe, this slender reed becomes an anchor.

"I let the river go."

At the end of the summer, Kevin decided to stay on with Dean in Colorado and reenroll at Berklee the following spring. With Dean attending his classes, Kevin had time on his hands, and he spent some days walking around the college town. While he did not experience a psychotic break during these weeks, we learned that his encroaching disease played an occasional cruel trick on his consciousness. He wrote to us that he was having spells of racist thoughts—which bewildered him, because he had never in his pacific life harbored a racist sentiment. Adding to this torture was a kind of dualism: even as these hateful thoughts gripped him, another part of his mind somehow stood apart, looking on, appalled and awash in guilt.

But a few wisps of grace were still available to Kevin, and he seized on one. The odds against the serendipity of this particular incident, and his spotting it, were long. But then so were the odds against his contracting the disease. On one of his strolls, Kevin spotted an African American man waiting at a corner bus stop. As he neared, he heard the bus bouncing along behind him, and then watched as it streaked past the would-be passenger. Kevin hauled out his mobile phone, retrieved the bus company's number, and reported the driver.

Sometimes the grace was even more amazing. Casually hacking

around the campus of the city's community college one early-fall morning, Kevin heard the muted sounds of jazz music coming from one of the buildings. Through the window, he could see some students playing horns, piano, bass, guitar. The door to the room was open, so he walked inside, where he saw several other students on folding chairs, and an instructor with a clipboard. He'd come upon auditions for the campus jazz band. Kevin stood watching near the entrance for a few minutes, then crossed the floor to ask the instructor if he could sign up. He didn't say he was enrolled at the college, but he didn't say he wasn't, either. When his turn came, someone loaned him an electric guitar, and he sat down on a folding chair to play. After he had finished a couple of pieces, the instructor studied him meditatively for a moment, and then remarked (as our son hastened to gleefully email us) that unless Pat Metheny walked through the door, the guitar slot was his.

The college allowed Kevin to enroll in one noncredit course (music, as it happened) for the sake of legitimacy.

Things went along fine until Thanksgiving.

Dean decided to fly home. Kevin asked if he could stay on. In the final instance of our ignoring warning bells, Honoree and I gave him permission.

Dean and I drove down to Concord, New Hampshire, for a rare getaway together—what the little boy Dean used to call a "vaventure." We joined John Kerry's presidential campaign bus there. I had arranged to interview the senator for the magazine of his alma mater, Boston College Law School. The topic was the mother of all softballs: Where (the heck) had he learned his gift for oratory? Kerry, as it turned out, was in no mood for an interview of any kind. He spent most of the allotted time glued to his cell phone, his face turned to the window, talking to his aides and friends about whether he had screwed up his previous night's televised debate against John Edwards. He seemed to regard the topic of oratory as unworthy of him. The interview—such as it was—never got published.

It didn't matter too much. Dean and I had our vaventure. And Kerry lost.

Honoree stayed in Middlebury. She later admitted to being gripped with terror for Kevin. She telephoned some of Dean's friends in Fort Collins and asked them to check on our son. They said they would.

Honoree was right to be terrified, as it proved. After five days with us, Dean returned to Fort Collins. It was dark and cold when he opened the door to the apartment they shared. The apartment was strewn with dirty clothes and dishes. Kevin sat slumped in a cushioned chair, his eyes glassy and unfocused. In broken sentences, he managed to ask his brother, as if Dean had never been away, if he could see the large blue three-dimensional musical note suspended in the air between them.

Dean called an ambulance to get Kevin to a hospital. His action probably saved his brother from deeper deterioration and possibly from a suicide attempt. I caught the next available flight to Fort Collins.

Two or three days passed before Dean and I were allowed to visit Kevin. We arrived at midday, lunchtime, and were directed to the psychiatric wing. We saw Kevin in the cafeteria, shuffling along in a line of shuffling patients clutching brown plastic food trays, all of them dressed in thin green scrubs. His eyes found us and he moved his lips in a ghastly parody of his lopsided grin. His lips were flecked.

The green scrubs jolted me. My son, green-scrubbed and generic, an integer in a slow-moving green-scrubbed undifferentiated mass.

Apparently he had stopped taking his antipsychotic medication after Dean left the apartment for Vermont. Like so many family members uninitiated in the brutal norms of the psychotic world, we had not entertained the thought of Kevin rejecting his prescribed medicine. With similar innocence, we had assumed that his original diagnosis— bipolarity, whatever that meant, a mood disorder of some kind—was, while unfortunate, at least mild when compared to some of the things that could happen to people.

It was under these illusions that I had flown west to Colorado, expecting simply to pick up my son and bring him home for some more rest and treatment. It was not to be. The resident psychiatrist attending Kevin, a good one, gave me his diagnosis bluntly on the first day we met. Kevin was schizophrenic.

Ten days passed before he would release Kevin. The psychiatrist, crisp and professional behind his rimless glasses, was a scrupulous man almost beyond the call of duty. My son was in effect a transient, so there was no time to form a therapeutic relationship. Yet the doctor wanted to accomplish as much as he could in the few days available. This mostly meant introducing a mix of medications every morning and monitoring their effects. The hours between medicating and testing were long. Dean and I took our breakfasts in a coffee shop before he went off to class. I spent the rest of each day walking around, catching a movie matinee, reading the paper. The headline one morning was that Saddam Hussein had been tracked down and lifted from a hole in the ground. I found myself wondering whether he had gone off his meds.

One day Kevin asked for his acoustic guitar, and I related the request to the nursing staff, knowing that "objects" of any kind were generally forbidden in psychiatric wards, especially objects with strings. To my surprise, the nurses consented. I like to think they perceived the gentleness in him, and the aching need he had to be roused and centered by music. I brought him his acoustic from the apartment. When Dean came with me to the hospital a couple of nights later, he brought his own axe along, and my sons worked up an impromptu gig for the other young patients and their parents in the common room. Both boys lowered their heads over their instruments. It was the first time I'd noticed that they had adopted identical playing postures. Kevin placed the sole of one hospital-slippered foot across the arch of the other, and then Dean did. The people in the room gave them their full attention and clapped between numbers.

Nothing in my life has ever matched the gratification I always felt watching my sons play together, trading off rhythm and melody in the four-bar blues, exchanging cues with subtle nods, flashing grins at some tiny glitch unnoticed by the listeners. In sublime communion.

I brought Kevin back home to Middlebury. It was his final airplane flight. Vermont boasts a better-than-average network of mental health services in its counties, and Middlebury was home to a good one. Kevin was assigned a "team," a consulting psychiatrist and a counselor, and they set up a regimen of meds and "talk therapy" with him. (The latest theories of schizophrenia therapy, as we will see, have rehabilitated "talk" therapy as a useful device and have incorporated it with medications as the most effective treatment.) For his part, Kev was cooperative, polite, and, as always, engaging. He promised to stay on his meds, and he kept the promise. For a while.

He wanted desperately to make it back to Berklee. The wish consumed him. By then, nearly every thought or wish was a consuming one.

We reenrolled him in January 2004. He managed to get his old apartment back. By this time we held no illusions about the state of his mental health. Yet we could think of no humane alternatives. To separate him from his music would be cruel; tantamount, without exaggeration, to separating him from his very identity. After reenrolling him, we came back home and hoped for the best. We now lived in a universe of Hobson's choices.

Once again, things went well for a while, quite a long while. Days and then weeks passed without a crisis. Kevin began work on a long and sophisticated jazz-guitar suite, recording multiple tracks to give it depth and resonance. He called it "Primoshadino." I never asked him about the name. Jazz titles are often whimsical. Honoree and I clung to whimsical.

Late in the spring—before the end of the academic year, but late enough for the major-league baseball season to have started—Honoree and I felt secure enough in Kevin's stability to plan a weekend trip to Daytona Beach. Honoree's adored niece, Adrienne, a striking and competent young woman and a rising officer in the Air Force, was getting married there. On a Friday night we checked into a motel near US Highway 1 that ran along the Atlantic Ocean, not far inland from the family home of the bridegroom-to-be. We changed clothes and drove over for a cocktail mixer that would bring the two families together.

There was merriment and old family tales retold and family photos hauled out of purses and billfolds and a ravishing buffet table, and the party swelled, and we caught up with a happy Adrienne, whose hair was even redder than my wife's, and Honoree's mobile phone rang inside her purse, and it was Kevin.

No crisis this time. Everything was fine. So fine, in fact, Kevin told his mother, that he was taking himself off his meds.

We got to know US Highway 1 very well that night. We left the party, climbed into our rented car, and, keeping Kevin on the line, drove the road's length in Daytona Beach for hours, up and back, up and back, up and back, talking to him, pleading with him as headlights in the approaching lanes grew sparser, as Mobil stations and Pizza Huts flicked off their logo lights, as supermarket plazas grew dim. We tried (again and again) the lost cause of reasoning with him: How hard is it to put a pill in your mouth and wash it down with a glass of water? What is the downside?

It was all duck feathers in the wind. Kevin listened affably, patiently, and then explained again that he was off-meds. Final decision. He was fine now. Case closed.

Anosognosia.

I caught a flight to Boston the next morning. Honoree decided to stay behind with the wedding party, but she was wrung out with worry. The phone in our motel room rang that morning as she was showering, and she scrambled out and sprinted for it, skidded across the wet tile floor and hit the baseboard with her foot, breaking a toe. In Boston, I checked into a Howard Johnson's a block from Fenway Park and a short walk to the Berklee School. The Red Sox were playing an afternoon game. Kevin and I had agreed to meet around three. As I put my hand on the motel-room door to leave, I was frozen by a sudden disembodied roar. It went on and on, yet there was no visible source. I thought of swarms of shrieking demons erupting from the Id. A Red Sox player had hit a home run.

Kevin was waiting for me at the agreed-on street corner. His lopsided grin was in place and the tips of his fingers were shoved into his pockets. We hugged, and I savored the warmth of his body. I thought of a summer afternoon twenty years earlier at our weekend house in Connecticut, when I had held him, a sleeping infant, on my lap in a chair at the back of our small cottage, his bald head propped in the crook of my crossed knee. I'd been half dozing myself, but I kept my eyes on a robin as it took its sweet time hopping from one end of the yard to the other, through long, dappled grass, and twigs, and acorns, stopping once in a while to pluck at a worm. I didn't move a muscle beneath my son as he napped on. That had been a good afternoon, in a sweet time.

Kev was his old self that weekend in Boston—cheery, boyish, happy to see me, the light of the days bringing up the gold in his hair and the blue of his eyes. We were easy together, as we'd always been. We hit some museums and took the MTA to the North End and stuffed ourselves with an Italian lunch. We walked a lot—through the Prudential Center, Boston Common, along the curving borders of the Fenway, following it down to Agassiz Road, over the waters of the Back Bay Fens and into the old Victory Gardens that dated to the urban subsistence-farming years of World War II. We talked casually about a lot of things.

But when I raised the topic of his meds—the topic that had brought me up to Boston, the topic that chilled me even as I kept it casual— Kevin deflected it. No hostility, no defiance. Meds were just something he didn't do anymore. After a while I let it go. I made myself concentrate on this otherwise perfect weekend with my son, and I willed my grieving into remission. The next day I called the well-recommended Boston psychiatrist whom Kevin had been seeing, and I asked him if there was anything he could do. The psychiatrist, who had treated his share of gifted and troubled Berklee students, told me there was not. The only choice, a ghastly one, was to let our son "crash" again and hope that he would learn a lesson from it.

He almost made it to the end of the academic year.

The inevitable crash didn't surprise us, but the robotic darkness in the voice on the other end of the line did. Kevin was accusatory and defiant. He believed that we were conspiring against him, and he wanted it to stop.

Paranoia.

This time Honoree made the run to Boston. We were trading off on these missions now. She drove to Kevin's apartment in the Fenway-Kenmore neighborhood. She invited him for coffee. As they walked along the street, Kevin began to believe that his mother was stalking him and told her he was going to call the police. She encouraged him to do so. When the squad car arrived, she explained the situation and the officers escorted our son to a local hospital. He went without resistance.

A few days there, a handful or two of meds, a haphazard examination by an overworked psychiatric team, and our son was pronounced fit to return home. Along for the ride were the voices that had entered his head. Once we were home, the head psychiatrist at Rutland Regional Hospital informed us that Kev's condition had deteriorated to schizo-affective disorder.

The weeks and months ahead formed a mélange that remains painful to revisit closely for the purpose of picking out discrete narrative strands. They were months of hopeful clarity and relapse, hospitalization and release, irrational hope giving way to benumbed acceptance that this was to be the way his life would play out. I had reworked a familiar metaphor to help reassure myself: the membrane. I made myself believe that the membrane supporting his schizophrenia was firm. Of course, it was not firm after all. And then the membrane tore, and our son plunged into free fall.

There were good moments in his final months. In the fall of 2004 Honoree enrolled him at Castleton College, close enough to our home that he could keep living with us and still play with the jazz band. A new young music director had come in, a saxophonist, and he understood Kevin at once, and invited him into a combo that played around Vermont and New Hampshire and Massachusetts. Sometimes the drummer was Gabe Jarrett, the brother of famed pianist Keith.

One frigid winter night the combo gathered at a bar in Ludlow, a town about sixty miles southeast of Middlebury. When we arrived, Kevin discovered that he had forgotten the cord that linked his Martin to his amp. I did a quick driving tour of the town's stores; they were all closed. The bartender remembered a guy who lived up on the hill across the main road, a musician. I ran out the door and across the road and up the hill and knocked on the door and talked the stranger into lending me one of his cords. The combo played great jazz that night, to an audience mostly of men seated at the bar in the next room, drinking beer and glued to sports on ESPN, their rear-end décolletage peeking above their blue jeans.

He finished composing "Primoshadino." It is a hell of a jazz suite.

He remained gentle and endearing. He wasn't talking much to us, though. He was tuned in to other conversations. We always knew when these were happening. He would look away from us, and his lips would move almost imperceptibly, and sometimes he would flash a trace of his lopsided smile. We comforted ourselves with the thought that the voices were friendly.

He yearned for the days of Booby, and tried to reconjure that fine band with a bassist and a pink-haired drummer at Castleton College. They called themselves Fall Lineup and played gigs around the state. Kevin always drove. These were nights when Honoree and I sweated out his return home, especially the nights when snow and ice covered the highways. But there was no keeping him from it. And he always made it home.

He maintained good relations with his in-town psychiatrist and counselor. He never missed a meeting, never complained about the meds he'd resumed taking—or so we thought—never was less than charming and articulate with them.

Maybe, Honoree and I let ourselves believe, this was the way it would always be. Far from a perfect future, but one we would safe-guard as long as we lived. And then, imagined Honoree, ever the opti-mist, he would find a sweet young woman who would love and take care of him.

And the winter of 2004 passed, and then came the summer of 2005.

19

Red Sox 17, Yankees 1

Friday, July 15, 2005, was a date marked on the kitchen calendar. We didn't often mark dates on the calendar. But this was the night that Dean and I were going to a Red Sox game.

We could not have picked a more auspicious date. Boston, the defending World Champion, was in first place in the American League East with a 50–39 record. They had finally erased the Curse of the Bambino the previous autumn in a four-game series sweep of my beloved St. Louis Cardinals. That was cool; Dean and I were die-hard Bosox fans now. The visitors were their ancient rivals the New York Yankees, in third place at 47–41, but just two and a half games behind Boston. Johnny Damon, with his flowing mane, was hitting a ton for the Sox at .346. Alex Rodriguez was leading the Ancient Rivals at a .316 clip. The game had all the makings of a showdown.

I had secured two tickets to this game several weeks earlier. I would pick Dean up at his newspaper office in Montpelier; the two of us would share the driving down to Boston and then back home the same night. None of the family had ever been inside Fenway. The closest I'd come was that motel across the street on my visit to Kevin the previous spring, when I'd listened to the invisible crowd release its home-run roar.

The portly southpaw veteran David Wells took the hill for the Town Team against journeyman right-hander Tim Redding of the Bronx Bombers that night. The Sox chased Redding in the second inning with the bases loaded and none out, and leading 3–0. Yankee reliever Darrell May got a force-out at third base on a ground ball by "Papi" Ortiz, with Mark Bellhorn scoring; but then Manny Ramirez golfed a fly-ball double off the Green Monster in left to bring home Edgar Renteria, "the Barranquilla Baby." Trot Nixon, next up, lashed a screaming drive past Melky Cabrera to the center-field wall that was good for an inside-the-park home run. Ortiz and Ramirez circled the bases ahead of Trot, and it was 8–0 Red Sox before all the fans were in their seats. Before it was over, Papi unloaded a grand slam into the right-field seats, his twenty-third round-tripper en route to forty-seven for the season. Dean and I never made it to the game.

Friday was garbage-pickup day in Middlebury. I awoke not long after dawn, as usual, to haul the bloated black vinyl bags from the kitchen down the basement stairs and through the garage to the driveway, where they would await the noisy trash-compacting white truck.

It was on my second trip down the stairs, just before I turned left to enter the garage, that I grew aware of a presence off to my right in the basement gloom, and I turned.

There was Kevin, his head bowed, a familiar posture. A dusty little window just under the ceiling, on his far side, allowed some weak morning light to play on his hair, not enough to fire up the gold. For just a fraction of a second I thought I had found him getting some early-morning practice in. Then I realized that he had not moved, and no sound came from his guitar.

20

Insanity and Icarus

We decided that he would be cremated.

He had been his old winsome self on the day of the night that he fastened one end of a short rope to a pipe beneath the basement ceiling and the other around his neck, the final task of his gifted fingers, and dropped from a kitchen chair. He'd taken an amiable ride with one of his Middlebury counselors that afternoon, talking casually about his future. Later in the afternoon, as I was signing papers for some money transaction, he had strolled over and cracked a joke, a pun. He was good at puns, though he rarely made them.

Honoree recalled much later that he had started to say something to her, something serious, that same late afternoon, but he had broken off.

I recall stumbling up the basement stairs after I'd glimpsed him, and then up the stairs to our second-floor bedroom, bellowing Honoree awake. I recall her leaping from bed and standing beside it with her fists clenched, crying out. I recall dialing the goddamn 911. And then returning to those basement stairs to sit and wait for the police and EMT crew, Honoree beside me. I recall how thirsty I was, parched, my throat a mass of cotton. I recall not being able to turn fully to the right to look at the figure I had glimpsed. I recall that my brave wife moved to him and touched him.

It seemed like it took hours upon hours for the EMT crew to arrive and cut Kevin down and place his body on a stretcher. I recall recognizing one of the crew as the host at a restaurant on the edge of town where we had eaten family meals together since the boys were young. Playing connect-the-dots on the children's menu and dabbing up Kevin's spilled orange juice. I recall realizing, when the crew transported his body to the ambulance in the driveway, that they were tracing the exact route that Kevin had covered after alighting from our van in 1988 to rush into the house. We asked the stretcher-bearers to pause there so that we could say good-bye to our son.

I recall asking close friends to drive us east, over the mountains, to Montpelier, where Dean was working as a reporter for a small newspaper. It was the route I had planned to travel to pick him up for the drive to Boston and the Red Sox–Yankees game.

I recall the howl that Dean released when I found him and blurted the news to him. I recall how, after several seconds, he forced himself to regain composure and begin planning what must be done next. Begin to guide and shepherd us.

Kevin's memorial service at the funeral parlor a few nights later drew a cross section of people whose lives he had touched, and letters and floral bouquets from others too far away to attend. The mourners filled the room and the staircase leading down to the crowded parlor and then to the front porch, and then on out into the night air on the lawn below the porch. Kevin's bandmates from Fall Lineup were there, and his teachers and guitar mentors, and the tall young woman whom he had defended in sixth grade against the future hockey star. She'd arrived with her mother about an hour early, and the two had sat motionless in their folding chairs the whole time, as others filled the room. On a table behind the dais rested Kevin's black Martin, beneath a bouquet sent by a group of my high school friends from Hannibal.

The Woods Tea Company, which was booked for a gig in another town that night, dispatched their banjo player, Mike Lussen, who had been onstage when I'd boosted Kevin up there that long-ago Sunday afternoon at the Boat House in Burlington. Michael had since become a close friend of our family. I looked into his eyes when he entered the room, and I couldn't place him.

Our writer and drummer friend from Chagrin Falls, Scott Lax, who had jammed with Kevin at Bread Loaf, made the journey from Ohio by car, and he offered a graceful remembrance.

Our friend Jay Parini delivered the eulogy. His first words were, "Life is suffering...," and he made the words sound not callous or dismissive, but loving, and absolutely right.

Honoree asked our friend Joe Mark, the academic dean at Castleton College, to read her remarks:

"If love could have saved Kevin, he would still be among us...

"If passion and hard work could have saved Kevin, he would be here with us today. With one so gifted, the effort is not always obvious. But I can tell you that he was devoted to music and to being the finest guitarist he could be...

"If goodness could have saved Kevin, we would have been celebrating his twenty-first birthday with him yesterday...

"For myself, as I experience the terrible pain of Kevin's loss, I turn to my cherished memories. I am so grateful for having known and loved this beautiful boy who was entrusted to us for a short, sweet time."

Dean was heroic that evening, as he had been since the moment he'd heard the news of Kevin's death. He stood straight at the dais and faced the crowd of mourners, and he delivered a simple, eloquent farewell to his brother and guitar partner. Dean had become our family's pillar. He had taken charge of things from the outset. He counseled us to collect and sequester all of Kevin's clothing, instruments, drawings, scrapbooks, musical CDs, and other artifacts that would give us pain when we happened upon them in the coming days and years.

He wrote a brave letter to our biweekly newspaper, the *Addison Independent*, that forthrightly explained Kevin's psychosis at the time of his suicide:

There is no rationality for his death that we will ever comprehend. Everything in Kevin's life was geared toward the future. He had a band with which he practiced and performed regularly. He was attending classes at Castleton State College. He was sending out press kits as recently as a day before he died.

I hope that his death can raise awareness about schizoaffective disorder. I hope that by dying, Kevin will give those among us who suffer from psychological disorders the strength to face their problems without fear of being stigmatized.

Kevin continued to improve by increments from the state of mind he was in after his last trip to the hospital. Occasionally he cracked a smile, and we were grateful for it. He had a great academic year at Castleton, making the dean's list. He and his mother had planned a visit to a spiritual retreat in California. He even joked a little on his last day.

He composed music and lyrics and his desire to do well in this world burned like a flame that shined brightest in my life: he cared for his family, he felt compassion for the indigent, and he was never violent. He was gentle and thoughtful. He had a disarming sense of humor.

Kevin's absence is one that I will feel all of my life. It hurts to move away from the last day that I spent with him. But I am grateful for the almost 21 years I was given with Kevin. And after God takes back a gift like Kevin, it is a small request to ask Him for enough hope and strength to endure the grief.

It was Dean who'd convinced his mother that the memorial service must be held in Middlebury, rather than Castleton, as she'd initially wanted. Honoree still believed that the town had turned against Dean, and thought of him as he had been publicly portrayed in the aftermath of the terrible accident. Dean's insistence on Middlebury allowed Honoree to see how many friends remained available to our family, and to us, and it gave her a measure of peace.

Aunts and uncles and cousins and friends gathered from around the country to help us through the first days after the service. They brought casserole dishes and prayers. Condolence letters and cards arrived every day. One card that moved us especially was sent by Amy, who had suffered the terrible injuries in the automobile accident.

The July days and nights passed, and our visitors departed one by one and two by two, bearing the empty casserole dishes and our gratitude. Soon we were by ourselves in the house.

One evening soon afterward, Honoree and I sat talking in front of our fireplace, she in a cushioned rocking chair and I on the sofa. I felt a presence, and for just a moment Kevin was in the room, standing over me, asking my forgiveness. I am not a believer in spiritual manifestations. I recognize the moment as classically psychological, perhaps a modified psychic break. I mentioned the sensation to Honoree. And then, less than a minute later, for some reason, I plunged my hand down into the sofa, between the cushion and the armrest, and brought up Kevin's mobile phone, which he had been missing. The one he had used in Fort Collins to report the bus driver who'd sped past the black man at the stop. I am certain that a rational explanation exists for that as well. Certain.

We left Middlebury that autumn of 2005 for Castleton, thirty miles to the south. Honoree had joined the administration at the college there. We spent that benumbed winter as caretakers of a two-hundred-year-old white-clapboard farmhouse that sat off to itself atop a knoll a few miles south of the college campus. The farmhouse was owned by a seventy-year-old former Rockette and dancer at the Copacabana, who lifted our spirits in the days before she departed for Arizona and winter with her relatives. A henna-haired diva of high style and peppery wit, Alice directed me to mix the gin-and-tonics in her living room ("Float the gin!") while she conjured her glamour years. She loved recalling the night at the Copa when she twirled her crinoline skirt at the edge of the stage and knocked a drink out of George Raft's hand. Raft was a movie star who specialized in playing gangsters. Ever the lady, Alice stepped out of the dance line and bent over to mop Raft's soggy lapels.

"What did he say?" I asked, always eager to hear a story's continuation.

"He said, '*My god, they're real!*'" Alice replied, beaming.

Honoree spent her days at the college; I spent them robotically walking the nearby dirt roads, and writing. In the evenings we huddled together on the couch, a fire going and blankets over our legs, and watched every classic movie in Netflix's inventory. In the greening-up spring, we searched for a house. We signed a purchase contract on the second one we looked at, a small low-slung chalet, its two stories built into a hill above Castleton, with a pine woods at the rear and a front view that faced the Green Mountains to the southwest. It is the house we live in now.

Dean's strength of character and his stability—his apparent stability—undergirded our family's recovery. (My wife and I have always wondered whether the shock of Kevin's death moved Dean's prodromal phase a little further along.) Dean was twenty-three when Kevin died, and he had gained experience in newspapering in Colorado and Vermont. He continued to write powerful political essays for the website OpEdNews. He held to a strenuous regimen of weight training and riding his bicycle in the hills of Vermont, or the West, or wherever he happened to be.

In the spring of 2006 he secured an internship at the *Nation*, and he lived for several months in an apartment in New York. At the end of his final day, he met Honoree and me in a departure lounge at Kennedy Airport for a weeklong trip to Positano, Italy. I could not help grinning when we spotted him striding slap-footed into the lounge under an enormous backpack, his thatch of dark hair uncombed as usual, and his nose buried with perfect unconcern in a bright-yellow book, *Italian for Dummies*. He proved to be no dummy during the flight to Naples: he chatted up two Italian flight attendants and got their phone numbers. Once in Positano, it took him all of one day to strike up a weeklong romantic friendship with a pretty, curly-haired young clerk in a bookstore a block up the hill from the coastal Saracen tower six hundred feet above the Mediterranean, where we stayed. The sunlight playing on the sea beyond the nearly vertical town, the hiking on the mountains above with his cheerful new companion gripping her basket of bread and cheese, the nights strolling with us along the sandy beach between the sea-scented harbor and the lighted string of outdoor restaurants that faced it—all this helped bring restoration to Dean, and it restored Honoree and me to watch him savor it. We boarded a bus departing Positano on a morning when a great rainbow arced out of the mountains into the Mediterranean, and we flew home from Naples and back into the flow of time.

Dean was our joy and foundation in those early years After, and he is our joy and foundation today. But the years in between presented a path to him, a path steeper and rockier, more forbidding, and more perilous than any he had cleared out in the Rocky Mountains during his college years. He had rid himself of his dependency on alcohol, for a long time, anyway. Yet the disease that took his brother's life still moved, on its own slow, insidious timetable, toward manifestation.

For a while, Dean lived a young adventurer's dream. In 2006, he set out upon a cross-country drive from Vermont to Albuquerque, where, through connections forged by his old man, he worked for a while on the location set for the movie *In the Valley of Elah*. He served as an unpaid assistant to the director, Paul Haggis, who graciously provided Dean with a small office, his name affixed to the door. Dean later remarked that the highlight of his moviemaking career was fixing a hot cup of tea for Tommy Lee Jones. An old girlfriend got in touch with him, and he decided that she was even more attractive than Tommy Lee. He paid his thanks to Paul Haggis and accompanied the young woman up to Portland, Oregon. Their romance dissipated, but in Portland he found an outlet for his political passions. He joined Working America, the progressive grassroots organizing group affiliated with the AFL-CIO. He went door-to-door in working-class neighborhoods, talking up the virtues of workers' rights and affordable health care. He was promoted to field manager, training freshly recruited teams in the skills of canvassing, persuasion, and leadership.

The organization returned him to Albuquerque in January 2008 with the title Canvass Director. He supervised a labor campaign office with a staff of more than twenty people who spread out through the city's neighborhoods, continuing the mission of building affordable-care advocacy. He joined the state's lieutenant governor and secretary of state to give presentations on the issue.

Correspondence from Dean was upbeat and hopeful during that time. Of course, living across the continent from him as we were, we could not keep up with every detail of his life. We didn't know, for instance, that he had stopped writing songs and had put aside his guitar. These things represented an era that was now painful to him, and he closed it off in his thoughts.

The reason for Dean's departure from New Mexico the following year, he told us, was that he missed New England. Although he had been doing spectacularly well with Working America out there, our first and only reaction to this news was that we were happy to have him nearer to home.

He took an apartment in Portland, Maine, bought an old green pickup truck, and found a canvassing job with the Maine People's Alliance, a group similar to Working America. Before long he was clattering around the small towns of the vast state in the truck, meeting with small-business owners to learn their views on affordable health care and talking up its benefits.

Dean held another motive for coming east. He had met a young woman online. She lived in Maine. He'd viewed her profile on an Internet dating site, a site that matched people who loved the outdoors. After pulling up roots and leaving behind a job that was rewarding his career hopes, and crossing the country with the fantasy of commencing a union with the love of his life—and, no doubt, ending his loneliness—Dean instead stumbled into emotional disaster. He found himself mired in the thrall of an archetypal figure, the Unattainable Other.

Most people are able to make peace with such rites of passage over time. Those with fragile neurological structures are less equipped to achieve closure. When the inevitable breakup happened, Dean buckled under the shock of it. In a decade's time he had withstood two, and perhaps three blows against his flawed scaffolding of sanity. His ability to pull himself back from the madness gathering in him, even as it occasionally abraded his thoughts and behavior, was in retrospect an almost unfathomable accomplishment. When compared with the virulence of Kevin's affliction and the rapidity of his brain's disintegration into irreversible ruin, Dean's case also offers evidence of how profoundly variable the "spectrum" of mental illness can be. It took this fourth blow, ironically the least of all of them in the scheme of things, to send Dean's scaffold crashing. His membrane of psychic protection shredded, he experienced this loss as a negation of his worth and a rebuff to his ardent love for the woman.

He stayed on around Portland for a while after the woman announced that it was over, disbelieving that it was true. He dated a few other women, but he no longer possessed the self-command that had shored him up for so many years. His intensity frightened women now, as did his intolerance for deviation from his expectations. (We pieced this together later, from his terse replies to our questions and from what we could see with our own eyes.)

The Maine People's Alliance, valuing his grasp of progressive issues and his gift for expressing them with confidence and clarity, was just then providing him a launching pad should he want to make a leap into professional politics. The Alliance sent him to Washington a few times for meetings with its two senators, who then were Olympia Snowe and Susan Collins. Back in New Mexico he had formed an acquaintance-ship with Governor Bill Richardson. He had developed into a forceful public speaker. His good looks and unforced charm seemed to pierce through the impersonal screens that political types erected between themselves and strangers. He won the respect of busy people in govern-ment with his forthrightness and grasp of issues while at the same time making them grin in spite of themselves over his boyish spontaneity. He was utterly without pretense, in the line of Kevin and their mother; and he assumed that everyone he met would be the same. Usually, thanks to him, they were.

Honoree and I had begun to feel that these factors might soon shape a career for him, one that would consummate his journey back from his years of pain and persecution and sense of guilt and devastating loss.

It wasn't to be.

The breakup with the woman who had so captured his heart delivered the final blow to his stability and self-esteem. He took a cou-ple of grease-monkey jobs at auto-repair shops, hoping to reforge his identity as a sleeves-up workingman, the sort of guy he had encountered again and again on his pickup-truck rambles around the state. And the sort of guy that the woman he'd come cross-country to be with had admired. (A favorite accusation of Dean's in those roiled years was that I had never taught him to work with his hands. It was true, and I had lived with this damning verdict as one of my failings as a father, until it struck me years later that, hell, nobody had taught me to work with *my* hands, either.) At any rate, Dean admired working people as much as he loved the wilderness and its rugged solitude.

Communications from him often were argumentative, or unrealistic regarding his goals, or—worst of all—rambling and out of focus.

And then, one autumn day, as if fulfilling Robert Frost's dictum—"Home is the place where, when you have to go there, they have to take you in"—Dean came home.

I spotted his green pickup when I turned off the hillside dirt road onto our driveway. He'd pulled it up against the rising pine woods behind our house. The sight of the truck didn't surprise me. Dean had never been one to announce his intentions. What did surprise me was the mastiff whose great muzzle suddenly filled my open window, its ears back, its brown eyes boring into me, a heavily clawed paw resting on either side of its jowls. This was Rooster, a ninety-pound mixed-breed boxer and pit bull (neutered) that Dean had adopted in Maine.

As I later recounted to friends, it took only a few seconds for me to realize that the dog was a pussycat, and a few applications of disinfectant cleaned up my car seat nicely.

Dean was home, and we took him in.

It would be wonderful, of course, to write that Dean's restoration was swift after he came home that autumn of 2011. It wasn't. More years would have to pass before a serious psychotic break, the third or perhaps fourth of that period, drove him into the care of a brilliant young psychiatrist in our state who earned Dean's trust, broke down his years of anosognosic rejection of antipsychotic medications, and steered him back into the light that Kevin had reached for.

His symptoms were merely distracting at first: long nightly soliloquies at the dinner table, not conversations, but rants, tirades. Interrupting them carried a price.

His alienation deepened as his disease now commenced its executive control over his thoughts and actions. His voice had dropped and thickened again to the tough-guy tones he'd used before his Colorado conversion. Paranoia moved in. Neither Honoree nor I knew when a casual, even deliberately innocuous remark would unloose a stream of invective that quickly would pivot and focus on subjects, and, sadly, ethnic groups, that are the usual targets of paranoid thinkers.

This was not Dean. This was the thing that had colonized Dean's brain. We knew this, but the knowledge brought us no comfort. To the contrary, it nearly incapacitated us with the same sense of helplessness we'd experienced as we had watched Kevin deteriorate. Since early adolescence Dean had despised medications, counseling, and hospitals. Unlike Kevin, he had gained the legal prerogative to refuse all of these. Dean was an adult when his schizophrenia resurfaced in force. He could not be admitted against his will to a psychiatric hospital or to accept psychotropic medication. That is, unless psychosis drove him into a state of emergency. Laws such as this, on the books in most states, are testaments to one of the most abject and—I almost wrote "maddening"—self-contradictions in the universe of mental health treatment. Their tight constraints, bureaucratically plausible yet recipes for calamity in life situations, require that a mental illness victim demonstrate "danger to self or others" before police and doctors can take control. In practice, this requires that a sufferer must come right up to the brink of committing demonstrable harm—violence—before restraints may be applied. The instances in which that "brink" is crossed are engraved in countless families' memories.

And so—as with countless families—Honoree and I sat back and awaited the horrible inevitable: hoping against hope that the crisis would hit the slender boundary between the imminent and the actual.

I don't think that either of us gave up hope entirely. I had studied Dean all of his life, as had Honoree. When I told her, as I did many times,

"He is a lion. He will come out of this," I was not whistling in the dark. I meant it. I just didn't have any idea how this would happen.

He continued to eat and sleep in our house while paring communication with us to near zero. He continued to refuse counseling and medications. He ceased his mountain excursions with Rooster. He ceased going outdoors much at all. A bulky fieldstone fireplace, doubling as a support pillar for the roof, separates our kitchen from our living room. Dean took to striding around this pillar, sometimes for hours at a stretch.

At intervals he would rouse himself from this torpor and make erratic gestures toward launching a small-business career. Clinging to his Portland fantasy, he decided to open an auto-repair shop. We loaned him the money to purchase a small Quonset hut on property just across the New York state line about twenty-seven miles west of Castleton. He bought a used camper and often slept on the grounds. He got the interior into shape. He put up new beams, new insulation, installed a new floor. I have a photograph of Dean wearing welder's glasses and staring at a flame in front of him. And then it went south. Dean lost all interest in rehabbing the hut or starting a repair business. This was—is—another common symptom of schizophrenia: the inability to sustain interest and enthusiasm.

It was now 2012. Dean was thirty-one.

One overcast afternoon late that fall, I approached the Quonset hut from the west. I was driving home from the Albany airport. I thought to turn off the highway and pop in for a visit.

Dean was sitting on a folding chair in the back of the camper a few yards from the hut as I rounded the corner. A few empty beer cans littered the little wooden platform in front of the door. Dean was hunched over, and it looked as though he had been weeping.

He got to his feet and let me hug him around the shoulders. "First time in a long time you've hugged me," he grumbled. I kept my arm around him and guided him to the car, and we drove home, where Rock Bottom awaited us.

Christmas Eve was hell, and Christmas Day was worse. We argued

fiercely over something or other that night—there was no avoiding it—
and Dean awoke keening the next morning. Soon he was out of the
house and striding down the curving dirt road, banging on doors and
announcing that he was the Messiah. Some of our neighbors, unaware
of Dean's condition, seemed to see this as an excessive celebration of
the Nativity. Telephone calls went out to the Castleton police. A call
from the Powers household was among them. By the time Dean reached
the bottom of the hill, a young officer stood outside his squad car waiting for him. Dean resisted getting in, and the officer was obliged to
use some force, tempered with patience. Had it happened in any of
many other locations around the country, Dean's struggle might have
been his last action on earth. I had never been so thankful for living in
Vermont.

The officer drove him to the hospital in Rutland, where he was
admitted as an emergency patient, sedated—this much was permissible
without patient approval in our state—and held over for a month of
examinations. Then, due in large part to Dean's obstinate yet articulate
arguments—truth be told, he could be a genuine pain in the ass in these
situations—the doctors decided to release him into the care of a nearby
recovery facility, one of the few of its kind in the country: Spring Lake
Ranch, a working hillside farm for drug and mental patients in rehabilitation, had opened in 1932. Kevin had spent some weeks there in
the last twelve months of his life and was helped, temporarily.

Dean agreed to spend three months at Spring Lake while accepting
medications. He begged out after a month.

Spring 2013 came, and the weather turned warm, and at Lake
George, New York, the resort area forty miles southwest of Castleton,
people were starting to take out sailboats and test the shallow waters
near the beaches for swimming. I had encouraged Dean to check out
the area for recreation and maybe for meeting a girl. Circumstances
came very close to making me wish I had never mentioned it. After
he had left the house one morning, an ex-girlfriend texted Honoree to
tell her that Dean had left a post on Facebook that suggested he was
contemplating suicide. Around noon, Honoree tried calling him on his

mobile phone. No answer; not even a ring. We drove to the Quonset hut. Dean was not there.

The familiar acid dread crept into our stomachs. We tried to think whom we might call. The possibilities were heartbreakingly few. We sat and looked out our living room window, hoping to see Dean's pickup churning up the road below us to the house. The truck did not appear. We telephoned the Castleton police and reported him missing. That night we hardly slept.

The following morning we reached the police department in Glens Falls, some twenty miles south of the beaches. Yes, the desk officer told my wife: men in his department had come upon an abandoned green pickup truck on a short dirt road near the lake that matched the description Honoree had given him. Its doors were locked. Through the window, the officers could see a mobile phone lying on the driver's seat. They decided to tow the truck to the department in Glens Falls.

Honoree gave the officer Dean's name and our telephone number, and then, as we had several years ago after Kevin's 4 a.m. call from Boston, we sat in our living room and waited for whatever was to happen next. Later, we both recalled how matter-of-fact it all seemed this time. We were numb, of course, and we silently braced for the moment when grief would burst through the numbness. Dean had muttered— albeit rarely—about suicide. Kevin had never mentioned it.

After an hour or so of silence from the telephone, I grew convinced that Dean was gone from us. Honoree did as well. I meditated dully on the question of what it would be like to live on with both our sons the victims of suicide. What it would be like to sleep, or try to sleep, or try to stay awake when the dreams were active, as they still were regarding Kevin. To arise and shower and dress in the mornings, buy groceries, pay tax bills, watch a television program, open the front door and step outside and get into the car and go off to risk making eye contact with a member of the damned human race.

To gin up the energy to give a shit about anything was what it all boiled down to. In my self-anesthetized state, the most optimistic thought I could manage was that neither of us would likely live that much longer anyway.

The phone finally rang between three and four in the afternoon. A Glens Falls officer was on the line to tell us that our son was in the hospital in the town. They'd identified him from the information Honoree had provided to the police department. A group of swimmers, heading for the wooded shore, had noticed Dean as he began to lower himself into the shallow water, on his back. He has since denied what we understood at the time to be true: that he had filled his pockets with rocks.

The swimmers hauled him out of the water. He did not resist. They called the Glens Falls police, who arrived and escorted him to the hospital. When Honoree and I arrived, Dean was in a sedated sleep, but he awoke to the sound of us. My wife and I later talked about his first moment of recognition. We had both noticed it, and each of us agreed that we would never forget it. His lids pulled back from his hazel eyes, and then his eyes came alive, and then he grinned. It lasted only a moment, that grin; and it has lasted ever since: a wide, unrestrained grin of pure joy. It was the grin of a child who had been through a nightmare experience and awakened to find his mother and father bending over him, embodiments, as they had been since time began, of the simple verity that things were going to be all right.

And they were to be. But—to quote Saint Augustine—not yet.

Again, our son was released after a few days of emergency care. The hospital was in another state and had no jurisdictional authority to retain Dean after that. Again, he came home.

His liberation from psychosis required one final harrowing episode. One further step toward the actualization of danger-to-self-or-others. That, and then the entry into his life of a psychiatrist who understood him: a young professional of empathy, insistence, and negotiating skill. He used all of these assets to wrest Dean from the gravitational belt of anosognosia, compelling our son to recognize that without an enduring commitment to regular counseling and regular medication, he would live the rest of his life in the fogbound cycle of psychotic crisis followed by temporary recovery. Or worse.

The psychiatrist's name was—is—Gordon Frankle.

It all came down in September of that year. I had decided, with Honoree's consent, to attend a writers' conference in Texas. What was the worst that could happen? I found out the answer via telephone from Honoree the morning after I arrived in Archer City, Texas. Dean was back in the emergency room. Not long before her call to me, she had heard his panicky voice as he made his way up from his downstairs bedroom. His shirt was splotched with blood. Dean had tried to plunge a pocketknife into his chest. The folding blade had collapsed against a bone. Honoree called 911, and the arriving paramedics rushed him to Rutland Regional Hospital. I caught the next flight home from Dallas.

This time his hospital stay was long and arduous. Even given his gesture toward suicide, a judge needed to rule on whether permission of involuntary treatment could be granted. Because of bed shortages, Dean was forced to spend the first two weeks in a barren, windowless emergency room without pictures, mirrors, or anything with color, nothing except a bed and sheets. He passed the time in a state of fury.

Gordon Frankle delivered our son back to us, and to himself.

Not overnight, though. Dean spent twelve days in a psychotic state without medication, and then several more weeks in a regular bed. Yet, despite his typically overwhelming caseload, Gordon Frankle brought our son along slowly and carefully. He tested and balanced Dean's regimen of antipsychotics by slow increments. Eventually he settled on a regimen of Haldol, delivered in monthly depot injections, which Dean maintains to this day.

Just as importantly, Dr. Frankle made time to talk with Dean; to talk seriously and probingly with him, measuring the length and intensity of conversations according to our son's capacity to understand and respond.

Confidentiality will keep Honoree and me from ever knowing the content of these conversations. Yet knowing the content is not essential. What seems essential to us is that they worked.

It was late autumn before Dean was released. By this time the colonizing demon was nowhere to be seen or heard. The boyish smile we had glimpsed months earlier in Glens Falls was back. He had been chatting with hospital staff members who weeks earlier had been obliged to grapple with his bellicosity. "Your son's a great kid," an orderly told us during an early visit.

He was released shortly after a November snowstorm. He called us to announce that he intended to celebrate by walking the fourteen miles from the hospital to our house. To home.

He made it halfway before it got dark and he called again to ask for a ride. The next day he asked us to drive him to the pickup spot so he could complete his triumphal walk home.

21

Someone Cares About Crazy People

The future of mental health care is being shaped along two trajectories. Along one of them races scientific progress. Along the other path inches social reform.

If science fails, it will not have been for lack of trying. A Rand Corporation study found that more than 220,000 mental health research papers were published between 2009 and 2014, supported by more than nineteen hundred funders worldwide.[1] The United States dominated the field, the report stated: as both the largest producer of research at 36 percent of publications, and as the largest recipient of government and private funding at 31 percent.

The recent trajectory of science and technology clearly has revitalized the hope—indistinct though it remains—of a cure for chronic afflictions such as schizophrenia. Progress in this area has been stunning. Neuroscientists speak of a golden age, borne along by such breakthroughs as the gene-editing tool CRISPR, the so-called "brain-to-text" decoding system, the revolutionary rise of optogenetics.*[2] In 2014, the

---

* "Optogenetics" defines two parallel methods for monitoring and influencing neurons in the brain: genetically encoded sensors and light pulses. Named the Best Method of the Year 2010 by the journal *Nature* for its use of fiber-optic cable to normalize certain brain circuits, optogenetics has been radically improved by a unification of the two methods. The team leader in achieving this new stage is Michael Hausser, a neuroscientist at the Wolfson Institute for Biomedical Research in London. Hausser has reported that now the system can record complex neuron signaling codes and "play" those codes back so that the brains of

Sweden-based global technology developer Luvata finished work in its Waterbury, Connecticut, labs on the leviathan INUMAC.* This most powerful MRI scanner—to date—contains a magnet capable of lifting a sixty-metric-ton tank and containing more than 125 miles of superconducting cable. The magnet and cable produce a field strength of nearly twelve teslas—units of measuring flux density—which greatly exceeds any MRI system. This will enable the giant instrument to produce ultra-high-speed, crystal clear diagnostic "snapshots" of events in the brain. It sells for about $270 million.

Advances such as these have virtually enabled scientists to set up shop inside the brain, creating submicroscopic observation posts in its neural pathways. In the words of one neuroscientist, "Fundamentally [they show] that bipolar disorder, and in fact all mental illnesses, are brain disorders of a biological nature that warrant proper investigation including scanning. And that that will be of clinical utility in the near future."

As for the past, it is hardly even prologue. Mental illness as a product of biology overrides the legacies of modern theorists from Sigmund Freud to Eugen Bleuler to Thomas Szasz. (Emil Kraepelin, his admiration for "racial hygiene" aside, granted biology its place in schizophrenic affliction, and is regarded as the father of "scientific" psychiatry.)

Such innovations, of course, require a reliable and constant infusion of money. Here, the picture is volatile, yet encouraging.

Private investment funding, a sine qua non of this research, and development, rises and falls, often dramatically, largely on the nation's economic health, and currently is on an upswing. Its general stability probably owes much to economists' faith in the potential wealth contained in those hundreds of global labs engaged in cognitive neuroscience: "the greatest untapped market of all,"[3] in the words of one.

---

animals will recognize and respond to them. This represents an important step toward controlling human neurons and eliminating or changing the faulty ones.

* The acronym covers most of the words in "Imaging of Neuro Disease Using High-Field MR and Contrastophores."

In 2013, President Obama introduced a long-term funding initiative for creating innovative hardware in the fight against neurological afflictions. The BRAIN project allocated $100 million for its first phase, creating the means to investigate the firing patterns of all neurons in a circuit toward the goal of controlling them.

As noted, such incursions have not yet produced a cure. And as we have seen, the demonstrated adaptability of CRISPR and other new instruments of gene-altering remains a matter of urgent ethical concern. Researchers and entrepreneurs have an enormous ethical responsibility to ensure that the cure and the disease do not merge.

Given all this sobering potential to reactivate the dream of perfecting mankind, applied science does seem to indicate that help is on the way.

Yet, while the global science/technology Ahabs sail resolutely ahead, hoping to finally harpoon a quarry that still eludes their swelling arsenal, our society and its political leaders seem largely content to lounge on the docks and wonder: "*What* whale?"

As mental health research flourishes, mental illness care in the United States remains in chaos. It has always been in chaos, yet in our time the chaos has accelerated and spread. And the chaos and its social effects grow normative, diminishing everyone's civic and private well-being.

As this book has shown, insane offenders against the law are routinely convicted and warehoused in jails and prisons, and the jail and prison populations swell beyond the limits of health and decency, and the watchdog groups issue statistics and the media report them, and people wonder what can be done, and then they cease wondering.

Sometimes a little reform does occur. The US Supreme Court ruled in 2011 that the overcrowding in California prisons was unconstitutional. This was four years before the state's district judge Lawrence K. Karlton made his similar ruling prompted by the overuse of Tasers, pepper spray, and solitary confinement, which traced to the same problem. (The judge died at age eighty shortly after his 2015 ruling.) The high court sternly ordered that the correctional system population be reduced—to 137.5 percent of design capacity.

Today, the systematic abuse of these prisoners by guards and wardens, often resulting in death or suicide, is reported with even greater frequency, yet is greeted with proportionate public apathy. Apathy is not a feature, however, amid the families of these victims, families who are largely African American and poor. It is impossible to quantify the collective erosion of happiness, optimism, productivity, and faith in civic institutions within this wronged and ravaged subpopulation. Yet it is hardly impossible to speculate. These erosions almost surely add up to a wider stain of civic withdrawal in these communities; a deeper contempt for the idea of citizenship in America.

Surviving prisoners who serve out their terms are tossed back into the world with their mental afflictions intact, and very often worsened by beatings, solitary confinement, and deprivation of psychiatric care and medication. A great many of these unfortunate social "throwaway people" have no real impetus or choice but to repeat the corrosive patterns introduced by the great asylum exodus of the 1960s and beyond: homelessness, drugs, street crime, rearrest (the lucky ones), conviction, reincarceration.

Mass shootings by people in psychosis create freshets of outrage—not over our poor and porous identification, care, and oversight of mentally disturbed people, but over the laxity of our gun-control laws. Gun-rights advocates hear these outcries, and call, not with any great passion, for mental health care reform. Then the conversation drifts to other things, until the next massacre.

Police shootings of mentally ill victims, mostly black and poor and unable to find help, inspire similar freshets, with similar results.

Suicides take the lives of thirty-eight thousand Americans a year. About 90 percent of suicides are the result of mental illness.

It is estimated that mentally ill people die earlier than sane people by an average of twenty-three years. They die as victims of violence; they die of suicide; they die of disease and neglect and exposure on the streets. Their average life expectancy is on a par with that of people in Bangladesh.

One might assume these and other symptoms of chaos in mental health care would long since have brought about a countertsunami of redemption and reform, a national initiative, perhaps, fed by support from federal and state governments, foundations, corporations, charities, Internet donors. Yet they have not. While it is true that a handful of legislators, journalists, academic figures, and individual citizens have made heroic attempts to garner sustained attention and support for the plight of the mentally ill, their efforts have yet to catch fire with the populace.

The national inertia certainly does not stem from a lack of information or ideas. The information and ideas are everywhere. The information and ideas flow in a daily stream from endless sources of expertise: the National Institute for Mental Health, the World Health Organization, the American Psychological Association, the National Alliance on Mental Illness, the American Medical Association, the National Institute of Science, the Treatment Advocacy Center, the Justice Department, mental health departments and divisions in every state, and an abundance of collectives, psychiatric associations, think tanks, seminars, journals, and bulletins. These sources, whose findings are filtered through the press and the Internet, often disagree. Often, their data-gathering structures, and thus their data, vary widely; definitive truth on any area of mental illness is as elusive as a cure. Yet one has only to reach out and pluck a handful of the million factoids that rocket through cyberspace to grasp the dimensions of this societal scourge.

The most troubling items in this factoid blizzard involve false economics. They paint a picture of an American society that does not want to pay for the care of crazy people and of state governments that happily gratify their wishes, chopping mental health budgets at every opportunity. Taxpayers and legislators alike seem generally ignorant of the extent to which they are being soaked by the hidden costs of this parsimony. For instance, public care costs far less than public jails. The National Alliance on Mental Illness has estimated that for every $2,000 to $3,000 per year spent on treating the mentally ill, $50,000 is saved on incarceration costs. Prisoners with mental illness, in NAMI's reckoning, cost the nation an average of nearly $9 billion a year.[4] Between 1998 and 2006, the mentally ill population of all prisons and jails in America increased four times, from 283,000 to 1,264,300. Reports of mental health problems among state prison inmates have reached a rate of 56.2 percent of the prison population, as compared to 11 percent in the general adult population.[5] As *National Affairs* declared in 2013, "The financial costs of large-scale incarceration are immense." The journal estimated that housing a prisoner for a year costs "between $10,000 for a low-security inmate...to more than $100,000 for maximum-security inmates in states with high prison-guard salaries."[6] The journal quoted Bureau of Justice estimates that total spending on prisons and jails in 2010 were to be nearly $50 billion—nearly $500 a year for every US household.

Nevertheless, between 2009 and 2011 and following a severe recession, states cumulatively cut more than $1.8 billion from their budgets for services for children and adults living with mental illness. California led the nationwide slashing with cuts totaling $587.4 million.

Thomas Insel, the former director of the National Institute of Mental Health, has estimated that mental illness costs taxpayers $444 billion a year. Two-thirds of that total is eaten up by disability payments and lost productivity. Only a third is spent on medical care. "The way we pay for mental health today is the most expensive way possible," Insel has said. "We don't provide support early, so we end up paying for lifelong support."

And speaking of medical care, NIMH has estimated that two-thirds of children with lifetime mental health problems never receive treatment.

The availability of psychiatric counseling, especially for those showing early signs of mental illness, is believed to be essential in staving off full manifestation of the disease. Yet psychiatry is receding as a specialty of choice for emerging doctors. The calling has never fully regained the prestige it lost in the 1960s under the assault of Thomas Szasz and his kindred mental illness deniers, even as current brain science repudiates their claims. As of 2010, the United States claimed

46,000 psychiatrists, a painfully small number in a nation of nearly 325 million. Although recent cutting-edge reform theorists now call for a revitalized system of psychiatric care conjoined with sophisticated psychotropic regimens, American medical students are rejecting psychiatry as a choice.

The shortages are especially critical in rural America and among poor African Americans and Latinos in urban neighborhoods. Only an estimated seven thousand psychiatrists specialize in consulting with children and adolescents—the groups most in need of such care.

The indifference to the suffering of mentally ill servicepeople and service veterans remains a national disgrace. The suicide rate among Army personnel, on a steady rise since 2000, reached a record in 2012 and exceeded the number of Army deaths in Afghanistan. In 2009, almost 76,000 veterans were homeless for at least a night, and 136,000 spent at least one night in a shelter.

Within this miasma of indifference, neglect, and budgetary foolishness, however, there are signs that the nation is being roused into action. Enlightened journalists, academic theorists, legislative leaders both state and federal, and a growing network of local/regional experimental rehabilitation movements are pointing the way toward an era of regeneration in the lives of the mentally ill.

Those mutual antagonists of activism, E. Fuller Torrey of the Treatment Advocacy Center and the fiery science writer Robert Whitaker, between them have contributed a long list of densely researched books that investigate all angles of chronic mental illness, its sources, spread, false doctrines, the damage done by false prophets and true profiteers, and the possible paths to support. Torrey and Whitaker continue along vigorously in their careers as thinkers, writers, and ombudsmen on behalf of the insane.

Another indispensable advocate is the aforementioned Pete Earley, the author of *Crazy: A Father's Search Through America's Mental Health Madness.*[7] The eminent social-justice journalist and author turned his furious attention upon the mental health care labyrinth when his adolescent son "Mike"—Earley has withheld his son's actual name— developed symptoms of bipolarity and nearly was devoured by the criminal justice system. After laying bare the Kafkaesque frustrations of trying to get help from the system, Earley began to travel the world speaking on behalf of the mentally ill. Through his website, http://www.peteearley .com/, he reports aggressively on abuses and reforms in this universe, and he offers guidance and advice to those in need of it.

If America can be said to have a political statesman of mental health reform, it would be Tim Murphy, the seven-term Republican congressman from the Eighteenth District of Pennsylvania. In 2013, Murphy, a lieutenant commander in the US Navy Reserve and a practicing psychologist with a PhD in child psychology, introduced the Helping Families in Mental Health Crisis Act. Murphy notes that "the federal government spends $125 billion on mental health, but there is little interagency coordination on programs."[8] His bill—in its original form—mandated creation of an assistant secretary for Mental Health and Substance Use Disorders, who would oversee mental health programs and policies, and a Serious Mental Illness Coordinating Committee composed of experts from the public and private sectors to collaborate on strategies for treating serious mental illness. The act authorizes $60 million in grants over four years to implement assisted outpatient treatment of the sort envisioned but not consummated half a century ago by the engineers of deinstitutionalization. This measure would allow courts "to order certain mentally ill individuals with a history of arrest, hospitalization, and whose condition will worsen without medical care, to comply with treatment while living in the community."

Murphy's bill would amend the problematic and often misunderstood privacy rules of the Health Insurance Portability and Accountability Act (HIPAA) to allow parents and other caregivers to receive the private health information of a mentally ill person under their care. Contemplating the plague of violent abuse by untrained police officers and prison guards against schizophrenia victims, the bill would require advanced training for people in such positions.

Murphy has recognized that even though small-scale community care is far preferable to the dismal asylums of the past, some patients' afflictions are severe enough that they need sustained treatment in an institution. A provision of his bill would remove regulations that prohibit "the same-day billing under Medicaid for treatment of physical and mental health in the same location on the same day for the same patient."

The Helping Families in Mental Health Crisis Act would also authorize $40 million in additional funding for President Obama's BRAIN Initiative. It would mandate the Department of Education to work with social-media companies in an effort to destigmatize mental illness. It would encourage badly needed professional volunteerism at community centers by providing Federal Tort Claims Act malpractice insurance for doctors who want to be of service.

The ideas encoded in Tim Murphy's bill amount to a historic departure from the passivity and ineptitude shown by the federal government in response to the chaos of mental health care. Yet they do not represent a consensus of advocates and reformers in the field. A sweeping denunciation came from the Washington-based Judge David L. Bazelon Center for Mental Health Law, a national legal advocacy organization and part of an extensive coalition of libertarian-leaning advocates. An unsigned editorial on Bazelon's website declared that Murphy's legislation, "if passed, would reverse some of the advances of the last thirty years in mental health services and supports. It would exchange low-cost services that have good outcomes for higher-cost yet ineffective interventions." Bazelon's core objections seem rooted in that most numbing and intractable of schisms that divide those who would remedy mental health care: the moral and constitutional legitimacy of intervention against a patient's will. The editorial continued: "Among the problematic provisions of Rep. Murphy's bill is…a grants program to expand involuntary outpatient commitment, under which someone with a serious mental illness is court-mandated to follow a specific treatment plan, usually requiring medication." The writer asserted, "The facts show that involuntary outpatient commitment is not effective, involves high costs with minimal returns, is not likely to reduce violence, and that there are more effective alternatives." The facts asserted by Bazelon well may exist, yet they were not presented in the editorial.

A private outreach organization with community-based goals similar to those outlined in Murphy's bill is Clubhouse International, a group that traces its conceptual roots to the 1940s.

Clubhouse is modeled after Fountain House, which sprang from the efforts of some patients who had been discharged from a New York state psychiatric hospital. Their idea was to invite mentally ill people into an enclave of kindred spirits from similar backgrounds who would provide them with companionship, care, and work/recreation opportunities. Fountain House continues today with an annual membership of some thirteen hundred people, and its structure has inspired similar programs in more than thirty countries. Clubhouse, prominent among the groups that followed the template, is now a worldwide nonprofit organization. Its members are supervised by staff members who guide them in learning workplace skills, forging strong personal relationships, finding adequate housing, and pursuing educational resources. Clubhouse does not provide therapy or administer medications, but it maintains ties with psychiatrists who offer those services.

Murphy's bill was passed in the Republican House of Representatives by a vote of 422 to 2. President Obama signed it into law in December 2016.

As we see through the work of impassioned pathfinders from Dorothea Dix to President Truman, NAMI founder Harriet Shetler, E. Fuller Torrey, Robert Whitaker, Pete Earley, and Tim Murphy, among many others, the crusade to eradicate the chaos of mental health care could not survive without the inspiration and breakthrough achievements of leadership and vision at the national level. The value of such figures is at once symbolic and real. The eloquent, charismatic Dorothea Dix awakened the hearts of staid, frequently officious men of power in the mid-nineteenth century and channeled their power to reforms. A pugnacious and plainspoken Harry Truman used his executive power to push through and sign the National Mental Health Act in 1946. A fresh cadre of such national figures is necessary in our time. Perhaps a new charismatic leader of the cause will emerge from within the communities of people bereaved by the loss of a loved one to a failure within the present chaotic system.

The future will be decided in a thousand American urban neighborhoods and suburban conference centers and small-town church basements and library meeting rooms and rural kitchens. It will be decided by selfless stewards such as my ruddy-faced fellow Castleton townsman Willem Leenman, who for forty years, along with several staff members, has directed an eleven-occupancy home for men afflicted with schizophrenia and bipolar disorder. The handsome old white-frame bears the unassuming name FortySeven Main Street. Leenman's parents founded the facility after the family moved to America from the Netherlands. It is supported entirely by private funding. Leenman has admitted that he doesn't realize much of a profit, yet his passion for the well-being of his charges has never faltered. To watch these men as they trudge along Main Street, slowly yet with dignified bearing, is to understand in one's heart that someone cares about crazy people.

The future of mental health reform will depend upon whether enough people gather in enough of such venues as these to complete the work of Dorothea Dix by joining to reject and extinguish our modern Bedlams, and replace these Bedlams with a reborn and more sophisticated and more enduring program of moral care. It will depend upon whether enough people will take notice of and be inspired by the rediscovery made by sociologists and psychiatrists: that kindness, companionship, and intimate care are demonstrable counterforces to deepening psychosis. Not cures, but counterforces, particularly when practiced in concert with psychotropic regimens that fit the specific nature of a person's affliction as well as that person's specific biosystem.

It will depend upon whether enough people will recognize and volunteer their participation in one of the several ventures around the country similar to that created by the innovative psychiatrist Courtenay M. Harding. In 1985, Harding, a pioneer of the current "recovery" movement, created the Vermont Longitudinal Study of Persons with Severe Mental Illness, an experiment that validated the notion that community care balanced with proper medication can help restore many severe schizophrenic sufferers to happy and productive lives.

The study drew upon the work of George Brooks, a Vermont hospital clinical director who in the early 1950s took a critical look at Thorazine, the first of the "miracle drugs." Brooks prescribed the drug to "back-ward" schizophrenic patients who had been considered hopeless. Less prone to marketing blandishments than most of his colleagues, he looked beyond the hype and noticed that many of his patients remained unable to leave the hospital despite receiving a high dosage of the new drug. Brooks crafted an experiment that resonated with the assumptions of moral care. He invited his patients to take part in a program of "psychosocial rehabilitation." As Harding wrote in a 2002 essay for the *New York Times*, Brooks, with the help of his staff, mentored his patients "in developing social and work skills, [and to] cope with daily living and regain confidence. After a few months in this program, many of the patients who hadn't responded to medication alone were well enough to go back to their communities. The hospital also built a community system to help patients after they were discharged."[9] It featured "home-like" conditions, complete with regular group therapy, the option of halfway houses and outpatient clinics, and job placement.

Harding, then a professor of psychiatry at the University of Vermont who knew of Brooks's work, joined with him in the 1980s. She recruited a team of psychiatrists to observe and track the fortunes of former patients in Brooks's original program. In 1985, the team conducted its last of several follow-up assessments of those patients who agreed to be interviewed. Harding wrote that 51 percent of the 168 subjects still living were rated as "considerably improved" or "recovered." She added, "The most amazing finding was that 45 percent of all those in Dr. Brooks's program no longer had signs or symptoms of any mental illness three decades later."

After that, Courtenay Harding repeated her evaluation protocols through more than eight years of assessing former patients at the Augusta State Hospital in Maine. These people were matched, as closely as possible, to the Vermont volunteers by age, gender, and other criteria. The results were not identical to the previous study: the subjects in Maine did not do as well as those in Vermont in a number of categories: productivity, community adjustment, and persistence of symptoms. Still, they showed a remarkable recovery rate of 48 percent.

(It is important here to stress a point I have made before: Harding does not equate "recovery" with "cure," though her criteria for the two conditions often seem nearly identical. "I define recovery," she has said, "as reconstituted social and work behaviors, no need for meds, no symptoms, no need for compensation.")[10]

These differences prompted Harding to make a "collateral" discovery that confirmed conventional neuroscience theory: that environment is an important factor in determining the onset and degree of schizophrenia. The Vermont patients were part of a cutting-edge rehabilitation experiment, whereas those in Maine received traditional care.[11] As Harding put it, "The Vermont model was self-sufficiency, rehabilitation and community integration. The Maine model was meds, maintenance and stabilization."[12]

Since then, Harding has held a series of faculty appointments as a professor of psychiatry, and she has lectured in the United States and around the world on the efficacy of disciplined, professionally supervised community care for chronically ill mental patients. Her philosophy, known among psychiatrists as "psychosocial rehabilitation," is practiced in an estimated four thousand "dedicated" programs around the country.

In reporting on the rise of community centers for mental health care, I do not categorically endorse them. Given that mental illness itself is subject to endless definitions and cultural biases, not to mention predatory claims by spurious healers of various sorts and by errors among the best-intended professionals, it would be foolish to believe that a decentralized archipelago of self-professed clinics and treatment enterprises is uniformly safe or even legitimate. My personal belief is that oversight and credentialing—by affiliated hospitals or state agencies—must be a mandatory component of any community system. The lessons of deinstitutionalization are too recent, too destructive, and too clear to ignore.

That said, the future of care for the mentally ill will depend upon whether Americans can recognize that their psychically troubled brothers and sisters are not a threat to communities, but potential partners with communities for not only their own but the community's regeneration. That the mentally ill need not be distractions from pursuing the good life. Instead, they can be instruments of the good life for others, even as they each enjoy a good life themselves. Their needs, their stories, their presence in our lives, and their capacity for responding to the outstretched hand of a neighbor can immeasurably enrich not only the ill person but the neighbor as well. The mentally ill people in our lives, as they strive to build healthy, well-supported, and rewarding lives for themselves, can show us all how to reconnect with the most primal of human urges, the urge to *be of use*, disentangling from social striving, consumer obsession, cynicism, boredom, and isolation, and honoring it among the true sources of human happiness.

To put it another way: the mentally ill in our society are awaiting their chance to heal us, if we can only manage to escape our own anosognosia and admit that we need their help.

Epilogue

I still dream of Kevin nearly every night. The motif changes through the years. At some point, fairly recently, he began to play his guitar again. We are in a downstairs coffeehouse, late; exposed brick walls, dim light, shadows. The patrons have all gone, but a few musicians linger in front of their beers at wooden tables, figures in a Caravaggio painting. Kevin is among them, yet isolated from them; he is the only one playing, and the source of light. The pick in his fingers feathers over the strings, which are somehow in the foreground, and infinite.

Or he and I are struggling along through an immense crowd in some city, near the bottom of marble steps that descend from a grand hall, where an important event has just ended, a concert maybe. The people around us are exiting the hall. Kevin is small, and people jostle and press in against us, and I hold his hand for fear of losing him.

In the most disturbing and redemptive dream of all, Kevin as a young boy has been struck and killed by a car, and I feel our dream-shock and dream-grief as intensely as I felt it in the actual event of his death; but Honoree gives birth to another baby, and the baby is Kevin.

Dean is thirty-five now, and he is doing fine. He seems in possession of himself, aware of his limitations, and ready to live on his own in the wider world. We have found a small house for him in Rutland. He will move into it soon. Honoree has been preparing him for the skills and duties necessary to live in a house. One of those skills is cooking. Dean has been an eager learner. The other day I walked to the edge of the kitchen and found the two of them huddled at the stove, Dean a head taller than his mother, absorbed in what she was showing him. I can't be sure, but I believe that she was teaching him how to cook chicken in fancy style.

Acknowledgments

Honoree Fleming, my dear wife and friend of thirty-eight years, all credit for this book begins with you. You set aside your years of quiet grief, and your natural reserve, and your aversion to revisiting the horrors that shattered our family's tranquility and our children's promise, and you established yourself as my ally and partner through the long months of researching and writing this. Infallible source on matters of science, tireless editor of my own fallible memory, uncompromising copy-reader, and stubborn adversary when the need arose, you have left the glowing imprint of your loving soul on every page. What a woman you are. What a presence.

Dean, our gallant lion: Thank you for so bravely giving me permission to open up the most harrowing, soul-threatening events in your tumultuous young life. You have made it possible for me to demonstrate that the mentally ill among us, even people in psychosis, remain fully, intensely human, with prospects for significant healing.

Jim Hornfischer, "Agent Jim," you understood the potential social value of this book instantly, and you represented it with great conviction, as you have all the projects on which we have been partners. You also saw the necessity of including Dean's and Kevin's stories, though I had decided against including them in my original proposal. You placed the book with a superlative publisher. And you were a tirelessly committed reader of drafts once the writing began.

Michelle Howry, my editor at Hachette, you came late to this project through no fault of your own, and you shepherded it to consummation with the skill, insights, and conviction of one who had been present at the creation.

David Groff, poet, teacher, and enabling friend of writers, you filled an editorial vacuum for several weeks before Michelle Howry was able to take up her duties. You read and thought brilliantly about every chapter, every paragraph, every sentence, every word, and you resolved many urgent questions of structure and coherence with serene confidence and great prowess. You made me a better writer than I had been before.

Maureen May, genetic counselor at the Allegheny Health Network in Pittsburgh, and my steadfast researcher, you provided reams of reliable data from the most arcane realms of neuroscience and neuropsychiatry.

Raj Narendran, Maureen's husband, you were among the coterie of clinical and research psychiatrists who helped me sustain the illusion that I know more than I do. Any damage to that illusion is exclusively my fault.

Jeffrey Schaler, psychologist and friend of Thomas Szasz, you opened yourself to my questions about him, though you understood that my interpretations might not be entirely favorable.

I am also in debt to generous assistance from the following people:

Ruth Grant, for lending her extensive neuromedical expertise to my exploration of brain-science issues;

Joe Mark, academic dean emeritus of Castleton College, for awakening me to the career of Thomas Szasz;

Lawrence S. Kegeles, associate professor of psychiatry and radiology at Columbia University, for sharing his research on the effects of cannabis use upon those afflicted with schizophrenia and for his critical readings of my sections covering the nature and duration of the prodrome and the nature of schizophrenia;

Vermont psychiatrist John Edwards for sharing his insights into schizophrenia and into the source of the fears and anxieties that cause people to turn away from the insane.

Notes

Epigraph

1. Dorothea Dix, "Memorial to the Legislature of Massachusetts," January 1843, from "The History of Mental Retardation, Collected Papers," Disability History Museum, http://www.disabilitymuseum.org/dhm/lib/detail.html?id=737&page=all.

Preface

1. Seep Paliwal and Brendan Fischer, "Walker Staff on the Mentally Ill: 'No One Cares About Crazy People,'" Center for Media and Democracy's PR Watch, February 21, 2014, http://www.prwatch.org/news/2014/02/12396/no-one-cares-about-crazy-people-walker-staff.

2. Steve Schultze and Meg Kissinger, "Politics of Mental Health Complex Occupied Walker Staff," *Milwaukee Journal Sentinel* archives, February 21, 2014, http://archive.jsonline.com/news/statepolitics/emails-show-scott-walkers-role-in-managing-mental-health-complex-crisis-b99209690z1-246333671.html.

Chapter 1: Membrane

1. The details in this episode are taken from the online files of a number of newspaper and television reporters in eastern North Carolina: most notably F. T. Norton of the *Wilmington Star News*, Christina Haley and Caroline Curran of the *Port City Daily* in Wilmington, Alyssa Rosenberg of WWAY TV in Wilmington, Jasmine Turner of WECT Television, and the CNN blogger Andrew Owens.

2. Caroline Curran, "Port City Daily Exclusive: DA, Defense Attorney Offer Different Accounts of Fatal Shooting of Mentally Ill Teen," *Port City Daily*, February 4, 2014, http://portcitydaily.com/2014/02/04/port-city-daily-exclusive-da-defense-attorney-offer-different-accounts-of-fatal-police-shooting-of-mentally-ill-teen/.

3. Jason Tyson, "Over a Year Has Passed, Yet No Trial Date for Policeman Who Killed Teen in Own Home," *State Port Pilot*, January 7, 2015.

4. Jasmine Turner, "Forensic Psychiatrist Testifies in Day 9 of Vassey Trial," WECT Television, April 29, 2016, https://www.google.com/webhp?sourceid

=chrome-instant&ion=1&espv=2&ie=UTF-8#q=Jasmine+Turner%2C+%E2 %80%9CForensic+psychiatrist+testifies+in+Day+9+of+Vassey+trial%2 C%E2%80%9D.

5. Hannah Patrick, "Vassey Testifies as Trial for Teen's Death Nears End," WWAY Television, May 3, 2016, http://www.wwaytv3.com/2016/05/03/ vassey-testifies-as-trial-for-teens-death-continues/.

6. As reported by F. T. Norton of the *Star News* on April 29, 2016, http://www .starnewsonline.com/article/20160429/NEWS/160429621.

7. F. T. Norton, "Former Detective Bryon Vassey Found Not Guilty in Shooting Death of Teenager," *Star News*, May 6, 2016, http://www.starnewsonline .com/article/20160506/NEWS/160509770/0/search?tc=ar.

8. Lindsay Kriz, "The Case of the Missing Screwdriver," *Brunswick Beacon*, May 17, 2016, http://www.brunswickbeacon.com/content/case-missing -screwdriver#.Vz23SHJQKLU.facebook.

Chapter 2: What Is Schizophrenia?

1. Julian Jaynes, *The Origin of Consciousness in the Breakdown of the Bicameral Mind* (Boston: Houghton Mifflin, 1976).

2. Ibid.

3. Veronique Greenwood, "Consciousness Began When the Gods Stopped Speaking," *Nautilus*, May 28, 2015, http://nautil.us/issue/24/error/consciousness -began-when-the-gods-stopped-speaking.

4. Jaynes, *Origin of Consciousness in the Breakdown of the Bicameral Mind*.

5. Maxine Patel and Mark Taylor in their Introduction to "Challenging perceptions of antipsychotic long-acting depot injections," a "Progress in Neurology and Psychiatry" supplement, sponsored by an educational grant from Janssen-Cilag Ltd., 2007, http://www.academia.edu/171819/Changing_Percep tions_to_Antipsychotic_Long_Acting_Deport Injections.

6. C. Leucht, S. Heres, J. M. Kane, W. Kissling, J. M. Davis, and S. Leucht, "Oral versus depot antipsychotic drugs for schizophrenia—a critical systematic review and meta-analysis of randomized long-term trials," *PubMed*, January 22, 2011, https://www.ncbi.nlm.nih.gov/pubmed/21257294.

7. Kelly Gable, PharmD, BCPP, and Daniel Carlat, MD, "Long Acting Injectable Antipsychotics: A Primer," PsychCentral, http://pro.psychcentral.com/long -acting-injectable-antipsychotics-a-primer/004332.html#.

8. Robert Kaplan, "Being Bleuler: The Second Century of Schizophrenia," *Australasian Psychiatry*, October 1, 2008, http://www.academia.edu/1362526/ Being-Bleuler.

9. Gary Marcus, "A Map for the Future of Neuroscience," *New Yorker*, September 17, 2013.

10. Pak Sham, Peter Woodruff, Michael Hunter, and Julian Leff, "The Aetiology of Schizophrenia," in *Seminars in General Adult Psychiatry*, ed. George Stein and Greg Wilkinson (London: RCPsych Publications, 2007).

11. Michael Hopkin, "Schizophrenia Genes 'Favoured by Evolution,'" *Nature*, September 5, 2007, http://www.nature.com/news/2007/070903/full/news 070903-6.html.

12. Michael C. O'Donovan, "Biological Insights from 108 Schizophrenia-Associated Genetic Loci," *Nature*, July 22, 2014, http://www.nature.com/nature/journal/v511/n7510/full/nature13595.html#corres-auth.

Chapter 4: Bedlam, Before and Beyond

1. Berthold Laufer, "Origin of the Word Shaman," *American Anthropologist* 19, no. 3 (July–September 1917), http://onlinelibrary.wiley.com/doi/10.1525/aa.1917.19.3.02a00020/pdf.

2. Michel Foucault, "Madness and Society, in *Aesthetics, Method, and Epistemology*, vol. 2, *Essential Works of Foucault, 1954–1984*, ed. James Faubion (New York: New Press, 1998).

3. René Dubos, *So Human an Animal: How We Are Shaped by Surroundings and Events* (New York: Charles Scribner's Sons, 1968).

4. Ibid.

5. Susan Piddock, "A Space of Their Own: Nineteenth Century Lunatic Asylums in Britain, South Australia and Tasmania" (thesis, 2002), http://studymore.org.uk/asyarc.htm#LandscapesBethlemMoorfields, a Middlesex University resource.

6. W. R. Street, *A Chronology of Noteworthy Events in American Psychology* (Washington, DC: American Psychological Association, 1994).

7. Urbane Metcalf, *The Interior of Bethlehem Hospital: Humbly Addressed to His Royal Highness the Duke of Sussex and to the Other Governors*, 1818, http://www.bible.ca/psychiatry/mad-doctors-mad-house-keepers-alienists.htm.

8. As described by Carla Yanni in *The Architecture of Madness: Insane Asylums in the United States* (Minneapolis: University of Minnesota Press, 2007).

9. Ibid.

10. Quoted by Dr. Andrew Prescott in *Masonic Papers: Godfrey Higgins and his Anacalypsis*, Pietre-Stones Review of Freemasonry, copyright 1996–2014, used by permission.

11. Gerald N. Grob, *The State and the Mentally Ill: A History of Worcester State Hospital in Massachusetts, 1830–1920* (Chapel Hill: University of North Carolina Press, 1966).

12. As quoted in E. Fuller Torrey and Judy Miller, *The Invisible Plague: The Rise of Mental Illness from 1750 to the Present* (New Brunswick, NJ: Rutgers University Press, 2001).

13. Grob, *The State and the Mentally Ill*.

14. Dorothea Dix, "Memorial to the Legislature of Massachusetts 1843," *Old South Leaflets* 6, no. 148, as quoted by Grob in *The State and the Mentally Ill*.

15. Thomas S. Kirkbride, *On the Construction, Organization, and General Arrangements of Hospitals for the Insane. Some Remarks on Insanity and Its*

Treatment, Yale Medical Library, http://archive.org/stream/39002086342939
.med.yale.edu/39002086342939.med.yale.edu_djvu.txt.

16. Josh Clark, "6 of the Scariest Abandoned Mental Asylums in America," Stuff You Should Know, http://www.stuffyoushouldknow.com/blog/gallery/6 -scariest-abandoned-mental-asylums-america/.

17. Paul Levy, "We Are All Shamans-in-Training," All Things Healing, http:// www.allthingshealing.com/Shamanism/We-Are-All-Shamans-In-Training -Parts-1/12825#.V2hfF7grK71.

Chapter 5: Eugenics: Weeding Out the Mad

1. As reported by David Fenn on AboutDarwin.com.

2. HMS Beagle Project, http://www.hmsbeagleproject.org/timeline/robert -fitzroy-takes-his-own-life/.

3. Martin Brune, "Theory of Mind—Evolution, Ontogeny, Brain Mechanisms and Psychopathology," *Neuroscience and Biobehavioral Reviews* 30, no. 4 (2006), http://www.sciencedirect.com/science/article/pii/S0149763405001284.

4. Charles Darwin, *The Autobiography of Charles Darwin: 1809–1882*, ed. Nora Barlow (New York: Norton, 1993).

5. Charles Darwin, *On the Origin of Species by Means of Natural Selection; or, The Preservation of Favoured Races in the Struggle for Life* (London: Murray, 1859).

6. Abdul Ahad, "Darwin's Theory Is the Mixture of Malthus's Theory and Lyell's Theory and Darwin Use [*sic*] Wrong [*sic*] Lamarck's Theory as Well as Believe [*sic*] as a Mechanism of Evolution," *American Journal of Life Sciences* 2, no. 3 (2014), http://article.sciencepublishinggroup.com/ pdf/10.11648.j.ajls.20140203.12.pdf.

7. Dialogue from Charles Dickens, *A Christmas Carol*, originally published in London by Chapman and Hall, 1843, widely reprinted.

8. Darwin, *On the Origin of Species.*

9. Andrew Carnegie, *American Experience*, http://www.pbs.org/wgbh/amex/ carnegie/peopleevents/pande03.html.

10. Francis Galton, *The Narrative of an Explorer in Tropical South Africa* (London: Murray, 1853), http://www.abelard.org/galton/galton.htm.

11. Francis Galton, *Memories of My Life* (Ulan Press, 2012); originally published in London: Methuen, 1908.

12. Paraphrased from a 1913 letter to Charles Davenport, the eugenics-friendly director of the Cold Spring Harbor Laboratory. An image of the typed letter with handwritten corrections is available courtesy of the DNA Learning Center, http://www.dnalc.org/view/11219-T-Roosevelt-letter-to-C-Davenport -about-degenerates-reproducing-.html.

13. Quoted by Jonathan Peter Spiro in *Defending the Master Race: Conservation, Eugenics, and the Legacy of Madison Grant* (Lebanon, NH: University Press of New England, 2009).

14. Madison Grant, *The Passing of the Great Race; or, The Racial Basis of European History* (New York: Charles Scribner's Sons, 1916), quoted by Spiro in *Defending the Master Race.*
15. Grant, *The Passing of the Great Race.*
16. Spiro, *Defending the Master Race.*
17. Ibid.
18. Ibid.
19. Statistics for the sterilization and killing of the mentally ill are drawn from several sources, including skepticism.org/timelines/tag/nazis/eugenics/order… 4/tmpl_suffix:_table/; the Holocaust Encyclopedia, http://www.ushmm.org/wlc/en/article.php?ModuleId=10005200; http://tiergartenstrasse4.org/Nazi _Euthanasia_Programme_in_Occupied_Poland_1939-1945.html; and the University of Minnesota Center for Holocaust & Genocide Studies, http://www.chgs.umn.edu/histories/documentary/hadamar/the_occurrence.html.
20. "The 'Final Solution': Estimated Number of Jews Killed," Jewish Virtual Library, http://www.jewishvirtuallibrary.org/jsource/Holocaust/killedtable.html.
21. Margaret Sanger, in "My Way to Peace," a speech delivered to the New History Society, January 17, 1932, retrieved from "The Public Writings and Speeches of Margaret Sanger," http://www.nyu.edu/projects/sanger/webedition/app/documents/show.php?sangerDoc=129037.xml.
22. Margaret Sanger, "The Function of Sterilization," from "The Public Writings and Speeches of Margaret Sanger."
23. Margaret Sanger, "The Morality of Birth Control," from "The Public Writings and Speeches of Margaret Sanger."
24. Sanger, "My Way to Peace."

Chapter 7: "When They Were Young"

1. Mark Twain, *The Adventures of Tom Sawyer* (Hartford, CT: American Publishing Company, 1876), republished by Oxford University Press, 1996, as part of The Oxford Mark Twain series, ed. Shelley Fisher Fishkin.
2. As noted by the blogger and former childhood denizen of the park Chuck Miller, http://blog.timesunion.com/chuckmiller/storytown-er-the-great-escape -in-kodachrome/4116/.

Chapter 8: Madness and Genius

1. R. D. Laing, *The Politics of Experience and the Bird of Paradise* (London: Penguin, 1969).
2. R. D. Laing, *The Divided Self: An Existential Study in Sanity and Madness* (London: Penguin, 1965).
3. Nancy Andreasen, "Secrets of the Creative Brain," *The Atlantic*, July/August 2014, http://www.theatlantic.com/magazine/archive/2014/07/secrets -of-the-creative-brain/372299/.

4. Sandra Bruno, "Creativity as a Necessity for Human Development" (AAAI Publications, 2013), http://www.aaai.org/ocs/index.php/SSS/SSS13/paper/viewPaper/5795.

5. Susan K. Perry, *Writing in Flow* (New York: Writers Digest Books, 1999), https://www.amazon.com/Writing-Flow-Mihaly-Csikszentmihalyi/dp/0898799295/ref=sr_1_1_twi_har_1?s=books&ie=UTF8&qid=1469990783&sr=1-1&keywords=susan+k+perry.

6. James C. Kaufman, ed., *Creativity and Mental Illness* (Cambridge: Cambridge University Press, 2014).

7. C. G. Jung, *The Spirit in Man, Art, and Literature* (London: Routledge, 2003).

8. Nancy Coover Andreasen, Arthur Canter, "The Creative Writer: Psychiatric Symptoms and Family History," *Comprehensive Psychiatry* 15, no. 2 (March–April 1974), http://www.comppsychjournal.com/article/0010-440X(74)90028-5/abstract.

9. Scott Barry Kaufman, "The Real Link Between Creativity and Mental Illness," *Scientific American* (October 3, 2013), http://blogs.scientificamerican.com/beautiful-minds/the-real-link-between-creativity-and-mental-illness/.

10. Robert A. Power et al., "Polygenic Risk Scores for Schizophrenia and Bipolar Disorder Predict Creativity," *Nature Neuroscience* 18 (July 2015), http://www.nature.com/neuro/journal/v18/n7/index.html.

11. As quoted by Arielle Duheim-Ross in *The Verge*, June 8, 2015, http://www.theverge.com/2015/6/8/8746011/creativity-genetics-schizophrenia-bipolar-decode.

12. As quoted in Ian Sample, "New Study Claims to Find Genetic Link Between Creativity and Mental Illness," *Guardian*, June 8, 2015, https://www.theguardian.com/science/2015/jun/08/new-study-claims-to-find-genetic-link-between-creativity-and-mental-illness.

13. Ibid.

14. Loren Eisley, *The Mind as Nature* (New York: Harper and Row, 1962).

Chapter 9: "If Only, If Only, If Only…"

1. Our sources were a letter that Amy wrote to her lawyer, and a book that the family published two years after the accident.

Chapter 10: Chaos and Heartbreak

1. Fernanda Santos and Erica Goode, "Police Confront Rising Number of Mentally Ill Suspects," *New York Times*, April 1, 2014, http://www.nytimes.com/2014/04/02/us/police-shootings-of-mentally-ill-suspects-are-on-the-upswing.html.

2. Fernanda Santos, "Justice Dept. Accuses Albuquerque Police of Excessive Force," *New York Times*, April 10, 2014, http://www.nytimes.com/2014/04/11/us/albuquerque-police-report-justice-department.html.

3. Ryan Boetel, "City Settles Boyd Shooting Case for $5 Million," *Albuquerque Journal*, July 10, 2015, http://www.abqjournal.com/610827/albuquerque-reaches-settlement-in-lawsuit-over-james-boyds-death.html.

4. Department of Justice Semiannual Crime Report, 2014, https://ucr.fbi.gov/crime-in-the-u.s/2014/preliminary-semiannual-uniform-crime-report-january-june-2014/tables/table-3.

5. Peter Wagner and Bernadette Rabuy, "Mass Incarceration: The Whole Pie 2016," Prison Policy Initiative, March 14, 2016, http://www.prisonpolicy.org/reports/pie2016.html.

6. Charles Colson Task Force on Federal Corrections: May 2015, "Consequences of Growth in the Federal Prison Population," http://www.urban.org/sites/default/files/alfresco/publication-pdfs/2000221-Consequences-of-Growth-in-the-Federal-Prison-Population.pdf.

7. Nicholas Kristof, "Inside a Mental Hospital Called Jail," *New York Times*, February 8, 2014, http://www.nytimes.com/2014/02/09/opinion/sunday/inside-a-mental-hospital-called-jail.html.

8. Jim Dwyer, "Mentally Ill, and Jailed in Isolation at Rikers Island," *New York Times*, November 19, 2013, http://www.nytimes.com/2013/11/20/nyregion/mentally-ill-and-jailed-in-isolation-at-rikers-island.html.

9. Jennifer Gonnerman, "Kalief Browder Learned How to Commit Suicide on Rikers," *New Yorker*, June 2, 2016, http://www.newyorker.com/news/news-desk/kalief-browder-learned-how-to-commit-suicide-on-rikers.

10. Michael Winerip and Michael Schwirtz, "Rikers: Where Mental Illness Meets Brutality in Jail," *New York Times*, July 14, 2014, http://www.nytimes.com/2014/07/14/nyregion/rikers-study-finds-prisoners-injured-by-employees.html.

11. As reported by Christopher Mathias in "Here's Kalief Browder's Heartbreaking Research Paper on Solitary Confinement," *Huffington Post*, June 23, 2015, http://www.huffingtonpost.com/entry/kalief-browder-solitary-confinement-research-paper_n_7646492.

12. Blythe Bernhard, "Family devastated by son's suicide in Farmington Jail," *St. Louis Post-Dispatch*, November 8, 2014, http://www.stltoday.com/lifestyles/health-med-fit/health/family-devastated-by-son-s-suicide-in-farmington-jail/article_6ef5a107-0f13-5d42-847e-5200fca72408.html.

13. "My Son Killed Himself: Josh Deserved Better!" Pete Earley website, November 4, 2014, http://www.peteearley.com/2014/11/04/son-killed-josh-deserved-better/.

14. Pete Earley, "Suicide in Jail Spurs Action After Mother Shares Son's Story," Pete Earley website, November 20, 2015, http://www.peteearley.com/2015/11/20/suicide-in-jail-spurs-action-after-mother-shares-sons-story/.

15. Ibid.

16. Ibid.

17. Ibid.

18. Ibid.

Chapter 11: The Great Unraveler

1. Thomas S. Szasz, preface to *The Myth of Mental Illness: Foundations of a Theory of Personal Conduct*, 50th anniv. ed. (New York: Harper, 2010).

2. Ibid.

3. Ibid.

4. Jeffrey Schaler, introduction of Thomas Szasz at the 1995 Conference for Treaty 6 First Nations of Alberta, titled "Alternative Approaches to Addictions & Destructive Habits," Edmonton, Alberta, November 7, 1995, http://www.szasz.com/albertaintro.html.

5. Ron Leifer, "Review of Existential Psychology and Psychiatry, V. XXIII, Nos. 1, 2, and 3, 1997," http://ronleifer.zenfactor.org/writings/psychiatric-repression-of-thomas-szasz.htm.

6. Paul J. Harrison, "The Neuropathology of Schizophrenia: A Critical Review of the Data and Their Interpretation," *Brain* 122, no. 4 (1999), http://brain.oxfordjournals.org/content/122/4/593.

7. Martha E. Shenton, Thomas J. Whitford, and Marek Kubicki, "Structural Neuroimaging in Schizophrenia from Methods to Insights to Treatments," *Dialogues in Clinical Neuroscience* 12, no. 3 (September 2010), http://www.ncbi.nlm.nih.gov/pmc/articles/PMC3181976/.

8. Rael Jean Isaac, "Thomas Szasz: A Life in Error," *Scientific American*, September 23, 2012, http://www.americanthinker.com/articles/2012/09/thomas_szasz_a_life_in_error.html?cpage=2.

9. Alfred Kazin, *An American Procession: The Major American Writers from 1830 to 1930—The Crucial Century* (New York: Knopf, 1984).

10. Szasz, *Myth of Mental Illness*.

11. As quoted by Melanie Hirsch in the *Syracuse Post-Standard* on February 19, 1992.

12. E. Fuller Torrey and Judy Miller, *The Invisible Plague: The Rise of Mental Illness from 1750 to the Present* (New Brunswick, NJ: Rutgers University Press, 2001).

Chapter 12: Surcease

1. Molly K. Larson, Elaine F. Walker, and Michael T. Compton, "Early Signs, Diagnosis and Therapeutics of the Prodromal Phase of Schizophrenia and Related Psychotic Disorders," National Center for Biotechnology Information, http://www.ncbi.nlm.nih.gov/pmc/articles/PMC2930984/.

Chapter 13: Debacle

1. President John F. Kennedy, Special Message to the Congress on Mental Illness and Mental Retardation, February 5, 1963, http://www.jfklink.com/speeches/jfk/publicpapers/1963/jfk50_1963.html.

2. Olga Loraine Kofman, "Deinstitutionalization and Its Discontents: American Mental Health Policy Reform" (Claremont McKenna College senior thesis, January 2012), http://scholarship.claremont.edu/do/search/?q=author_lname%3A%22Kofman%22%20author_fname%3A%22Olga%22&start=0&context=1652366.

3. As quoted in "About Dr. Thomas Szasz," CCHR International: The Mental Health Watchdog, https://www.cchrint.org/about-us/co-founder-dr-thomas -szasz/about-dr-thomas-szasz/.

4. Kathleen Stone-Takai, "Mandating Treatment for the Mentally Ill: Why So Difficult?" (thesis, California State University, Sacramento, 2009), http:// www.csus.edu/ppa/thesis-project/bank/2009/stonetakai.pdf.

5. As quoted by Ellen Dewees, Lanterman's former administrative assistant, in "Legislation for the Mentally Ill," letter to the *Los Angeles Times*, December 5, 1987, http://articles.latimes.com/1987-12-05/local/me-6108_1 _mental-health-lanterman-petris-short-act-commitment-procedures.

6. Vera Graham, "Peninsula's 'Little Lady' to Let Psychiatric Community Have It," *San Mateo Times*, August 25, 1977, https://www.newspapers.com/news page/39052999/.

7. As quoted by NAMI, referencing the PBS documentary *When Medicine Got It Wrong*, May 4, 2010, http://www.nami.org/Press-Media/Press-Releases/ 2010/Mother-s-Day-and-the-Myth-of-the-Schizophrenogenic.

8. Robert Whitaker, *Mad in America: Bad Science, Bad Medicine, and the Enduring Mistreatment of the Mentally Ill* (New York: Basic Books, 2010).

9. Darrell Steinberg, David Mills, and Michael Romano, "When Did Prisons Become Acceptable Mental Healthcare Facilities?" Stanford Law School Three Strikes Project, February 19, 2015, https://law.stanford.edu/publications/ when-did-prisons-become-acceptable-mental-healthcare-facilities-2/.

10. Ibid.

11. Ram Subramanian, Ruth Delaney, Stephen Roberts, Nancy Fishman, and Peggy McGarry, "Incarceration's Front Door: The Misuse of Jails in America," Vera Institute of Justice, February 2015, http://archive.vera.org/sites/ default/files/resources/downloads/incarcerations-front-door-report.pdf.

12. Steve Forbes, "Why the Treatment of Our Nation's Mentally Ill Is an American Disgrace," *Forbes*, January 21, 2013, http://www.forbes.com/sites/ steveforbes/2013/01/02/an-american-disgrace/#430a37e128e2.

13. Dominic Sisti, Andrea Segal, and Ezekiel Emanuel, of the Department of Medical Ethics and Health Policy in the Perelman School of Medicine at the University of Pennsylvania, quoted in "Penn Medicine Bioethicists Call for Return to Asylums for Long-Term Psychiatric Care," Penn Medicine news release, January 20, 2015, http://www.uphs.upenn.edu/news/ News_Releases/2015/01/sisti/.

Chapter 15: Antipsychotics

1. Ronald P. Rubin, "A Brief History of Great Discoveries in Pharmacology: In Celebration of the Centennial Anniversary of the Founding of the American Society of Pharmacology and Experimental Therapeutics," *Pharmacological Reviews*, December 2007, http://pharmrev.aspetjournals.org/ content/59/4/289.full#title7.

• *Notes*

2. As reported in Bovet's *New York Times* obituary, written by Dennis Hevesi and published on April 11, 1992.

3. Steve D. Brown and Paul Stenner, *Psychology Without Foundations: History, Philosophy and Psychosocial Theory* (New York: SAGE, 2009).

4. Philip Seeman and Shitij Kapur, "Schizophrenia: More Dopamine, More D_2 Receptors," *Proceedings of the National Academy of Sciences*, July 1997, http://www.ncbi.nlm.nih.gov/pmc/articles/PMC33999/.

5. "Chlorpromazine (Thorazine, Largactil) Advertising," https://www.google.com/webhp?sourceid=chrome-instant&ion=1&espv=2&ie=UTF-8#q=thorazine%20advertising%201954.

6. "Thorazine Advertisement, 1954," http://prescriptiondrugs.procon.org/view.resource.php?resourceID=005734.

7. "Clozapine," World eBook Fair, sourced from *World Heritage Encyclopedia*, http://worldebookfair.org/articles/Clozapine.

8. As reported by Robert Litan and Hal Singer in "Unlocking Patents: Costs of Failure, Benefits of Success," *Economists Incorporated*, November 2014, http://walkerinnovation.com/wp-content/uploads/2015/02/Litan-EI-Inc-Study-November-2014.pdf.

9. Roy Levy, "The Pharmaceutical Industry: A Discussion of Competitive and Anti-Trust Issues in an Environment of Change," Bureau of Economics Staff Report, Federal Trade Commission, 1999, https://books.google.com/books?hl=en&lr=&id=unDWS8j7ZRoC&oi=fnd&pg=PR9&dq=The+Pharmaceutical+Industry:+A+Discussion+of+Competitive+and+Antitrust+ . . . &ots=DRVg7ORFZx&sig=usjUjKdwkG2Fs9ceVjUR_9WVxlc#v=onepage&q=The%20Pharmaceutical%20Industry%3A%20A%20Discussion%20of%20Competitive%20and%20Antitrust%20 . . . &f=false.

10. As reported by the IMS Institute for Healthcare Informatics.

11. Ed Silverman, "How Much?! Global Prescription Drug Sales Forecast to Reach $987B by 2020," http://blogs.wsj.com/pharmalot/2015/06/16/how-much-global-prescription-drug-sales-forecast-to-reach-987b-by-2020/.

12. As reported by Julienne Roman in *Tech Times*, November 19, 2015, http://www.techtimes.com/articles/108119/20151119/drug-spending-worldwide-to-hit-1-4-trillion-in-2020-ims.htm.

13. "Risperdal Lawsuits," Drugwatch, http://www.drugwatch.com/risperdal/lawsuits/.

14. "Risperdal Verdicts and Settlements," Drugwatch, http://www.drugwatch.com/risperdal/settlements-verdicts/.

15. http://www.quitam-lawyer.com/sites/quitam-lawyer.com/files/11.3.09-%20Omnicare%20Settlement.pdf.

16. As described by Alex Berenson in the *New York Times* article "Merck Agrees to Settle Vioxx Suits for $4.85 Billion," November 9, 2007, http://www.nytimes.com/2007/11/09/business/09merck.html.

17. "Two Johnson & Johnson Subsidiaries to Pay Over $81 Million to Resolve Allegations of Off-Label Promotion of Topamax," United States Department of Justice, April 29, 2010, http://www.justice.gov/opa/pr/two-johnson -johnson-subsidiaries-pay-over-81-million-resolve-allegations-label -promotion.

18. "Avandia Heart Attack and Congestive Heart Failure," Drugwatch, http:// www.drugwatch.com/avandia/heart-attack-congestive-heart-failure/.

19. "Abbott Labs to Pay $1.5 Billion to Resolve Criminal and Civil Investigations of Off-Label Promotion of Depakote," United States Department of Justice, May 7, 2012, http://www.justice.gov/opa/pr/abbott-labs-pay-15 -billion-resolve-criminal-civil-investigations-label-promotion-depakote.

20. "Justice Department Recovers Over $3.5 Billion from False Claims Act Cases in Fiscal Year 2015," United States Department of Justice. December 3, 2015, http://www.justice.gov/opa/pr/justice-department-recovers-over-35-billion -false-claims-act-cases-fiscal-year-2015.

21. Erik Gordon, a pharmaceutical analyst and clinical assistant professor at the Ross School of Business at the University of Michigan, in Duff Wilson, "Merck to Pay $950 Million Over Vioxx," *New York Times*, November 22, 2011,http://www.nytimes.com/2011/11/23/business/merck-agrees-to-pay -950-million-in-vioxx-case.html?ref=topics.

22. Dr. McDougall's Health & Medicine Center, https://www.drmcdougall .com/health/education/videos/advanced-study-weekend-experts/peter -gotzsche-03/.

Chapter 16: "Something Unexplainable"

1. P. Batel, "Addiction and Schizophrenia," US National Library of Medicine, National Institutes of Health, March 2000, http://www.ncbi.nlm.nih.gov/ pubmed/10881208.

2. S. Potvin, E. Stip, and J. Y. Roy, "Schizophrenia and Addiction: An Evaluation of the Self-Medication Hypothesis," *PubMed*, May–June 2003, http:// www.ncbi.nlm.nih.gov/pubmed/12876543.

3. Batel, "Addiction and Schizophrenia."

4. Theresa H. M. Moore, Stanley Zammit et al., "Cannabis Use and Risk of Psychotic or Affective Mental Health Outcomes: A Systematic Review," *Lancet*, July 28, 2007, http://www.thelancet.com/journals/lancet/article/ PIIS0140-6736(07)61162-3/abstract.

5. R. Radhakrishnan, S. T. Wilkinson, and D. C. D'Souza, "Gone to Pot: A Review of the Association Between Cannabis and Psychosis," US National Library of Medicine, National Institutes of Health, May 2014, http://www.ncbi.nlm .nih.gov/pubmed/24904437.

6. Ibid.

7. Samuel T. Wilkinson, "Pot-Smoking and the Schizophrenia Connection: Medical Research Shows a Clear Link Between Marijuana Use and Mental

Illness," *Wall Street Journal*, July 21, 2013, http://www.wsj.com/articles/SB1
000142412788732463750457856609421781599 4.

8. As reported by Governing the States and Localities, retrieved from http://
www.governing.com/gov-data/state-marijuana-laws-map-medical
-recreational.html.

Chapter 17: "We Have Done Pitifully Little About Mental Illnesses"

1. R. Srinivasa Murthy and Rashmi Lakshminarayana, "Mental Health Consequences of War: A Brief Review of Research Findings," *World Psychiatry 5*
(February 2006).

2. President Truman, November 19 message to Congress, http://www.trumanlibrary
.org/anniversaries/healthprogram.htm.

3. David McCullough, *Truman* (New York: Simon and Schuster, 1992).

4. As reported by Jaap Kooijman in…*And the Pursuit of National Health: The
Incremental Strategy Toward National Health Insurance in the United States
of America*, a Google eBook, 1999, https://books.google.com/books?id=wCs
3kKiL9UcC&dq=dr+ross+mcintire+there+is+no+way+of+appeasing+that+cr
owd&source=gbs_navlinks_s.

5. President Truman, November 19 message to Congress.

6. David Blumenthal and James A. Morone, *The Heart of Power: Health and
Politics in the Oval Office* (Berkeley: University of California Press, 2010).

7. Jill Lepore, "The Lie Factory: How Politics Became a Business," *The New
Yorker*, September 24, 2012, http://www.newyorker.com/magazine/2012/09/24/
the-lie-factory.

8. Ellen Herman, *The Romance of American Psychology: Political Culture in
the Age of Experts* (Berkeley: University of California Press, 1995).

9. D. M. Giangreco, U.S. Army Command and General Staff College, "The
Soldier from Independence: Harry S. Truman and the Great War," speech to
the Society for Military History, the Frank Lloyd Wright Monona Terrace
Convention Center, Madison, Wisconsin, April 7, 2002.

10. Robert Traynor, "Hearing Loss in the Trenches of World War I," in *Hearing
International*, April 1, 2014, http://hearinghealthmatters.org/hearing
international/2014/hearing-loss-trenches-wwi/.

11. Cited in "Occupational Noise Exposure," the Occupational Safety & Health
Administration, https://www.osha.gov/SLTC/noisehearingconservation/.

12. The U.S. Army Environmental Hygiene Agency's Noise Hazard Evaluation,
February 1975, //www.google.com/search?q=U.S.+Army+Environmental
+Hygiene+Agency's+Noise+Hazard+Evaluation%2C+February+1975&oq
=U.S.+Army+Environmental+Hygiene+Agency's+Noise+Hazard+Evaluation
%2C+February+1975&aqs=chrome..69i57.4340j0j7&sourceid=chrome&es
_sm=93&ie=UTF-8#q=U.S.+Army+Environmental+Hygiene+Agency%E2%
80%99s+Noise+Hazard+Evaluation,+February+1975&nfpr=1.

13. Michael M. Phillips, "One Doctor's Legacy: How one of the most divisive figures in American medical history, Walter Freeman, steered the VA on his view toward lobotomies; outrage over ice picks in the eye socket," *Wall Street Journal* special report, part two, December 2013, http://projects.wsj.com/lobotomyfiles/?ch=two.

14. Ibid.

15. Quoted by Allen M. Hornblum, Judith L. Newman, and Gregory J. Dober in *Against Their Will: The Secret History of Medical Experimentation on Children in Cold War America* (New York: St. Martin's, 2013).

16. Norbert Wiener, *Cybernetics: Or Control and Communication in the Animal and the Machine*, 2nd ed. (Cambridge, MA: MIT Press, 1965).

17. Alex Beam, *Gracefully Insane: Life and Death Inside America's Premier Mental Hospital* (New York: Perseus, 2001).

18. Stephen T. Paul, professor of psychology and social sciences, Robert Morris University, "[A] Very Brief History of Lobotomy," http://www.drspeg.com/courses/00-general/lobotomy.html.

19. Karl Menninger, *Whatever Became of Sin?* (New York: Hawthorne, 1973).

20. This was Frederick Hacker, quoted by J. E. Carney in "The Freudians Come to Kansas: Menninger, Freud, and the Émigré Psychoanalysis," published in *Kansas History*, summer 1993, https://www.kshs.org/publicat/history/1993summer_carney.pdf.

21. Kate Schechter, *Illusions of a Future: Psychoanalysis and the Biopolitics of Desire* (Durham, NC: Duke University Press, 2014).

22. Jeremy Safran, "Who's Afraid of Sigmund Freud?" *Public Seminar* 1, no. 1 (2013).

Chapter 21: Someone Cares About Crazy People

1. Alexandra Pollitt, Gavin Cochrane, Anne Kirtley, Joachim Krapels, Vincent Larivière, Catherine A. Lichten, Sarah Parks, and Steven Wooding, "Mapping the Global Mental Health Research Funding System," *Rand Health Quarterly* 6, no. 1 (2016), http://www.rand.org/pubs/periodicals/health-quarterly/issues/v6/n1/11.html.

2. Ben Thomas, "Using Light to Monitor and Activate Specific Brain Cells," *Scientific American* (January 22, 2015), http://blogs.scientificamerican.com/mind-guest-blog/using-light-to-monitor-and-activate-specific-brain-cells/; also, Elise Walker, "Optogenetics: Lighting the Way for Neuroscience," *Helix*, May 8, 2014, https://helix.northwestern.edu/blog/2014/05/optogenetics-lighting-way-neuroscience.

3. Harry M. Tracy, "The Neuro Funding Rollercoaster," *Cerebrum*, June 1, 2016, http://www.dana.org/Cerebrum/2016/The_Neuro_Funding_Rollercoaster/.

4. Ron Honberg, Angela Kimball, Sita Diehl, Laura Usher, and Mike Fitzpatrick, "State Mental Health Cuts: The Continuing Crisis," NAMI, 2011, http://www.motherjones.com/documents/681590-nami-state-mental-health-cuts.

5. "U.S.: Number of Mentally Ill in Prisons Quadrupled," Human Rights Watch, September 5, 2006, https://www.hrw.org/news/2006/09/05/us-number-mentally-ill-prisons-quadrupled.

6. Eli Lehrer, "Responsible Prison Reform," *National Affairs* (Summer 2016), http://www.nationalaffairs.com/publications/detail/responsible-prison-reform.

7. *Crazy* was published in 2006 by G. P. Putnam's Sons.

8. Tim Murphy, congressman, Eighteenth District of Pennsylvania, "Detailed Summary of the Helping Families in Mental Health Crisis Act," https://murphy.house.gov/uploads/Section%20By%20Section%20Detailed%20Summary%20of%20HR3717.pdf.

9. Courtenay Harding, "Beautiful Minds Can Be Recovered," *New York Times*, March 10, 2002.

10. Patrick A. McGuire, "New Hope for People with Schizophrenia," *Monitor on Psychology*, February 2000, http://www.zoominfo.com/CachedPage/?archive_id=0&page_id=6915122515&page_url=//www.psychrights.org/Research/Digest/Effective/APAMonV31No2.htm&page_last_updated=2014-10-01T20:44:25&firstName=Courtenay&lastName=Harding.

11. M. J. DeSisto, Courtenay Harding et al., "The Maine and Vermont Three-Decade Studies of Serious Mental Illness. I. Matched Comparison of Cross-Sectional Outcome," *PubMed*, September 1995, http://www.ncbi.nlm.nih.gov/pubmed/7496641.

12. McGuire, "New Hope for People with Schizophrenia."

Index

About the Author

Ron Powers is a Pulitzer Prize–winning critic (*Chicago Sun-Times*, 1973), an Emmy-winning TV commentator (*CBS News Sunday Morning*, 1985), and the author or co-author of fourteen previous books. He lives in Castleton, Vermont, with his wife, Honoree Fleming, PhD; their son, Dean; and Dean's dog, Rooster.